ISBN: 9781313567350

Published by:
HardPress Publishing
8345 NW 66TH ST #2561
MIAMI FL 33166-2626

Email: info@hardpress.net
Web: http://www.hardpress.net

BERKELEY
GENERAL
LIBRARY
UNIVERSITY OF
CALIFORNIA

Ex
libris
Don Horter

C. D. Heathcote
London
10th August 1899.

"It has also been complained to me that "The Rod in India," 2nd Edition is too expensive. I am sorry for it. It was my mistake in introducing superior plates by a first class artist, and other things which altogether cost me over £400. which has not come back again."

Preface to Tank Angling in India by H. S. Thomas
Madras. December 1887.

The Rod in India.

"Pleasant is the fisher's life
By the waters streaming."

"O laborum dulce lenimen."

"Dulce est desipere in loco."

* * "neque semper arcum
tendit Apollo."

THE

ROD IN INDIA:

BEING

HINTS HOW TO OBTAIN SPORT,

WITH

Remarks on the Natural History of Fish, their Culture, and Value;

AND

ILLUSTRATIONS OF FISH AND TACKLE.

BY

HENRY SULLIVAN THOMAS,
OF
MADRAS CIVIL SERVICE,
F.L.S., AND F.Z.S.

Second Edition.

LONDON:
HAMILTON, ADAMS & CO.,
32, PATERNOSTER ROW.

1881.

LONDON:
HARRISON AND SONS, PRINTERS IN ORDINARY TO HER MAJESTY,
45 & 46, ST. MARTIN'S LANE.

PREFACE

To the Second Edition.

THIS Second Edition is nearly half of it a new book.

In my First Edition I sought the co-operation of brother anglers. Kindly have they responded, some direct to myself, some through the medium of the Press Many told me things that I had learnt myself in the interim: such matter is introduced afresh in this edition as my own, as it none the less is; but I thank correspondents all the same. Some told me things I did not know: such matter, wherever it appears, is honestly acknowledged by name or initial, both that the reader may know who is the authority for it, where I am at liberty to quote the full name, and also that he may recognize the advantage of the kindliness.

All such communications as have been made direct to myself, and consequently appear for the first time in print, have been printed in the same type as my own matter. Such communications as have come to me through the Press, even though it may be kindly stated in them that they were penned in answer to my invitation, are, as extracts, printed in smaller type; partly to distinguish them from what is quite new, and partly to save my book from becoming unwieldy, not in any way to imply less value.

Of these last communications I have had to clip some not a little because they repeated what was to be found elsewhere in the book. I trust I may be forgiven by the writers.

I have enlarged the page, so as to be able to present better plates, but I have not enlarged the type to suit. If I have sinned against printing rules in this matter it is that I may keep my book from being too bulky to be still an angler's companion.

I have admitted in the contributions of others though, as promised in the earlier preface, I have excluded from my own matter, narrative of sport achieved, because I thought it likely to prove interesting, and an incentive to take to Indian fishing. And this it is hoped the Chapter on Fishing Localities will help my readers to find their way to, as the rest of the book may aid them to accomplish.

If old hands, nevertheless, find nothing new in these pages, will they kindly consider that it is mainly their own fault for knowing too much. But why should I apologize to such, for really good fishermen will not expect to learn, and if they concur, even in part, they are sure to be friendly.

It only remains to cordially wish you the good sport which this book aims at helping you to obtain.

H. S. THOMAS.

Guernsey, July, 1881.

PREFACE.

To the Angler.

I PROMISE that you shall not be wearied by long yarns about the fish that I have caught; the object is to set your rod bending, and your heart leaping.

Do not be afraid of the natural history. There is not more of it than a good fisherman ought to know, and as it is expressed simply I trust it is not very uninteresting.

To the Non-fisherman lover of Natural History and Pisciculture.

As you may not care to wade through the whole book for the bits likely to interest you, and as those bits are necessarily scattered where they are applicable, a special Appendix will enable you to pick them out without trouble or waste of time.

You must kindly excuse the unscientific language used for the sake of fishermen pure and simple, who will probably be my chief readers. I plead and follow herein, the example of that distinguished and pleasant naturalist, Charles Waterton, who had both the courage and the position to be able to say he had "confined himself to a "few simple words in preference to a scientific jaw-"breaking description;" so that young naturalists might understand him at once, which was all he aimed at.

Ye giants in natural history, for whom this simple little book is scarcely fitting fodder, but who may yet dally with it for half an hour for the sake of the few crumbs to be gathered here and there, bear with me if in my little effort to follow, *longo intervallo*, the style of such a naturalist as Waterton, I timidly shelter myself under another quotation from his Essays on Natural History; it will serve to explain my reasons for taking him for my model. "I "verily believe that if an unfortunate criminal just now "were defended by a sergeant-at-law, without his "professional wig and gown, and then condemned to "death by my lord judge in plain clothes, the people "would exclaim 'that poor devil has not had a fair trial.' "So it is with natural history. Divest a book on birds, "for example, of its unintelligible nomenclature, together "with its perplexing display of new divisions, and then it "will soon be declared deficient in the main points, and "be condemned to slumber on the dusty shelf. If in this "little treatise on monkeys I shall succeed in imparting a "love for natural history into the minds of my young "readers, and at the same time convince them how much "is gained in the field, and how little in the closet, my "time and labour will be well repaid. I will introduce "no harsh words to confound them, nor recommend to "them systems, which at best, are unsatisfactory inven- "tions. All that I have got to say shall be placed before "them in so clear a point of view, that every reader, be "his education light or solid, will be able to comprehend "my meaning, and nothing more than this can be "required." Like my model, my aim in this respect is to impart a love of natural history to fishermen, and to gain amongst them more friends and coadjutors for pisciculture in India. In my Official Reports to Government also, all the members of which are not necessarily pisciculturists, I have ever studiously excluded all hard words from the text, and have pushed them unceremoniously into the margin; so also in this little book any phraseology of science will be found condemned to a foot-note, or to the close company of a plain Saxon synonym. Thus disposed no exception can well be taken to its presence, especially in the names of fish where, without such accuracy of expression, it would be hard to know for certain which fish it was that was being spoken of.

But lest this seeming rudeness to natural history should scare away some that might otherwise do me the honour of at least a cursory reading, I think I had better present my letter of introduction. The following letter and the handsome accompanying Medal, which I had the unexpected honour of receiving from the Acclimatization Society of Paris, is the best evidence that, though in a humble way, I have still given some painstaking attention to the subject on which I write :—" J'ai l'honneur de vous " informer que la Société d'Acclimatation, sur la proposi- " tion de sa Commission des récompenses, vous a décerné " une médaille de 1ere. classe pour vos travaux de pisci- " culture dans l'Inde."

To the Critic.

" Spare the Rod !?"

Acknowledgments.

For two of my plates,* the Mahseer and the Murrel, I am indebted to the courtesy of Dr. Bidie, Curator of the Government Museum in Madras, who very kindly afforded every facility to my draughtsman. The *Barilius Bakeri* has been copied by permission from Dr. Day's " Fishes of Malabar."

H. S. THOMAS.

Mangalore, April, 1873.

* These plates have not been used in the present edition.

CONTENTS.

CHAPTER I.

INTRODUCTORY.

CHAPTER II.

THE MAHSEER.

CHAPTER III.

THE NATURAL HISTORY OF THE MAHSEER.

CHAPTER IV.

CIRCUMVENTING THE MAHSEER.

CHAPTER V.

SPINNING FOR MAHSEER.

CHAPTER VI.

HOW, WHEN, AND WHERE TO FISH FOR MAHSEER.

CHAPTER VII.

FLY FISHING FOR MAHSEER.

CHAPTER VIII.

GRAM FISHING FOR MAHSEER.

CHAPTER IX.

LIVE BAIT FISHING FOR MAHSEER.

CHAPTER X.

THE CARNATIC CARP.

CHAPTER XI.

SMALL FLY-TAKERS

CHAPTER XII.

BOTTOM FISHING FOR LABEOS.

CHAPTER XIII.

FRESHWATER SHARKS.

CHAPTER XIV.

THE MURRAL.

CHAPTER XV.

EELS.

CHAPTER XVI.

FISHING ON THE NEILGHERRIES.

CHAPTER XVII.

FISHING IN ESTUARIES.

CHAPTER XVIII.

ROD AND TACKLE.

CHAPTER XIX.

FISHING GEAR AND OTHER SMALL BEER.

CHAPTER XX.

THE TAME OTTER.

CHAPTER XXI.

SPAWNING.

CHAPTER XXII.

STOCKING PONDS.

CHAPTER XXIII.

MISCELLANEOUS.

CHAPTER XXIV.

FISHING LOCALITIES.

CHAPTER XXV.

A PLEA FOR RIVER FISHERIES.

CHAPTER XXVI.

A PLEA FOR SEA FISHERIES.

CHAPTER XXVII.

LITHOGRAPHS.

WOODCUTS.

CHAPTER I.

INTRODUCTORY.

Apologia pro libro meo.

NOT a few lovers of the gentle art are condemned by their calling to pass the best years of their existence in India, sighing, amongst other things, for the banks of Tweed, or Usk, or Bush, looking forward to the too far distant time when furlough, or other favouring circumstance, shall take them home to the land where they may again beguile the speckled beauties from the stream, or once more do battle with the lordly salmon. To such it may be a comfort to know that they need not wait so long for the "good time coming," that there is as good fishing to be had in India as in England; and to minister such comfort to exiled anglers is my present philanthropic object.

I fancy there are not a few fishermen in India, good fishermen too, who know well how to fill a basket in England, who are nevertheless entirely at a discount in India. Indeed I have met such, and do not mind confessing that I am myself a lamentable instance of that distressed class, for whether or not I knew how to circumvent a trout in England, I certainly could make nothing of the Mahseer in India, and lost all too much time in learning the manners and customs of that oriental gentleman. Sad indeed is the retrospect of golden opportunities lost! What would I not have given to any one who would then have put me in the way of seizing them! To give this helping hand, the benefit of my little experience, to brother anglers is my object in writing. It is not that I have the assurance to think I am the right man to undertake the task. On the contrary, I know that there are many who have enjoyed much better opportunities of sport in Indian waters, and who have consequently more experience, as well as better leisure. They are the men who ought to write a book on the subject, but they do not, and it is not my fault that they do not.

It is not that I have nothing better to beguile the tedium of a P. and O. Steamer voyage back to India, though that may be my opportunity for scribbling. It is that I have an idea it is a sort of thing some fellow ought to do out of purely philanthropic motives for his brother anglers; and as nobody else will do it, I suppose I must. It seems so selfish to have discovered that there is right good fishing to be had, and then to keep it to oneself. In short, I cannot do it; so "here goes."

There may be some six hundred books or thereabouts on fishing in general, but there is not one that I know of on fishing in India. The subject is scarcely overwritten, therefore, in spite of the six hundred books aforesaid.

Englishmen have few relaxations indeed in this land of their exile. Very, very differently situated in this respect is the Public Servant in India and his congener in England. "All work and no play makes Jack a dull boy," but I venture to say from experience that an energetic Mahseer telegraphs such an enlivening thrill of pleasurable excitement up the line, down the rod, and through the wrist and arm, to the very heart of the man who has got well fixed, that it makes his pulse beat quicker, and is altogether as good as a tonic to him. Be he ever so cool in the management of a heavy fish, even the old hand cannot but experience a certain amount of exhilaration.

> "The stern joy which warriors feel
> In foeman worthy of their steel."

I maintain that a few such electric currents before breakfast do a man good, and send him into his daily work much more wide-awake and cheerful. Pulvermacher is nothing to it. Considering the amount of refreshing good it does a fellow, it is a wonder an enlightened Government does not keep a man in rod and tackle, and allow treble hooks to be included in the annual "Sadirwarid."*

Furthermore a successful fisherman is calculated to take more interest than his neighbours in a matter which has grown to be acknowledged in England, in Europe, in Australia, in New Zealand, in Canada, in America, in Japan, as of national importance, to wit, pisciculture, or in other words, the means of increasing the

* An annual indent for pens, pencils, knives, scissors, needles, thread, and suchlike miscellaneous articles.

supply of animal food yielded by fishes. A really good fisherman is a close observer of piscine nature, and not unfrequently of insect nature too, and is therefore likely to bring more experience than others to the furtherance of the object. If in my official report on Pisciculture in South Canara I have been able to give any information about the habits of the Mahseer, its food, its time, manner, and place of spawning, and the consequent dangers to which its fry are exposed, and the protection that can be afforded them, it must honestly be confessed that it is entirely to my fishing rod that I owe it. These fish live in such deep and strong waters, among so many rocks and snags, that they are not approachable by the net till the rivers have subsided in the dry season, till the fish, formerly spread all over the river, have congregated into the fewer remaining pools. It is obvious, therefore, that if net-caught specimens had been the only ones available, conclusions on their habits would necessarily have been formed on data very much limited as regards both locality and time; limited, in fact, to places and periods which my rod proved would have given no information at all, for the net-caught fish would have been only those captured in the lower waters and in the dry season, whereas my rod showed that it was in the high waters that they spawned, and that they had completed that operation before the dry season. By the friendly aid of my rod only was I able to take Mahseer at intervals over several months, and in both the upper and lower waters of the rivers. The native anglers are very poor hands at catching the Mahseer, and I should have leaned on a broken reed indeed had I been dependent on them, for they were very few specimens that I got by that means, not half a dozen in all, whereas by the aid of my own rod I was enabled to examine the ovaries and the stomachs of between seventy and eighty Mahseer, and to gather therefrom reliable evidence of the state of advancement of the former at different times and places, as well as the most satisfactory proof of what the fish was in the habit of feeding upon. I say this not from any conceit with reference to my own individual fishing, but in common fairness to rods in general, in acknowledgment of how greatly pisciculture is dependent on the aid of angler sportsmen, as well as by way of encouragement to observant fishermen, and in explanation of one of my motives in writing on fishing, for my idea is that if I can do any thing towards making a man a successful fisherman, I have advanced one step towards making him, if not a pisciculturist, at any rate an aider in acquiring knowledge on the subject, and thus an advancer of its progress.

Very much has been done at home for the advancement of the science of pisciculture by the newspaper communications of sportsmen, and though the matter thus obtained is considered and arranged and utilized by the pisciculturist, it is to the intelligent angler that he is after all indebted for most of his facts. In this respect the Indian pisciculturist labours under peculiar disadvantages, for he not only has to work through the medium of foreign languages, but also without the aid, as in England, of a thousand intelligent observers, all ready to communicate freely through the medium of special papers like "The Field" or "Land and Water." I write, therefore, also in the hope that anglers may be induced to lend their kindly aid from time to time towards increasing the knowledge of the habits of the fishes found in Indian waters, and as a consequence to forward the efforts of those seeking the best means of increasing the supply of this sort of food.

Still I write primarily for fishermen. In doing this, however, it is a little difficult to know how to write. Though there are many good fishermen in India there are also many who, from early absence from England, know practically very little about it, although they are ready enough to take to it, if they can only see their way to getting sport. I have therefore two opposite courses to follow simultaneously. I have to make myself intelligible to the novice, and at the same time to endeavour not to weary the fisherman by re-writing what he has already read in different shape in some half dozen of the six hundred books already alluded to. By way of getting safely through this Scylla and Caribdis I must commence by presuming my readers' knowledge of books such as, "A Book on Angling," by Francis Francis, Publishers Longmans, Green & Co., Paternoster Row, London, in one volume octavo, price 15 Shillings, cloth; "The Sea Fisherman," by J. C. Wilcocks, Publishers Longmans, Green and Co., London; and if he has not read these books yet, I can only recommend him to do so, as it would be idle for me to go again over ground already so well and so pleasantly described. It is better that I should confine myself as closely as possible to the Indian side of the subject, and endeavour to give my reader only what he cannot get better elsewhere. Still it is impossible to do so altogether, and yet be intelligible to the tyro; when I am more than ordinarily tedious therefore to the practised fisherman, I can only hope that he will give me all he can spare of that commodity of which he is generally believed to have such a plentiful supply, to wit, patience.

If brother anglers reading these pages feel inclined to give me the benefit of their further experiences, I shall hope to embody or quote them in some possible future edition. The collected wisdom of all anglers in all parts of India might thus grow into a very complete book, sufficient to show the best means of securing the best sport available in different localities in India.

This invitation, thrown out in my first edition, has been very kindly responded to by anglers. Not a few have written to me direct, and others have contributed papers to the "Field," and to the "Asian," some professedly in answer to this invitation, others in the same spirit of helping fellow fishermen to sport. For myself I beg to tender cordial acknowledgments to all who have thus helped in what I must call the kindliest manner. I am confirmed in the conviction, always fixed in my mind, that it is very rare for a good fisherman not to be a good fellow. For others, readers of this little volume, the result is happy, for they will not be confined to my ideas only, but will have the opinions and the experience of others also. Believing that my readers will be glad to have the views of others, as well as my own, and recognizing that India is too large a field for any one person to cover unaided, I have endeavoured to bring together in this volume all the information kindly afforded by others. That contained in newspaper contributions will be found in Chapter XXIV, on Fishing Localities, the source and the *nom de plume* being always given. Some of my readers may find double interest in, and attach increased weight to, these contributions, from recognizing under a *nom de plume* a friend well known by them to be a master in the art.

Besides the contributions of unknown writers, I am able to give my readers two interesting communications, one from the pen of Colonel J. Parsons, and the other by Colonel W. Osborn, Commanding 9th M.N.I. Sportsmen will find them both valuable.

The further experience had since 1873 has also enabled me to introduce not a little additional matter of my own.

If sportsmen think that the above invitation has resulted in any advantage to themselves, perhaps they will allow me to renew it in this edition. Though I cannot be sanguine that this book will live to a third edition, still stranger things have happened, and it is just possible that it may again come to pass that anglers, who have put themselves to the kindly trouble of co-operating through the press or direct, may find that, in the total of experiences put together, they get more than any one of them could individually contribute.

Anglers are in England a numerous class, whereas in India they form a very small minority of the lovers of sport. Whether for love, or for money, shooting of any sort, and more particularly heavy game shooting, is so much more difficult to obtain in England than in India, that many who in England perforce content themselves with the rod, would in India be seduced by the ruder attractions of the boar-spear, the rifle, and the gun. For myself I can well remember a day in camp, "marked evermore with white," when rising at dawn I heard over my early cup of coffee the trumpeting of elephants, knew that there was a fair chance also of Bison, Sambre, and Spotted-deer, knew also that there was a Mahseer river in the valley. In one corner of the camp hut was the battery, in the other were the rods and tackle. Which shall it be? I may get up to those elephants in a quarter of an hour, I may trudge ten miles and not get a shot. I know that I can make a certainty of the Mahseer. I chose the latter, and brought home six fine fish before breakfast, and never regretted my choice. But I think there are not a few who, in like circumstances, would unhesitatingly have preferred the rifle to the rod. And thus it comes about that anglers are in India comparatively few. They are all too few to help each other adequately with information over so wide an area as India; all too few to make it worth while to write a book on the subject, except for the love of the thing, therefore there is all the more reason why they should continue to help each other as much as they can.

CHAPTER II.

THE MAHSEER.

"By sports like these are all their cares beguiled."

GOLDSMITH.

Of the fish to be caught in Indian waters the best is, in my opinion, the Mahseer, the best, I mean, as regards sport, and we may as well begin with the best. Its size depends much on the size of the river in which it is found, as will be seen in Chapter III.

In my own opinion, and in that of others whom I have met, the Mahseer shows more sport for its size than a salmon. The essence of sport, or in other words of the enjoyment of any pursuit lies, I take it, in the exhibition of superiority therein, whether of skill or courage, not the exibition for others to see, but the difficult attainment of it for our own satisfaction. It would be a tame affair to be pork butcher to a village pig, but to spear the "mighty boar" is quite another thing. Why? Where lies the difference? Simply in the fact that—

"Youth's vigour, manhood's fire,
Firm hand, and eagle eye,
Must he possess
Who would aspire
To see the grey boar die."

Entering more or less into all sports, even into such peaceable pursuits as chess, whist, or billiards, there are a thousand different gradations of "the stern joy which warriors feel in foeman worthy," whether mentally or physically, "of their steel." It is the love of conquest. What is wanted is not conquered worlds, but "more "worlds to conquer." Who cares to pull out a dead pike on a night line? The pot-hunter, not the sportsman. To battle with a heavy salmon, or kill a good game trout on a very light line, is quite another matter. From this point of view it is that I say a Mahseer shows more sport than a salmon. Not that you can kill more of them, which you may also do, but that each individual Mahseer makes a better fight than a salmon of the same size. I am prepared to expect that on this point, as on most others not capable of being proved to demonstration, some will disagree with me. *Quot homines tot sententiæ.* For my own part I can only say that my prejudices were all in favour of the salmon, both as being a salmon, a sort of lion of the waters, whom I had grown up looking on with respect from my childhood, and as being a fellow-countryman. But the Mahseer compelled me to believe in and honour him in spite of my prejudgment to the contrary. I came to the conclusion that though he might not make so long a fight of it as a salmon, he yet made a much more difficult one, because his attack was more impetuously vehement, his first rush more violent, all his energies being concentrated in making it effective, though his efforts were not, and from that very cause, could not be, so long sustained. Trying to account for this I had the curiosity to measure and compare the size of his tail and fins with that of his body, and I found that the superficial area of his propelling and directing power amounted together to as much as the superficial area of the whole of the rest of his body. The proportion which the tail and fins of a salmon bear to the rest of his body is very much smaller. The Mahseer having then so much greater means of putting on steam, and having also the habit of always putting it on at once energetically and unsparingly, it is readily intelligible that his first rush is a mighty one, and that, that made, his strength is comparatively soon exhausted. Other rushes he will make, but his first is the dangerous one. Then it is that the final issue of the campaign is practically decided. Be one too many for him then, and you may be grimly satisfied that all else he can do will not avail him; you may count on making him your own. Then it is that you must wait upon him diligently. If you have not got all free, the connection between you and your new friend will be severed within a moment of your making each other's acquaintance. If you have carelessly allowed the line to get a turn round the tip of the rod, or let any slack near the hand become kinked ever so little, or twisted over the butt, or hitched in the reel or a button, then it is that not a moment's law is given you for the re-adjustment of this little matter; there is a violent tug, and an immediate smash;

The waters wild
Go o'er your child,
And you are left lamenting.

You must fish in a state of constant and careful preparedness for this sudden and impetuous rush; for there is no use in hooking a fish if he is to break you immediately. Even your very reel must be looked to that it runs easily, that it is not fouled and clogged by use, that no treacherous sand has got in from laying down your rod and reel by the river side, for when a heavy fish goes off with racehorse speed, he will take no denial, and woe betide you if you cannot promptly oblige him with the line he wants. If he cannot get it fast enough to please him, he will break it. All this may be true of the salmon too, but it is pre-eminently so with reference to the Mahseer, and more than ordinary attention should be paid to it accordingly.

A single turn of the line round the top of the rod does not always catch the eye at once, and is much more likely to occur while spinning than when fly fishing. It is well therefore to test from time to time whether or not all is free. This can easily be done by taking a pull at the line close to the winch. If it runs freely through the top, well, but if it does not, get your bait out of the water as quickly as possible, to avoid accidents. Out with it at all costs without a moment's hesitation. Never think of risking it, for it is not a mere risk but a certainty that if you have the misfortune to get a run in that plight you will also get a smash somewhere, and not improbably of your rod. If you are too lazy to remedy the evil immediately let me venture to suggest that it would be better that you should retire from business.

A pliable rod is in my opinion a matter of great moment in Mahseer fishing. The rush is so sudden and so violent that the hand, be it ever so light, cannot answer to it sufficiently quickly, and with a stiff rod the mischief is done in the very first tug. Whereas if you have a pliable rod it yields instantaneously to the tug, it yields before you have felt the tug down at the other end of the rod in your hand, and the first thing you are aware of is the noise of the revolving check winch. If you have a stiff rod you will require to strengthen your tackle, that is, you will be at the disadvantage of not being able to fish so fine.

It is friction that you get rid of in a pliable rod; or, to speak more correctly, you get rid of undue friction, and have a greater command of the friction which you utilize. The friction caused by two or three turns round a capstan or about a belaying pin amounts almost to a dead lock, and so, in a less degree, the friction caused by a single right angle is considerable. The latter is about the friction caused by the line at the point of a stiff rod. In a pliable rod the point yields quickly, reduces the angle, and so reduces the friction, till you raise the point and renew and increase the friction at your discretion.

The friction of the winch or reel is another item not to be left out of your calculations in considering the amount of tension that your line will bear. If you want to realise this, take your winch off the rod, and, holding it in your hand, satisfy yourself that it runs quite easily. Then tie the end of the line to a post or anything firm, and holding the reel in one hand run away as if you were a fish, only run as fast as a fish swims, and you will find that the friction of the reel, which seemed to be next to *nil*, will, when multiplied by the velocity, amount to such a tension that it alone will break any but a strong line. Consider, again, the wonderful velocity with which a fish swims. So quickly does a trout dart away that you can scarcely see it pass you. When you hook a fish it is frightened at the restraint, and exerts itself to flee therefrom at its utmost speed. Nothing prevents its fleeing at that speed except the resistance of your tension; and if the fish is so big that the resistance makes no sensible difference to it at first, as a man's weight does not much reduce the speed of a horse, the velocity with which the line runs out will, with a heavy Mahseer, be very great indeed, and the tension from winch friction alone will become very serious. When the pace is reduced you may fall back on the rod for additional friction, but till it is you will, in the case of a very heavy fish on which you can make no impression, find that you instinctively let the rod be pulled down to the angle of about 45° or 50° from the water, and that nevertheless you still have to use very strong tackle for large Mahseer.

Still you should also be "hard" on your fish, keeping the line as stiff as a wire from the fish to the point of the rod, so as to avoid slack line, a state of affairs which not only facilitates a hook dropping out, but also gives opportunities for a "foul" round a rock. Hold the point well up so as to keep the fish free of any snags at the bottom. You will find that in deep water a Mahseer will, like a Grayling, always bore down to the bottom. If there is a depth of 20 or 30 feet of water down he will go to the bottom, your whole collar will disappear below water, and when at length you again catch sight of the knot that unites the collar to the running line, you may commence "chortling in your joy," for he is giving in, your strain is telling on him, as he will never come up willingly, he will never spring into the air after the manner of the Salmonidae. The moment he comes upwards pull him towards the shore. Put in your claim for being the conqueror.

Well, all being ready for paying out line at any required pace at a moment's notice, and it not being supposed that it is to be given gratis, far from it; how is full toll to be exacted for every inch? This is usually done by raising the point of the rod more or less according to circumstances, and thus compelling the fish to bend it before he can get the line to run, and to bend it more and more as you feel you can steadily raise the point still further, till eventually you "show him the butt," a contemplation that must be anything but pleasant to him.

Different men kill their fish differently, some taking twice as much time about it as others. My preference is for having my fish out of the water as soon as safely may be. Brute force is of course out of the question, but short of that I am for putting on all the strain the rod and tackle is calculated to bear, and it is a matter of some little nicety to know exactly how much your rod will bear. But, above all, I am for keeping on the strain *unremittingly* without a *moment's respite.* Do not give the fish an instant to think, or it may occur to him to take up a position in which he can sulk at the bottom, and that is dreadfully slow work. You must then try all the remedies usually prescribed for a sulking salmon, but it is a tedious business at the best, and it is losing time while you might be trying for another fish. My faith is that by sufficient *promptitude* you can prevent his ever taking to sulking at all. The very moment he ceases rushing, commence winding up, and wind away as vigorously as you dare without a second's hesitation. Do not wait for him to shape the course of events, but shape it yourself. Rely a good deal on the force of "pure cussedness" in a fish. Whatever you do his first idea is to do the exact opposite. He is afraid of your restraint, which is novel to him, and his first impulse is to break away from it. Subsequent yearnings he may possibly have, and doubtless has, when he comes to think of it, for the shelter of some deep corner where he is used to solace himself, his own fireside. But it is a novel experience to him this restraint, and it is no new work to you, and you may pre-occupy his mind, and occupy his tail, not a little, if you show prompt generalship. The master mind may come in here as well as in the fall of empires, and it is surely a pleasure to find you have that commodity somewhere about you. Of course you have it. We all knew you had it. And now it is proved! The very instant the fish hesitates wind him in. It is not impossible you may land him at once, getting him on shore before he has well made up his mind what to do. But the probabilities are that as he finds himself nearing the shore, and gets a clearer view of the great big trowsered biped that is bothering him, he will summon up all his strength for another rush. All right, that is just what you want; you only want to make him keep on exerting himself unremittingly, and he must soon be yours. Is there no music in that whir whir whir of the check reel, the rod bending bravely all the while! Surely it was of this that the sporting poet Shakspeare said some hard things with reference to

> "The man who hath no music in himself
> Nor is not moved with concord of sweet sounds."

Fire away, Mr. Mahseer, discourse sweet music on the long-stringed winch. The more the fish fights the better, the better for sport, the better for speedily killing him; any respite is recovery of strength, and a good sulk makes him almost as bad to kill as a new fish.

The ground on which I lay such stress on *continuity* of pressure, more even than on the strength of the pressure, is simple enough when it is considered. Under any extraordinary exertion the muscles call on the blood, and the blood on the lungs, for speedy renewal of speedy waste, and the result is being what is called out of breath, and the muscles, though by no means tired out, can do nothing till the breath is regained, shall we say till the blood has been re-oxygenated. Never give a moment's grace then for this re-oxygenating of the blood, and you may kill a large fish in a very short time. The average time for killing a big fish with a salmon rod is a pound a minute. A twenty pound fish should be your own in twenty minutes or thereabouts, according to the water in which you have to fight him. By continuity of pressure, unremitting strain without one moment's respite, you keep the fish out of breath, and thereby neutralize the latent muscular power which a little breathing space would soon renew, and give you all your work to do over again. This is how it is that some people play an ordinary salmon for long hours, and think they have a most extraordinarily game fish on. It is the same principle on which "the mighty boar" is speared. Press him to his very utmost speed from the first, and keep him at it, and you will soon overhaul him, but let him go at his own pace, a pace that will not distress him, and he will keep you at an English hunting gallop till he walks away from you, the horse giving in before the boar, that is, if he is at all a *travelled* pig.

I have a theory that if the strain on the fish is kept as much as possible at right angles to the current, it has a greater effect on him than any other strain. If the fish is down stream playing lazily about, not vigorously, perhaps meditating sulks, it is obvious that he is at a great advantage, he has the whole weight of the stream in his favour, and you distress him very little in comparison to the pull on your rod. He is practically resting and recruiting. But get the pull to bear at right angles to the force of the current and he cannot help exerting himself to keep his nose straight to the stream. If he allows himself to be pulled out of his position, and gets ever so slightly side on to the stream, in he comes towards shore immediately, is frightened at the prospect, and dashes off again just as you would have him. Thus you keep him at it, and very soon tire him out. In deep water, however, you may be equally satisfied you are wasting no power by pulling the fish upwards, for the specific gravity of a fish being *very* little greater than that of water, he gains next to nothing by his weight while *in* the water, and he must keep on exerting himself to swim downwards, with his head down and tail up, to resist your upward strain, and as in that direction he can never swim beyond the bottom, you are ensured against any violent rush. A friend wrote to me of a fish boring at first, and then making a free fight with a good deal of spluttering on the surface. I do not look upon this spluttering on the surface as fighting, but as an indication that the fight was over, the fish was beaten, and had no longer the power to bore down to the bottom. As soon as ever a fish begins to splutter, the pulling upwards should cease, the point of the rod should be lowered and pulled sideways, not upwards, so as to bring the fish to shore without having its head out of water. Spluttering is dangerous and to be discouraged, for direct communication through the air means the absence of the yielding cushion which the water supplies in easing off each jerk on the line ; it means, also, that the fish gains the advantage of his specific gravity being greater in the air than in the water. It is an ugly time when a jack shakes his jaws in the air, and never is a trout so likely to get off as when springing into the air. With fish that have not such vices naturally it is a great mistake to help them to being troublesome. No Mahseer, indeed none of the Indian carp, are up to those little tricks, so never bring them to the actual surface, but play them short of that till you land them.

Briefly, then, my idea is be heavy on your fish, and be unremitting, be prompt, scan your battle-field, and choose your ground, and shape the course of events as much as you can yourself: in a stream pull generally at right angles to it, in deep water pull upwards, get your fish on *terra firma* as soon as possible, it is the safest place for him.

An extra reason for having the line as taut and straight from the fish to the top of your rod as possible is that you may lessen the chances of the fish fouling it round a rock and cutting you. So try and keep well over him till he is beaten.

I do not believe in running down the bank. I think it is resorted to much too readily, the result being that the command over the line is more than half lost the while, and not nearly enough steady pressure is maintained. Hold your ground and hold on to your fish, and the odds are you will have him. If he keeps going, and your line is coming towards the end, follow the fish only at such a pace as leaves you still full master of the rod and the pressure, and do not move any faster till close on the last extremity. To endeavour to race your fish on a practically loose line is equivalent to racing an express train.

When the fish is tired you feel each struggle as you feel the strides in a tired-out horse. Every beat of the tail is telegraphed up the line. Before the fish was tired you seemed to have on a [illegible] impression. [illegible]

[illegible]

[illegible]

[illegible]

There are some people who [illegible]

fish tastes like. To my mind that is a very secondary matter. It is, moreover, a matter on which it is well known that people are not calculated to agree, so much so that "*de gustibus non est disputandum*" is an axiom. Is it fair, then, that I should be called upon to say whether or not the Mahseer is good eating? All I can say is that I have tasted Mahseer in such high condition that they were excellent, they were so rich that one could not eat any melted butter or other sauce with them, and so well flavoured that they seemed to me to stand between the salmon and the trout for the table. Such a fish must be one that has not even commenced partially spawning, much less one that has completed that operation. The best size for flavour is in my opinion about 6 lbs. or 7 lbs., say from 2 to 10 lbs. When less than 2 lbs. they are too bony, when much larger than 10 lbs. they are apt to be too gross and oily for European tastes; but they are always thought thoroughly edible by your camp. Natives, whom I have supplied with more than they could eat fresh, said it salted well, but I never tried, and tastes differ, though rich fish do as a rule salt well.

You will want one attendant with you to land your fish and carry them, as well as to carry and prepare bait, as we shall see hereafter, and to relieve you of your heavy salmon rod between whiles when clambering over rocks from one good place to another; in short to take off your hands all the drudgery of fishing, and to leave you only the sport. Pick out one or more likely fellows therefore, and train them.

But I have been rather putting the cart before the horse, indulging in the sport given by a Mahseer before saying how to hook him, seemingly forgetting the wise saw "First catch your hare." Perhaps it was by way of offering some inducement to anglers to accompany me out fishing in the next chapter but one, for they can skip the intermediate short chapter or not, according as they care or do not care to know anything about the natural history of the Mahseer.

CHAPTER III.

THE NATURAL HISTORY OF THE MAHSEER.

"I in these flowery meads would be;
These crystal streams should solace me;
To whose harmonious bubbling noise
I with my angle would rejoice."—
IZAAK WALTON.

"*ἀνείλκυσα χρύσειον ἰχθύν
παντᾷ τοι χρυσῷ πεπυκασμένον*."—THEOC. ID. XXI.

"I landed him, a fish compact with gold."—
CHAPMAN'S Translation.

It may be interesting to some that a few words should here be introduced on the natural history of the Mahseer. The Mahseer is a carp, though, as we shall see hereafter, very different in size, flavour, strength, activity, and so forth, from his ignoble name-sake in England, or rather from the fish that we have been accustomed from our boyhood to call *the* carp, as if there was not a very large family of them. So if you like it better, you can call him a barbel. His genealogy may be given as follows:—

Animalia.
Vertebrata.
Class. Pisces.
Sub-class. Teleostii.
Order. Physostomi.
Family. Cyprinidæ.
Sub-family. Cyprininæ.
Genus. Barbus.
Sub-genus. Barbodes.
Species. Barbus (Barbodes) tor.
or Species. Barbus tor.

Those who have read my first edition may perhaps notice that

Teleostii. Greek, *teleos*, perfect; *osteon*, bone.

Physostomi. Greek, *physa*, a bladder; *stoma*, a mouth; the swimming bladder communicates with the digestive canal by a duct.

Cyprinidæ. Latin, *cyprinus*, a carp.

Barbus. Latin, *barba*, a beard.

this classification is different from that adopted before; the former one, though correct at the time it was used, being out of date now. They may notice also that our mutual friend the Mahseer is no longer *Barbus mosal* as then, but is now *Barbus tor.* In 1873 we had more names than one given us by Cuvier and Valenciennes, by Dr. Hamilton Buchanan, and continued by Dr. Day in his monograph of Indian Cyprinidæ.

But in Dr. Day's more recent work "The Fishes of India," published in 1878, the two names *Barbus mosal* and *Barbus tor* are clubbed under one, to wit, *Barbus tor.* I therefore follow the nomenclature of the latest authority on the subject, and subjoin the following complete quotation of Dr. Day's remarks under the species *Barbus tor,* together with his foot-note, because it serves to show the dubious that we are talking of the same fish.

15. Barbus tor, Plate cxxxvi., fig. 5; and cxl., fig. 1*.

Cyprinus, tor, mosal, and *putitora?* Ham. Buch. Fish. Gang., pp. 303, 306, 388; Gray and Hard. Ind. Zool.; McClelland, Ind. Cyp., pp. 271, 303, 337, 388, pl. xli., f. 3; Cuv. and Val. xvi., p. 197; Jerdon M. J. L. and S. 1849, p. 311.

Labeobarbus macrolepis, Heckel, Fische aus Kashmir, p. 60, t.x. f. 2; Bleeker, Beng. p. 60.

Barbus progeneius and *megalepis,* McClelland, Ind. Cyp., pp. 270, 271, 334, 337; Jerdon, M. J. L. and Sc. 1849, p. 311.

Barbus macrocephalus, McClell. Ind. Cyp. pp. 270, 335, pl. 55, fig. 2; Cuv. and Val. xvi, p. 201; Bleeker, Beng., p. 60; Günther, Cat. vii, p. 131; Day, Proc. Z. S., 1869, p. 556.

Barbus mosal, Cuv. and Val. xvi, p. 200; Bleeker, Beng., p. 60; Day, Proc., Z. S. 1870, p. 372.

Barbus mussulah, Sykes, Trans. Zool. Soc. ii, p. 356; Bleeker, Beng., p. 60; Jerdon, M. J. L. and Sc. 1849, p. 313.

Barbus Hamiltonii, Jerdon, M. J. L. and S. 1849, pp. 311, 312.

Labeobarbus, tor and *progenius,* Bleeker, Beng., p. 60, and Cobit, and Cyprin., Ceylon, 1864, p. 10, t. 2.

Barbus macrolepis, Günther, Catal. vii. p. 131.

Burapatra,† Assam: *Poo-meen-candee*‡ Tam.: *Naharm,* Hind.: *Kukhiah,* Punj.: *Joongah, Petiah* and *Kurreah,* Sind.

* For an account of the natural history of the Mahseer, and the sport it affords, see "The Rod in India," by H. S. Thomas, Mangalore, 1873.

† "Hatti Shikaree," *i.e.,* Mr. J. E. Welborne, a resident in Assam, gives the Assamese as *Junga Petia.*

‡ I think the Tamil word should be spelt *Bŏm-min,* as explained a few pages

* B. iii, D. 12 ($\frac{3}{9}$), P. 19, V. 9, A. 7–8 ($\frac{2-3}{5}$), L.l. 25–27, L. tr. 4 4. Last undivided dorsal ray osseous and entire.

Length of head 4 to 5, of caudal $4\frac{3}{4}$ to 5, height of body $4\frac{1}{3}$ to $5\frac{1}{2}$ in the total length. *Eyes*—diameter $6\frac{1}{4}$ to $7\frac{1}{2}$ in the length of the head in moderately sized specimens, but much larger in the young (at 3·5 inches in length, being $3\frac{1}{2}$ in the length of the head; at 5 inches, $4\frac{1}{2}$), 2 to $2\frac{1}{4}$ diameters from the end of the snout, and 2 apart. Interorbital space flat. Opercle $\frac{1}{4}$ higher than wide; the maxilla reaches to below the front edge of the eye; snout pointed; jaws of about the same length: lips thick, with an uninterrupted fold across the lower jaw, and both the upper and lower lips in some specimens produced in the mesial line. Dorsal profile more convex than the abdominal in some examples, not so in others. *Barbels*—the maxillary pair longer than the rostral ones, and extend to below the last third of the eye. *Fins*—the dorsal arises opposite the ventral, and is $\frac{3}{4}$ as high as the body, its last undivided ray is smooth, osseous, strong, and of varying length and thickness. Himalayan, Bengal, and Central Indian specimens generally have the spine strong, and from $\frac{1}{2}$ to $\frac{2}{3}$rd the length of the head, it rarely exceeding this extent. In Canara, Malabar, and Southern India, where the lips are largely developed (*see* Pl. cxl.), the spine is very much stronger, and as long as the head excluding the snout. Pectoral as long as the head excluding the snout, it reaches the ventral which is little shorter. Anal laid flat does not reach the base of the caudal which is deeply forked. *Lateral line*—complete, 2 to $2\frac{1}{2}$ rows of scales between it and the base of the ventral fin: 9 rows before the dorsal. Free portion of the tail longer than high. *Colours*—silvery or greenish along the upper half of the

further on in this chapter. *Poo-min* would mean flower-fish in Tamil, and be incorrect for the Mahseer. It is very difficult indeed to get correct vernacular names. The only way is to get them written down for you by some native who really knows how to spell them in his own language, and then to transliterate them yourself on a correct system. The Canara Canarese name is *Perueal* or *Harale-minu;* the Mysore Canarese, *Hăllămînu;* the Malayalim, *Merurŭl:* the Tulu, *Heragulu* or *Perural;* the Hindustani, *Maha-sir.*

* B iii.	Branchiostegals iii.
D	Dorsal fin.
P	Pectoral fin.
V	Ventral fin.
A	Anal fin.
C	Caudal fin.
L.l.	Lateral line.
L.tr. =	Lateral transverse.

body, becoming silvery shot with gold on the sides and beneath. Lower fins reddish yellow.

This fish is the celebrated "Maha seer" of sportsmen in India. The various large barbels in Assam are termed *Petiah*, with a specific name prefixed to denote the species alluded to.

Barbus macrocephalus, McClelland, from along the Eastern Himalayas and Upper Assam, has not the length of the head, "$\frac{2}{9}$ths only of the total (without the caudal)"—(Günther); but *without the head or caudal*, or $\frac{2}{7}$ths of the total excluding the caudal fin. It has rather a longer head ($4\frac{1}{4}$ in the total) than is usual, its eye is nearer the front end of the head, whilst the upper bone of the suborbital ring is very wide.

Barbus tor H. B. or *progenius* McClell., shows great variation in the length of the head, which seems to augment in proportion with the size of the fish; the body is often much higher, whilst the lips are very much more developed than in the last variety.

Habitat.—Generally throughout India, but in the largest size and greatest abundance in mountain streams, or those which are rocky.

Without being in a position to prove it, I still adhere to the view advanced in 1873, that there are more Mahseers than have been named, and that if it were possible that as much accurate attention could be given to the Mahseer as has been devoted to the Salmonidæ of Great Britain, of Europe, and of America, it would be found that the Mahseers of India would likewise grow in numbers. No one who has not tried it can form any idea of the amount of labour required to collect specimens sufficient to clear up a moot point, to decide which differences are only accidents of local colouring, which the ordinary result of the change of season, which indicate only varieties, and which serve to constitute separate species. To satisfy an accurate mind specimens must be collected from many rivers, in many localities, at various ages, in various seasons, and in goodly numbers; and all details of capture must be reliably noted at the time; all these facts which form the basis of conclusion should also be retained for the satisfaction of other enquirers. I did enough of this to know what a labour it is, enough to know that it would be impossible for me to find sufficient leisure in the intervals of business to exhaust the matter to my own satisfaction; not enough, as I have admitted, to *prove* my view that there are more Mahseers than have been named, and yet enough to indicate its probability. These indications may be not uninteresting to my readers, there-

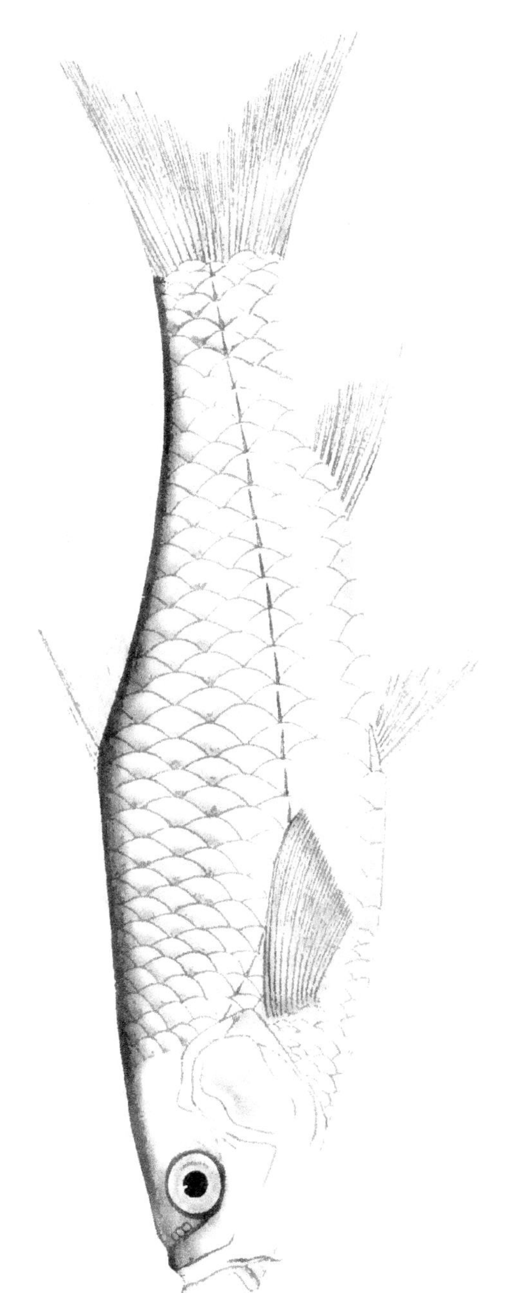

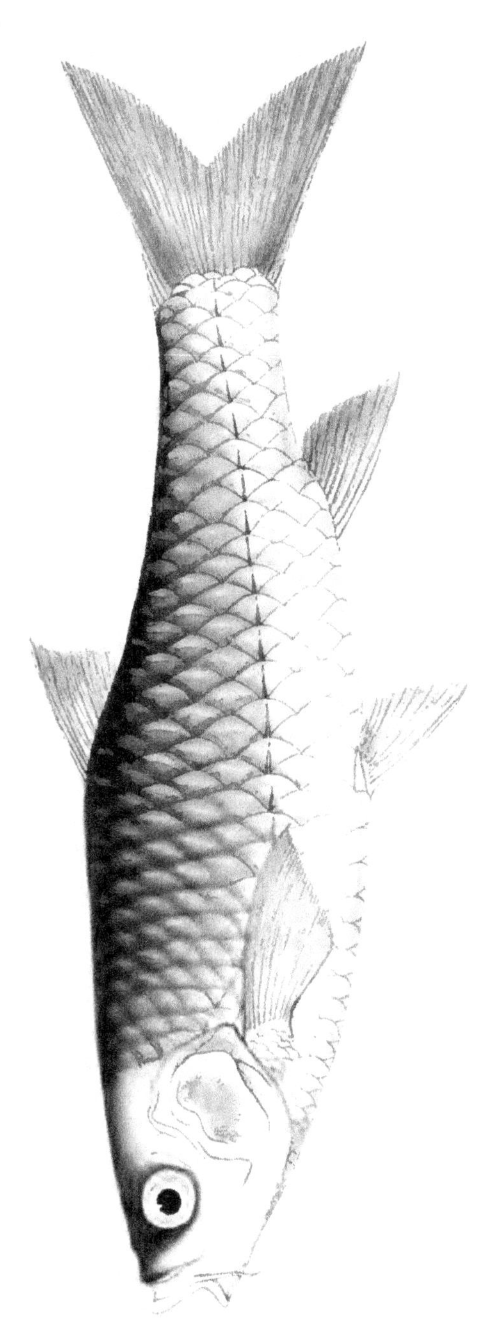

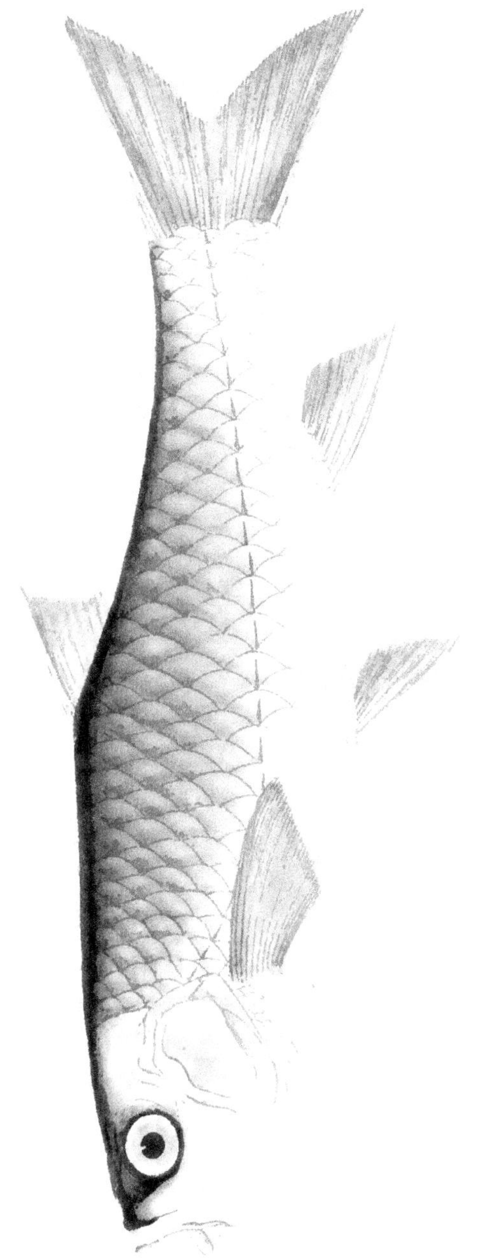

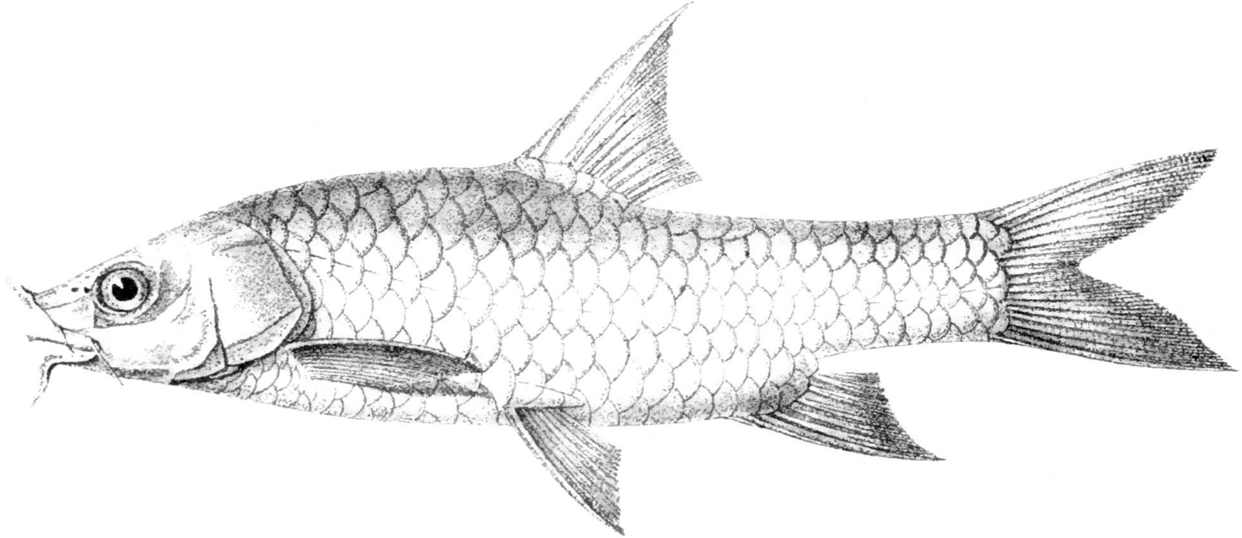

Mintern Bros lith.

BARBUS [illegible]

fore, without claiming for my fish any other than the one name *Barbus tor*, I will present drawings of several Mahseer. The light brown Mahseer, Plate I, was caught at a place called Subramani, in the South Canara District of the Madras Presidency; the grey and gold Mahseer, Plate II, at Sirâdi, in the same district; and the light blue Mahseer, Plate III, near the far-famed Falls of Gairsoppa, in the Mysore territories.

These Plates I, II, and III are from drawings executed by a native draughtsman in Canara. At the time they were done, some seven years ago, I examined them closely enough, as I then thought, but now I am not without doubts that they are faulty in some minor details, and I have no means of re-comparing them with nature. I can only present them as fairly close approximations.

A pretty painting of a 5lb. Mahseer caught in the Arienkavu Pass, near Courtallum in the Tinnevelly District of the Madras Presidency, was kindly sent me by a friend. In that the fish is represented as having a deep chocolate-coloured back and fins, the colour blending into golden brown on the sides and gills, and fading into white on the stomach. The iris of the eye is a bright vermillion, instead of the ordinary light yellow, the pupil black as usual. I am sorry that I cannot reproduce the painting, but the drawing is an artistic sketch without sufficient accuracy of detail in the matter of scales and fin rays. Plate IV, is a copy, by kind permission, of Figure 1, Plate CXL, in Dr. Day's "Fishes of India." It shows the large development of adipose continuations of the upper and lower lips. The flaps are exhibited erect in the drawing which shows well how they can stand free; but they ordinarily lie close against the fish. I have found this peculiar formation occurring both in the fish represented in Plate I, and also in that shown in Plate II, and I have sometimes found it in the Plate II fish in the Gairsoppa river as well as in the Canara rivers. It cannot indicate a mere variety for I have found it so frequently. Does it indicate a species, or is it a temporary growth like the beak of a male salmon in the spawning season. I do not think it is the latter, because I do not clearly remember to have ever seen it half developed, and yet my memory is not quite positive on this point. I am certain, too, that I have observed it in small immature Mahseer of 1 lb. in weight and even under; but that may or may not point to Mahseer breeding at an early age.

Plate V is a drawing of the Bawanny Mahseer. The Bawanny is an affluent of the Cavery in the Madras Presidency, a river that runs eastwards. The rivers which hold the Mahseer named above all run westwards. The Bawanny Mahseer, it will be observed, is much deeper and more high backed than the other Mahseers. To insure accuracy of drawing, every detail of form has in all cases been taken life-size by compass, and then the reduction from that drawing has not been made by eye, but in numerous comparative squares, so that we are insured against even a single scale being too high or too low.

I am sorry that I cannot represent the colours of this fish. It was a most handsome fish. It would have been difficult to do justice to the rich golden hue which shone on the gill covers, and was the predominant colour of every scale. It is from this colour that the natives of that locality call it *Bom-min.* (The *o* like the *o* in kingdom, the *i* long like *mein* or *mean*) which is the Tamil for gold fish, from *pon* gold and *min* a fish. The colour is not at all that of the little Chinese gold fish, to which we are accustomed in glass vases, but something between the colour of a bright new sovereign and that of bright shining copper fresh from the mint, the burnished copper the colour of the outside of each scale, and the tinge of brighter gold flashing through the centre of each scale, and coming out almost all over the gill covers, and showing itself freely in parts of each fin.

How could any artist do justice to such colouring without the actuals before him. And even with the living fish before him it calls for a good artist to seize truth and represent it, for truth in fish colouring is evanescent. My learned readers will readily recall to mind how noble Romans had at their sumptuous feasts live mullet laid upon the table that they might watch the beautifully changing hues of the expiring fish. Have my readers watched a high conditioned Mahseer in like manner? Let them; and they will see that the colours change every second after the fish is out of the water. The eye travels from individual scales to gill covers, to the head, the fins and tail, and before it returns to the original spot, a change has come over that spot, and it is perceptible. The next survey is made more rapidly, but still there is a noticeable change. Thus to notice the changes is easy; but to catch each fleeting shade of colour before it is gone is very

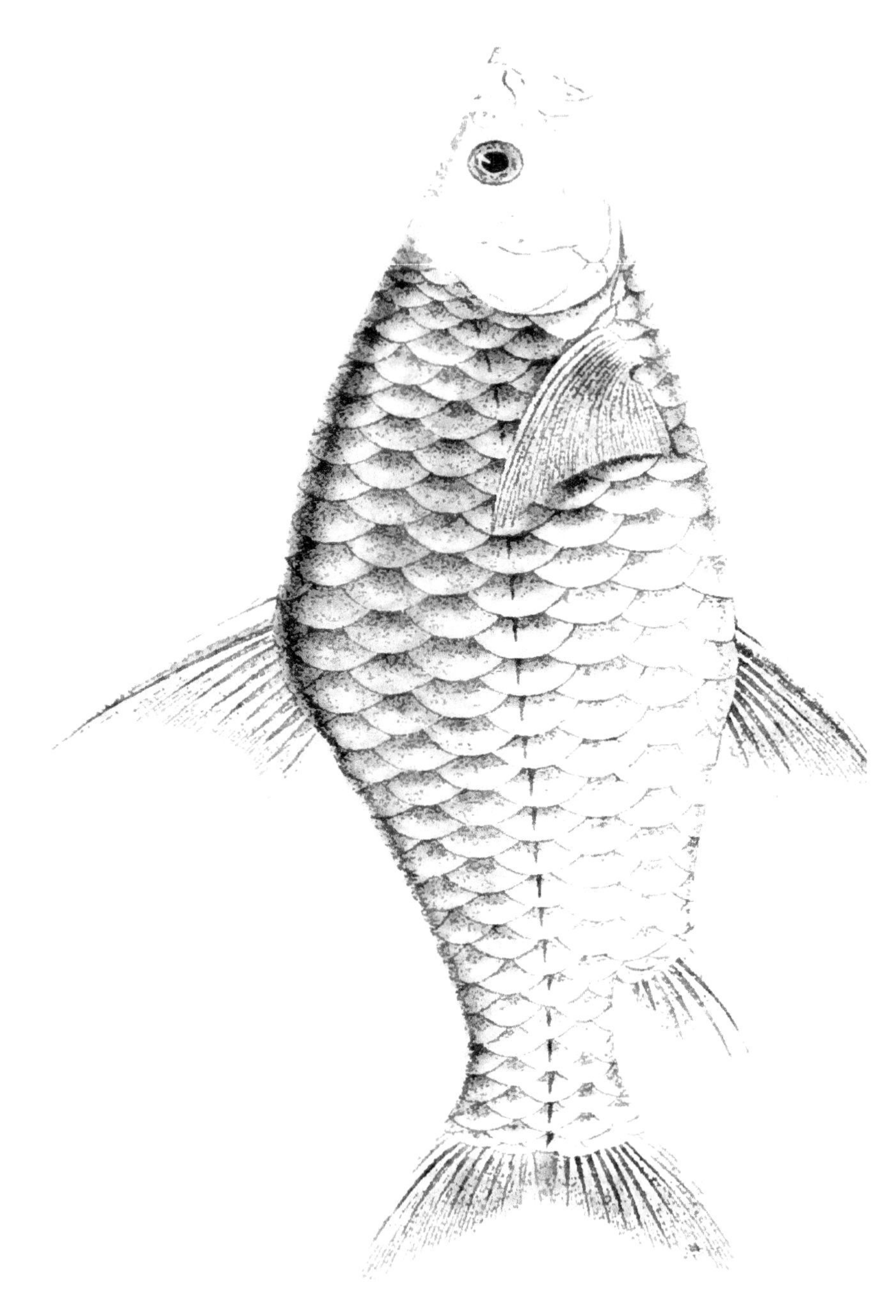

very far from easy. This is what I have essayed to do. I did not care to present my readers with the corpse-like colouring of dead and dying fish. I wanted the resplendent hues of healthy living fish as nature paints them when rejoicing in their element. How did I essay it? I took an artist with me to the water's edge. He had ready rough drawings of fish in any number, and his colours, brushes, &c., were handy. The moment I landed a fish he hit the colours, and roughly and rapidly filled them in. I did the same by his side. We compared notes. We were conscious that change had been going on as we coloured, and that it was hard to say wherein the earliest and wherein the later colours had been correctly seized. So another fish was caught, and the colours of the painting compared with it the instant it was on shore. Necessary corrections having been made, another was captured, and yet another, and these all had to be captured at a season of the year in which the fish were in high condition, with a healthy colour. The result is that I have colouring which some have told me must surely be too bright, whereas I affirm that the failure is rather in the opposite direction. I cannot get sufficient resplendency. I cannot add to each colour the look of burnished metal. I cannot give the changing reflections of each angle of light on the glistening coloured scales, the varying hues of semi-transparent fins showing differently with a dark or a light-background. Enough that I have done my little best to help my readers to recognize our mutual friends of whom we chat together, and that, where I had not the means of making even such a remote approach to a just representation of my beauties, I have preferred leaving the drawings uncoloured.

Keen fishermen will understand that it is no easy matter to lay down the rod and take up the brush when the fish are on the run. There are times when it could not be done at any price, no not for an annual gold mine. There are times, too, when appliances are wanting. Hence it is that some fish are left uncoloured. Friends have engaged to colour fish for me in places inaccessible to myself, and finding the same difficulties have abandoned the attempt. Others have most kindly supplied paintings which unfortunately could not be accepted for want of accuracy.

The Mahseer having been more fished for in Bengal than anywhere else it had grown to be the common idea that it was exclusively a Bengal fish, and at the time I wrote my first edition there was a general impression that there were no Mahseer south of the Nerbuddah. That idea is now exploded.

People talk of *the* Mahseer, just as they talk of *the* carp, as if there was only one of them, whereas the name Mahseer is loosely used for many of the larger carps of India, which differ with the countries in which they are caught, and when fishermen who have caught Mahseer in the North of India, on the West Coast and on the East Coast of Southern India, get together, and describe the redoubted Mahseer somewhat differently before a circle of eager listeners, and thence come to disputing with each other as to who is most accurate, one is reminded of the old fable of the gold and silver shields which the two knights saw and fought about, and as a fisherman my advice would be, the less *carping* about it the better.

The name Mahseer is seemingly derived from the Hindustani words *maha* great and *sir* (pronounced *seer*) head, and as the carps (Fam. Cyprinidae) make up in India a little family of several hundred species, and as the larger carps also are not few in number, it is as well to confine the use of the name Mahseer to the large-headed or large-mouthed carps. The distinction will be found useful to anglers, for large-mouthed and small-mouthed fish of the same family feed differently, and the baits to be tendered to them should in consequence differ accordingly. The want of this simple distinction has led to the Carnatic Carp being called a Mahseer, and to some loss of sport thereby, as will be seen in the Chapter on that fish.

The size of the Mahseer depends much on the size of the river in which it is found, and possibly on other circumstances also with which we are not acquainted, but certainly on the size of the river. The size of salmon at home is similarly found to be not a little dependent on the size of the river they frequent. Size in a river affects both the feeding and the life-time of fish, for a large river affords a greater quantity, a greater variety, and in India a more continuous supply of food than a small river does, and it also ordinarily affords greater opportunities for evading capture. The consequence is that there are rivers in which the Mahseer do not run above 10 or 12 lbs; there are others, again, in which 40 lbs. or 50 lbs. is by no means an exceptional weight. We hear of captures of fish weighing more or less about 100 lbs., and I have in my possession two heads of Mahseer that weighed, approximately, by estimate, 90 lbs. and 150 lbs. each. They have always hung in my hall, and numerous friends have asked me their weight, and quoting from memory I have for seven years given them as 150 lbs. and 180 lbs. respectively, and the mistake became so thoroughly impressed on my memory that in a hurried moment I wrote without verification to the "Asian," 30th September, 1879, that I had such heads of such weights. In wading, however, through a fearful bundle of letters, before committing myself to mis-statements or loose statements in this book, I have discovered my error, and honesty compels me to admit it. The truth must be told in the words of the narrator and donor of the heads, Mr. G. P. Sanderson, author of "Thirteen Years among the Wild Beasts of "India," a book that every sportsman, old or young, must be interested in, and most, even old hands, may profit from. Young hands should not essay heavy game without having read it. These Mahseer were caught by Mr. Sanderson with a night line in the Cavery River.

"As to my big fish I put it down at 150 lbs., the other 50 have "been added in the telling. I had no means of weighing it, but "I found it was as much as I could lift a couple of inches from "the ground by hugging it in my arms; no one but a big Mussul- "man peon in camp could do as much as this. I imagine that "a man of 11 stone should have no difficulty in lifting a man of "his own weight off the ground if lying on his back; I have since "lifted a man of over 10 stone with greater ease than the fish. "A native overseer with me, who was formerly in the Ashtagram "Sugar Works, put it down at 5 maunds (or 140 lbs. Mysore); he "said they were accustomed to deal with 5 maund bags, and he "knew the feel of them pretty well. The measures of the fish "were: length, including tail, 60 inches; greatest girth 38 inches; "inside lips when open, circumference 24 inches. The skin and "head are in the Bangalore Museum.

"Of course my rough estimate of the fish's weight is valueless "as fact, but you may believe that I was not out many pounds. It "was an astonishingly thick and heavy fish for its short length. "I have caught them 5 ft. 6 in., but not much more than 80 lbs.

" It had a shoulder like a bullock, steeply hanging over. I have " caught about 50 of them, but my next largest was about 90 lbs. " I have no doubt in my own mind that they run over 200 or 250 " lbs., as I have seen teeth and bones of them far larger than my " 150-pounder; they are often caught by the natives."

So huge were these heads that one of them fully covered the skeleton of an unusually fine sambre's head, and I had arranged it in my hall with the sambres head inside the Mahseer's head, and the grand antlers coming, as if naturally, out of the Mahseer's head, when a friend called. He looked round at the various spoils of bison, sambre, fish, &c., till he cast his eyes on this. "Rather a " rare buffalo isn't it?" said I. "Have you ever shot one like " it?" "Buffalo! Buffalo!! It's not a buffalo," he said, "but " it's something of the cow tribe." I had owed him one. But he was not long before he left me again in his debt.

Dr. Day, in his "Monograph of Indian Cyprinidæ, Part II, under *Barbus (barbodes) tor*, writes: "A noted sportsman in the " N.W. Provinces writing to me says, his largest fish taken with " a rod and line was captured in the River Poonch, 24 miles from " Jhelum; it measured from snout to bifurcation of tail 3 feet " 11 inches and weighed 62lbs. . . The cube of a fish's length " gives his weight in pounds; fish may vary a pound or two " according to condition, but the test is wonderfully correct." I confess to a lack of confidence in the rule myself, for I think that fish of the same species vary much, not only with the condition of the same individual at different seasons and in different rivers and climates, but from individuality of figure, contracted probably from accidents of feeding in earliest youth. Observe the difference in the weights and lengths of the fish contrasted immediately above by Mr. Sanderson.

Though purely fresh-water fish, Mahseer are more or less migratory in their habits, ascending during the floods considerable heights, two thousand five hundred feet to my knowledge in the Canara district, ten pound fish being there found half way up the Mereara Ghat, and travelling long distances for the sake of spawning. When the streams are swollen by the monsoon rains they are able to ascend to parts of the river till then unapproachable for want of water. There they find fresh feeding grounds that are inaccessible to them at other times. There they linger till the diminishing stream warns them to be moving downwards. There they deposit their spawn, and thus secure for their fry, when hatched, waters then dwindled to dimensions much better suited to their puny strength than the deeper current of the lower river. The spawning done, the parent fish keep dropping gently downwards with the continually decreasing waters, and before the spawn they have deposited is hatched, they are completely cut off by paucity of water from their fry, so that till the commencement of the same monsoon in the following year they cannot return to devour them.

But they must not, after the manner of salmon, be considered back fish or foul fish when descending the rivers. Careful examination of the ovaries of many fish has satisfied me that the Mahseer does not spawn like the salmon all at one time, but just as a fowl lays an egg a day for many days, so in my opinion the Mahseer lays a batch of eggs at a time, and repeats the process several times in a season. How many batches it lays in a season cannot be positively said, but I should judge from the appearance of the ovaries that there were three batches.

Fishermen can judge for themselves, and may be interested in doing so. For this purpose cut the fish open from the vent to the mouth, and the ovaries will be found lying close against the back-bone. There is no mistaking them, a thin skin, more like a quill in size than anything else at first, with the little round dots of eggs evidently apparent through. That these are in states of development differing among themselves in any individual fish will be easily recognizable; but which are more or less approaching complete ripeness for being laid, can only be learnt by the experience gained from comparison of different fishes. When nearly ripe the eggs will be hanging more loosely together, and the vent will be inflamed. After a batch has been laid the lower part of the tail, and the ventral fin, or the fin on the stomach, will be more or less worn, bearing marks, in short, of having been used to work out a hollow in the gravel for the reception of eggs. This ragged frayed appearance of tail and fin will indicate, therefore, that one or more batches of eggs have been laid, although others for future laying may still be found in different stages of development in the ovaries.

If the fisherman sees no eggs in the long thin quill-like bag lying close against the back-bone, between it in fact and the intestines, then he may be sure that he has got hold of a male with milt.

The salmon, we know, completely exhausts itself by the mighty effort of laying at one time about as many thousand eggs as it weighs pounds, and it is not surprising that it should then be in such a weak state as to be unfit for human food or sport, unable almost to take care of itself; and even after it has somewhat recovered, and become what is called "well mended," it cannot be expected to be the same fish in the river that it is in the sea. It is a sea-fish, and the river is not its proper element any more than India is yours and mine. It still pines for shrimp sauce and a furlough in the sea. The case with the Mahseer is, however, very different indeed. It gets through its egg laying on the same principle as the fowl, not exactly one egg a day, but in batches at intervals, and does not feel the same drain on itself as if it had laid them all at one time. Moreover, it is all the while in its own element in the river, is getting as good feeding as it can ever have, and is recouping itself between the several layings. The consequence is that I do not remember ever to have come across a Mahseer looking so emaciated as to appear unfit for human food, though I have observed them to be in poorer condition at one time than at another. But that is very different from looking as a spent salmon does, big and bony headed, lank and thin-shouldered, pale and haggard as if he had been to a ball or a pool till small hours every night for a month. It is a general rule that every animal, and for the matter of that every grass, &c., is in its finest condition when preparing to reproduce its species. A hen is never in better condition than when full of small undeveloped eggs, and about to commence laying them. It may fairly be concluded, therefore, that the Mahseer which is prepared to lay one or two more batches of eggs is in good reproducing condition, is in fact in high condition, although it may have already laid one or more batches that season. When it has completed its spawning for the year it has much deteriorated in flavour and lost all its richness, though it is not unwholesome like a spent salmon.

A reason for the Mahseer laying in batches may be interesting. Indian rivers are very variable in their depth, a tropical sun and a thirsty land drying up the streams that feed them, and reducing them rapidly to very much smaller dimensions than they boasted during the rains. The change in their size is both greater and more rapid than in European rivers. It would not be well, therefore, for the fish in them to spawn by the same rule as the fish in European waters. The ova laid in one place might be high and dry in a few days, and the whole laying lost. It would be like committing an army to the Great Eastern, instead of dividing the risks by consigning it to several troop-ships. By laying in several batches not only are the chances of success multiplied, but the fry are more widely dispersed over the rivers, and by happy experience discover for themselves the force of the proverb "the fewer the better the cheer." There is little doubt the fry of the Mahseer eat, amongst other things, the fry of the smaller sorts of fish; these are much bred in the smaller feeders. Where such streamlets fall into the river, therefore, each batch of Mahseer finds a separate *table d'hôte.*

An inventory of the contents of a Mahseer's stomach ought not to be without interest to a fisherman, for unless he knows what the fish is in the habit of eating, he cannot tell what bait to offer it. If he expects to be successful, he must offer natural food or something resembling it, for a fish is not so foolish as to take anything that is offered to it on the sole faith of the advertisement. Only reasoning beings do that. Let us then turn out this gentleman's stomach, and discover his weaknesses, as Prince Henry and Poins did Falstaff's, from the contents of his pocket. What do we find there? Aquatic weeds of all sorts, some taken intentionally, some when grabbing at the insects that live on them; seeds of the *Vateria Indica* or Dhup of the West Coast, which are about the size of a pigeon's egg; the seeds of many other trees also which hang over the river where it is forest-clad; bamboo seeds; rice thrown in by man; and unhusked rice, or paddy, as it is washed from the fields; crabs, large fresh-water crabs as big as the palm of a man's hand, and with back and claws so thick and hard that it is astonishing how the fish can have the power to crunch them into the small pieces in which they are found in the intestine; small fish, earthworms, water beetles, grasshoppers, small flies of sorts, water or stone crickets, shrimps, and molluscs or fresh-water snails are also found there, the latter shell and all, and smashed to pieces like the crabs.

Of all this category the easiest food for the fisherman to present in a natural form is a small fish or imitation fish.

It will also be observed that the food taken on the surface of the water is little in comparison with that taken under it, and at the very bottom. The fish, beetles, crickets, shrimps, are all found well under water; the crabs, worms, molluscs quite at the bottom; and from the proportionate quantity found in them, the crabs, molluscs, and fish, seem to be their favourite food.

This is what Paley would call "internal evidence." But we have also external evidence to the same effect, deducible from the formation of the outside of the mouth. The four fine feelers hanging down, two on each side of the mouth, which give him the scientific name of *barbus* or bearded (from the Latin *barba*, a beard), are indications of a bottom feeder.

What the thick lips are for I cannot say, but I hazard the surmise that it is not impossible they are to enable the fish to detach from the rocks the water-snails on which they so largely feed.

The upper lip is capable of being extended beyond the lower lip, and brought down to the same level, so as to form a cup on the bottom of the stream, and cover any small body, such, for instance, as the aforesaid molluscs detached from their hold by the upper lip, and being washed rolling down the bottom of the stream. The molluscs being thus detached and covered, are readily drawn up into the mouth by suction, the process by which a fish always gets its food into his mouth: for how else could it do it rapidly and easily in water? Let any one try to catch a grain of falling rice or other light substance in his hand in a bath. If he moves his hand quickly, the motion will be communicated through the water to the object, which will consequently evade his grasp. How else could a trout take down a water-bred fly that sits jauntily on the water ready to rise again if alarmed. I have seen Mahseer sucking in their food in countless crowds at places where they were habitually fed by the worshippers and priests at a native temple, and have heard their loud sob-like noise as they sucked in air as well as water in their hurry to secure the grains in the scramble. Dr. Frank Buckland has written something about certain tame codfish doing much the same. Anybody who has watched gold fish in a globe will have seen them constantly sucking in water, drinking it as people used to think in the dark ages, really breathing it, that is sucking it in, and passing it through their gills, which are their lungs for the purpose of getting out of the water the oxygen contained in it. By the very same process a fish sucks in a mouthful of water, and with it the fly sitting on it, and down goes the fly, down the little Maelstrom thus created. In the same way probably does the Mahseer suck up the detached molluscs, his peculiar formation of mouth enabling him to do it from the bottom where another fish could not.

To test their power of sucking up, I have fed them at a place where they were accustomed to be fed, and tempted them nearer and nearer, till they were well within observation, and having then thrown in a good handful of rice, so that much of it must sink to the bottom before they could get it, I watched them taking it off the sandy bottom. They sucked it up with great rapidity, so that it wanted close observation, but I watched them very carefully for some time, and distinctly saw the upper lip thrust out from its socket, and brought down over the rice, and then there was a clear act of suction for each grain, though the grains were taken up one after another nearly as fast as a fowl picks up corn. The fish the while were not swimming level in the water, but with their tails just enough inclined upwards to allow the pectoral fins to work without touching the bottom. The pectoral fins were so near the bottom that the motion contributed to the water by each vibration stirred up the fine sand, but they did not touch the bottom. By the suction from the mouth, however, I could not perceive that any sand at all was disturbed. They picked up the single grains of rice cleanly and cleverly, and quickly.

The Mahseer, then, is an accomplished bottom feeder.

The means by which the large crabs, shells, and other hard substances are reduced to a mass of small pieces by the Mahseer is doubtless the formidable set of teeth in the throat. Every carp has teeth in its throat, placed so far down that they are not visible in the mouth; but the teeth of the Mahseer's throat are unusually formidable, and the bones out of which they grow are beautifully formed with a great surface at the back for the muscles to play upon, and that not directly, but with the advantage of a good leverage. If any *blasé* individual thinks this "very like a whale," just let him slip a finger down a live Mahseer's throat, and I promise him the luxury of a new sensation.

These pharyngeal or throat teeth are not set in sockets like human teeth, but are continuations of the pharyngeal bones.

Unlike other teeth, in fish instead of dentine, they have a coating of enamel, which is continued to their base. There seems to be no provision for renewing them in case of loss, no adjoining row of teeth as in the shark, no second tooth below as in the human being; and in an instance in which I noticed that two were wanting on one side, the place where they should be was quite smooth. They are not used for capturing food at all, but for crushing it in its passage down the throat. The fine perforations through which they are supplied with nerves and nutriment are easily seen. The attachment of the muscles to the pharyngeal bones is also very apparent and in keeping with what we know of the power with which they are used.

Professor Spencer F. Baird, Commissioner of Fish and Fisheries in the United States, says in his report for 1875–76, that the pharyngeal teeth of the common carp, *Cyprinus Carpio*, are shed annually a little before spawning time. Whether or not our large Indian carp, the Mahseer, does the same is a point that it may interest some to observe. I do not think it does. I certainly have not examined carefully for this specific purpose, but I have caught Mahseer before their spawning time and have never noticed any indications of such shedding, and I think I should have noticed them if they had been there. For instance, I have seen broken teeth unreplaced, and I have never seen loose teeth, or incomplete young teeth. If the teeth are shed one can readily imagine that it would influence the feeding of the fish at that season of the year. I certainly have found times even with clear water, when the Mahseer could not be induced to look at a fly or fish, and I have been utterly puzzled for a reason. Still it does not follow that want of a new set of teeth was the reason, and it may quite as well have been the east wind. There the question is, however, for enquiring anglers to investigate, do Mahseer shed their pharyngeal teeth annually as a stag sheds his horns, and if they do, when do they shed them, and how long are the new teeth in coming on, and what is the food, if any, during the toothless period?

The Mahseer has also great power of jaw by means of which it is able at a blow to stun a live fish, and to make up by compression for the absence of the teeth usually found in the mouth of predacious fish. That it makes other use of it also to the detriment of the angler will be found in the next chapter.

CHAPTER IV.

CIRCUMVENTING THE MAHSEER.

"'Take my bait,' cried Hiawatha,
'Take my bait Oh king of fishes!'"
LONGFELLOW.

SOME people complain that the Hindu does every thing in a way opposite to that which you would naturally expect of a sane man, because opposite to that way in which all Europeans are accustomed to do the like acts. On entering a house he has not the ordinary politeness to take off his hat, but instead thereof, he kicks off his shoes; in place of making himself a little extra civil before a big wig, he folds his arms, and stands bolt upright, and so forth. Similarly the Mahseer, being a thorough Asiatic, does many things by contraries. If you expect him to take better, as any decent salmon or trout would, when there is a spate in the river, you will be very much mistaken. Except for a live bait not a fin will stir then. If you see the river discolored, you had very much better not waste your labour and your patience on it, for you may be sure you will not catch a single fish either with a fly or spinning. You must wait till the river is clear again, wait till just the time you would consider the most unfavourable for trout or salmon. Though I have taken Mahseer freely when the river has been the least bit tinged by a thunderstorm, still I hold to the opinion that, for a fisherman who keeps carefully out of sight, clear water is best, that in short the Mahseer takes best in clear water, and for the reason, I fancy, that he sees best then. It is not the season of the year that prevents the Mahseer taking; it is not because the river has been swollen by rainfall, and contains perhaps other more attractive bottom feeding. The result on the Mahseer is just the same when, without any swelling, the river is coloured in the middle of the fine season by the drainage from rice fields, freshly ploughed and swamped for the second crop cultivation. Similarly artificial colouring of the water has on trout the same effect as natural colouring from rainfall, and it is a semi-poaching dodge, never condescended to by me, dear reader, to puddle a small stream, and then take them out with a worm, and this at times when the day is so hot and bright that they will not look at a fly. This peculiarity of the Mahseer is more against good fishermen than it is against tyros, because it is exactly opposed to all the experiences of the former, and those who do know something about fishing in England are consequently more likely to be on the wrong tack in India, than those who know nothing or next to nothing about fishing in general, for they would naturally arrange to fish at the very time when in India they are least likely to have sport. I have, however, tested this question pretty thoroughly, and am quite satisfied that it may be laid down as a safe rule, that it is useless to fish for Mahseer except in clear water; it must be at least so clear that you can see the small pebbles at the bottom with ease in 4 feet of water, and it may be as much clearer as ever you like. You need not be the least bit afraid if it is as clear as crystal, indeed it ordinarily is so through all the best fishing months of the year. I have fished in vain with the water so far cleared after a spate that I could see the small pebbles in 2 feet of water, and that with great patience and diligence in known, good, easily commanded water, and with a large and very bright spoon, and yet I only stirred two fish, and even they ran short. I conceive I must, from knowing localities, have taken my bait very close to their noses, and kept it dallying there provokingly, and that even then they missed it from visual obliquity in the coloured water. I am for bright water, therefore, and in this respect the English fisherman must forego his old creed, and adopt a new faith as fully as did the thorough going young scamp of an undergraduate who, unable otherwise to find fit expression for the radical change for the better that had taken place in his resolutions, informed his friends that he had not only "turned over a *new leaf*," as parentally entreated, but *several libraries*.

One mode of fishing for Mahseer there is that may be followed in coloured water. I was not aware of it when the above remarks on bright water were written in the first edition, but those remarks are thoroughly applicable still to all the ordinary methods of fishing for Mahseer, and are worthy to be impressed as contrary to ordinary ideas, and live bait fishing is somewhat of an exceptional way to fall back upon in coloured water, rather than to use by preference to fly-fishing or spinning. I will therefore let the above remarks stand in all their unqualified force for the benefit of the great majority of fishermen, and will refer the man unfortunately overtaken by a spate, and the man who prefers that mode of fishing, to a separate chapter on live bait fishing for Mahseer.

To any one with an eye for fish a single glance is sufficient to show that the Mahseer is a carp. It has a leathery mouth without a vestige of a tooth in it anywhere, the ordinary conclusion would be that carp-like it is not calculated to prey on small fish, but more likely to be taken with dough or a lobworm. An examination of its stomach has, however, told a different tale (page 29), and thence it was that I first learnt how great a fish-eater the Mahseer is. It has the same weakness for a fish diet as its congener the English chub, only it has it to a much greater extent.

But we have not yet done with our friend's Asiatic contrarieties. This mealy-mouthed gentleman, who looks as if his soft leathery lips could not hurt anything, has a peculiar way of killing his fish. He has no teeth in his mouth wherewith to hold any slippery little fish he may catch, and prevent its struggling out again before he can swallow it. In lieu of this he is therefore provided with great power of jaw, and he kills, and holds his fish, by compression, violent compression. It is difficult to conceive how so soft a mouth can give the bite it does, can bear to give the violent crush it does; but there is the analogy of the tiger, which has a yielding springy pad, on which it treads noiselessly as on velvet, with which it can however strike a blow that will break the backbone of a buffalo, and crush in the cranium of a man. That the Mahseer can exert great power of compression with its soft mouth I once had clearly proved to me. My spoon bait, which was nearly new, and for weight's sake unusually stout, and in thorough repair when I cast it in for a spin, was doubled right in two, and crumpled up like a piece of paper, when I landed my fish, and took it out of his mouth. He must have happened to catch it edgewise in his mouth as it spun, and thus been able to exert his strength on it; for had it not been exactly edgewise on, it would have turned and slipped away from his jaw as he pressed it, and thus it would have got flat in his mouth. Probably few fish get a fair bite at a spoon at the very angle of the spoon in the very part of the mouth required to produce such an effect on such a hard substance; the chances must be much against it, and that would account for my having seen such a result but once. But once seen there was *no* longer room for doubt about the power of the fish; the spoon was whole and sound when cast in, was cast in deep water clear of rocks, was not run against anything by him, for it was well inside his mouth when I took it out directly he was landed. Had I tried to produce the same effect, it would have required a good downright blow, with a hammer and anvil to help me. I then bethought me of the spoon of a friend which was thinner than mine, and which was much indented as I had thought at the time by rocks. I bethought me too of the many hooks I had lost unintelligibly; I knew I had a light hand acquired by killing trout on fine tackle, and yet treble hook after treble hook had been smashed, sometimes before I had felt my fish at all, and some of them had been curled up like a ramshorn, and curled inwards as from outside pressure, not outwards as from tension. The murder was out; they had been crunched up by the Mahseer's power of compression, and the treble hooks had suffered more than the single, because they had offered resistance, while the single hooks had turned in the mouth and evaded it. When further considered from this point of view the object of the mouth being soft instead of bony is apparent, for it would be easier to hold a struggling slippery object between two compressing sides that yielded enough for it to partially embed itself, than between two unimpressibly hard sides that could get no grip on the object. These my views on the Mahseer's power of compression have, like not a few others put forward in the earlier edition of this little work, been only confirmed by the further experience of myself and other anglers, and stand no longer on comparatively few instances however striking. But it would be tedious if I were continually pointing my readers to confirmations, and I shall indulge the hope that they will be kindly content to take my word as they did at the first.

These three main points, then, being borne in mind, the necessity for fishing in clear water, the Mahseer's love of small fish, and its power of smashing by compression, we shall be in a better position for arranging to circumvent it.

There is yet another point which may as well be reverted to before proceeding further, and that is the bottom-feeding habits of the Mahseer. This was deduced in the last chapter from the evidence of the contents of the stomach, an organ not given to telling fibs, and from the formation of the outside of the mouth. I lay stress on this habit from a fishing point of view, because I am convinced that a due appreciation of and allowance for it will lead to better sport. I lay stress on it also because I know it is commonly disregarded. It stands to reason that you are more likely to catch a fish by seeking it on its feeding grounds, and there offering it its natural food, than by requesting its attention in a somewhat unusual direction, the surface, and there too to a novel object, not much like any thing in creation, a gaudy salmon fly. I lay stress on this point because so many fish for the Mahseer with an artificial fly at the surface of the water, and the salmon-fisher is from more reasons than one very loth to give up his fly. The fly is cleaner and much less troublesome than any other lure. It is much easier to throw a salmon fly than to spin a fish, and Mahseer doubtless *are* caught with a fly.

The Brahmin, who is as punctilious about his food as a much-fished trout, describes a pariah as "one who eats without asking," and if the Mahseer were not in respect of food as omnivorous as a pariah, it would never take down such an unearthly thing as a salmon fly in the promiscuous manner it sometimes does. Though it does take it, and there is some sport to be had with the fly, still in my opinion it is not a natural bait, and therefore not the best lure that can be offered, and the sport thereby obtained is decidedly inferior to that to be had by spinning. Trout are doubtless to be caught in England by very poor fishermen, with very incorrect fancy flies, still if the correct fly be used, that is, a good imitation of the natural fly at the time on the water, it is undeniable that the chances of sport are sensibly increased. Similarly, if the reader will waive his prejudices for the fly, and will spin deep with a small fish as bait, I will engage that he shall not only kill more, but also better fish, than with a fly. I think I may safely say that if he can spin as well as he can fly fish, he will kill three Mahseers spinning to one with a fly, and that the total weight in pounds shall be more than three to one.

Still he may say that he prefers the fly, that he loves the excitement of the swirl on the surface, and the rapid approximate guess at the weight of the fish he has just missed, has all but caught, and has at least had the pleasure of seeing, or better still loves to form a rapid idea of the size of the fellow he is well into, and is in for a fight with, and means to take all the more pains about taming now he sees he is such a grand one.

He may say he prefers the fly, and prefers it so much that he would rather kill fewer by that means than more spinning, on the same principle as he would rather catch fewer with the rod than more with the net. If so, by all means let him stick to the style of fishing from which he derives most pleasure, and I will admit that, besides the advantages already conceded, the fly has this still further recommendation, that it can be thrown further than a minnow. There are pools and runs the best parts of which cannot be reached with the minnow, but that can be well covered with a fly, and there are sometimes places in which, from rushes or weeds, the water cannot be reached at all spinning. For such occasions I always carry a fly collar in my fly book, and bend it on till I come to ground where it can be exchanged again for the spinning tackle.

But as there are places where it is impossible to bring spinning into play, so are there places where the river is so overhung with forest on all sides that it is difficult enough to get to the water's edge at all, and impossible without a boat to find room to throw a fly. In such places even the staunch advocate of the fly will find it advantageous to have a spinning collar in his pocket, ready for exchange till such time as he can revert to his favourite lure. If he spins at all well, the result may induce him to keep the spinning tackle on a little longer, and perhaps may eventually convert him.

But if he still prefers the fly, or at any rate wishes to use it on occasion, I must request him to be good enough to repair to the chapter specially devoted to his subject.

In either case, however, let him remember above all things that he is fishing in clear water with a bright sky, and that he must consequently be much more careful to keep out of sight than if he were fishing in England, on a cloudy day, by a river more or less coloured.

CHAPTER V.

SPINNING FOR MAHSEER.

"That fish that is not catched thereby
Alas! is wiser far than I."—
DONNE.

THE inventory which we took in a former chapter (Chap. III) of the contents of this Asiatic gentleman's intestinal canal showed that he was as omnivorous as the mortal Mr. Samuel Weller was omnibibulous. Metaphorically speaking, the accommodating answer of each of them is "all taps is vanities;" but the particular vanity of the Mahseer, or at least that which we are best able to oblige him with, is, as we have seen, a small fish; and the question next arises how is the dish to be served.

Every one knows that fish is good for nothing if it is not fresh, and a pike or perch carries this maxim so far as to prefer them "all alive, alive oh." A little roach all alive and kicking has peculiar charms for a jack, but well nigh irresistible though it may be, and many staunch advocates though it may have in consequence, still I am not one of them. Except it be for a trimmer, I should prefer not to use it; my idea being that with a dead fish you can cover so much more water, that you can show your spinning bait to ten or twenty fish, where your stationary live bait will be seen by only one, and perhaps not that for a while. Advertise freely and you will be sure to find a "claimant." May he be as heavy as Sir Roger. By the ordinary law of chances the odds are you will come across more taking fish out of the ten or twenty than in the one who happens to live in or near the hole into which you have cast your live bait; and you cannot be constantly moving your live bait or you will kill it. You must just quietly drop him into a likely hole, and leave him to "paddle his own canoe;" whereas with a spinning bait you can take it saunteringly all through those deep eddies that ought to be full of big fish, just under those big rocks, and as close to their edge as you like; you can playfully dally awhile in front of any pet corner; you can hark back after a little respite to where you have seen a fin move; in short *you* can "paddle your own canoe" when and where you like, and not be at the mercy of your live bait, and then if you can really paddle well, your bait will be as tempting as most live baits. The sequence in my mind is that a good spinner will kill more jack than a live bait fisher; but of course all depends on his being a good spinner, a natural painstaking one. The live bait lover certainly has one very great advantage, which is of more importance than he is probably aware of; that is, that he is generally more out of sight. Out of mere idleness, perhaps, without any preconsideration, he lays down his rod, and sits leisurely down a little way off, and this is in truth *the* most weighty reason why he should catch more fish than the dead bait spinner, who is perhaps standing prominently out in fine relief on the very edge of the bank, and constantly moving his legs and arms in the action of walking and spinning. How men can think a fish is such a fool as to take a bait, when it sees the "*vultus instantis tyranni*" on the bank, I cannot make out. Still they do think it, or at least ignore the visual organs of the fish, and go on fishing all their days after the manner of Hiawatha, jawing at the Sturgeon Nama,

> "'Take my bait,' cried Hiawatha,
> 'Take my bait Oh king of fishes!'"

"Hiawatha's fishing" is a very pretty study of what *not* to do, unless by the way you really want to get inside a sturgeon, in which case I say good bye and part company, for I am not game to play Ajidaumo.

If the spinner of dead bait will be careful to conceal himself from view of his desired prey as thoroughly as the live-bait-lover unconsciously does, he will not be at the great disadvantage he otherwise generally is; on the contrary, he will be at an advantage, in that he tries so much more water with his lure.

And as to his lure, too, I am convinced he is not at the discount he is commonly thought to be. If he manages it badly, of course he cannot expect to fare well, but if he is really a good hand at spinning, his bait will look every bit as natural as a live fish, and, strange to say, sometimes even more so. Watch a live bait and a well spun minnow and compare them. I will back the spun one. The live bait has, perhaps, a great hook all unconcealed and too apparently sticking out of its lip; or if baited in the side, it is soon lying somewhat unnaturally on its side; or it has managed in its lively gyrations to make a tangle of its line, and encircle itself therein; or it is more dead than alive, and looking somewhat suspicious; or may be it is off altogether, and the angler is in happy ignorance of the fact, and in blissful expectancy of a momentary run at a bare hook.

My sentiments then are that, if the angler will be at the pains to spin delicately, will take the trouble to conceal himself thoroughly, and will bait his fish neatly with the hooks well concealed, he will in clear water kill more by spinning a dead fish than by using a live bait.

In coloured water the objections to prominent hooks may not be so pertinent, but of that hereafter. Only here be it remembered that, in live bait fishing, the hooks must of necessity be obvious for they cannot be embedded in the flesh as much as in a dead fish.

I have killed Mahseer with a spoon, with a phantom minnow, and other imitation fish of sorts, and with a dead fish, and there is something to be said for each of them, something that will commend itself differently to different anglers in proportion as they like taking trouble or not.

The spoon bait is, of course, only an imitation of a fish, and about the rudest imitation we are in the habit of using. Still it is by no means to be contemned, and does a great deal more business than would be supposed, one side being copper or gilt, and the other, the inside, being silvered, it flashes as it revolves, and is seen a long way off in consequence. But if too closely inspected the rudeness of the imitation is so apt to be discovered, that it is seldom used in England except in coloured water; but as it is of no use fishing for Mahseer in any thing but clear water, the spoon is at a further discount in India. Still it does very good service if used judiciously. It stands to reason that in water clear as crystal its use should be confined to the runs and eddies: for in the quieter waters you could not get it to revolve rapidly enough for deceit, without pulling it faster through the water than is advisable. In a good strong run you may even keep it stationary, nay, more, may also lower it slowly down stream, the stream doing all the spinning for you.

In consequence of this necessity for using it in running, and chiefly in rapid water, I prefer the spoon to be somewhat heavier than it ordinarily is in England; for if it comes to the surface it ceases to have a hold on the water, and consequently ceases to spin. Having regard, moreover, to the bottom-feeding propensities of the Mahseer I prefer to spin deep.

As to the different sizes of spoons a word may be better said in the chapter on tackle. I will only mention here that I have been so hard pushed for bait in camp that I have been thankful to lay hands on a mustard spoon, and convert it to the much more useful end in existence of being a beguiler of good Mahseer.

Apropos of this I may be allowed to tell a little incident. I was fishing in a densely forest-clad part in which a guide was necessary. I was fishing with a spoon, and my guide sat watching me listlessly till he saw me get hold of, play, and land a decent Mahseer. Then he woke up and was all attention. He closely watched me unhook the fish, and straightway begin spinning again with the same spoon, and soon catch another Mahseer. It was too much for him. He could contain himself no longer. Is it lawful for me, he asked, to see the hook. Certainly, I said, and handed him the spoon. He turned it over and over in his hand and scrutinized it closely and deliberately. Then, with a motion of the head, and a look of being thoroughly satisfied that he had got to the bottom of the mystery, he solemnly handed back the spoon. He asked no explanation of me, so I gave none, but went on fishing and caught more. That evening he got a wrapt audience round him, and expounded the whole matter. "That gentleman catches Mahseer by magic of hand, he puts on no bait at all. I saw it with my own eyes. It is pure magic of hand." He verily believed it.

A spoon has this further advantage that it is much lighter than a dead fish, and if you use a springy fly top, as I do, in preference to a stiff spinning top, as used in trolling for pike, you will find that its comparative lightness will allow of your throwing a spoon of ample size, whereas with a natural fish bait you are restricted in size by the weight which your top joint will lift and swing out without being strained or broken.

This is probably the reason why stiff spinning rods have come to be thought the right rods for Mahseer. But more of them anon.

There is something very slippery about a flying spoon; you cannot catch hold of it without coming well on to the hook, and I think that you loose less runs at a spoon than at any other bait. A fish cannot lay hold of it anywhere without slipping off it straight on to the hooks.

The spoon is also as clean fishing as the fly. As soon as you have killed a fish and removed it from the hook, your lure is ready again.

Moreover, you may not always be able to procure bait; at any rate not immediately on your arrival at your fishing quarters, and the first evening's or morning's sport may be lost if you are not prepared with a spoon or an artificial fish.

I have used a phantom minnow too, and other artificial minnows with advantage, and any salmon minnow will kill, but it should be specially dressed for this country, as will be seen in the chapter on tackle, or it will be quickly demoralized. There are fishermen, also, who have used an artificial dace or roach, such as are made at home for pike fishing, and had good sport with them. But they are not fitted for all waters, only for the larger rivers containing much heavier fish than do the smaller ones.

Of all bait, however, the one that I consider the most killing, when available, is a dead fish on light spinning tackle. Any small fish from 3 to 6 inches in length will do, but if I am picking out of many in a bait-can I select, and use first, those that are exactly 4 inches long, tail included. I prefer this length both because it is a nice edible size, and generally appreciated, I fancy, by the majority of Mahseer, and also because it is a convenient weight to throw out from the ordinary fly top of a light salmon rod. If you have a much heavier bait on, it will rather strain a fly top to be constantly throwing it, and if you put on a special trolling top for the purpose, you cannot change from spinning to fly fishing at will, or at least you cannot change without more trouble, and the loss of more time, than it is worth; whereas you ought with the aid of an attendant to be able to do it under the minute, and to take just a dozen casts over that pretty bit at the far end of the pool which you could not quite reach with your minnow, and which it would be a positive sin to leave untried, before passing on to other water, and replacing your fly collar by your spinning trace, the former being wound round your hat, or better still, thrown down for your attendant to crown his turband with at better leisure than you can possibly be expected to have while so deeply engaged.

These were the considerations that first led to my spinning with a fly top in old experimentalizing days, when also I wanted to make a fair trial which was the more killing bait, a fly or a fish. I came thereby to learn, however, that a pliable top carries with it very much more important advantages. The Mahseer takes its fly perhaps much as a salmon does, rising at it and descending quietly to its old place at the bottom till it feels the hook, but even then its first rush after feeling the hook is very much more violent than a salmon's. It is this grand first rush that is the glory of Mahseer fishing. But in spinning there is added to it yet another danger, the Mahseer does not ordinarily take its fish quietly as if it knew it would be unresisting like a puny fly, but it seizes it, not always, certainly, but not uncommonly, with an angry blow that gives a sudden jerk to the line; it comes at the fish bait with a swoop like a hawk, and seizing it passes swirling by at speed. To this angry jerk is very quickly added the grand rush that follows on feeling the restraint of the hook and line. Then it is that you find out, as mentioned in Chapter II, that no hand is light enough. The Mahseer is too quick for you. Before you can drop the top the mischief is done. There has been a sudden smash, and your friend has gone. You think, dear me, that was a splendid fish, my tackle was not strong enough. I venture to say that the probabilities are that the fish that broke you was not a bit heavier than the last you killed on that same line, and that if you had only got on terms with him at starting, by means of a pliable rod, you might equally have killed him also. I do not deny, be it remembered, that the Mahseer do grow very large, and do want very strong and fresh tackle, but I maintain also that much of their violence may be neutralised, and the necessity for very coarse tackle obviated, by the use of a pliable fly rod in preference to a stiff trolling rod. I say not only fly rod, but pliable fly rod, for fly rods for salmon are made both stiff and pliable, and I prefer the latter. The rod is in effect only the hand end of the line. It is the last connecting link between the fish and the hand. I do not understand the term Mahseer rod as if it were necessary to have something *sui generis*. An ordinary pliable salmon rod is the one on which I rely by preference, and I hold that if you strengthen your rod by stiffening it you must necessarily proceed to strengthen also your line, your collar, and your snood; and having done that, you are fishing with a barge pole and a cart rope. You are substituting brute force for skill. Don't call it sport. Sport is the delicious triumph of skill. The man with the barge pole gets very little of that poor fellow, and he has the labor of carrying a heavier rod and a heavier winch than is really needed. Give me the magic wand that promptly "stoops to conquer," that is sensitive of every plunge, that aids me like a friend in meeting it promptly, that works with me hand in hand throughout the fight, almost speaks to me of the next effort of the enemy, always anticipates me in foiling it, and when the battle is won, draws himself up as straight as an arrow, and breathes again for fresh contests. Ah well! I have some dear friends among my rods with many mutual confidences, shared with none else. They have had as much to do with the killing of many a fine fish as I have.

They have had to do with it in more ways than resisting the first rush. I have, after some play, killed a marral of some 5 or 6 lbs. which had one hook pressing against a tooth, and not embedded anywhere, and which dropped off as the landing net took the weight off the line. Would such a thing have been possible with anything but a springy top? I have after a vigorous fight in rough water shelved a Mahseer of some 5 lbs., as memory serves me, which had one hook embedded half way up the barb in the hardest part of the gill cover, in short, it was only pressing at right angles against the bone, and dopped out as I took off the tension. Who did that? Not I, but my springy top. Once more. In very rough water I hooked a Mahseer, which, after a mile of exposure on a coolies shoulder in the sun, scaled, I see in my notes, 30½ lbs. in camp. Away down stream he rushed like a madman, screaming out the line, though the basket boat was started after him as promptly as possible; presently he stopped, and the basket boat, with its way on, overshot him. Of course I was telling the boatman what to do, and he was paddling and I reeling up, all we knew. In the heat of the action as we were making downwards towards still water, where there was plenty of elbow room and a bit of shelving bank, everywhere else huge precipitous rocks overhung us, there was a cessation of vibration, the telegraphic commu-

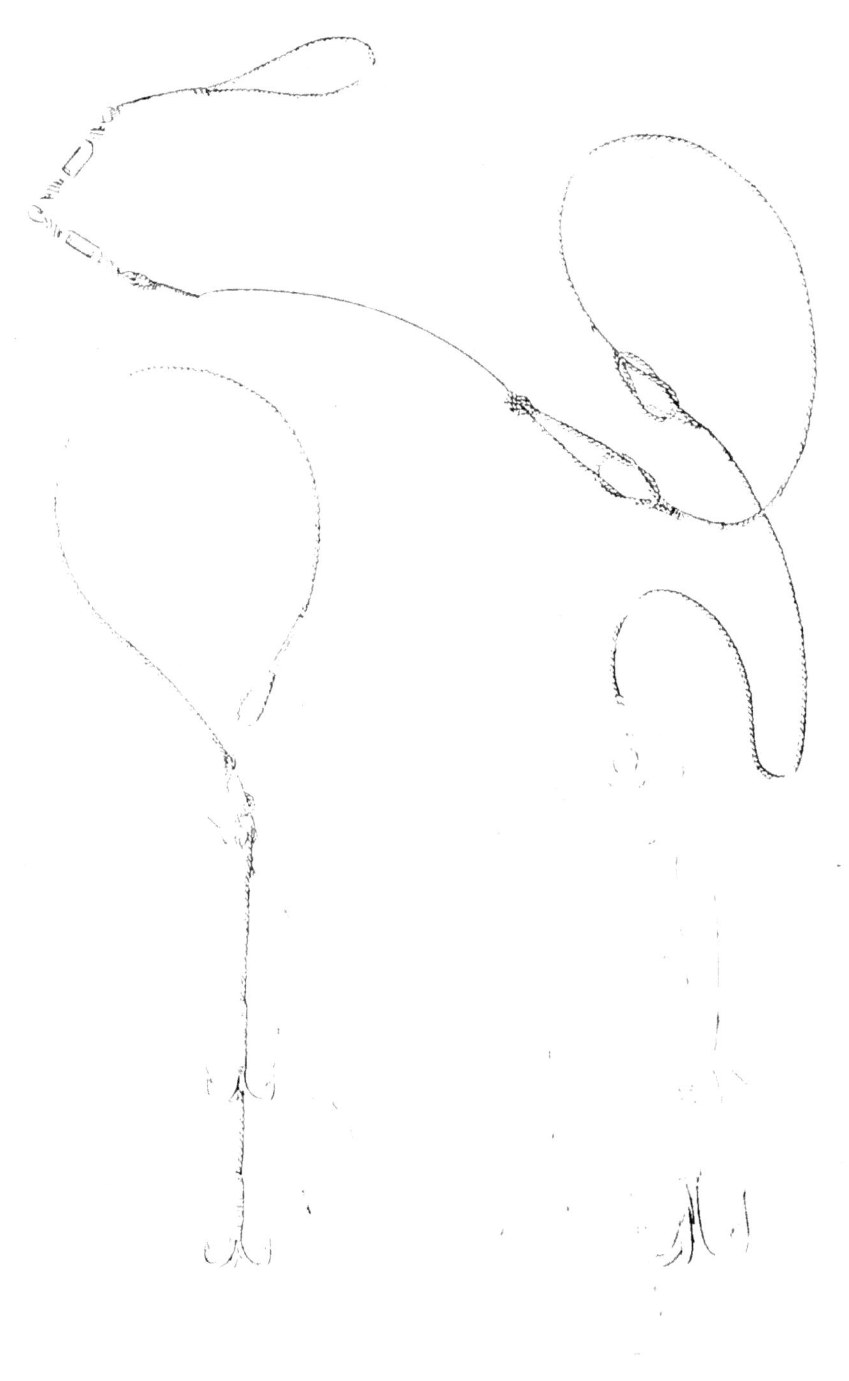

nication between me and my fish was interrupted. Promptly we paddled above him, got him out of his arm chair on some rock at the bottom, and began conducting him, foot by foot as he gave way, down another division of the river away from his friendly arm chair, which he hung on to like a dentist. For the first time I got just a momentary glance of the commencement of a 9 ft. spinning trace. It was refreshing to see signs of getting better acquainted. But down it went again into the dark depths. Finally I landed, got the boat and the natives out of the way, and after 52 minutes of good hard fighting shelved my friend. As I stooped down to unhook the fish, the hook tumbled out. It had only been round one ray of the tail fin all the time, and the hook had been so small a one that it little more than encircled the ray at its base. Now, who killed that fish? Not I, certainly, but my springy rod. I defy the best fisherman going to have killed that fish with a barge pole. This, then, is one of the advantages of a springy elastic rod. I know of an angler going so far as to say that with such rods he did not want any barb to the hook, and preferred them without for trout, as they pierced more readily. There, however, I cannot follow him; and as regards playing a fish generally, the argument is equally applicable to other fish. It is with special reference to the first rush that the speciality of a Mahseer rod should be pliability, elasticity, on no account rigidity.

I have two ways of baiting. One is more troublesome than the other, but it is in my opinion the more killing, so I give it first.

Having selected your bait alive and fresh out of the bait kettle, humanely kill it thoroughly with a flip or two on the back of the head, but temper your physical energies with a little discretion, so as not to knock it about.

"There is wisdom in sucking eggs," and there is a right and a wrong way of killing a bait even. If you have the loach-like *Ophiocephalus gachua* to deal with, as hereafter recommended, you may flip away at his head for a long time without killing him, and though you may half stun him, you will be horrified, when putting the baiting needle through him, to find he is still alive and kicking, whereas if you give him one good squeeze in one hand so as to crush his internal organs, he will die instantly. If he is too slippery for you, a little river-side sand will soon get over that difficulty.

You must not follow this same plan with the dace-like fish, however, for if you do, the silvery scales will all come off, and it will at once look dreadfully dishevelled. Moreover it is not necessary, for the dace-like fish have as thin a cranium as a snipe, and a flip on the head soon does for them, and with them it is that you must be careful not to be too rough.

Your bait being dead, then insert the baiting needle, point foremost, at the anus, and bring it out at the open mouth. Before pulling it through, hook the loop of the gut on to the eye of the baiting needle. Then pull the baiting needle out at the mouth, drawing the gut after it through the fish till the hook comes home to the anus. In doing this, humour the baiting needle by giving it a turn, as a doctor does an instrument, so as to tear the vent hole as little as possible in getting the loop through it. I prefer a single treble hook of the sort described in the chapter on tackle, and about the size shown in Plate VI, figure 2, which is No. 1 in Plate VII of the scale of treble hooks. I used to use No. 7, but I find the hook is so well concealed in this mode of baiting that one can afford to use a larger hook, and the larger hook gives of course greater chances of hooking, and a larger hook hold. When the hook is home to the vent, embed one of the three thoroughly in the fish, so that the two remaining hooks of the treble shall be lying close against the fish. In this position they are scarcely perceptible, whereas if one hook is carelessly only half embedded, the other two stick out and show unnecessarily. It is always worth while to bait very carefully and neatly, because all your subsequent efforts centre on the nicety of your baiting. Then you must have a sinker, also described in the chapter on tackle. Pass the baiting needle through the loop or ring attached to the sinker, and run the sinker down the line, and push it, thin point foremost, down the fish's throat, so that it is entirely concealed within the mouth of the bait. Then remove your baiting needle, and hold the line so as to come out of the bait's mouth exactly in the centre; and so as to keep it in the centre, and make the bait spin true, as well as keep the lead from coming out, sew the bait's mouth up as follows with a common needle and thread. Close the bait's mouth, pass the threaded needle through both lips so as to bring it out at one of the nostrils in the upper lip, insert it at the other nostril, and pass it through both lips again, keeping the

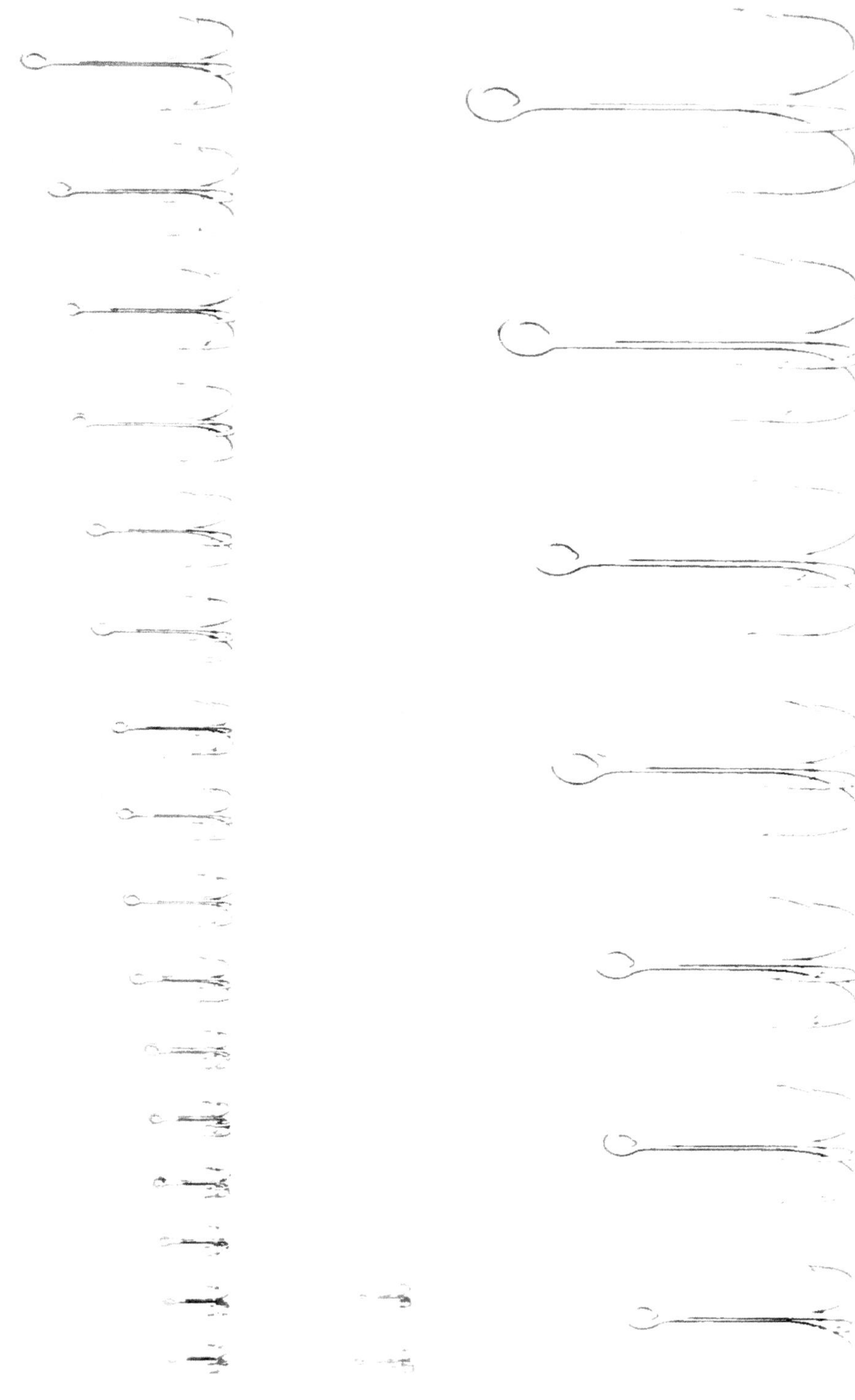

line between these two stitches. The two ends of the thread will then be over at the chin of the bait; draw them together just gently enough to avoid tearing the bait, and yet tightly enough to keep the mouth well closed. Tie a sailor's knot, *not* "a granny" or grandmother's knot, and cut off the ends. Do not use white thread for this, because it will show, but stout black thread double, or any dark coloured knitting silk double, say brown for preference. Your bait is then ready for use.

This may seem a long, troublesome, and fidgetty process, but it should not occupy as long in the doing as it does in the describing, and if you have an attendant with you, he can always be preparing a bait for you while you are fishing, and whenever your bait is spoilt by a fish, or by long or rough usage, you can at once change it for a fresh one, by using the double loop recommended in the chapter on tackle, in the manner there suggested. This change can be effected in about ten seconds, or may be less, and the soiled bait left for the attendant to remove from the hook and replace by another fresh one.

If you have not got a treble hook, a single bare salmon hook can be used very well for this purpose, the hook being pulled into the vent after the line shank foremost, till the fish is well down on to the bend of the hook, and there is really little more than the point showing. A No. 4/0, 5/0, or 6/0 Limerick hook will do very well for this purpose.

The only objection I have heard made to this mode of baiting is that the bait is apt to bend too much by draggling down on to the hook, because there is nothing in the line to give it rigidity and keep it straight. But I have not found this myself if care is taken not to embed the hook further away from the head than the vent hole, and if it be a fault it is one that is easily remedied by inserting the baiting needle not at the anus, but a trifle nearer to the head. In such case insert it not in the stomach, which is liable to tear away, but in firm flesh half-way up the side, and take care to pass the baiting needle, not simply under the skin, but through a good piece of flesh so as to give a hold, and also embed one of the hooks thoroughly well into the side till the other two lie quite flat against it. Pass the baiting needle out of the mouth and proceed as before. This for objectors, but I prefer the use of the vent hole as it tears less, and is in my opinion not at all too far back; indeed I sometimes insert the one embedded hook a little further aft than the vent, because the vent is differently placed in different fish, and some require a little more bend to make them spin. The opposition of the water makes the bait hang back on the hook, so as to draw up the tail, and create bend enough to make it spin.

But there is one objection to this mode of baiting which I will freely admit. If your bait is not the *Ophiocephalus gachua*, but of a less tough sort, or if from not being quite fresh it is inclined to get rotten, which it will very quickly do in India, then, as the bait softens from being sodden by use in the water, the sinker in the stomach slips down the line, and by its weight breaks a way for itself out of the stomach or vent, and trailing visibly outside your bait spoils its appearance utterly. For such spoiling, too, there is no remedy but a fresh bait, and of these you may not have too many. At any rate you grudge the time lost in changing, especially if the fresh bait is not with you, but with your attendant, who, for better concealment, is not quite at your side. In such case use the sinker outside as in Plate VI, figure 2, placing it a good foot or foot and a half away from the bait. This plan, again, is not without objection, for it is not quite so easy to cast quietly a line that has two separate weights at the end, as a line which has all its weight at one point, the end. So you must make your own choice of comparative advantages and disadvantages. Perhaps the difficulty might be got over by using an outside lead cap over the nose of the bait with a perforation through the centre of the crown for the line, as in minnow spinning for trout. I never tried it however, and never saw such caps made large enough for a four or five inch bait, and I should fear that they would fray the line.

But for those who are too idle for baiting after this manner, and have not an attendant trained to do it for them, I have another simpler plan which will do nearly as well though it is not quite so neat. It consists of a treble hook and a lip hook with a looped sinker as before. Put the line though the loop or ring of the sinker, and let the sinker run down to the lip hook. Put the sinker thin end foremost into the bait's mouth and half down its throat, close the mouth so as keep it in by passing the lip hook through both lips. Then embed the treble hook into the side of the dead bait parallel with the vent. You are ready for action. But this bait will not last so long as the former one, because it is given to tearing at the mouth, especially in rough hands which jerk it unnecessarily in swinging it out for a spin, and when the second hook is not put in so as to share the strain with the lip hook. When properly baited it should give the bait the slightest curve imaginable. But Francis Francis has chapters and two sets of plates on this one subject alone, this line of beauty curve, and H. Cholmondely Pennell has more apparently in "How to spin for Pike." Between these two, therefore, the reader should have more than enough on the subject, and I have already promised not to trouble him with what he has in English books. To these and other authors then I refer him, but with the request that he will bear constantly in mind the one marked and very important difference between English fishing and Indian fishing, that whereas you seldom spin or troll at home in water that is not more or less coloured or tinged, and not unfrequently under a cloudy sky, you never ought to spin out here for Mahseer except in clear water, and if you get any thing but a bright sky above, you are in luck's way indeed. The consequence is that it is necessary to be doubly particular about having as fine tackle with as few hooks as possible; and flights of numerous hooks that are considered quite "according to Cocker" at home, look in our bright waters so truly terrible that no Indian fish would be fool enough to come within a yard of them. When I use this kind of tackle I use only one treble as above stated. But I find most people prefer two, and not a few three trebles, so I beg you to be content with two, and let them be small ones as shown in Plate VI, figure 1. Say No. 7 on Plate VII of the scale of treble hooks, and of course "extra strong," as described in the chapter on tackle.

Furthermore, a multitude of hooks, even if they were not repellant, as they obviously must be in bright water, are not at all necessary out here. They are made at home for fishes whose mouths are so full of teeth and scarcely-covered bone, that the surface presented to the hook is so hard that the chances are sadly against a hook penetrating, and getting a hold, and therefore the hooks are multiplied with a view to increasing the chances of hooking a fish. But the Mahseer's mouth and lips are soft, tough, and leathery, presenting a perfect hookhold all over, so that one hook is enough, and two is certainly ample. Moreover, the Mahseer closes his leathery mouth very tight on his fish as I have shown, and the chances are much against his escaping being hooked.

On all grounds, therefore, I am for as few hooks and as fine tackle as possible with the Mahseer. With some other fish with which we shall have to do hereafter the same necessity may not exist.

Presuming, then, that I have contrived to seduce my reader into a preference for a dead fish on fine tackle, as being more natural and consequently better calculated to stand closer fish-eyed scrutiny in clear water than any artificial bait, the next question that arises is whether any particular sort of small fish is more killing than another. This I have endeavoured to ascertain by identifying the fish found in the several Mahseer killed; but their digestion is so marvellously rapid, that it is very seldom indeed that the small fish there found are recognizable. Not only have their scales and fins almost always disappeared, but their very shape has been lost. Though I have once or twice recognized one of the dace-like fish called *Barbus sarana*, or, in Canarese, *kijau*, it does not thence follow that there may not have been several other sorts amongst the ones I could not make out, such as the young of the *Barbus chrysopoma* or of the *Barbus filamentosus*, of which plates will be found further on, or of somewhat similar fish. Though I have seen the Mahseer taking dace-like fish freely in the natural state, it is no sequence that they do not as freely take other fish, which I could not see them take, simply because they are small fish that inhabit the bottoms of rivers, and are consequently not within sight. I cannot say, therefore, if the Mahseer have a preference for any particular sort of small fish, and as they seem to take them all alike, little caring which is Caesar and which is Pompey, the question rather is which the fisherman prefers. The dace-like fish shows furthest from its white shining scales, but that is not much of a point where the water is clear as crystal, and they are a tender bait, and soon tear on a hook and look dishevelled. The young of the *Chela argentea* are a favourite bait with some, because they are so very bright and silvery. But they are most frail. Any of these sorts of baits can be readily caught by a throw or two of the casting net in the shallowing edges and tails of the pools of the very river in which you are fishing. Your boatman is probably a fisherman by caste, and has only to be warned to bring his casting net with him. The *Ophiocephalus gachua*, however, a somewhat loach-like fish in general appearance, and called in Canarese *morant*, in Tamil, *koravai*, and in Hindustani *dok*, is much tougher, and consequently keeps its good looks much longer on a hook. Its lips, which is a great point, are stronger, and its mouth being wider, it readily takes in a larger sinker. It may be easily recognized by the similarity of its general appearance to that of the marral, *Ophiocephalus striatus*, figured in Plate XIX, for it is one of the same family and genus, though small. It has small scales, looking to the ordinary observer like a scaleless skin. It is a bottom-feeder, always among the stones, and the young are to be found in any small pool adjoining rice-fields, whence they can be readily taken by bailing out, or by small boys with a worm, or by damming up any small stream and turning it on to a dry reaped rice field, when they will follow the stream out on to the rice field and are easily caught. This is the simplest way of catching a number in a short time. Your grooms or other camp followers can do it for you. These fish keep alive in a bait-can longer than any fish I know; but they are great hands at jumping out if it is not closed.

Though I say loach-like, the reader will please understand that I mean like in general semblance only to the eye of the casual observer, and not in characteristics to the closer examiner; for it is really of the same genus as the marral, though a span is its utmost length. My desire is to make myself intelligible to the general reader, the more critical one must therefore please not quarrel with me for, or conclude ignorance from, laxity of expression like the above, any more than he would conceive a person ignorant of the earth's rotation for saying the sun set.

As to what is the best size for a bait to be, it must, I think, remain a moot point, dependent very much on the fancy of the fisherman. Some have an idea that the larger the bait you use, the larger will be the fish you catch. But my humble opinion is that we do not always take as big a bite of cake as ever our mouths will hold, and I am quite sure very fine pike and 30 lb. salmon have been killed with a very minnow for bait. I have myself seen a pike of 3 feet taken on a roach not as many inches in length. The use of a large bait may perhaps serve the purpose of choking off the smaller fish, and allowing the bigger ones to have it all to themselves, but I very much doubt it, for it is astonishing how huge a bait, in comparison with its own size, a small fish will sometimes go at if he happens to be more than ordinarily peckish. On a spoon of 2¾ inches in length I have pulled out a greedy little Mahseer of only a quarter of a pound in weight, whereas I have also taken a twelve pounder on a spoon of only an inch and a quarter in length. I measure the spoon in the spoon part only without calculating the ring and hook fore and aft. Pike, again, have been known to take other pike of more than half their own size, and in one case every bit as big as itself, though in the last instance it might have been more intent on fighting than digesting; anyhow it won't do it again, for it died of suffocation. Of course if you go to such a length, as was recently done with success, of baiting with a 7 lb. jack for an individual pike of 50 lb., known to reside in a certain locality, it would trouble any small pike to take such a bait, and you might fairly calculate on strong probabilities of your taking the particular pike you wanted, or none at all. But you do not always happen to have a personal acquaintance so intimate as to be able to provide the special dish which your friend alone shall particularly affect. Furthermore, I hold that as a preventitive measure against indifferent fish a large bait is not a necessary precaution. My belief is that if there is a big fish on the feed within reach of your bait, though small, and you work it naturally enough for him to desire to take it, he will have it, and woe betide the cheeky little fish that presumes to come between him and his dinner, for "a hungry man is an angry man." Again and again have I seen a large fish sail majestically up to his bait, and take it leisurely in, as if thoroughly conscious that none of the smaller fish around dare step in before him. There is a calm resolute look in his eye, and an angry little twitch of his tail, that the smaller fry understand the meaning of right well. It means business, and they make way for his majesty most apparently. But if there is any doubt in his mind, and he shows no sign, they can read that too, and in they go at the bait, as they are probably hungrier and less wary than he is. And that is how it is that a good fisherman generally kills finer fish in the long run than an indifferent fisherman, even though both fish with precisely the same bait. The finest fish are the oldest, the most experienced, most wary, and in a position to be the most fastidious. The deception that satisfies them must consequently be the most perfect; but if it be quite satisfactory, then they are thoroughly competent to look out for themselves, and well able to prevent the smaller fry from rudely rushing in and carrying off their intended dinner. There is a very decided, dignified, awe-striking, keep-your-distance expression in the countenance and general bearing of a large fish about to feed, and in a handsomely attired trout an unmistakable *odi profanum-vulgus* look, quite enough to make any small fry shrink into their shoes. Though I have not yet arrived at the point of recognizing the varying lines in the face of a large Mahseer, there is no doubt in my mind but that the small fish are thoroughly conversant with them, for I see a knowledge of a certain something there so clearly reflected in their behaviour, that I cannot question it, and myself am often able to gather something from his general demeanour, his lordly lineaments, even before he leaves his station for the bait. His daily satellites the small fish must, however, have much more closely studied his physiognomy.

Still the rule cannot be considered by any means absolute. Small Mahseer must rush in and take their risks of punishment sometimes, just as half-grown chickens do in a yard, and get a good peck now and again for their pains. Nothing venture nothing have. Your small bait may also be taken by a small Mahseer before it comes within the ken of the large fish which is in another part of the pool or run, a part you have not yet spun over. An argument this for spinning through the best bits first; a reason again why the best fisherman catches the best fish. He divines intuitively where the best fish ought to be, and he fishes accordingly. Furthermore, the best fish having taken up their position in the best localities command only a limited radius therefrom. If the smaller Mahseer never got a chance of a small fish they would be badly off.

There is no doubt, however, in my mind but that the large fish is able to make the smaller ones understand that he means to have such and such bait in sight, and that they are not to think of anticipating him. It is quite intelligible that he should do it almost without a sign, just as you would intimate to your second gun-bearer that you are prepared for the approaching beast or bird, and that he is to keep motionless. He does not need to be told the last half of the idea, it is a natural sequence; it would be a work of supererogation to tell him he must not move before you; he never dreamt of such a thing, for he has been too well drilled. The position of the small fish is a parallel one. They only need to see in the big fish's eye a look of preparedness to take the bait, and they understand the rest. He will take it at the time he considers best for surprising what he conceives to be a live fish, just as you will take your shot when you get a fair view of the shoulder, though there be a little delay it should be quite as comprehensible to the small fish as it is to the gun-bearer that the master is only waiting his opportunity, for there is a look in his eye that means 'business,' and that is enough.

Do you doubt that fish have ideas and are able to communicate them? It might be proved abundantly that fish can think for themselves; and that they should be unable to communicate their ideas to each other would be contrary to the analogy of all nature. Let it suffice to ask a few questions which can admit no reply but that fish can and do think intelligently. Small fish see a large one going to spawn; they follow her in a crowd and wait patiently till she has worked out a hollow in the gravel and commenced to spawn therein, and then they feed busily on the stray ova that are washed down to them. Have they not recognised in the appearance of the female, or in the companionship of the male, an indication that the act of spawning is about to take place, else why have they assiduously followed her? Have they not been confirmed in the idea by seeing her working out a hollow in the gravel, else why have they continued to wait upon her? Maybe they have done the same before and got a good dinner by it. If so, they have memory. Maybe the majority of them crowd after her simply because they see others do so, and conclude that there is probably something to be gained thereby. If so, it is drawing certain conclusions from certain premises, which is the process of reasoning. Anyhow, depend upon it they are no fools, and the angler who hopes to be successful must commence by disabusing his mind of the idea that he has a fool to deal with. Every man that lives from hand to mouth has of necessity to be wide awake to his immediate surroundings, [illegible] draw conclusions, and prompt to act upon them. It is the case with civilized man, it is still more markedly so with the savage, while with the animal kingdom it is presumedly the sole field of thought. Still it is thought, and sometimes followed out through a surprisingly long chain, and fish are no exceptions to the general rule, even though their intelligence may not be so educated as that of the domesticated animals that have been brought into closer communion with the superior intellect of man; and may not be so much noticed and appreciated by man, because exhibited under the water, an element with which he is necessarily less conversant than earth and air.

Fish have a brain, why then should they not use it, though it is not as heavy as Cuvier's or Byron's or Thackeray's? It has even been suggested that there is a comparison between the weight of brain and intelligence of different fish.*

Why is it that you use a transparent, almost invisible. material like silkworm-gut to attach to your hook? Why do not you use whipcord or string? It would be both stronger and cheaper. Why! because the fish is observant, would notice it, would conclude, would *think*, aye *think*, there was something wrong, and would not be such a fool as to take your bait.

Not to multiply examples too much, how is it that the trout in a much-fished river are much shyer than in less frequented waters, and require finer tackle and better fishermen to catch them? They are not really shyer of anything but man, they are not less greedy of food than they were, but if anything the reverse, because of their fewer opportunities of feeding, they are only more discriminating, more educated, more intelligent. They have learnt to distinguish between an artificial fly and a natural one; they recognize the figure and the shadow of a fishing man, and dash away; while they feed securely on in presence of the ox grazing on the bank. They may not be a "cooking animal" like you and me, but they are thinking animals all the same, and no fools either, and if we wish to do anything with them we should not take them for anything but intelligent beings. If you do, and only then, shall we be inclined to think there is some sense after all in Johnson's well-

* "The proportionate weight of brain in a Pike as compared with its body, is as 1 to 1,300; in a Shark as 1 to 2,500; and in the Tunny, a remarkably stupid fish, but as 1 to 3,700."—The Angler-Naturalist, H. Cholmondely Pennell.

known definition of the angler, "a stick and a string with a worm "at one end and a fool at the other," albeit the learned man spake it in ignorance.

I repeat, again, the fish at least is no fool. Eradicate that idea. Take a new creed. Say rather he is a thinking animal. I might go on multiplying examples to prove it, but I should weary you. Pray do not breath a word about reason and instinct, or I shall have to begin again and write a whole chapter on that well-worn though interesting subject. Do just please concede for peace sake that my fish is a reasoning being, and I will go on to the next subject, his talkativeness.

I have stated my belief that fish are able to communicate their ideas to each other, and I hold this opinion on two grounds; the first, that it would be contrary to the analogy of all nature if they could not do so, and the second, that I think I can recognize indications of their exercising this power.

My belief, then, is that all the higher animal life that we know anything of has the power of communicating ideas.

Has any one the hardihood to assert that monkeys cannot converse? Watch them moving quietly along in a large crowd. One of them gives a little sound of satisfaction, and there are soon plenty with him to share the fruit he has found. That mamma monkey calls to its young one that it is time to be off sharp as there is a man coming, or that it should not dawdle so as there is fruit in front, and it very evidently understands and repairs to its mother hurriedly or leisurely according to the nature of the maternal command. This is very marked. And then how mamma croones over it. Is it all meaningless? I will be bound there is not so much nonsense in it as in half the stuff talked to babies by nurses and mothers; about blessing their little tootsi-wootsies and so forth. Let one of the herd see a crocodile where they are about to drink, or a panther, or anything that alarms them, and only listen to the jabbering caught up and carried on by all. Do you say it is all gibberish? It is intelligible enough to them, and all with one consent take precautions accordingly. They do not run wildly hither and thither, as if overcome by an uncertain fear, but they have a clear idea of what is the matter, and what they ought to do under the circumstances. The state of affairs has been intelligently communicated.

Try again. Strike gently, so as not to cow, or threaten to strike, that captive monkey, and see if he does not face round, and give you a bit of his mind at once. He commences talking with great volubility and though you cannot understand him he means a great deal. It is very evident from his demeanour he does, his face and bearing being full of rapid expression.

I have often thought it a very good thing we do not know all that quarrelsome dogs say to each other, for there must be some frightfully bad language used sometimes. The very style of the growling of some of them makes one shudder, it sounds so full of coarse oaths. But they can talk civil talk to each other also. I had a fine heavy dog, half fox-hound, half Cuban blood-hound, which had an excellent nose. He came on the scent of antelope, and followed it up till it was warm, and he could make it out. Knowing from sad experience that he was much too portly to catch an antelope himself, Jim abruply left the scent, and went in search of Juno, the fleetest of the kangaroo hounds, then hunting for herself about a quarter-of-a-mile off. Back the two scampered together in a great hurry, he picked up the old scent, and followed it up, till he fairly laid her in view, and then away she went, he keeping her in sight as best he could by cutting corners. To bring her away from her own chances of sport, and that so promptly, and to get her to accompany him back in such a hurry, he must have conveyed to her mind a very clear idea of some definite sport immediately in hand. No human being interfered. They did it all themselves. But dogs can also make themselves intelligible to men, for we have lived so much with them that we have in some measure learned their language. Though we do not know all they say about it, man can well understand from the manner of a dog's giving tongue, when it thinks it has hit upon a scent, and when it is sure it has a warm one, and when it is in view. A dog's whimper, its giving tongue, baying, barking, growling, moaning, howling, yelping, are all distinct sounds, with a distinct significance, which man has learnt to understand. He has learnt a little also of the many different intonations in those sounds, of the differing force of expression in them, and of the looks of face, and motions of tail, and sometimes of paw and tongue and raised bristle with which they are accompanied. If he knew more he would understand also how dogs speak to each other in silence by signs, or expressions of countenance, or in audible words, that man cannot follow.

How does a bison tell its calf that it must run in front of the herd and lead the pace, and having told it this, how does it make it understand the line of country to be taken? All this it does in apparent silence, and you may observe the little one looking back when in doubt for instructions.

How does an antelope, on the approach of danger, tell its little one, not yet old enough to run, to lie down instantly, and not to stir for its life till called?

How does a sheep call its particular lamb out of a hundred, or more, a great distance away, and that particular lamb comes at once, and no others offer to move? When it wants to reassure its lamb, and to tell it not to come, it employs a very different sound, and the lamb shows by its conduct that it comprehends.

Tigers make very different noises when searching for their prey, when apalling it, when rejoicing over it, when calling each other, when angered. Man can distinguish the difference therein. But there is doubtless much more means of intercommunion which man cannot follow. For instance, tigers and wolves and wild dogs not unfrequently hunt in concert, some lying in ambush, while others beat towards them, and they must have conversed together to preconcert the plan of the campaign.

Birds also converse. See how constantly mynas are chattering away to each other, especially the hill myna (*Eulates religiosa*), and swallows before migrating seem to be busily discussing some subject or other. I presume it is their journey. Rooks hold great assemblages, and make much nose thereat, and the end of it all is rational behaviour, for they are admittedly very learned about various things, and are evidently not without rights of property in last year's nests. They have also decisions executed by the multitude in the cases of intruders or offending individuals. Indeed, it is difficult to conceive how any creatures who habitually live in collected numbers could possibly order their conduct so as to live harmoniously, unless they had the power of freely interchanging their ideas.

How could the sociable grosbeak, or sociable weaver bird of South Africa (*Philetarus socius*) conjointly construct for the whole colony one large umbrella-shaped collection of nests connected like the houses in a town; how could they arrange all the necessary details without communicating ideas and arriving at a joint understanding? Sociable animals must necessarily converse.

I should not be surprised to find it some day proved that not only do birds have language, but also separate languages for different species, as we have for different nations, and variations of voice for each individual and sex. Without such variations of voice it would be difficult to understand how, in the pairing season, for instance, each individual sparrow can not only call a sparrow and a mate, but its own mate, as it evidently does without mistake, in the midst, too, of a clamour of other voices. That the bird's ear is formed for the accurate distinction of voices is traceable in the grey parrot, the raven, the jackdaw, the myna, and others, which not only repeat words, but catch so exactly the intonation of the human speaker that they are sometimes undistinguishable.

That there are different voices for different sexes we can ourselves recognize in the varying voices of domestic poultry, and man can so copy the voice, and parrotwise probably the words also, of a she bear that a male bear shall answer it from far away in the forest, and keep on answering and drawing near as called. I have seen it done on the Animalais, till we had to desist because we were unarmed. The gentleman who did it said that there were junglemen who could thus call a male bear within easy shot. Many of us have heard natives so copy jackals crying over their prey, that others shall answer and come even within striking distance of a club. This subject might be enlarged on, but I only wish to lead up to my fish.

Take just one example from insects, in addition to those from beasts and birds. Watch the ants moving in long columns along some conjointly cleared road, in some particular direction, evidently with some common object. How did they agree about and communicate to each other that common plan? Put your finger, or any other obstacle, in the line and stop them. There is immediately excitement amongst them all, and parties swarm up to remove the obstacle with a readiness that seems to say the state of affairs has been rapidly communicated, and a course of conduct resolved upon and ordered by authority. See two ants meet and cross feelers rapidly, and then go on their several ways. What have they been doing? Fooling? All their history is against the supposition.

They would seem to have been conversing. Watch them dragging a cockroach up the side of a wall. It is about fifty times the size and weight of any one of them, but there they are on all sides, some upholding, some dragging, some pushing, others indicating the way, and others coming as reliefs, but all evidently understanding each other, and consequently working with a unanimity of purpose which alone could make it possible to accomplish their end as they do. They clear fields, sow seeds, cultivate them, and in due course cut, carry, and store crops in granaries built for the purpose. They forage for, capture, stall, feed, and milk cows. They maintain armies and take prisoners. They have a well ordered society. It is impossible that they could do all this without being able to communicate freely with each other.

Though arguments to this end might be multiplied at pleasure, and are to be found in convincing force in the writings of Sir John Lubbock, in "Mind in the Lower Animals," by W. Lauder Lindsay, M.D., and such like works devoted to the subject, enough for the purpose of this work has probably been said, in passing, to satisfy the reader generally that beasts, birds, and insects can and do converse as freely as human beings, and consequently that there is a presumption in favour of the same faculty being possessed by fish. There being no apparent grounds why fish alone should be an exception to the general rule, and all analogy being favourable to their being able to communicate ideas, we may examine with less incredulity, without any presumption to the contrary, and consequently with more fairness, whether or not there are any indications of their exercising the power which they may well possess.

I instance first the example above given of a large fish deterring smaller ones from anticipating him in the matter of food; and I beg a re-perusal of those remarks with less incredulity and more seriousness, than was, perhaps, given to them before. I have seen the same with chub also, as well as with Mahseer. I have seen six or eight chub attracted by my floating cockchafer, and apparently meditating taking it, when they hung back, divided, and made way for a comparatively much larger chub of 2¾ lbs., who sailed majestically up to the bait, and took it leisurely down, with a seeming confidence that the others would not presume to anticipate him. He must have made them understand, even though he came from behind them, that he desired to have that cock-chafer himself, and he must have felt confident that he had expressed himself explicitly, and would be attended to. The same conclusion seems to be pointed at by the frequently deliberate way in which a large trout sucks down his fly, in contradistinction to the hurried dart of the smaller trout.

Furthermore, how is it that when a river is much whipped, the fish all get very shy? I do not suppose they have all been pricked by the hook and got away, so as to have gained wisdom each by personal experience. Surely there are too many thousands in the river for that, and too many more thousands fresh born every year. Those that have been hook-pricked, not an inconsiderable number certainly, are not improbably able to communicate the fact to the others, and not till a large proportion of the community have thus suffered, is much weight likely to be attached to their warnings, in opposition to the cravings of nature.

Certainly there is much to be urged in the contrary direction also, as, for instance, the fact that fish will keep on biting in one particular spot, though they see their neighbours being pulled out before their very eyes. Still men do things quite as foolish. They engage in trades dangerous to life, and continue to follow them, though they see their fellow workmen falling off around them from diseases which have been calculated to result with certainty after a stated number of years. If the pressure of circumstances, *res angusta domi*, be too strong for the wisdom of the human being, why should not the cravings of nature be allowed to have outweighed the caution of the fish, rather than be deduced as conclusive evidence that he knows not the risk he is running. It is at least an open question, and analogy and observation incline me to the belief that fish can communicate ideas to each other.

I may not be able to deduce as many, or as striking examples, as in the case of birds or beasts, but that, as I have already shown, is the natural consequence of fish inhabiting an element in which we are necessarily less at home than in our own.

It is not necessary to my argument that the communication should take place by means of oral sounds as with human beings, though fish have the sense of hearing. Dr. W. Lauder Lindsay says: "Various fish kept in pleasure ponds in gentlemen's demesnes "also know their own masters' voice or call, and sometimes even "footfall or footstep, from those of all other individuals. They "attend to the one and are indifferent to the other." And Sir J. Emerson Tennent, in his very interesting "Natural History of Ceylon," has remarked, not without force, that "organs of hearing "have been clearly ascertained to exist not only in fishes, but in "mollusca. In the oyster the presence of an acoustic apparatus of "the simplest possible construction has been established by the "discoveries of Siebold, and from our knowledge of the reciprocal "relations existing between the faculties of hearing and of pro-"ducing sounds, the ascertained existence of the one affords "legitimate grounds for inferring the co-existence of the other in "animals of the same class." Still it is not necessary to my argument that the communication should be made even by sounds inaudible to the human ear. It is equally comprehensible that, as in the case of ants and animals, they may be made by distinct means, means of which we have no knowledge.

It has been remarked above that it is difficult to conceive how any creatures who habitually live in collected numbers could possibly order their conduct so as to live harmoniously, unless they had the power of freely interchanging their ideas. May not such a remark have equal pertinence to fish as to birds? Is it not equally applicable to such fish as swim in shoals? Porpoises, for instance, act very obviously all in concert, and the change, from one unity of purpose, to another unity of purpose, is made with such rapidity, and such a complete embracing of every individual of the school, that it is easier to believe that the new idea was in some way communicated, than to believe that it was not. Gregarious fish, such as the herring and the pilchard, could scarcely conduct their migrations in unison if they had not all a common intent arrived at by communication. The simultaneous manner in which a vast shoal of fish will descend from the surface of the sea to deeper water points also in the same direction. It is well known to anglers that you may catch dace after dace out of a shoal till you have hooked and lost one in the landing, and that then you will ordinarily get no more dace out of that shoal. How is this to be accounted for except on the supposition that they have powers of communication analogous to those of gregarious animals on land? Exceptional days there are certainly, that come once or twice in a twelvemonth, when nothing will dissuade the dace from taking as

fast as you can throw in your fly. But those exceptions militate not against the general rule, and the conclusion I have drawn; they only indicate, as in an instance above, that on those exceptional days appetite overmasters prudence, despite communicated cautions. The male stickleback is known to build a nest, and then to find and bring a female partner to it. Why should it not be believed that the male stickleback made a communication that induced the female to accompany him, just as much as such communications are believed to be made by dogs and other animals which live on the land? The fact of living wholly on the land, or much in the air, or wholly in the water, does not seem to affect the question. It affects only our facilities for observation by limiting them sadly. But, as far as observations go, they seem to indicate that there is no difference in this respect between fish and other animals. They all seem to need, to have, and to use, the power of conversing, whether by articulate sounds, or by what Dr. W. Lauder Lindsay calls "non-vocal language."

One more thought occurs to me. I will not put it among the indications of language, because I am not sure that it fairly is one, though it may be. Many anglers will have noticed that in playing one fish it is not infrequently followed about through all its struggles, by its pair fish, in the case of the marral, or by a crowd of fishes as with the Mahseer. Why is this? Is it merely that the others are curious? If so, what is it that they are curious about? Is it about the strange demeanour of the played fish? They follow it very closely. Or can it be that the hooked fish has expressed astonishment or fear, or has asked for aid? Do they want to ask him what is the matter?

This brings me to another sense, the sense of smell in fishes, in connection with the immediate subject of this chapter.

It was out of the question of the size of the bait to be used, that this discussion of the intelligence and communicative power of fish grew; and the next question is whether it is advisable to preserve bait in any way, against the eventuality of not being able to procure it fresh when wanted. It is obvious it will not do to let it take care of itself, for it will very soon get so rotten as not to stay on a hook for five minutes, besides being offensive; consequently bait are commonly salted in England, and thus kept on sale. Some fishermen have objected to the salt on the ground of its injuring the hook, and prefer fish preserved in spirits. I, however, have an objection to bait preserved in spirits, and I base it on the strong sense of smell known to exist in fishes ; a sense considered to be very perfect, and second only in power to the organ of sight in fishes. A bait preserved in spirits of wine has a very strong smell even after it has been on the hook, and used in the water for half-an-hour ; and I cannot think that a fish will be unmindful of it, and recklessly take such a strange smelling thing into its mouth ; I have often thought, in using such a bait, that I have lost many a run I should otherwise have got. I have seen fish follow it and turn away. Of course I cannot say positively that it was the smell that turned them away from it, for they will do just the same to any bait they mistrust ; still I was fishing very carefully, the bait was neat, and I thought it was the smell. Salt-fish I have used with effect, and if you must use preserved fish, I would prefer that method of preserving them. At best they are very inferior in appearance and toughness to a fresh fish taken alive out of the bait-can, and baited immediately on being killed.

But the kindly reader who has been good enough to travel thus far with me must be right weary of this chapter, and anxiously looking for an end at which he can put down the book and rest. Further remarks on spinning will therefore be reserved for another chapter.

CHAPTER VI.

HOW, WHEN, AND WHERE TO FISH FOR MAHSEER.

> "Give me mine angle; we'll to the river there.
> * * * * * "I will betray
> Tawny finned fish; my bended hooks shall pierce
> Their slimy jaws."—SHAKSPEARE.

BEING provided with the right lure, be it fly or spinning bait, there is still the question how to use it. Suppose we consider the spinning bait first, in continuation of our last chapter. How should we spin, with the stream, against the stream, or across the stream? Those who advocate spinning with the stream, or drawing your bait in the same direction as the river is flowing, do so on the same ground as fly fishermen, namely, that all fish lie habitually with their heads up stream, and that consequently you bring your bait down to them, into their mouths as they say, instead of pulling it away from them up stream. But the cases are by no means parallel. What is natural in one case is unnatural in the other, and the secret of good fishing is so closely to imitate nature, that the fish shall not be able to distinguish your bait from its ordinary food. Though the fly lights, or mounting from the bottom sits, on the water's surface, and is carried unresistingly down the stream, the behaviour of the small fish which you have to imitate is very different. It swims up stream just as much as down stream: indeed, if it did not it would find itself down at the sea in a single season. It swims across also, as much as up and down. Certainly it does sometimes allow itself to drop down stream tail foremost, and that action as well as others may be imitated occasionally, but it is not a common action, and only adopted when the fish has but a short distance to go, or in a rapid. When a fish, whether large or small, wants to go down stream it almost invariably turns round, and swims down head foremost, for the obvious reason, that it can then see before it, and avoid rocks, snags, falls, etc., though when the rapid is strong it requires to descend tail foremost, so as to regulate its pace by partial swimming. When swimming down head foremost, what with the force of the current and its own swimming, it ordinarily moves more rapidly than when sauntering up stream. Besides which, it never goes down stream, except in rapid pursuit of some food that has been carried past it, or for the purpose of returning to, and again taking up, the post of observation it has lately left. Whereas, when coming up stream, fish often saunter upwards, watching for what the stream shall carry down on either side of them, lazily stemming the current, and frequently remaining stationary. At such times when moving most leisurely, and when most intent on their own food, they must offer much better opportunities for being surprised by big fish than when moving more rapidly; I should conclude, therefore, that it is the position in which the larger predacious fish are most on the look-out to take them at advantage. It is, therefore, a movement which I should think it advisable to imitate, or rather I should imitate it much oftener than I should the swimming down stream. In pulling your bait up stream, also, it is easy to vary the motion by letting it be stationary, at times, where the current is strong enough to make it spin, and to keep it off the bottom, and where the stream is more than ordinarily rapid, you can occasionally imitate the motion of a fish letting itself be lazily carried downwards by the stream. To do that you must not slack off entirely, because if you do, your fish will be carried downwards like a dead thing, whereas it should appear like a fish just keeping its nose to the stream, but letting itself drop backwards. Do not take off the tension on your bait altogether, but lessen it, continuing to just feel it, so that you will be keeping your bait's nose to the stream, and be ready to feel at once if you get a run. But if you draw your bait across the stream, you will show it to many more fish, and therefore have, in my opinion, a much better chance of taking one; and that is on the whole my favourite throw, sometimes letting the bait describe a semicircle by simply keeping the top of the rod still, and letting the stream, when strong enough, do the rest; and sometimes drawing the bait right across, or half across half up, varying it each throw so as to search all water, and because it is said that "variety is charming."

Much depends on the pace at which you draw your bait. Many draw it a great deal too quickly, under the impression that it is all important that it should spin round and round with lightning speed. But there are other things also which are important. The only object of the bait spinning round and round on its own axis is, as far as I am aware, to conceal the hooks, and perhaps also to give the general appearance of a fish moving by vibration of the tail. But chiefly, I believe, to conceal the hooks. My idea is that it is better to attain this end by having few and well concealed hooks, than at the sacrifice of natural motion in the bait. It is true that from paucity of hooks you sometimes have a run and do not hook, because your bait has been taken by the tail where there is no hook. But I would rather have that disappointment than not have the run at all by way of diversion; and my belief is that you get more runs on fine tackle with few hooks, than you do when you have a bait bristling with hooks enough to scare away the most strong-minded of fish. Moreover, the Mahseer ordinarily takes the bait in head foremost, as a trout does, not crosswise as a pike does, consequently a tail hook is not needed, except to avoid occasional missing of the bait, and I certainly would not use it just to guard against such an accident. I would rather rely on the fish missing the bait altogether, and coming at it a second time. Again it will be remembered that the leathery mouth, and the habit of compressing its prey, both point to fewer hooks being needed for getting hold of a Mahseer than are ordinarily used for trout and pike and salmon. Besides, there is a great advantage in fishing slowly. Predatory fish do not ordinarily hunt down flying game like a dog; they take it unawares like a cat, and if they feel they cannot seize it at a spring, or a rush, they give it up, and watch for another opportunity. Consequently, if a bait passes them rapidly, they take no apparent notice of it, considering the attempt at surprise likely to be vain. Many and many a time have I watched them do the same with a passing live fish. The young fellow is probably not unaware of the dangerous quarters he is passing through, and makes a dash of it accordingly; the old fellow sees with half an eye that he is wide awake, and makes no effort to overtake him. So little notice does he take, although the small fish has come close by him, that you are disposed to think he is not a taking fish, not on the feed, but a thoughtful beggar reflecting on the immoral tendencies of cannibalism, and seriously meditating the giving of it up. But keep your eye on him now, as that other little fish which is sauntering leisurely upwards comes by him, there is the slightest possible undulation of his tail, he takes just one step backwards* as if preparing for a spring, then suddenly makes one lightning dash, and the small fish has undergone deglutition. That is evidently the motion that pays. Imitate it then. But you dare not trail your bait so lazily, so listlessly, about in bright water if you have a multitude of obvious hooks. For slow spinning in clear water the necessity for light tackle with but few hooks, and those well concealed, is therefore imperative; consequently I prefer the method of baiting with one hook given on page 47, to that with a lip hook also on page 50. And I prefer the second arrangement, too, with the lip hook and only one treble, to flights of hooks invented by English fishermen for English waters, to which they are better suited than to the bright waters and bright skies of the Indian angler. Besides its being unnatural for a predatory fish to give chase to, and hunt down, a small fish or bait that is passing at such speed as to indicate a preparedness for flight, and to put him at a disadvantage for seizing it at a single short dash, like a tiger's bound upon its prey, it is also to be considered that he may not have seen it at all, or it has passed out of his sight, or reach, all too quickly.

Here I must acknowledge obligation to L. J. for the following kindly communication made in the "Asian" of the 23rd December, 1879. I will quote here only his postscript, because that only is to our present point. The rest of his letter will be quoted further on. I will only premise that the rest of his letter shows a capture in thirteen days of 958 lbs. of fish, a little fact that gives weight to his evidence. He says:

"P.S.—I have thought once or twice of writing to Major Thomas† "about Mahseer *chasing* fish. In page 79 of his book he says, "referring to Mahseer: 'Predatory fish do not hunt down flying "'game like a dog; they take it unawares like a cat; if they feel "'they cannot seize it at a spring or a rush, they give it up and watch

* The reason for the slight backward movement will be seen hereafter in remarks on the swimming of fish.

† Not Major or Dr., as elsewhere promoted, but simply a member of Her Majesty's Indian Civil Service.

" 'for another opportunity.' I am not one of ye giants in natural "history, and therefore I am not going to pit* myself against the "Author, as I should only get the worst of it, but I just want to tell "him that I on two occasions saw Mahseer hunting.

"On the first occasion I was playing a fish on a long shelving sand, "where I could see my fish some 30 yards off. It was late in the "afternoon, I saw a small fish come full speed from the deep water, "and pass close to my feet (I was standing in about a foot of water), "followed by a Mahseer who came tearing along until his dorsal fin "stood out of the water. He was so close to me that had I not been "playing a fish, I should certainly have tried to throw myself on him "and tried to catch him in that way. He evidently did not see me in "his hurry until he almost ran against me. He appeared to be a fish "of about 25 or 30 lbs.

"On the second occasion I saw a lot of small fish regularly hunted "into a corner by two Mahseer, and then the gobbling and splashing "that took place must have made it very lively for the little ones."

These observations of L. J. certainly militate against my quoted view, and yet I will venture to be "of the same opinion still." Not that I doubt or undervalue L. J.'s observations in the least. I accept them fully, and yet I think there is plenty of room for us both to be right. My view, is I think, still the rule; so it will be seen that I still stand by it, qualifying it only with the one word "ordinarily." Indeed, most general rules have to be qualified, for animals are not like machines that move with never deviating precision, and are incapable of change. In the matter of the size of the bait, and elsewhere, I have mentioned that the rules which I may have indicated cannot be considered absolute. Nevertheless, it is useful, I think, to indicate what is the ordinary rule, for though animals may deviate from it, we shall have more sport if we fish in accordance with the rule than with the deviation. Again, I have been perhaps just a little bit afraid of being tedious and wanting in connectedness and perspicuity, if I mentioned and argued out every qualification, as in the present one. In the sentence questioned, I have instanced the habits of capture in the dog and cat, but even those instances are not to be accepted without qualification. The dog ordinarily hunts down flying game

* Pitting should be out of the question between brothers of the angle. I am only very much obliged to L. J. I hope he will take in good part my venturing to be of the same opinion still, and my reasons therefor.

by continuous pursuit, but sometimes, as in efforts to catch birds, it steals up and makes a pounce like a cat. I have known a pair of dogs beat a hedge in this way, one on each side. The cat, too, and the tiger are not absolute in their ways. At times they will follow up their prey in hot pursuit, and tigers will also drive their prey, as L. J.'s Mahseer drove theirs, into a place where it may be taken at advantage. Tigers will post one of their number in a gorge for others to drive towards. Some friends of mine found themselves being thus quietly edged up. Wild dogs and wolves will thus beat towards their ambushed fellows, yet it will not be objected to that it is the generally accepted view, and it will be admitted as a fair description, that the wild dog and the wolf capture their prey by hunting it down, the cat and the tiger by surprising it. In like manner, I think, I may hold to my description of the manner in which the Mahseer captures its prey as a right one, L. J.'s manner being the exception, which, however, it is interesting to know and note. In connection with remarks on striking, I have myself noted a pertinacious hot pursuit of the bait by Mahseer; nevertheless, I did not think it the rule when the prey is moving rapidly. Trout will also chase small fish in the shallows, but their rule is rather to watch for what the stream brings within reach of the station which they have taken up.

While it is comforting, therefore, to know that the Mahseer may sometimes hotly pursue your bait a long way, even though spun too rapidly, it is better to trust to slow spinning, so as to give him an easier opportunity.

Furthermore, there are more or less educated Mahseer, as there are highly educated trout. Much fished trout, it will be admitted, require to be fished for with finer tackle, and less obvious hooks, as well as with greater skill than do others. Similarly there are unsophisticated Mahseer, dwelling in uninhabited wilds, that are capturable with ease by almost any fisherman; while there are others that have learnt caution from their growing acquaintance with "that arch deceiver man," and have to be fished for with more care and more knowledge. Such fish, especially the larger, older, and more experienced ones, are more constantly on the look out for man, more suspicious, and more intelligent in their criticism. I have heard say, that once upon a time there dwelt in fair Thames a trout so much fished for with all sorts of tackle, and grown so experienced therein, that not only could he detect an artificial minnow at a glance, but he could tell even *the shop it came from!* I am afraid I cannot produce a Mahseer quite up to that, but they are on the way to it.

My belief is that Mahseer, and other predacious fish, prey rather on sick fish than on others, and for the simple reason that the sick and weakly are the more easily captured. The same rule obtains with tigers, jackals, and other beasts of prey, the sick or wounded deer falling speedy victims where the hale and strong escape. I remember once fishing a pool with a small fly for Chela, Barils, and such-like. The pool was full of them, so that the Mahseer had no lack of small fish whereon to feed, but I saw no Mahseer feeding till I hooked one of these little fellows on my small trout fly. Immediately a Mahseer came at it, and I was in fear and trembling for my little trout rod. My conclusion was that the Mahseer had noticed that the fish I had hooked, and was pulling in, was in some way distressed, and was therefore more easily capturable. This theory may comfort you in spinning, for a spun fish looks rather like a fish in difficulties, than like a hale and active one. It is also another reason still for spinning slowly, for a distressed sick fish moves slowly and wearily, not with vigorous speed like the too quickly spun fish.

I think a fish's range of vision laterally *in the water* is very limited, and that, however quickly it may see any thing reflected against the light or in the air, it does not see nearly so far laterally under water. Though clear-sighted, it is, I think, short-sighted under water. It is the consequence, in my opinion, of the density of the element. Try yourself, in a large swimming bath, and you will find you cannot see very far about you at the bottom. It is true that the short-sightedness of a man under water is not worth much as an argument, to prove short-sightedness in the same position of an animal formed for existence in that element. Still I just throw it in, in conjunction with other facts tending to the conclusion, that, the density of the element as well as the diminution of light, has the same effect on the visual powers of the fish also. On no other theory could I understand how it is that large fish and small fish manage to exist in such close proximity. You see any number of small fish in one part of a pool; and in another part of the selfsame pool any number of the very fish that prey upon them; and those fish are on the feed too, though not noticing the little ones, for directly you spin one of those same little ones *near* them as a bait, it is taken; whereas if the big fish had seen the little ones, I cannot conceive why they should let them alone, and immediately take your bait. These little fish, it should be remembered, have no thick coverts in which to hide, like deer from the tigers that prey upon them; nor have they greater fleetness by which to escape in the open. The substitute for their protection seems to be the density of the element in which they live, which makes it difficult for even a fish to see any great distance through it laterally, and without a back-ground of light. Fish can dart exceedingly quickly for a short distance, so that a small fish that gets a start before the larger fish is in motion can be very quickly out of sight. Probably only the unwary are taken by surprise, the others relying on the density of the element to save them. Whether by surprise or pursuit the sick could not avail themselves of this means of escape, and would therefore be especially affected by the predatory fish. If there were no such means of escape it would be difficult to understand how small fish could live and feed with any pleasure in the presence of their habitual devourers. With such a retreat close at hand, however, they feed with a sense of security in full sight of their enemies, just as a rat does, enjoying his meal and eyeing you the while, well knowing that his hole is close by, and that he can be into it in a second. It is the hypothesis of short-sightedness only that makes it intelligible to me why a fish which suspects your bait, follows so very close behind it, within a few inches instead of feet or yards, examining it before it makes up its mind, and requires to follow it for some time too, scrutinizing at those close quarters, before it can satisfy itself about it. This theory of short-sightedness laterally in the water has special application to running water, in which the line of vision is much broken by the disturbances in the stream, not necessarily violent disturbances as in a run or stickle, but as in a gentle eddy, as in any part of a river in which some water is passing other water, and thus breaking the line of vision. This must be constant in all rivers, for there is always friction between particles of water in the flow of the stream, and always a back draught or upward flow along the edge of every river. There is more or less friction, according as the stream is more or less rapid. Through perfectly clear and still water fish may be able to see, somewhat indistinctly, some little distance laterally, as through thick plate-glass, but when the water is broken their plate-glass becomes to them like ground-glass. At least that is my theory, and I think fishermen will find that adoption of it, and attention to it, will influence their sport.

It is true that large and small fish ordinarily frequent slightly different parts of a river, still they are not so far apart but that the big fish ought to be able to see the little ones, if the density of the element did not curtail their length of vision, and the broken rays refract it. This my belief becomes a reason in my mind for spinning in right places, for showing your bait exactly where a fish is likely to be lying, and one of the several explanations why a good fisherman, who knows such places intuitively, kills more fish than a tyro. It is one of the grounds for my opinion that a spun dead bait is preferable to a live bait, which, from being stationary, is not shown to nearly so many fish. It is to their short-sightedness under water that I trust, and find I trust rightly, in wading in to fish, in preference to standing on the bank. If they could see far laterally in water, they could not fail to see the fisherman's two legs and trowsers all in the water up to the fork, and seeing, they would refuse his lure. And yet all fishermen find that it pays very well to wade.

This argument of short-sightedness is in favour, therefore, of spinning slowly, so as to let a fish see, and to give it a chance and a confidence of catching your bait. The chances, I say, as well as nature, are against spinning quickly. For my part I like to dawdle a bait about, up and down, under this bank, close by that big stone, and let it peep into every little nook and cranny likely to hold a big fish.

But, perhaps, you may see a big fish eyeing your bait, what is to be done then? You feel disposed to cease pulling it away from him, and to let him have a better look at it. The first impulse is to stop altogether, and wait for him. Such a course would be fatal. Spin quietly on as if you had not seen him.

If he has already suspected your bait, you will not mend matters by letting it fall dead before him. But if, on the contrary, he is simply eyeing it, to see if it gives him a fair opportunity for surprising it at a spring, then let that opportunity appear, by continuing its listless dawdling motion in the same direction, and the chances are he will make up his mind with a promptitude that will astonish you; and so sudden will be his dash that, before you have well seen him move, you will feel he has taken your bait. But if he does not, try him again with another throw or two, bringing your bait by him in different ways, but not too obtrusively. I remember one of the first times I tested these tactics. Two decent fish of the perch family (*Lutianus roseus*) were deliberately following my bait. They were side by side, and about a yard behind my bait, but they kept on following it deliberately, and eyeing it intently without offering to come a bit nearer. "Oh, my heart went pit a pat, pit a pat;" but I screwed it down resolutely, and I bethought me what should I do now if I was a nice little fish, with two great ugly brutes like that behind me. Why, if I knew it, I should bolt like mad instanter, and if I did not know it, I should just go quietly paddling on exactly as I am doing now, and then I should probably get masticated for my listlessness. So the end of my cogitations was that my bait was made to act out this little pantomime, to pursue the even tenor of its way seemingly unconscious of the devouring element behind. But oh, the agony of suspense! This spin can't last for ever. Will they never take? In another yard or two the bait will have come so home to me, that I shall have to pull it out. I was rewarded: one of the two, probably the unsuspecting and inquisitive female, had made up her mind that it was "O. K.," and had dashed so suddenly on the bait, that all I was aware of, was her disappearance from the side of her companion, and a tugging at my rod. The consequence was that she and I became very much attached to one another, and my rod kept on bowing elegant approval, while we had a lively dance together, at the end of which I led her to a seat in the boat. So ended this "spin."

Fishing in bright water as one does, and as I have explained should do, in India, many a little pantomime of this sort is seen throughout, and something learnt therefrom of the manners and customs of the scaly aborigines. But it should always be remembered that two can play at that game. If you can see the fish easily, so too can he see you, and much more easily than you can see him. He has every advantage over you. Though I have twice touched passingly on this subject already (pages 39, 41, 42), it is well worthy to be gone thoroughly into, because it is at the very bottom of all good fishing, cannot well be made too much of, and finds proper place here on remarks how to fish. The very first principle, the most important rule of fishing, is to keep well out of sight, and to accomplish this end too much pains can scarcely be taken. Again and again have I urged this as *the* main secret, on brothers of the angle, who questioned how on earth I managed to get my basket so full of trout. But again and again have I found that all the same they have only half admitted its force, concluding, ostrich-like, that because they could not see the fish, the fish could not see them. I feel, therefore, from the experience aforesaid, that it is almost a hopeless task to convert my reader from the general neglect of this maxim, to a thorough belief in the all importance of keeping it constantly in view, and of acting up to it with the amount of painstaking care that is necessary to command success. Indeed, I find I constantly have to be taking my own self to task for not being *sufficiently* careful in the matter, thoroughly though I believe in, and practice what I preach.

Properly to appreciate the necessity for exercising unusual pains to keep out of sight it is as well to consider the facilities which the fish has for seeing. To begin with, its sight is, I believe, as good as ours, perhaps keener, for the formation of its eye is said to be very good ; and it is natural that it should be, for it is, of all others, the sense on which it is mainly dependent for its existence, and with what rapidity it sees the minutest objects passing in the water a little observation will soon show. *Cæteris paribus* then, it ought to see us as quickly as we see it. But other things are not equal by any means. It has great advantages of size, colour, position, and element, of all of which it naturally avails itself. It is not a tenth of the size of a man, and in mutual observations the larger object is obviously calculated to be seen first. Then its colour, like that of most, I may say all, animals, is beautifully adapted to conceal it in its usual habitat, whereas a man who clothes himself by his own imperfect lights and his tailors, does so in direct variance with all the rules of nature. The object of his fashions is not so much to conceal his existence, as to be "the observed of all observers," and *sometimes*, indeed, to be comfortable. What more readily attracts the eye than a white paggaree, and an almost white coat to reflect the sun? A black coat is very little better, and is noticeable, as every sportsman knows, at a great distance. Then consider the difference of position. The fish is against a back-ground, the bottom, of nearly his own colour, whereas the man is standing out in bold relief against the sky. The fish, furthermore, is motionless, while the man is waving about a great stick of 10 or 16 feet long, moving his arms to do it, and cannot even keep his legs still. He is moving the whole of his comparatively big person, as he walks along the very edge of the stream, and not unfrequently on the top of a high bank. Motion catches the eye.

But besides these obvious advantages of comparative size, of colour, of position, and of being motionless, the fish has still another very materially favouring circumstance in the element in which he is. Water refracts, or breaks back the line of the rays of light. Newton says, "Refraction out of a rarer medium into a denser is "made toward the perpendicular," and as water is denser than air, the fish can see you round a corner; he can see your white paggaree before it is in a line with his eye. This is very simply demonstrated in the old illustration about a shilling. Put a rupee into an empty tea cup or a slop basin. Retreat gradually till it is just out of your line of vision. Let a second person pour in water, and you will see the rupee come into sight again. It is true this cuts both ways, enabling you, as well as the fish, to see round a corner, but as you neither of you should see each other, it is an argument for keeping further away from the bank than if you both saw in a straight line.

If you are not fishing, but wanting to observe the habits of fish, and can afford to be perfectly motionless, that is quite another thing. Much may be seen by creeping very slowly and imperceptibly up, with a rock or tree-trunk for a back ground, and remaining perfectly motionless. It is movement, the slightest movement, that catches the eye. It is by sitting motionless as a stone for hours together that the cat kills a squirrel. Motion is a sign of life, and when it is absent, animals, as well as men, are prone to doubt their eyes, and to take the object for some inanimate thing.

But do not trust to this if you are fishing, for it is as unnecessary as it is difficult that you should see your fish at all, and as above shown, the chances are about ten to one that he sees you before you see him, and then your catching him is a thing out of the question. You do not want to interview the fish, you want to catch him. Take a distant survey of the water, and when you see a likely looking bit, take its bearings, and decide whence you shall make your approaches on the enemy's position. Then stalk it as you would a sambur. Stalk not any particular fish, but stalk all the positions in which any fish are likely to be; in short, stalk the pool as if it were a living thing full of eyes, which, in fact, it is, and if any one of them sees you, and its owner darts frightened away, the probabilities are that the rest also will take alarm from his movement, and not a fish will you take in that pool. Do not stalk for too close a shot either; you do not need to be nearer than just to see your line fall, than just to see the surface of the water you are fishing, so that you may keep clear of rocks and snags, and fish it properly. But you do not always require to do even that. If from your first distant observations you know that the coast is all clear in a certain direction, then fish it round the corner of a rock without even seeing it. This is the best position in which you can possibly be. You do not need to see. You will feel fast enough if a good Mahseer has got hold of you, and then all you have to do is to return the compliment by holding on to him. If your hand is practised, you will know how your bait or your fly is deporting itself, though round a corner and out of your sight.

In so stalking, perhaps, you have attained a snug position in which, by lying down or otherwise, you are invisible to the fish, but in attaining it have unavoidably shown yourself at some awkward corner that you had to get round. If so, do not begin fishing at once, but wait long enough for the scare to pass off. When confidence is re-established you may again invite speculators to take shares. Many a goodly trout, like his betters, has been taken out of inaccessible retirement by such tactics. There is a peculiar charm in being even with the wary one that has baffled you and every one else up to date. The basket is the proper place for him, you always had an idea it was, and in he slides most satisfactorily.

There now, I have been very heavy and very long winded on this subject; but if I have converted you, I know you will not quarrel with me in the end, whatever the non-fisherman reader may do. A fuller basket will make a friend of you.

In Chapters II and V I have said that I prefer to spin with a pliable fly rod with a fly top, just such as I would use for fly-fishing for salmon; so I suppose I ought to say just two words on how to use such a rod for spinning, for there are good pike fishermen who are accustomed to trolling for pike with a stiff rod, but whose manner of casting the bait would soon break a fly rod. With a stiff rod the line is gathered in near the reel by the hand after every throw, and spread at one's feet, till the length between the bait and the point of the rod is less than the length of the rod; then the bait, which must be heavy, is swung out with some force, and the force and the weight of the bait carries all the line out through the rings. The force necessary for such casting would very soon break a fly top. My way is therefore different. I never gather in any line with the hand. I reel it up if need be for change of ground. But ordinarily I do not change the length of line which I have out. I swing the bait like a pendulum, and when it is at the end of the swing back a very little lift, *if well timed*, that is, if made exactly at the end of the swing back, will send the bait out to the full length of the line. I ordinarily have about as much line out as a length and a half of the rod. It is better to begin with less, and you will soon find that you can cast in this way with a line about twice the length of the rod. Say the rod is 16 feet, and the line out 32 feet, then if you cast this amount of line straight out, and drop the point of the rod so as to have it pretty straight in the direction of the cast, you will find that you have dropped your bait 32 + 16 = 48 feet away from you. A cast in this fashion of 45 feet to 50 feet may not be as much as can be managed with a stiff rod and the ordinary way ot throwing a heavy bait, but it is enough for sport, and covers a good deal of water, and the loss of a few feet in the length of the cast is, in my opinion, very much more than compensated for by the aid which the pliable top gives you in meeting the suddenness and violence of the Mahseers onslaught, as already set forth in Chapters

II and V. As the bait is on the point of falling into the water it should be just felt with the top ever so slightly, so as to make it fall lightly and noiselessly. To do this well in a long throw is a delicate operation, requiring, to my mind, a very great deal more skill than is needed for casting a fly lightly for trout. I do not hesitate to say that it is a very much higher art to spin well in this fashion than to cast a fly well, whether for trout or salmon. Besides the casting, there is also so much more room for skill, in the life-like management of the bait in the water, than is needed for the right handling of the fly. But the very difficulty makes the skilful accomplishment all the more pleasurable.

For such throwing the bait must, as I have said, be light. If you use a fish you are somewhat restricted in size; sinker included, you cannot well swing a fish more than six inches long without straining your top. The lightness of the phantom minnow and spoon allows of their being used much larger.

It will be found convenient to hold the rod with one or more fingers of the upper hand above the running line, and the other fingers below it; when swinging the bait for a throw, close the upper finger on the running line to prevent its being jerked out, when spinning take it off, so that the line may be perfectly free to run out the instant a fish strikes.

If fishermen would spin in this manner they would not be so wedded to stiff trolling rods for Mahseer fishing. It is because they have been told that they must spin for Mahseer as for Pike, that they have taken to a thing like a Pike rod, and then, finding they have a much finer foe than a Pike to fight with, they have had their tackle broken, as was to be expected, and have put down the breaking to the fish, instead of to their using the wrong rod, or rather spinning wrongly so as to compel them to use the wrong rod.

I daresay you will tell me I have said this more than once already in different words. I don't care. I shall say it again. Other fellows have been preaching the barge-pole and cable theory so frequently, and so positively, with all the force of men of experience, that everybody has taken to believing them, you among them. Confess it. Every letter to the "Field" about Mahseer preaches this one doctrine, and now it is my turn to have a nag at you, and it is for your good, dear reader. "Doon" is the one only writer who has lifted up his voice against barge-poles, cables, and meat hooks. I wish I knew who he is that I might shake hands with him.

But the heading of my chapter is How, when, and where, and the next point is when to fish. When as to season of the year, when as to time of day. The season of the year must necessarily be dependent on whether the place in question is subject to the influence of the south-west or of the north-east monsoon, for the time to fish is from the time the rivers clear down after monsoon floods till they are again discoloured by the rains.* This on the West Coast is from the end of September, at the very earliest, till the end of May, though September can scarcely be relied on, because of the occasional showers that come down and spoil sport, and May is apt to be a trifle feverish in the interior, so that you will stand a chance of catching something else besides fish. The time to fish in a gentlemanly comfortable sort of way, with security of sport, and immunity from fever, is from the 1st of October till the falling of the April or mango showers, or till the end of April. During this time every day is good for fishing for six or seven months without interruption, and the fish are not so variable about taking as are the trout at home, which will take well one day, and the next, or perhaps during a part of the very same day, will take a fit of sulks, and will not look at a fly, because forsooth their delicate sensibilities have warned them, or the natural fly, or both, that there is a thunder storm coming on, and instead of trout rising, you see innumerable eels lying lounging about the bottom, like coast guard men before a storm. There is a change in the state of the atmosphere, less ozone in it according to one observer, and the consequence is the trout have lost their appetites. But you will not be often troubled in that way in India, for the climate is not so variable, you are sure of fine weather for months together, and you are fairly sure of taking fish. Then's your time, *carpe diem*, for you will get a carp a day, or rather several Mahseer. You must not, therefore, mind the one drawback of your sport being spoilt by discoloured water, because it almost always occurs during fixed periods which you can calculate on beforehand, and during the months which I have named, it only troubles you once for about a fortnight in the end

* In Bengal the fishing is liable to be spoilt by the discolouration of the water from the melting of the Himalayan snows.

of October, or beginning of November, when the rice-fields are being reploughed for the second crop, and the muddy water from them is allowed to run into and discolour the river. Where there is a large area under rice on the banks of a river, the discolouration may last as long as a month from first to last; but where the river runs through forest only, you will be quite free from this nuisance. From October to April then, inclusive, may, as a rule, be counted on as good fishing months in all rivers which are fed by the south-west monsoon. I have found it the same not only in the rivers which run into the sea westwards, but also in rivers that have their heads near the Western Ghauts, and run away from them to the east through Mysore.

The right months for fishing in clear water in the rivers which are under the influence of the east coast monsoon will be further noticed in connection with the Bawanny, in the Chapter on Localities; and the right months for the rivers of Northern India will similarly be found in connection with those rivers, in the same Chapter, as given from the local knowledge of those who have so kindly supplied the bulk of that Chapter.

The time of day is also a thing to be considered. Fish will run all day long, especially on cloudy days, but I don't much believe in them between 11 and 3, and I think the best hours are before 9 A.M. and after 4 P.M. till sunset. Directly after sunset they cease running at a spinning bait, though they will take a night line. I presume this is because they do not see well enough in the dark for the moving bait, and are guided to the stationary bait of the night line chiefly by scent. As to the uselessness of going on spinning after dark, the keenest reader may I think be content to take me on trust, for, when by the river's side, I have been so keen myself as to go on fishing into the dusk and dark, though the place was densely forest-clad, and the margin marked with fresh tracks of crocodiles and panthers, only taking the precaution of having a man behind me with a loaded rifle, and trusting to his having sufficient care for his own vile body to keep a good look out in the rear of mine.

And now for where; where, in the two senses of in what waters, and in what parts of those waters. Mahseer, I believe, are to be found in every large perennial river in India. I know that they are to be found in every river on the west coast that I ever heard of. I know they are to be found in the Mysore rivers; I know they are in the Cavery, the Bawanny, the Kistna, and the Toongabadra. I hear of them in all the good rivers of Northern India. The lover of the picturesque will find them, admiring with him the adjective-exhausting falls of Gairsoppa, and dancing in the glad waters of Hoginkal, and other falls of Cavery; and I believe they have every bit as much right as the Artillery to the motto *Ubique.*

But they mostly affect the rocky mountainous parts of rivers. I had almost said they are confined to such parts, and are not to be found where the river grows broader and shallower with a sandy bed. There are no doubt instances where they markedly cease as the river leaves the mountains, and I have known them called an essentially mountain fish in consequence. But they are to be found again where rocks recur lower down the river than the sandy flats, and there are deep pools and heavy runs among the rocks; and they are even to be found in deep, still pools without a rock in them, so that it is not clear what rule, if any, governs their selection of locality. But I think there is no doubt that they chiefly affect the rocky mountainous parts of rivers, and that very many more and finer Mahseer are to be found in such parts than lower down a river. To such parts, therefore, I would recommend the Mahseer fisherman to confine his attention.

We speak here of the whereabouts of the Mahseer only. The localities in which to find other fish will be mentioned separately in connection with each fish, and some peculiarities of position will be noticed in the Chapter on Localities.

It may be of service to the fisherman to have a list of good angling stations, after the manner of "The Angler's Diary" in England, together with hints as to how to get to them, and to exist at them; for though a river may be a good one, there are sure to be particular parts in it in which the runs and pools are deeper, and better, and more approachable than elsewhere. A little information, therefore, on this head I shall endeavour to give in a separate chapter. But it is obvious that, for such a vast area as Hindustan, a list made out by any one man must be exceedingly meagre, and I would suggest that if brothers of the angle would contribute information about the different localities they have tried, we might very soon get together a goodly batch of information, so that new comers from England would be at no loss where to spend a little leave or leisure, and even old hands would find, when transferred by business or pleasure to new localities, that they could tumble better on their legs than they could without this information, and that there were a lot of other fellows besides themselves that "know a thing or two." To the charitably disposed, therefore, I make my appeal on behalf of brother anglers.*

This appeal was thus made in the first edition, and kindly has it been responded to, both by direct communication and by letters to the "Field" and "Asian." The result appears in the Chapter on Fishing Localities. It falls, however, very far short of what I had hoped to attain to, and as it is the chapter which may well be the most useful part of the whole book to really good fishermen, I will let the appeal still stand, in the hope that brothers of the angle may continue to communicate their knowledge of localities.

But supposing we have arrived at the river's side at a good locality, where in it are we to find our fish? An old hand does not need to be told, for he knows instinctively, though he has never seen the river before in his life. You can tell well enough from the outside of a house whether it is a poor man's cottage or a gentleman's mansion, and if you have an eye for the water, you will be able to make a very shrewd guess as to where the best fish lie. As a rule the swell is to be found in the best house, except in Ireland, by the way, where the finest structure in the villages is the poorhouse. But then every thing goes by contraries in "poor owld Ireland," even down to the cereals, for there Paddy raises the riot, instead of the Ryot raising paddy, as he does here. Still, out of Ireland, the rule holds good, and the swell fish, as well as his brother biped, is to be found in the best quarters; and those are readily recognizable.

Look for a Mahseer in just such water as you would expect to find a salmon, in the deep runs, especially where a fall enters a pool, and in the eddies of those runs.

The depth should not be less than up to the fork, and after that the deeper the better; though Mahseer, like trout, visit the shallows in search of small fish, etc., when the water is discoloured, and at night when the water is bright, returning with light to

* My present address is Madras, but any communication through my publishers, or through Messrs. Arbuthnot & Co., Madras, will always find me.

the deeper water. When the water is very slightly discoloured I have "found my account" in fishing where the river shallows just above the head of a run, in water so shallow that you would think a big fish could scarcely lie in it, water scarcely up to the knees. The Mahseer seem to visit it then for the better capture of small fish. If you attempted to fish in such places in bright water you would be seen.

For a Mahseer you may fish a run all its length. I have taken them quite at the tail of a run, and I have taken them in the very white water of the fall. They are not afraid of the water. But midway in the run is about the place for the highest hopes. I have, however, a special weakness for the eddies, though they are the most difficult to fish, because I think the best fish are generally found in them, and I prefer one good big fellow to two or three smaller ones. But in fishing the eddies, try and bear in mind that there is generally one on your own side of the river, just as good as the one under the opposite bank. Why should you be seized with that "*ulterioris ripæ amore*" which seems to be almost universal? Why? Probably because you had not prospected the place before you came to it, as I recommended, and are standing right over it, before you were aware of its existence, and have consequently spoilt it for all fishing purposes. Whereas had you prospected, and stalked the place, as I recommended, you would have shown nothing but the tip of your rod over the bank, and with a short line would have dropped your bait in close under it. It is time enough to try the run, and the opposite bank, after you have tried your own. The opposite bank or eddy is, in nine cases out of ten, more difficult to reach than the one under your nose, and, from the breadth of the river or run, frequently quite unapproachable. Do not, therefore, neglect the eddy on your own shore.

The still deep pools also are not to be neglected. From a boat they are the easiest fishing of all, and yield the biggest fish. On this account some prefer to fish the pools only. I have done very little in this direction myself, but the plan is simply to let out plenty of line so that your bait may be spinning far away from the boat, which might otherwise frighten the fish, and deep, because big fish ordinarily lie near the bottom, and the deeper the pool the better the fish as a rule. Having let out the line the bait is spun by the motion of the boat, so that it is really spun by the boatman not by you. When you realise this awful fact it strikes one that it is very similar to shooting sambre that have been driven out to you by the beaters, instead of stalking the stag *yourself* like an honest sportsman. In letting out the line, of course you will take care, having the boat in motion, to keep the bait off the bottom, for you do not want to catch that, like the man in "Punch," who got fast into the Kingdom of Scotland. Commence at the lower end of the pool, and row up against the stream, regulating the pace by the stream. Fix the rod with the reel free, or hold it as you prefer. In the lakes in Scotland it is usual to fish thus with two rods, one out of each side of the stern, and, the depth being known, to tie a little piece of bright coloured silk round your running line at the required distance from the end, generally, if I remember rightly, about 30 yards, so that when you see the little bit of silk pass out of the ring at your rod tip you may know how much line you have payed out. Whether you prefer to let out 30, 50, or more yards must depend much on the depth of the pool and the weight of your bait. If you have only one rod you can work it slowly across and across the stern if you like, but always with a taut line, and giving time after each crossing for the bait to swing round; this will cover more water than simply trailing. If you are trailing two lines the second one must be rapidly reeled up by an attendant the moment you have a fish on No. 1 or you will get into difficulties.

Use dead bait, spoon or phantom, as you prefer. I have told you which I prefer, and that a dead bait need not be spun so rapidly as a spoon or phantom.

Though I say fish deep, still do not be too keen about getting your bait very close to the bottom, for many more fish will see it if it is well off the bottom. Bear in mind that a fish can see an object moving across a light back-ground, much better than one against a dark back-ground, can see an object between it and the light which is above it, better than one between it and the dark bank on the side of it, and that above it, it can, within certain limits, see it the further the higher it is. For instance (*see* Francis Francis' "Book on Angling"), an object at A, which is twice as far from the bottom as B, will be seen over the whole base C D, which is twice as big as the base E F; in other

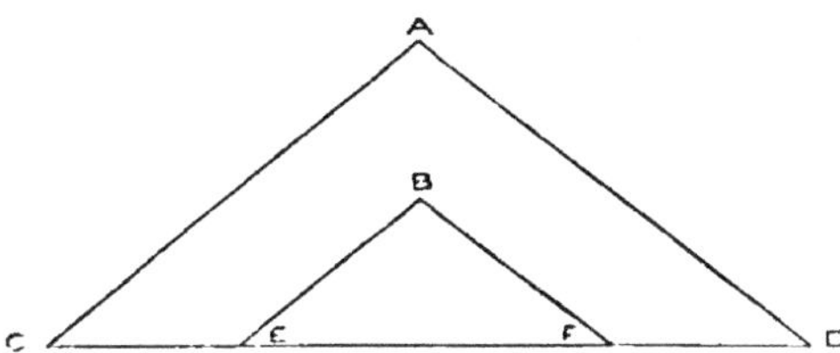

words, your bait at A will be seen by a Mahseer lying at C, which would never see it if it was spun 2 feet lower at B. On this theory you may say a fish will see further if you spin on the surface. But, on the other hand, we do not know how far a fish can see laterally, or at any angle out of the perpendicular under water, nor how far from the bottom a large Mahseer may feel inclined to come up after a bait, when the water is 20 feet deep. I should say, therefore, spin about mid-water, and I think you will show your bait advantageously to most fish.

If you are often fishing the same water, you should remember where you kill your best fish, for where one good fish has been taken, another of the same size is pretty sure to be found; the reason being that those fish which lay wait for, instead of searching for, their bait, those which stop in one place waiting and watching for what the stream shall wash down to them, look out for the best places, the places where the chief current of the stream will carry the most food by them, or a favouring eddy will bring it round to them, and there they take up their station behind a rock or stone, so that they themselves may be in comparatively quiet water, but yet in a good position for watching passing events, and as any food comes by them, out they dart, take it, and return to their station. Some such stations are better than others, and the strongest fish take the best. With them it is naturally

> "The brave old rule, the simple plan,
> That they should take who have the power,
> And they should keep who can."

And when that fish has been taken, and his place is vacant, the next strongest takes it. This is markedly the case with trout in English streams, the proportions of which do not vary much from month to month, and is, in my opinion, more or less the case with Mahseer too, though to a less degree, because the rapidly varying size of a stream will in a month or two make a favourite station an indifferent one. But a proper fisherman will readily recognize the most comfortable looking quarters for a good fish. The power of making a correct diagnosis will be acquired by practice, though there is a spice of *nascitur non fit* about it too.

How soon a vacant place is ordinarily reoccupied I do not know. Sometimes the very next day, if I remember rightly. How do fish find out that there is a vacant tenement? It would seem that they must be giving a look in from time to time to see.

Since the above was in printer's hands, I have come upon the following in "My Life as an Angler," by William Henderson, London, William Satchell and Co., 12, Tavistock Street, Covent Garden, W.C., 1880, a book that is *very pleasant* reading:—

> "I remember a tale told me by Johnny Younger, which shows how "surely the angler may rely upon this habit of the largest trout. On "one of my visits to his workshop he mentioned three evenings' fishing "which his son had recently taken in the Tweed. On the first of these, "when fishing upwards, I believe with the worm, he came to the stream "which flows immediately below Merton Cauld. The hour was late, the "gloaming far advanced, and the angler had captured several trout "of the usual size, when on trying one particular spot which he knew "by experience to be the best, he succeeded in taking a fish of, if I "remember rightly, 3 lbs. weight. On hearing this, Johnny observed "that no doubt this was 'the tyrant,' and advised his son to try the "same spot on the subsequent evening, as the fish next in size would "no doubt be found there. The prophecy proved true; a fish some- "what smaller than the last was basketed. On the third evening, "another trout still rather less was captured, but the three were far "heavier than any others taken."

CHAPTER VII.

FLY-FISHING FOR MAHSEER.

"Away, then, away,
We lose sport by delay;
But first leave all our sorrows behind us,
If misfortune do come
We are all gone from home,
And a-fishing she never can find us."
COTTON.

Is any one of our readers half as fond of fly-fishing as I am? If so,

"A sudden thought strikes me;
Let us swear eternal friendship,"

for stoutly though I have argued in favour of spinning for Mahseer, as being the most killing way of fishing for them, and unable though I am to retract, still I could wish that fly-fishing were as killing a way, for it is to my mind the most fascinating style of fishing going. I refer particularly to fly-fishing with a single handed rod and very light tackle for trout. The nicety of skill that has to be brought into play, to make anything of a bag amongst good and wary trout, is sometimes very refined. It is quite distinct from fly-fishing for salmon, and is a much higher branch of the art; though there is an exultant ruder joy certainly in the hand-to-hand fight with a lordly salmon, when once you have got him on. But any man who is a good trout fisherman will readily fall into salmon-fishing; though a master at salmon-fishing may be but a rude trout fisherman. But both the real trout fisherman, and the salmon tamer, will want to know what can be done in India by their favourite style of fishing.

Suppose we commence with the Mahseer fisher. I'll be bound the very first question he asks will be an awkward question; he will want to know what fly to use for Mahseer. This is a question to which there is no answer with a good reason for it, such as I should like to have at the back of my beliefs. There are pretty nearly as many opinions on the point as there are salmon-flies, and not one of them is satisfactorily supportable, that is, be it added with becoming modesty, in my humble opinion. As far as I can see, it is simply a matter of fancy. I can recognize no principle underlying the colouring of a salmon or Mahseer fly, nor can I conceive why a salmon should care a button whether or not every one of all the variously hued feathers that go to make up some of the more expensive salmon flies, are duly inserted, or more than half of them are forgotten. Take any one of the more elaborate instructions for tieing a salmon fly; I should very much like to see the salmon that could tell at a glance, as the fly passed him in the water, whether or not the brown mallard, bustard, peacock, and blue and yellow swan strips, and half a dozen more feathers, were all duly in their place. I do not believe in such a salmon ever having been hatched, no, not even "north of the Tweed." Why, you could not tell yourself without taking the fly in your hand to have a close look at it, nor could the very man that tied it; no more can the salmon without taking it in his hand to feel, if not to see. So that is just what he does. He sees something passing him which he cannot quite make out, it may be good for food, it may not; he will investigate; so he takes it in his mouth, which is his only hand, with which he is accustomed to feel and to taste doubtful objects, passing too rapidly to be quite made out by the eye, retaining those that are approved, and ejecting the others. He takes your salmon fly in his hand, meaning to throw it away if disapproved, but, before the spirit of enquiry in him is satisfied, your hook is into him, and he is entering on new experiences.

This is doubtless a very heretical doctrine that I am propounding. I know that the great majority of good salmon-fishers are of the contrary opinion. To them the colours of their flies are as sacred as the strands of their tartans; they would not let you alter one feather; and they will say something about blending colours. I am afraid they will be down on me heavily for this piece of heresy, and I should be overwhelmed by their numbers and weight. There rises before me the fate of poor Prometheus, who got making experiments with electricity. They called it stealing fire from heaven, and ran him in. But they let Franklin off for the very same crime. Perhaps I, too, may escape. I will trust to the enlightened age. I wish very much though that I could find some theory on which to base fly-fishing for Mahseer. I only look to salmon fishing to help me in this matter, but I look in vain. As far as I can see the principle at the bottom of all fishing is, the presentation to the fish of a hook, so concealed under something which is its natural food, or which is so like its natural food, that it is taken unsuspectingly in place of food. This principle is thoroughly acted up to in the tieing of artificial flies for trout, they being the closest possible imitation of the actual flies on the water, and the fisherman changes his fly every hour of the day that the fly on the water changes. But what on earth a salmon fly is meant to represent no one knows, nor, indeed, why it is called a fly at all, except from the trout fly having given the idea that salmon also might be fished for in the same manner, only with a larger fly. It is only surmised that it is taken by the salmon for a small fish or shrimp, or some other thing unknown. My belief is that it is simply taken for the thing unknown, and experimented on by the salmon in the manner above suggested. In brief the fly is dressed more to suit the fisherman than the fish. The fisherman must have a fly he believes in; he cannot possibly fish well if he has no faith in his lure. A fly of your own fancy always kills best. If the fish are in a taking humour, that is, are eagerly on the look out for food, they will take any fly you throw in sight of them. If they are not they will only take the fisherman's fancy fly. Therefore, if you have any fancy fly use it for Mahseer; if you have not, then take somebody else's fancy, mine if you will. For with only fancy and no rationale to guide us, and the necessity for having a fancy of some sort, all we can do is to look about till we find a man who has had the good fortune to kill pretty often with any particular fly, so that he has grown to have a confidence in it, and to use the same till we find a better. Now I have a very thorough belief in black as the colour. I had arrived at such a belief, unbeliever though I am, in 1873. I have been only confirmed in it by subsequent experience. Aye, wedded to it. And I find I am by no means alone in my belief. I find numbers of men use a black fly in preference to any other, and I have been surprised on asking good fishermen at great distances what was their pet fly, to get back from them simply my old friend the black. I believe that anything black will do business. I have tried black wings and legs with various bodies, with black worsted body, black floss silk body, orange body, peacock harl body, with and without silver twist, with and without tail, and somehow, gradually, I have come to think that the more glossy and shining it is the better, probably as catching the eye sooner. I have made as many experiments on the Carnatic Carp as on the Mahseer, and the fly with which I have done most business was one roughly dressed on the above fancies, out of the materials available on the river's side, to wit, almost entirely of peacock harl and silver twist, with just a little bit of glistening peacock feather for the legs. I had peacock harl tail, ditto body very full with tag, and two or three turns of silver twist, peacock feather legs, and a great bunch of harl for wings. Of course it was a bungling looking fly, but it did its work; that is, till torn to rags; for peacock harl is too fragile a material for wings, and does not last long. I shall therefore commend to my reader a fly tied on the same principle, to wit, as black as I can get it glistening, but of better materials, and I shall call it by the same name as my less gaily dressed friend of earlier years, the Blackamoor, and as I never use any other fly now, I will not give you any other. If you *will* have others you must pick them up for yourself from those who recommend them. You will find them in the extracts thrown together in Chapter XXIV, and you will be able to get at them through the medium of the Index.

Why black should be a better colour than any other I cannot tell you. Perhaps it is taken for the black tadpole so common in Indian rivers, and so juicy, and so relished by the Kingfisher I know, and I imagine by fish too. I was very nearly trying a dish of them myself one day. Perhaps it is that black is so readily seen in clear water against a clear sky. Perhaps it is only that it is oftener used, and with more reliance than other colours. In the case of the Carnatic Carp, perhaps, it is that it is mistaken for a broken piece of waterweed. But whatever it is mistaken for it is taken, and that's the great point, and as it has treated me and my friends well, I am ready to stand security for it that it is an honest fly.

Having thus settled the colour to our mutual satisfaction, the next question is the size of the fly. Here, again, it is *quot homines tot sententiæ;* and here, again, I have my own ideas, and will submit them to your judgment for what they may be worth. Salmon flies are generally supposed to differ in size with the size of the water, the finer flies being used in the finer water, the larger in the heavier water and larger rivers. The same ideas are carried into Mahseer fishing by salmon fishers. Accordingly I have seen Mahseer flies of all sizes from No. 3 Limerick to No. 10/0 Limerick, the latter being nearly as big as a swallow. Indeed, I have heard of an angler who, having tried his fly in vain, had given it up, and, taking up his gun by way of diversion, shot a swallow, which fell into the water. To his astonishment there was a big swirl and the swallow disappeared. Of course he shot another swallow, baited and fished with it immediately. It, too, was taken down, and he landed a Mahseer. What the weight was I do not know. On the other hand, I know an excellent fisherman who uses always a No. 3 Limerick hook. My own fancy is to have three sizes, No. 1/0, 2 and 3, of which I more generally use No. 2.

I am quoting sizes from my own scale annexed, and I would beg the reader's special attention thereto in order to save him from disappointment. In my former edition I quoted from the scale given in Francis Francis' "Book on Angling," overlooking the caution which he gives, and which I may as well quote: "Hooks are "varied so much in size, not only by different makers, but even by "the same makers, and the numbering and lettering becomes so "troublesome and complicated, that I have given a scale of Limerick "hooks of sizes numbered for reference, as the easiest and simplest "mode of expression." The value of this caution I learnt to my cost in this wise. Having planned a fishing trip with certain friends, I wrote to England for flies for us all, quoting Francis Francis' numbers, but not saying that I quoted from him. In consequence out came the flies beautifully tied, just as ordered, but all on hooks of sizes that were useless. Francis Francis' Nos. 11 and 12, which I was ordering for Carnatic Carp, would have been Nos. 5 and 6 on my scale, whereas Nos. 11 and 12 on my scale were perfectly useless, and that was the scale that came.

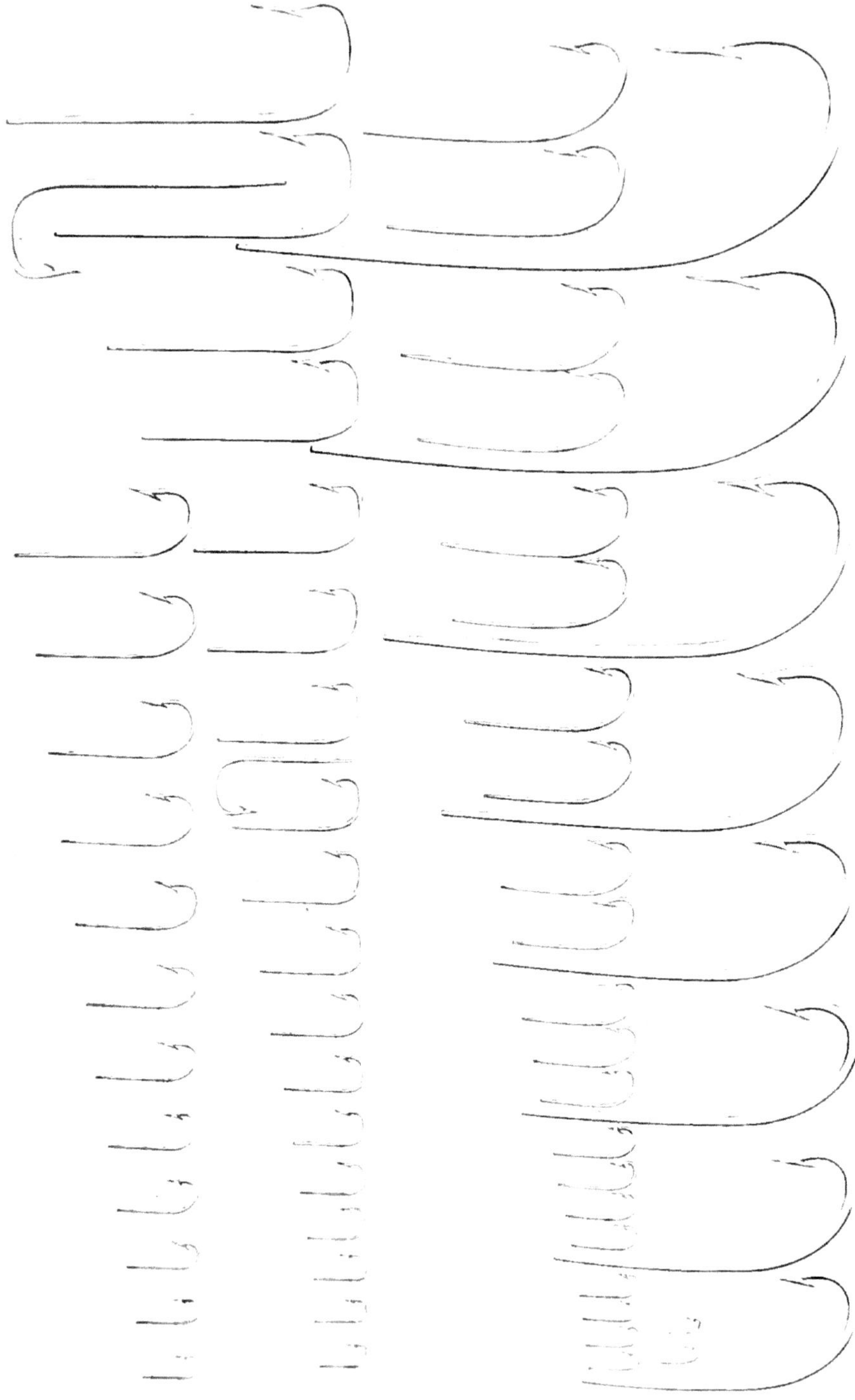

What was to be done? There was no time to write again, and we were all too busy men to tie flies for ourselves. We had not the time. What was to be done? My friends had relied on me, and . . . . well, it was very vexatious. I had to look about for a likely native,* and a friend and I taught him, and so we got our flies just in time after all. But it was very nearly being a worse disappointment. In ordering flies, therefore, be sure to quote, not only the number, but also the author of the number. If you take Francis Francis' number, say so; if mine, say so, and your tackle maker will know what you want. If you do not he is not to blame if you suffer a like disappointment to my own.

But why have I given you a different scale from Francis Francis? It is very annoying, doubtless, and I am very sorry to do anything to annoy you. Still less had I any silly fancy for setting up a standard of my own. I would very much rather have followed Francis Francis' scale, but unfortunately that scale did not go as far as was necessary for Indian fishing; it did not give the larger sizes or the smaller ones; it only gave medium sizes, such as he wanted for his own reference only. I saw no way of adapting his numbering to that of any hook maker that I knew of. Other books quote other numbering without giving any drawing of the scale, *e.g.*, the Adlington scale. I went to several leading tackle shops, and was at a good deal of pains to find an accepted scale. But in vain, there was none. I then did the next best thing I could think of. I wrote to more than one of the manufacturers recommended by the leading tackle shops, and had my drawings made from the scale of the manufacturer who took the most trouble to give me a perfect scale. My acknowledgments are due to Messrs. R. Harrison. Bartleet and Co., of Redditch, for the same. Messrs. William Bartleet and Sons, also of Redditch, have a similar scale.

I mention all this because I think it is very much to be

* Anthony Solomon Dorasamy Pillai, Head Taxidermist, Government Central Museum, Madras.

He will do the same for you by the kind permission of the Curator of the Museum, who, being himself a fisherman, has his heart in the right place for brother anglers. Of course the Taxidermist only does it out of office hours, so you must give him a little time. But if not in a hurry, get your flies tied at your own tackle shop in England.

regretted that some arrangement cannot be come to in the trade for the adoption of one scale in hooks. It would be intolerable if there were the same uncertainty in guns, so that you could be never sure of the gauge of your gun. There seems no reason why the same uniformity should not be attained in hooks as in cartridges. Surely the tackle makers could and should, in the interests of the public, establish a standard scale, not in Limerick hooks alone, but in all hooks.

Francis Francis' scale of Limerick hooks corresponds with mine thus far, that his numbers 1 to 12 approximate closely to the sizes of my numbers 7/0 to 6, skipping my numbers 1/0 and 4, thus:—

His 1 = my 7/0		His 7 = my 1½	
„ 2 = „ 6/0		„ 8 = „ 1	
„ 3 = „ 5/0		„ 9 = „ 2	
„ 4 = „ 4/0		„ 10 = „ 3	
„ 5 = „ 3/0		„ 11 = „ 5	
„ 6 = „ 2/0		„ 12 = „ 6	

Having thus come to an understanding, or to a misunderstanding, which you will, but at least to something definite about the sizes of Limerick hooks, I will describe the flies to be tied on them, adhering, of course, to what I call my own scale, though it is not mine, but that of more than one large maker.

THE BLACKAMOOR.

Tag: three or four turns of tinsel. Tail: two or three sprays of peacock harl from the end of the tail feathers that end without an eye, and are feathered only on one side. Body, peacock harl very full and ribbed with two or three turns of tinsel. Legs or hackle, commencing small, a little short of the tail end of the body, and carried up to the shoulder, hackle increasingly large and increasingly thick, and forming also the shoulder hackle, which may be full. For this use the tip end of one of those tail feathers of the peacock that ends without an eye, and that has harl on one side only, as those are much the brightest, and of a convenient length for the larger flies; for the smaller, the feathers taken from the back of the peacock may be substituted. Wing: the glossiest, deepest black procurable, *e.g.*, the black crane, the raven, the glossy blue-black feathers of the magpie's tail, with a sprinkling of the same peacock harl from the eyeless tail feathers to make it shiny. In the smallest fly on No. 5 Kirby the almost black blue from the wing of the mallard or magpie may be preferred to simple black.

For Mahseer, I use 2/0 and 2 of my Limerick scale, and more generally No. 2. Some use 6/0 and 7/0; and one excellent fisherman I know delights specially in No 3. But I think 2/0 and 2 are your best sizes, especially the latter, and that if you want anything bigger than 2/0 you should use a fish bait. For Carnatic Carp the same fly on No. 5 and 6, my Limerick scale, but more generally No. 6, for the tail and first drop fly. For the second drop, the same just a size smaller. It is convenient to have it tied on a different sort of hook so that it may catch your eye quickly, when selecting it for the drop fly, so, say No. 5 Kirby. This last may be tied on a single salmon gut. All the others should be tied on a gut eye,—treble gut eye for No 2/0 and larger, single salmon gut eye for No. 2 and smaller.

For Mahseer I fish with a single fly as for salmon; for Carnatic Carp with a collar of three flies as for trout, but a collar of single salmon gut.

For the benefit of those who are newly compelled in India to tie their own flies, I may mention that the hook of all salmon or Mahseer flies will of course be tied, not on single gut, as in the case of a trout fly, but on stout salmon gut doubled, so as to leave at the head a short loop, between a quarter and an eighth of an inch in length. The object of this is to give the gut stiffness, to prevent it from constantly doubling under the weight of the hook, and thus fraying, and eventually giving way, close up to the hook. The precaution is necessary in the case of salmon flies because of their weight; and when the fly is large, treble gut also is thus looped instead of single gut.

Hooks draw very much, however, in India, because the great heat dries the wax and shrinks the gut, and as a consequence hooks not freshly tied are very liable to draw. The precaution should therefore be taken of tying a knot in the gut laid against the shank of the hook; when it is covered with dressing it will not show.

Fish with the fly for Mahseer, just as you would for salmon; that is to say, that if you are a salmon-fisher I can give you no advice, you are sure to follow your practice. But if you are not, I may as well mention that the general idea is, that you should not draw your fly with a steady pull through the water, but with a succession of little jerks, with slight pauses between, so as to give it a shrimp like motion, the theory being that with every jerk the feathers will be compressed against the hook, and with every pause they will spread out again, thus making a greater show, and giving an appearance of life to the fly, an appearance of kicking out for a swim. That is, I believe, the theory and the general practice, but I may be allowed to add I do not believe in it. I believe the constant twitching only disturbs the water, and tends to frighten the fish, and the uneven motion of the fly increases the risks of the fish missing your fly when he rises at it. My way is to be careful to throw a perfectly straight line, and then to keep it just taut and no more, drawing my fly steadily and as slowly as possible, sometimes not drawing it at all, but letting it swing round with the stream, varying the throw and the draw so as to cover all likely water.

Mind you do not pull too fast. Many a fish will not be troubled to rise at a fly that passes him in too much of a bustle. Possibly it may have passed him before he has well seen it, or even if he has seen it, it is in too much of a hurry for him; he is not inclined to rush after it and scramble for it with his next door neighbour, who is just as wide awake as he is. Be that as it may, work your fly slowly: more fish are killed thus than by quick fishing, and less fish rise short.

And as to that much disputed question the striking of a Salmon or Mahseer, whatever rule you accept in one case, is equally applicable in the other. My plan is to strike as quick as lightning with a trout, but with a Salmon or a Mahseer, not at all. If your line is thrown straight and always kept taut, as it should be, you will feel a Salmon or Mahseer, and no mistake, when he has your fly well in his mouth; you need not watch the swirl, as for a trout, you will feel fast enough if he has caught your fly or missed it, and if you feel him there "belay there, belay," hold on to him hard enough to drive the hook in well past the barb; hold on, not by touching the line, but by raising the top of your rod, and making him bend the rod as much as you safely dare. He will do the rest for you in his violent efforts to break away. There is no occasion to strike with a jerk as for trout or small fish. If you do, the chances are you will be just too quick for him, and will pull the fly out of his mouth; and if you do that you frighten him, and he will not come again, which he might do, if he was not conscious of anything but having made an ass of himself, and missed a good thing. Remember, also, he is taking it unconsciously and leisurely, not in a hurry to catch hold of it before you shall snatch it away. In short, hold on to him when you feel him and not before, just as you would to a stumbling horse. But to do this properly you should not only have no slack line, should not only be just feeling your fly with your rod top, as you just feel a horse's mouth with the weight of a finger, and no more, so that you are keeping up communication with your fly, and are in a state of constant preparedness to act when called upon, but the point of your rod should be held almost at a right angle to the direction of the line, so that the fish when taking the fly, and striking himself by his weight, may do so against the full play of the elastic rod. If the rod is held with the point towards the fish he gets a straight pull on the line direct from the reel, with no spring to ease off its suddenness, and the result is in most cases a break, either of tackle or hook-hold.

The advantages of the non-striking principle are clearly seen in spinning. How often does a fish miss your bait, and if you do not pull it away from him with a jerk by striking, go at it again. No doubt it is hard to keep cool under the circumstances, for "it gives one quite a turn" to see a big fish roll over your bait, with every appearance of having taken it, and it is almost an instinctive process to strike. But it should not be done. If he has taken it, it will be unnecessary, for his weight will both hook him and tell you. If he has missed it, it is quite a mistake to jerk it rudely away from him, and it will only put him out. To exemplify the advantage of not striking, I may mention a $6\frac{1}{2}$ lb. Mahseer coming up at my spinning bait, and turning over as if he had taken it. As I did not feel him, however, I pulled steadily on as if nothing had happened. He immediately turned and rushed at it again. Again he missed it, and my little bait went spinning demurely on, as if there was no such thing as a Mahseer in the river. Round he turned and went at it the third time. The line tautened, and virtue was rewarded. I felt all over just like little Jack Horner, felt "what a good boy am I." The thing occurs daily, and, for my part, I cannot understand why people dispute about whether or not you ought to strike a salmon. It is clear to my mind both that you need not, and you should not. With trout and small fish, it is quite another thing. The rationale of the matter will be found further discussed, however, in the Chapter on the Carnatic Carp.

I may add, that the salmon fly has yet another redeeming point, over and above those mentioned in Chapter IV. Though, in my opinion, you catch fewer Mahseer with the fly than spinning, still I think you have a better chance of a variety of fish with the fly, than with a small fish. Other fine carps more or less like the Mahseer have much smaller mouths comparatively, and cannot therefore readily take the same sized fish-bait, as the Mahseer. These take the fly better, and as a consequence do not feed so much on fish. But they must have a chapter to themselves.

CHAPTER VIII.

GRAM-FISHING FOR MAHSEER.

> "The pleasantest angling 'tis to see the fish
> Cut with her golden oars the silver stream
> And greedily devour the treacherous bait."
>
> SHAKSPEARE.

THERE is another way of angling for Mahseer, of which I am fain to confess that I have myself no personal experience, and of which, therefore, I ought not perhaps to write; but it is a way of fishing which has so many friends in certain localities, that I feel it would be a grave omission to leave it unnoticed. I have also at my elbow a good spirit to prompt me, in the shape of a brother-angler* who has made many a good bag in this way in the Nerbudda, near Jubbulpore; and who is consequently in a position to guide my pen.

Make up your mind where you are going to fish, and send a servant, a day before, to ground-bait the place. Some ground-bait two or three days before; but one day is enough; the places selected should be deep strong runs into pools, and it will be sufficient to bait two or three such places. The baiting is done with Bengal gram (*alias* Chenna), the servant taking ten or twenty measures of it, and throwing in a handful every now and then, for hours together, till all the fish in the neighbourhood have congregated to get it.

The gram is said to require some preparation, though with what object I do not know, for no amount of parching, short of burning to a cinder, makes it at all more buoyant.

The established practice, however, is to soak it in cold water for about two hours, which is long enough to make it swell as much

* Major George Chrystie, 3rd Madras European Regiment, and Superintendent of Police

as it ever will, and then parch it in a frying pan, without the everlasting ghee or any such thing, till well browned and crisp, just as you would like to eat it. It will not actually float till fried to a cinder, but it is more or less buoyant, as it is more or less fried.

This, then, is your ground-bait, and the bait with which you fish should be just the same, with the one addition, that it must have a hole through it, large enough to admit the gut and the shank of the hook, but not to allow the barb to pass. Boring this hole is rather troublesome, for the grain, after frying, is very hard. It can be done with a very fine brad-awl, but the best way is with a red hot needle, set at the end of a handle, that you can expose to the fire. A dozen, or a dozen and a half, bored berries are quite enough for a day's fishing.

The hook used should be a No. 1½ Limerick (my scale) on a single gut. Whatever I may have said to the contrary in other places, no knot should be tied in this gut, or it may not pass through the hole in the gram. Singe the end of the gut before binding it to the hook, and whip your loop, and for both of them use fine silk, so as to avoid thickness. Put the loop of the gut through the hole in the gram, and so string on gram enough to cover the whole shank of the hook, the first strung piece of gram resting against the barb, and being kept by it from slipping off.

Before setting to work, let your man get the fish together, by a cast or two more of ground-bait. The fish ought to be visibly bobbing up their heads, and crowding together for the gram. Then let the man throw in a handful, and with it cast in your line into the middle of the bobbing, gobbling, crowd. You will get one every throw. To use a Shaksperian simile "it is as easy as lying:" you have not got to strike, or to do any thing. You just feel your bait is taken, and you pull him in as soon as he'll let you. You may go on taking one after another out of the same run. They do not seem to mind it, at any rate not till you have made a sensible impression on their numbers. I suppose they do not begin to think of the hotel bill till after they have had their dinner.

Fish the rapid heavy runs, not the pools, and when you have established a funk in one place, then try another of the previously baited runs. Two or three such runs will suffice for a morning or evening.

The season for this fishing is the same as for all other Mahseer fishing, the bright-water weather; and the time of day the same also, namely, the morning and evening.

There does not seem to be any necessity to hide yourself, as in other fishing. You may fish openly from the water's edge, for the misguided creatures think you are a public benefactor. In short, you may follow the fashion of the age, preaching "universal philanthropy," "the solidarity of humanity," and so forth, while in plain English you mean death to others, and gain to yourself.

Though you throw your bait like a fly, you do not draw your bait like a fly or fish; you simply let it float down, or rather be carried down under water. Your collar should be of single gut, as in fly-fishing. The thickness of the gut depends on what you expect to catch. The fish caught this way are generally small, but I see in the "Field" that the late Major Geoffrey Nightingale caught a Mahseer as much as 40 lbs. in weight, in this way, on a single gut. I presume it was salmon gut, or something approaching it. A single scale of this fish measured 2⅝ of an inch in diameter, in a life size engraving in the "Field" of 9th October 1869.

Possibly the large fish are shy, unless the angler is as thoroughly concealed in this sort of fishing as he should be in any other, and that it is only the youngsters that are taken in with communistic clap-trap.

Since my first edition I have tried the above plan very carefully, and have also tried it with what seemed to me a more natural bait, the fruit of the banyan (*Ficus Indica*) which I used in large quantities in admirably well adapted localities. But on every occasion it was a signal failure, albeit the description was verified as correct by a good fisherman, Colonel K. G. I do not remember having had an offer even. I think it is pretty clear that this style of fishing will not suit Madras Mahseer. It seems to be confined to localities in which the fish have been thoroughly educated to it by having been long accustomed to being fed by man.

In the "Asian" of the 25th November, 1879, W. T. F. says,

with a kindly compliment which modesty compels me to omit, that your humble servant "is rather out in his description of the "fishing at Jubbulpore," adding considerately "but then he does "not write from personal experience." He has also been good enough to write the following, which I extract from the "Asian" of 12th October, 1880, together with a suggestion by T. A. B. in the same paper, under date 9th November, 1880. Comment of my own, adjudicating in any way between the informants, I cannot presume to make, for the fishing is such a local one that I cannot be expected to know it personally; still I may not leave it unmentioned, because of the many likely to be interested.

The mode of fishing for Masheer in the Nerbudda, near Jubbulpore, being peculiar to that place, will no doubt be interesting to some readers of the "Asian."

I think this is the only place in India where parched gram, called in Hindustani *Chabena*, is used as a bait; at least I have not heard of it at any other place. The queer thing about it is that not only is the gram the best bait, but it is the only bait, except dough, which will catch fish. I suppose they have been educated to like gram, and gram they must have, and nothing else. I have tried one thing after another—flies, minnows, frogs, beetles, both natural and artificial, dead and alive, as well as spoons, but the fish will not look at any of them.

Jubbulpore was my first station in India, and having been accustomed to salmon fishing in the north of Ireland, I was delighted to find that I could still follow my favourite sport in India.

The river is very easily got at, being only about five miles off; but as it is necessary to procure the bait before proceeding to the river, I think a description of it ought to precede that of the river.

The simplest way to get the gram is to send to the bazaar for half a seer of fried *chabena*. I have often tried to parch the gram myself, and though I have watched the *bunnias* doing it, I could never succeed. It is done in hot sand, kept continually moving to prevent it being burnt, but as it is procurable in every village of any size, there is no use trying to make it oneself. When procured, the gram is seen to be loosely covered with the cracked outer shell; this has to be removed, and then the gram appears of a yellowish-white shiny colour. A hole has now to be drilled through it, large enough for the gut and shank of the hook to pass through, as the gram is very soft (it can even be crushed between the finger and thumb); this is very easily done with a fine brad-awl, but as a brad-awl is very liable to break it, I had a special instrument made for the purpose. This was simply a spear, the size of the head of a pin, very flat and sharp. Being flat it allowed the particles, as soon as cut away, to fall down, which the brad-awl did not, and thus prevented the gram from splitting. Several of the grains will be found already split, and it is very important to pick out only the perfect ones, as the more perfect they are the longer they will remain on the hook. A lot of these ready bored must be provided, say a match-box full, as they get used up very fast, for as soon as the gram gets sodden with water, which it will do in five or ten minutes, it breaks off and another has to be put on. This is the one great drawback to gram-fishing, for as each grain has to be threaded on the hook, and not forced over the barb, it is necessary each time to remove the hook, and having threaded on the gram to replace it on the casting line. As this occurs sometimes after one or two casts, it becomes a nuisance, and to lessen it as much as possible, I always arranged that, while I was fishing, my servant stood behind me with another hook ready threaded with gram. I thus lost very little time removing the old hook, and putting on the new, but even this dodge is only a slight improvement, and the old nuisance remains. The only real remedy is to use artificial gram. I have made this for myself by using a very white hard wood (I have forgotten the name), and after carving out the grain of gram, covering it with a thin coating of shellac varnish, this gave it the slight yellow tint of the natural grain, and also prevented it from getting dirty, and soaked with water. I found I was just as successful with this, as with the real gram, but as it used to take me hours to make a single grain, and that even then only every third or fourth one was at all like the original, I thought the game not worth the candle, and soon reverted to natural gram. No doubt if Farlow or some other tackle-maker could be induced to make them it would be a boon to fishers at Jubbulpore.

Having got the bait we now go to the river, and get the tackle ready. For a casting line I used double gut, twisted just enough to keep the strands together; the hook also was tied on double gut, but the loop for joining it to the casting line must be tied with silk, not knotted, otherwise the knot would not pass through the hole in the gram. For the hook I used a No. 7 Limerick, or the same size Sneck bend. This size just held the two grains of gram, and was not too heavy to prevent it from floating, which it did naturally on account of the lightness of the gram. I think I preferred the Sneck bend to the Limerick; the bend of the latter hook is very sudden and it broke the grain, but the former being square, the two grains fitted comfortably on it; they also could not slip over the barb as they sometimes did with the other hook.

To make a bag a man had to be sent a day or two, or even more, beforehand to bait the runs. This he did by occasionally throwing in a handful of parched gram at the head of the run. This floating down the river attracted all the fish for a long way down, and in a short time they had all collected in the pool, the biggest ones near the head of the run. Of course the first throw you made into this you hooked a whopper, but after taking two or three out, the rest got shy, and would not come again till next day. You could always get fish, and big ones too, without baiting the runs, but not so many as if the run had been baited beforehand.

As I said before, the nearest part of the river, and the most accessible place, is about five miles off, where the Nagpore road crosses it. It is called Goari Ghaut, and as there is a pucka road, it is an easy ride or drive. The ghaut itself is a good place to fish, as the fishes are regularly fed there by the priests of the numerous temples on the bank; but though there are a lot of them, they seldom run bigger than one or two pounds in weight. The Brahmins never once objected to my fishing there, and I think the rice and other grain is thrown into the river, not so much to feed the fishes, but rather as a votive offering to Mother Nerbudda. However, I soon got tired of catching tame fish, as these practically were, and went up and down the river looking for new places.

I used to get two dug-out canoes, and tie them together with planks placed across, this gave one a seat, and also prevented the boat from capsizing, which a single dug-out is very liable to do. In this way one could quickly drop down the river, fishing all the likely places on the way, and with four men to paddle, it did not take so very long to get back again, though of course there was a strong current to be overcome.

About a mile below the ghaut the river narrowed considerably; a hill jutted into it, forming a deep pool on the inside, and a splendid run at the point of the rock. I got the best fish I ever caught in the Nerbudda in this run, and many a one I have pulled out of the pool using a large hook, and lump of dough. One day, I shall never forget, I had successfully stalked a large fish I had seen rising at the very point of the rock, and having landed him after a prolonged fight, I was very proud of myself, and sat down to breakfast, previously changing the hook and putting on an enormous lump of dough. I threw this into the deepest part of the pool, and putting my rod down on the ground, I began my breakfast. In a short time there came a slight tug at the rod, and again all was still. I thought the fish had failed to hook himself, and finished my meal. But on taking up the rod I found there was a big fish on. I had to follow him across the most break-neck places, and was several times in danger of cutting the line, but I landed him at last. These were the two largest fish I ever caught at Jubbulpore—12 and 10 lbs. The average size is only 5 or 6 lbs., though I believe the fish in the river go up to 30 lbs. or more. The Nerbudda is a very large river, though nothing compared with the great Punjab rivers, and of course the fish will not run to the same size. I was greatly elated at getting these two fish on the same day.

About two miles below Goari Ghaut there were some large islands in the middle of the river, and the runs on each side were very good. There were good places all down the river, and at Behra Ghaut, especially just below the Marble Rocks, I was very successful.

The Marble Rocks are about 11 miles from Jubbulpore, but as there is a pucka road almost all the way, one can easily go out for a day's fishing by sending on a horse half-way. There is also a dâk bungalow there, and three days' leave can be spent very pleasantly. I was never tired of looking at the beautiful cliffs, which give the fishing there a peculiar charm; at home half the delight of trout fishing is the lovely scenery one has to pass through; but in India the wide, dry, sandy, or stony bed of the river sadly mars the beauty of the scenery, and it is only in the rainy season, when the river is full, that it can be appreciated.

The river enters the marble chasm by a fall of 30 feet, and once while fishing above it, I hooked a fish within 40 yards of the brink of the fall. It was very exciting trying to keep him from rushing down, and I don't think I ever played a fish so hard; it was a terrible strain on my rod and tackle while it lasted. There is a railway station for the rocks, but unless you could interest some of the railway officials in your favour, and get the mail train stopped there, the station was seldom used, as the other trains did not suit. I once went down by train to where the railway crosses the Nerbudda, about 20 miles, as well as I can remember, from Jubbulpore; there was very good fishing there. Up the river above Goari Ghaut there were lots of good places; one road went along the Rifle Range, and let out at a place where there was a village on the opposite bank. I cannot now remember the name of the place, nor have I any map by me to refer to. There was always a ferry-boat waiting on the near bank to carry the villagers across, and this could be hired for fishing from.

About 4 miles out on the Mandla road was the Gaur Nuddee, a small river flowing into the Nerbudda. This river was very well stocked with fish in the early part of the cold weather, October to December; after that the water got very low, and the big fish retired to the deep pools, whence they could not be enticed. The road crossed the river by an Irish bridge or causeway, and below this, and fishing from the causeway, I have got many a good bag. I don't think the fish ran bigger than 3 lbs. or 4 lbs. To have good fishing one had to arrive there at daybreak: and a sharp ride from cantonments on a cold frosty morning in December was invigorating, if not very pleasant. Clouds of steam were rising from the stream at this hour, showing how warm it was compared with the air, and it was quite a relief to wade in and warm one's perished feet. As soon as the sun peeped above the horizon your rod and tackle should be ready for the first cast, and if you did not have some fun for the next two hours you had bad luck. There were several good runs up the river, but the causeway was the best place.

Where this river joined the Nerbudda was a favourite place for fishing, but it was not very easily got at, there being nothing but a path through the fields; while proceeding there in the early part of the cold season, just after the rains, and before the ground had become dry and hard, I have often had to turn back. It is calculated to make you angry, if after having sent your rod on in advance to a certain place, you find you cannot get there on a horse, but could fish some other part of the river, if you could only recall the man with your rod. It is humiliating to say the least of it, to have to ride back the 5 or 6 miles, and when asked "what luck?" to have to reply that you could not reach the river.

* * * * *

I took a great fancy to fishing with gram, in spite of the nuisance of having to change the hook so often. The baited hook is not heavier than a salmon fly, and the fishing approached very closely to fly-fishing. By throwing in a single grain of gram every few minutes, and letting it float down stream, you could tell at once when a big fish was on the feed, and where he rose. I think that stalking a particular fish, which you see rising, is much greater sport than flogging a river on the chance of a fish coming to you: you had to throw the gram just as nicely, and let it fall just as gently on the water over a rising fish, as if it had been a wary trout, and you exult much more after landing the fish, which perhaps you have been watching for a long time, or have failed to catch on a previous occasion.

When at Poona some years afterwards, I often asked whether

there was any fishing in the neighbourhood, but invariably was answered "No," that there were lots of fish, but no one could catch them. The river at Poona is a good size and I thought I would try and get some of the fish which I made sure were in it. The first two days I tried everything I could think of as bait, but failed to touch a single fish. The third day, a happy thought, I determined to try the old Jubbulpore plan of parched gram, and very successful I was, that day getting several fish, one 11 lbs. in weight. They were not Mahseer, but some kind of carp, very deep in the belly compared with the length. I did not keep the secret to myself, and many good bags were afterwards made. The fish did not give much sport like Mahseer, but after being hooked, used to sulk in the bottom of the river, and I was three hours landing the above 11-pounder.

W. T. F.

* * * * *

I have read with much interest the letter from "W. T. F." about fishing near Jabalpur. I, too, have fished in the Nerbada, and adopted the plan mentioned by your correspondent: indeed it is about the only way in which you can catch fish in this river. "W. T. F." mentions that he found some difficulty in getting parched gram to stay on the hook: what we used to do was to soak some raw gram in water, till it was soft enough to pass a stout darning needle through. We would then thread as much bait as was required on to the common country thread sold in every bazaar. The bait was wrapped up in damp cloth, and all we had to do was to take off a grain or two when required for the hook. Let "W. T .F." try this plan and see how it succeeds.

T. A. B.

If you like to bottom fish for Mahseer you can. I never tried it, however, and do not mean to; and seeing how few the natives catch this way, even though they ground-bait beforehand, I would not recommend you to do so either, although the Mahseer is, as already explained, a bottom feeder. The natives use a lump of dough, a large worm, a water snail, a bit of plantain fruit, the entrails of a chicken, or almost anything. Read up the inventory of this gentleman's stomach (page 30), and you will have an idea of the variety of things he swallows, and can make your own selection of what dish to offer him.

If you are a Barbel fisher, and think to do as well with the Mahseer as with Barbel, bottom fishing, I warn you that I am afraid you will be disappointed; for though the Mahseer is a bottom feeder, as already explained, he is much more predatory in his habits than are Barbel, consequently you may expect to do more with a live fish bait; and if you must bottom fish for Mahseer, in preference to other styles of fishing for him, I would recommend Colonel Parson's way of bottom fishing.

If you are a poacher, I commend to you the following ingenious dodge, for which I am indebted to one who has since risen above such practices:—

"I am ashamed to say that we do not catch them here by "spinning, but by bottom fishing: I regard it as a kind of poaching "as compared with fly fishing or spinning. The method I follow is "this, and is the same as the natives employ, improved.

"A shingly bed in the deepest pools is ground-baited (not "actually necessary) for some evenings, with balls of ragee paste. "The fishing is night-work. I usually have 3 or 4 reels out, with "300 or 400 yards of line each. They should not be thrown out too "far: the reels are planted vertically on the bank, and have an "arrangement of bells to signal a fish on. The line has a couple of "turns round a stone of 3 or 4 lbs. to strike the fish. I have seen "these stones jerked 10 feet away into the water. The bait used is "a bunch of big crabs, a fowl's entrails, or a ball of ragee paste as "large as the fist. From 8 till 12 P.M., and again towards morning, "are the most likely times. With a mattress and coffee and cheroots "one can pass the night in fine dry weather very pleasantly. I have "had 11 runs in three nights from heavy fish. One cleared out "with 350 yards, despite every effort to stop him. The river there "was about 200 yards broad, clear of rocks, but running 11 feet "deep, and strong. As the reel was all but out, I was obliged to "call a halt, when the line went like rotten thread. I have no "doubt my big fish was a minnow compared to this one."

CHAPTER IX.

LIVE BAIT FISHING FOR MAHSEER.

"Thus have I cleared the field of my worst foe!"
THE SPANISH STUDENT. Act II, Scene V.

ALL the previous chapters have treated of fishing for Masheer in clear water, for, in the matter of fishing for them in discoloured water, anglers of any Indian experience have hitherto been agreed that it was simply useless. Whether from melting snows, or from heavy rainfall or irrigation drainage, a flood or discolouration in the river was considered an insuperable bar to all fishing. There was nothing for it but to pack up one's tackle, and give it up as a hopeless case. And thus there was the great objection that Masheer fishing was confined to clear water, that a change of weather might at any time make the fishing trip a complete failure and disappointment. But anglers will rejoice to hear that there is yet a way in which this worst difficulty may be overcome, yet a way in which the mighty Masheer may be taken even in the dirtiest water. We are indebted, and that not a little, to Colonel J. Parsons for the discovery; so I shall, with his permission, give it in his own words, as kindly communicated to me. He writes, under date 8th July, 1878:—

"A friend has lent me your book 'Rod in India.' I observed "that you invited hints on fishing. I am not aware whether you "still seek them or not; however, I think I may as well tell you "of my way of fishing when the river becomes thick. It is not "original, but merely an improvement of a native method I "saw practised many years ago at the Jumna, in the hills "between Mussoorie and Simla.

"I fish with live bait picketted, as it were, in the river; the "bait may be any size up to ½ lb. in weight (as Mahseer don't "doubt them—'sardines' if they look large). A bullet is "secured to the line about 2½ feet from the live fish, to give him "room to swim about if he wishes, and then the end of the fishing "line, with bait and bullet, is deposited in any likely place in "the river, and the rod is 'set' on the bank, with reel free to run "when required. The best place to put in your live bait is in "one of the eddies near the head of a rapid; a favourite place is "in the backwater, of 2 feet or so in depth, between two "channels of a rapid. In the deep pools Bowalis, a fresh water "shark kind of fish, and eels (I once caught one of the latter "18 lbs. weight in this fashion) are likely to take the bait and "give trouble. It is not improbable that Mahseer can feel* "about well with their leathery mouths, if they cannot see in heavy "water. Anyhow, the above is a very successful way of catching "Masheer when the water is too thick for spinning or a fly, for, with "close upon thirty years' experience of fishing in India, I have "invariably found that neither minnow nor fly are of any use in "heavy water. I never lose time myself in trying them; but it is "difficult to persuade others till they have tried their own "patience in the matter. I have caught very heavy fish with live "bait thus used, and this is not surprising, for, as you mention, "Mahseer are bottom feeders—and I have, moreover, caught nearly "as many in a day in muddy water with live bait, as I have in "bright water by other means. I mention one instance only, "Major S. . . . fished a few miles up stream from Naoshera "on the Towi River (which is met on the Bhimbur route to "Cashmere), and, though a really good fisherman, could not get "either run or rise; before his return, in less than four hour's "time, I had caught and landed five good fish in the pool close to "our camp; the water was like pea soup, and the fish were all "caught, as above, with live bait. I might probably have caught "double the number if I had set a couple of rods. I have caught "many large fish varying from 10 lbs. to 50 lbs. in this way, and "what more could be wanted from the river, when trolling or "fly-fishing is impossible? The bait, if neatly put on, and not

* I should incline to the conclusion that it is by their sense of smell that they are mainly guided, for a live fish leaves a scent under water as much as a live animal does on land,—witness the way in which an otter will follow a live fish scent under water, as I have seen. I think that fish are also guided mainly by their sense of smell in taking bait on night lines, for it is very certain that fish cannot see as well at night as they do by day. Native fishermen know this well enough, and accordingly spread their nets at night.

"pulled about frequently, will live for an indefinite period. I "have generally found his existence shortened very rapidly by "Mahseer.

"I give you a sketch of the bait," Plate IX. "The body hook "is inserted while the point of the *shank* is held next to the tail, "and then turned over so as to let the shank lie on the side "of the bait. The bait, of course, must not be curved. The mouth "hook is put in last. Attach the bullet with a bit of thread to "the line, so that you lose bullet only in case of a foul. The bait "itself rarely fouls. The curve of the side hook stands out at "right angles to the side of the bait, so that it may speedily act "when the bait is taken. The hook at A is passed through the "thin flap in the upper lip. The dotted line at B is where a bit "of the shank of the body hook is under a bit of *skin* of the bait. "The points of both hooks are well exposed.

"In Upper India, December and January are blank months "for Mahseer fishing, use any bait you like.

"One hundred yards of line is enough for any fish. K. says "200, but look at the account of his monster run, less than "100 yards (page 253 of your book). The fish was 4 feet 5 "inches. I have caught 4 feet 6 inches that never ran 50 yards.

"This method of fishing may occasionally succeed when the "water is clear, particularly in rough parts, but never so well as "in thick water: indeed, it is only then excusable as a substitute "for fly and minnow."

Colonel Parsons kindly sent me at the same time a pair of hooks tied as he uses them. They are "peculiar-eyed Limericks," answering to No. 6 0 and 4 0 on my scale of the ordinary tapered Limerick hooks (Plate VIII), the larger one being the side hook, and the smaller the lip hook. They are mounted in the simplest way possible on a single piece of salmon gut, and he writes that the mounting of them took him just 45 seconds, which, of course, is a great recommendation to any man who is pressed for time, and the majority of Indian officials have very little of that commodity to spare.

I am informed by a tackle maker that these eyed-hooks were at one time tried for salmon flies, but were condemned on the ground that the iron cut the gut. I presume it was when laid by for months in the fly-book that they rusted into the gut, for I should hardly think that they would cut the freshly-tied gut in a single fishing trip, provided care is taken, by thoroughly well soaking the gut before tieing the knots, that there may be no crack at the knots. I always use eyed trebles myself in spinning, and never found this objection. Colonel Parsons writes: "Being, like yourself, "frequently pressed for time, I have of late years almost discarded "the use of silk and wax in mounting bait and spinning casts. On "artificial minnows I use eyed strong double hooks, which are "mounted in a 'twinkling;' and for spinning natural bait, or "securing live bait, I use eyed single hooks."

There is no doubt in my mind that, for spinning tackle in India, eyed hooks are much to be preferred to bound hooks, as there is much greater danger of losing a fish, from the hook drawing or the binding being rotten, so rotten as to rip right up, proclivities too common in India, than from the hook cutting or rusting the gut. Besides, the danger with the binding is not noticeable, till a big fish comes and finds it out for you; whereas, any rusting of the gut is easily perceived, and as easily remedied. Many a man will not hesitate to snip off and re-knot a doubtful piece of gut, when he would think twice of looking out silk and wax and re-binding it.

Those who prefer to use eyed hooks for other purposes also may be glad to know that what are called "peculiar-eyed Limerick" hooks, that is, Limerick hooks with the eye very neatly fined off, are made of sizes corresponding to Nos. 10/0 to 1/0 in my Plate VIII, and that more roughly-eyed Limerick hooks, having the wire simply bent round for the eye, are made of all sizes from 10/0 to 16, and called "ringed," at least so I find them in Messrs. Harrison Bartleet's Illustrated Price List, where also are "ringed" Kirby hooks from 10/0 to 10, and "ringed" sea hooks and eel hooks. Messrs. P. Hutchinson and Son, of Kendal, also make very neat eyed trout hooks, which they call the "Adlington hook," and number 10, 9, 8, 7, 6, 5, 4, 3, 2, 1, 0, 00; they are practically Kirby bend hooks, answering to Kirby sizes, 3, 4, 5, 6, 7, 8, 9, 10, 11, 12, 13, the last one, 00, being between 13 and 14 in size. I put in these remarks because I cannot forget that Indian anglers have very little time as a rule for binding hooks, and are between 7,000 and 9,000 miles from English tackle shops, and long posts from Indian tackle shops.

Colonel Parsons' live bait flight of hooks is mounted as follows: —A single length of good stout salmon gut being doubled in the middle, so that the two ends lie equally side by side, a common knot, such as one ties at the end of a whip lash, is tied at the end of the gut, so as to keep the ends together, and to keep the knot that follows from slipping. Close above this is tied just such another knot, but this time through the eye of hook B (Plate IX). The necessary space being left, just such another knot is tied round the shank of hook A, and another through the eye of hook A. The knots on A can easily be slackened and worked further from or nearer to B, so as to accommodate the intervening space to the size of the bait. With reference to the bait, Colonel Parsons writes: "Six inches in length is a good size for a Mahseer, "but you will observe that if you can't get the size of bait you "like, the small, or mouth hook, can easily be shifted up or down "to suit a larger or smaller bait. I have frequently used a bait "1 lb. in weight, and occasionally as much as 1½ lb., the fitting up "of a mount to suit him is only the work of a minute, as I have "larger eyed hooks.

"I am afraid you may consider me somewhat of a barbarian,* "but press of time, and the not over susceptibility of the Mahseer "in rough or thick water, induced me to these inventions. In "slack, clear water of deep pools, the Mahseer is a very wary "wight, and I advocate care, and as neat tackle as is consistent "with the great strength of a large Mahseer to effect his capture. "How very seldom one gets two large Mahseer in one day out of a "clear slack pool? No. 1 may succumb to a minnow, skilfully "worked by a knowing hand well out of sight . . . . but No. 2 "betakes himself to cover for the rest of the day, at any rate when- "ever he sees anything in the form of a line or cast."

In a subsequent letter, Colonel Parsons writes: "I have paid a "short visit to Tangrot (the proper name is Dhangrot). I found "both Jhelum and Poonch flooded with snow-water and thoroughly "discoloured, instead of the crystal streams of the early year. The "Bungalow book informed me that the locality had lately been "visited by a good fisherman, who, the boatmen informed me, had "worked hard at spinning with spoon for Mahseer with blank

* Far from it. The contrivance is neat and simple, and I doubt not my readers will feel as much indebted as I do to our friendly mentor.

"results, being helpless in such a state of affairs. I anticipated the "same at this time of year (17th March, 1880), as both rivers are "fed by the Himalayan snows, now melting daily, and had brought "a casting net for live bait. The result of my mode of fishing with "live bait in troubled stream is this:—

"First morning (12th March), a 12 pounder.

"Evening, lost a heavy fish by the snapping under the barb of "one of Bowness and Bowness' best salmon hooks.

"Next morning (13th), a 9 pounder.

"Evening, a 19 pounder.

"Next morning (15th), a 32 pounder, length 45″, girth 23″.

"Evening. Lost an enormous fish (*fully* 5 feet long, and I "estimate fully 70 lbs. weight), after playing him for two hours, "and until he was fully exposed to view in a semi-exhausted state "by the bank, at which critical period the line fouled. I imme-"diately saw the danger and felt uncomfortable, but thought the "fish was ready for landing; he, however, suddenly rallied, and by "his vast weight parted a new treble salmon gut trace, and through "a huge self-created wave dived into the Jhelum, not to be seen "again for some time, I should say. Disconsolate, I embarked in "my skiff to my dinner on the opposite side of the river, the fish "having worked me from 5 to 7 P.M., at last in a faint glimmer of "moonlight, which, by-the-bye, was not very favourable for the "landing process of such a fish under a straight bank. I have no "doubt he felt very weary, poor fellow, but it might have "consoled him had he known how he made my biceps ache "holding him up pretty tight, through runs and sulks for two "hours, with a 19-feet salmon rod.

"Next morning (16th, yesterday). A 15 pounder, and in the "evening I moved from Dhangrot, well satisfied with my first visit "to that far-famed fishing ground.

* * * * *

"I only fished a comparatively short time morning and evening . . . .

"The above fish were all Mahseer. Aggregate weight of the "five, 87 lbs.; average, 17$\frac{2}{5}$ lbs. Tells well for Tangrot, and also "for live bait! At the same time I prefer the fly and spinners "when the state of the water admits of their use, there being "variety and choice of casts."

I have never tried the above style of fishing myself, and certainly should not, unless driven to it by an untimely flood, for, like Colonel Parsons, I very much prefer spinning or fly fishing. But I think the size of the fish taken, much more than the number, is a very satisfactory proof of the effectiveness of the method of fishing, and it is a very great matter to have got over our hitherto insuperable difficulty, the coloured water, and we can henceforth fish at such times as well as in clear water.

I am glad, however, to see that Colonel Parsons, while giving us this new method of fishing for Mahseer in coloured water, thoroughly endorses all I have urged with reference to all other styles of fishing for Mahseer in such water.

With reference to other fishing, I have recommended the *Ophiocephalus gachua* or *dok* of Hindustani as a bait; but it would not do for this style of fishing, because, like the murrel, it requires to come frequently to the surface to breathe the air, and would be drowned by being picketed to the bottom by a bullet.

A friend who was an ardent pike fisherman used to set several rods with live bait in Slapton Lea, well apart, and he picketed a daughter over each with a book and a whistle. If a bait was taken, the alarm was sounded, and my friend ran to the rescue, and played the fish. If you practise this fishing with water at all clear, of course you will warn your watchman not to indulge his curiosity in watching the line or the top of the rod, but to sit well away from the bank and listen for the whirr of the check winch.

CHAPTER X.

THE CARNATIC CARP.

"Rura mihi et rigui placeant in vallibus amnes,
Flumina amem silvasque inglorius."—
VIRGIL. GEORGIC II, line 85-6.

MAY I have the pleasure of introducing to you a new friend, *Barbus Carnaticus* (Jerdon). In view to your being better acquainted, suppose we stand on no ceremony, and anglicise the name into the Carnatic Carp.

I must be pardoned this little liberty with his patronimic, for the reasons set forth below.

The Carnatic Carp, let me tell you, is not at all a bad fellow. He is not to be set aside lightly as if he was a mere carp, like the fish (*Cyprinus Carpio*) commonly known by that name in England. He is much more like the mighty Mahseer, the king of carps; indeed, he has been frequently mistaken for a Mahseer, and it is for that very reason that I must lay stress on not allowing that he ought properly to be called a Mahseer. That word Mahseer has been too elastically used by fishermen. They have made it cover almost any big Carp. It should, at least, not include any that have not large mouths. Still, though I cannot concede that *Barbus Carnaticus* is properly a Mahseer, I ask for him a sort of brevet rank, by which, though a carp, he may be promoted above the level of the common English carp known to our school-boy days. The Indian carps, mind you, are very different from those in England. The Indian Carps run, in the Mahseer, up to 200 lbs., as the Indian cats do to tigers, and ferns to trees. (*Alsophila latibrosa*, a tree fern). Viewed thus in its proper light, it is no disgrace to be a Carnatic Carp, and his acquaintance is worth your cultivating. He runs to 25 lbs., and takes a fly.

My objection to his being called a Mahseer lies, as I have said, in his mouth, and my reason for urging it is that the smaller

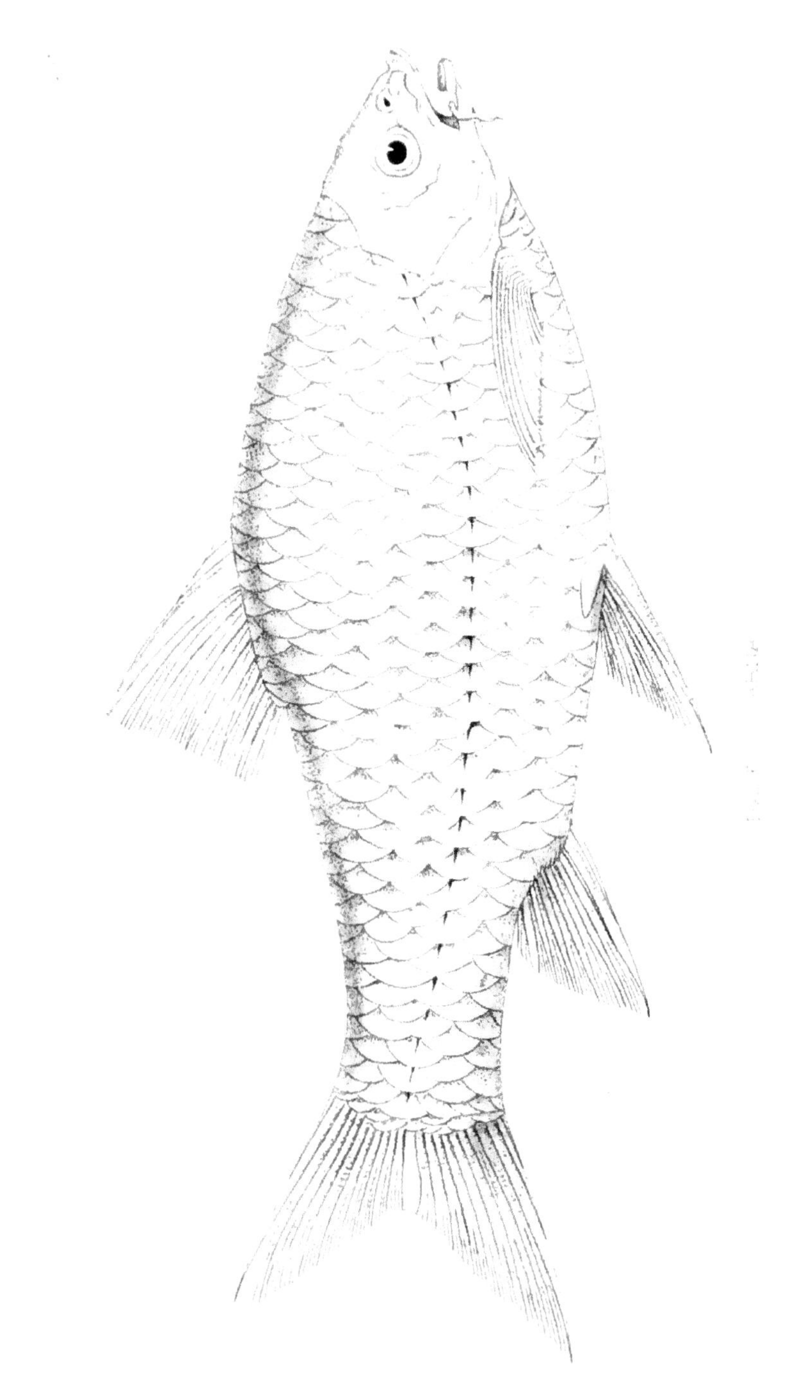

mouthed Carps feed differently from the large-mouthed, and must necessarily be fished for differently; and hints for the taking of the Mahseer would only lead to disappointment if applied to the hero of this chapter, under the impression that it was much the same fish. Indeed, I know cases in point, of fishermen who confounded them, and consequently confounded their style of fishing, with the result that they did not get as much sport as if they had critically adapted their manner of fishing to the fish they sought. One of these was also no mean master of the salmon wand. But they did not vary their fishing with their fish, they used large flies where they should have used small, and small flies where they should have used larger ones; and they threw a fly where they should have spun, and *vice versâ;* and they sought for both fish in like places, whereas they should have chiefly tried the deep pools and gentle eddies in the one case, and the runs in the other. All this came of their thinking them both Mahseer; and as they had caught the Mahseer in such and such a way, they thought they could do so again. Now it would make me unhappy if you did the same, if you should call this fish a Mahseer, and you should apply to him all the advice given in the "Rod in India" about the Mahseer, and should consequently be disappointed in your fishing, and perhaps angry with your faithful mentor, and that, too, after all the pains taken with your education. "But why cannot you call him a Chub," you say. True, he is more like a Chub than a Carp in his ways. But then he would not stand alone, there would be other claimants for the title of Chub, or Barbel, or Roach, or Bleak, or Dace, or Rudd, and I should only mislead you by indicating a similitude which was not close enough, and which had more than one claimant, for there are about sixty kinds of Carps in India. It is better to start fair altogether without any English preconceived ideas to be got rid of, and I think the simplest way is to take the name given him by his sponsor, Dr. Jerdon, the naturalist's name, the name recognized by Ichthiologists, and anglicise it as closely as possible. Such names are ordinarily indicative, first, of the classification; secondly, of the peculiarity of the fish in question, though they are sometimes named after friends, which naming, though it may be a kindly recognition, occasionally hard, perhaps, to avoid, is not useful descriptively; for, though the fish may be bearded and moustachoed, and so far be all right, still you know it cannot have two legs and Bond Street breeches, like the owner of the name given it. In this case the name is descriptive of habitat only, and therein I sincerely hope it is erroneous, and that the Carnatic Carp may be found over a much wider area than that assigned to it by Jerdon and Day. An exact description quoted from Day's "Fishes of India" will be found at the end of this chapter. It may aid fishermen and naturalists to recognize it elsewhere.

Barbus Carnaticus being then simply a Carp of the Carnatic, with your leave we will call him the Carnatic Carp. Don't be vexed with me now for this formal introduction. It is just as well not to pick up a new friend too quickly. Better know something about him first. But now you know his family, we may safely proceed to a closer acquaintance, nay, even to an attachment, so to speak, by means of rod and line.

You will do very little business from the shore. Indeed, I would not attempt it. You must have a boat, and there is none better than the common basket-boat or coracle of the country. It shoots the rapids, bumps the rocks, skims the shallows better than anything else, and when you come to an utterly unnegotiable waterfall, it—the boat, not the waterfall!—is very easily taken out and carried round by one man, your boatman. For this reason you should have a small one, just so small that one man can carry it. It will hold you and your boatman comfortably, and all the fish you can catch. It will hold a third man too if you want him, it will hold three safely, but as a rule you do not want a third man, for your boatman can lend you a hand with the landing net when you want it, and a third man only lessens the buoyancy of the boat, which is not an advantage when shooting a shallow rapid. As to a second fisherman being in the same boat, it is out of the question, for there is not room to manage two fly rods from one such small boat. Each fisherman must have a boat to himself. However, you and I will get into one boat just for half-an-hour, and you shall have a cast with my rod, till you get on terms with our new friend. I will take the liberty of supposing you are like a man I had the pleasure of being out with after these same fish, the Carnatic Carp, a thoroughly good sportsman, good in the pigskin, good with the rifle, but whose education had, for lack of opportunity, been lamentably neglected in the fishing line, and who was pleased to place himself under my tuition therein. It was about the only flaw in his otherwise estimable character. Still, you will admit, it was a very serious flaw. However, it has been effectively remedied now, so we will say no more about it. "Caught Salmon?" I began. "No," said he. "Nor Trout?" No," said he, "never threw a fly in my life, but I fancy "I've got it in my bones." He was right. He took three or four nice little fish from 1 lb. to 3 lb. each that very morning before breakfast, and after less than half-an-hour I had let him alone as big enough to take care of himself. Between you and me there are some men whom you could not make fishermen of, even though you brought them up by hand on cod liver oil, and weaned them on nothing but sardines and anchovy paste. But we will hope you have "got it in your bones."

Here we are on the Bawanny, an affluent of the Càvèry. We have got into the basket-boat at the top of a large pool from a furlong to half-a-mile long, say 150 yards broad, and from 2 to 20 feet deep, with a grand salmon run rushing in over the rocks, and continuing some way into the pool. Lower down the pool has scarcely any apparent motion except the eddies near the shore; and the banks are steep and well above the water level, huge forest trees overhanging the margin of the river. We will begin at the top, and work down river, for the simple reason that it is hard to work the basket-boat against the stream. This is a deep, strong run, and though just the water for a Mahseer, it is a little too much for the Carnatic Carp. Still, do not neglect it, for I have had big rises even in the heavy water, but try specially the edge of the run, and the eddies and back water between two runs, and the tail of the run where it is losing its force in the deeper water of the pool; try right down till the run merges in still water. Ah, there you are! Missed him! He wasn't a bad fish either. Somehow the biggest fish are always those one *doesn't* hook.

Never mind. Stay the way of the boat, boatman, and we will try him again. There he is again. Felt him this time didn't you, but couldn't get hold of him? You didn't strike quick enough; or you hadn't a straight line and *could* not strike home enough. But you will find out more of that difficulty when you come to fish the stiller water.

Now that the run is over, try the bank edge. In most

places along the steep bank edge, where the water is at all deep, you will notice quiet eddies, formed by the opposing forces of the stream and the backwater.* Fish there, especially when they are under overhanging trees or near reeds, always presuming that the water looks at least 2 feet deep. Kuti, the boatman, thoroughly understands, without your telling him, that he must keep the boat so far out from shore that at your longest throw at right angles to the shore you can just drop your tail fly within about a foot of the shore; commence throwing therefore, and he will soon see and gauge the length of your throw, and will let the boat go drifting quietly down the stream, but slightly staying its way, and keeping you exactly facing the shore, so that you can throw with ease, and draw your fly towards you, just as slowly as suffices to keep the line taut while it floats down the stream. And so you keep on trying fresh water every throw. If you fancy a place tell him, and he will paddle against the stream just enough to keep you stationary. If you rise a fish tell him at once, that he may keep you within reach of the fish while you throw over it again immediately. Do not wait and give the fish time for forgetfulness as you might with a salmon or trout, but throw at once, because you cannot depend on its remaining in the same place for any length of time. It may remain, and probably will, but it may roam, for it is not its habit to lie like a salmon or trout behind a stone at the bottom, but to roam about more or less in a swim. Fast in one at last. Hurrah! Back away, Kuti. Back into mid stream. Never mind whether the fish takes out line or not, back away hard all. There, now, you have deep water and plenty of elbow room, free of snags below and boughs above, and, what is of more importance still to your sport, you have drawn your fish away from his fellows, and are killing him in a place by himself, for this fish commonly swims in shoals like a dace, and it is better to disturb the rest of the shoal as little as possible. It is quite possible that you may not have disturbed the rest of the shoal at all, for it is quite possible that the fish you have, left the shoal, and followed your fly some little way before he made up his mind to take it, and you hooked him. At any rate we will hope for the best and do all we know. "'Tis not in mortals to command success, but we'll do more, Sempronius, we'll deserve it."

* This backwater is explained in a foot note in Chapter XVII.

The wisdom of killing a fish by itself, is amusingly recognized in the Tamil proverb that the Paddy-bird or Indian Egret never takes a fish out of a shoal, but waits till a solitary one passes. The proverb was told me apropos of a criminal prosecution. I was running the trail of a first class plunderer, a regular tiger, amongst the poor sheep committed to my protection as a ruler. There was a very twin to him left as unnoticed the while as if I was utterly ignorant of his goings on. But lookers on, who wanted to see justice overtake the tyrant, told me afterwards. "We understood you, Sir, you were like the Paddy-bird." And so the story came. In this, then, prudent reader, be like the Paddy-bird.

Cannot you get a pull on him at all yet? Wind him in whenever you get a chance, either from his swimming in your direction, or yielding ever so little to your steady unremitting pressure; take every inch you can; still don't be in a hurry, don't attempt to put on more pressure than your rod will bear, only keep on the pressure you have on *unremittingly*, and whenever you feel it lessen ever so slightly take as many turns of the winch as he will let you. Wind him in fast, but keep your hand very lightly on the winch ready to let go in a second if he makes a plunge. Kr-r-r-r goes the winch, and he has made a dash off on catching sight of you and the boat. The rush is over. Quick, and wind him in again. Ah, it is about his last run. Now steady, wind in cautiously till you have got the line just such a length that you can bring him up to the top at the side of the boat; but keep him off the boat. Don't attempt to lift him out by the rod; he is too big, and would break your top; still less dream of touching the line, Kuti knows all about it. He has got the landing net out, a big salmon landing-net, about 1 ft 3 in. across the mouth, and 2 ft. 6 in. deep, and very full so as to let the fish lie across directly it is in the net. Bring the fish slowly towards him that he may take him into the net head foremost if he can. Be on the look out, however, to keep a constant taut line on the fish, for he will evade the net as it nears him. Never mind the boat tilting to within two or three inches of the water; Kuti knows exactly how much his boat will stand; only do not you stand up or otherwise move from your seat. It is not worth while going to the shore to land your fish, besides there is no approachable shore within a reasonable distance, for it is for a long way so forest-clad that you could not get to land with an upright rod. Well netted, Kuti, into the boat with him. Five pound if he is an ounce. You have taken nearly a quarter of an hour over him. You ought to have had him in very little over five minutes. You see his mouth is much smaller comparatively than a Mahseer's, and he is a somewhat thicker built, less active-looking fish. However, we can discuss that hereafter. Do not waste time looking at him now. Let us get back to the same place, and try for another out of the same shoal. It was just a little below the trunk of that large wild mango tree up there that you hooked him. You have floated down a little and must make up to it again. Fish all about that place. Well, that is not so bad, taking another 2½ lb. and a 1½ lb. fish out of the same swim.

You see the advantage of working a shoal when you have lit upon one. But do not work it to death. They are not rising to you now. They seem to have had *quantum sufficit.* Depend upon it some wary old fogie has "twigged" you and "blabbed," with one of those wise shakes of the head about the imprudence of youth, and they are all looking at him to see if he is right, or only a fogie. If you throw again you will give him a chance of venting a provoking "I told you so." It is better they took him for a fool than you for a rogue. So move on to "pastures new," and after you have gone, there will be a row in the house. Natural food will come down stream, the old fellow, full of his croaking, will abstain and advise all to be "varra carefu,'" but some youngster will take it, smack his lips, and turn the laugh against the canny one; and the next morning, when you come round again, you will find his sage advice has been dissipated, and even his own beliefs so shaken, that you will be as warmly received as ever, and, may be, take in the old fellow himself.

Do you see those monkeys moving about feeding in the trees down there? Mark the place, for we must fish it very carefully when we come to it; my impression is that when monkeys are moving in trees overhanging the water, the result is that more fruit and more insects drop down into the water than ordinarily, and that the fish congregate more or less from the neighbourhood to watch for them. As you get nearer, and the monkeys notice you, they will commence vociferating and violently shaking the boughs, which will still further improve the position; meanwhile we will not neglect the water between, but fish it regularly down, till we come to the monkeys. Never mind its looking almost still without any ripple on it, it may all hold fish. Drop an enquiring line to know if there are any fools at home. You're sure to find some, for the river is nearly as full of them as the world is.* What *should* we do if it was'nt!

Kuti says he has seen a fish rise just about a yard below that bough. Depend upon it he is right. He never takes any notice of those little bits of fish which are too small for our present flies, the *Chela argentea*, say *silvery chela* (Tamil, *Vellachi*), and he will tell you like a European whether the swirl is that of a good fish, or of a smallish one.

This same Kuti is no chicken. He and I were in a boat approaching a rapid, only half of which could be seen from the pool above, and that half was anything but prepossessing; as the river went roaring down the steep incline, which was so long that you could not see the end of it, and could not therefore see, or even guess, how it behaved itself at the far end. I confess I did not like the look of it, and I asked suggestively. "Will the boat go?" He would not take the hint, but answered with perfect indifference, "Don't know," letting the boat glide on the while. "Have you never been here before?" "No." "Are you going to try it?" "Yes." It was a case of sit well down in the bottom of the boat, and hold on to the edges, so as not to be overbalanced, for in another moment the basket-boat was in the middle of it, being tossed about like a feather on the waves, and flying down at great speed, while Kuti jockeyed it with consummate skill, and cool collectedness, taking in intuitively, from the shape of the water, the position of each submerged rock, deciding whether to ride over this, or dodge that, and all with such rapidity and such power of paddle. And how the little boat obeyed him! Now and then it would seem as if it must be all U P. But the fellow was as cool as a cucumber, and the next moment we were past the danger, still riding rapidly on, and after having had ample opportunity for fully appreciating the advantages of holding on tight to the edges of the boat to avoid being pitched out, there was a flop, and we had taken a drop into

* Carlyle says tersely, I quote from memory, "There are three hundred millions "in the world, mostly fools."

the pool. Kuti promptly gave three or four vigorous paddles, and was out of the main current, the little boat riding quietly on the still water close under the rocks at the edge of the run. No one who had not been at it from a boy could possibly have done it. Kuti's own elder brother, who, like himself, has been on the river from childhood, who also has the name of Kuti, and is also a good boatman, even he had thought better of this one rapid, had taken his boat out at the top, carried it round by shore, and put it in below the run. I think he was the wiser man of the two; still Kuti minor is a broth of a boy. It is a pity he only talks Tamil. It suits me well enough, and we hold long conversations as we work away together, the one at the rod, the other at the paddle, and when a good fish rises and is missed, he takes it quite to heart, and cannot repress an involuntary sound of regret: still it is a pity he cannot talk English for the sake of other anglers.

Now we will get ashore and let you put up your own rod. Mine, you see, is a 16 ft. light made pliable salmon-rod, with 120 yards of Manchester Cotton Twine Spinning Co.'s waterproofed line on a $3\frac{1}{2}$-inch diameter check-winch, with a 9 or 10 feet cast of single salmon gut, carrying three flies, as for trout, the two end ones being on No. 5 or 6 Limerick hooks, according to my scale, dressed very full, and all the way down the shank, and the first drop on No. 4 Kendal-Kirby, or round bend, which is just the same size as No. 6 Limerick, but being short and fine, it is a much smaller fly. The flies are all nearly the same colour, being as black or dark as I can put them together with a glistening shiny appearance. Nothing kills better than a fly all peacock harl, body, wings, and all, and full. But peacock harl is frail, and wears out soon, and objection may be taken to it on that score. Still it kills fish while it wears, and I have an idea that is about what we want, is'nt it ?*

My rod is a 16 ft. light-made, pliable salmon rod by Farlow, and I am thoroughly contented with it. Still it is a matter of opinion, for a friend who was fishing with me came home one evening very cock-a-whoop at having killed a 5 lb. Carnatic Carp on

* The reason why this fly was thus tied is explained in the chapter on fly-fishing for Mahseer. The Blackamoor, as there described, but tied on No. 5 and 6 Limerick, mostly tied very full, but some few on No. 6, tied fine, may be accepted instead, for the reasons there given.

a single-handed 11 ft. trout rod, and having had so much fun out of it, that he declared he would never use a salmon rod again. There was no gainsaying that argument, but against it there is the consideration that you kill many more fish with the salmon rod, for the simple reason that you can throw a much longer line; and this is a matter of some importance, when you are fishing mainly in still, or almost still, water, and you want to get your fly so far away from you that the fish may not see you or the coracle; for if they see it your chances are of course *nil*, as already fully expounded in previous chapters. The coracle is such an obvious object that the necessity for a long line is greater then than when fishing on foot, and able to conceal yourself. I have killed the Carnatic Carp in heavy runs, and in shallow stickles, which you can approach more nearly with impunity, because of the ripple on them; but I have killed many more and better fish of this sort in the deep, almost still, eddies near the steep banks under the overhanging trees; therefore it is for this sort of fishing that you should be best prepared, and for this I like the long cast of the salmon rod. Again, three large No. 5 Limerick hook flies are just a trifle heavy for an 11 ft. rod. Once more, we are not quite sure how heavy may be the fish you may get in this manner of fishing. It is true that of the fish caught by my friends and self the great majority were 5 lbs. and under, and that $7\frac{1}{2}$ lbs. was the biggest Carnatic Carp we took; still Day says they run to 25 lbs., and such a distinguished naturalist is not likely to have made such an assertion without having tested it by something better than native hearsay; tested it probably by net-caught specimens. Natives have told me that they run to nearly a cubit in length; we know they are a very deep fish. Whether a 25 lb. Carnatic Carp will rise to a fly or not has, I fancy, got to to be discovered, but if it will, surely such a fish would be a trifle too much for an 11 ft. rod. And one lives in hopes of getting such a fish on, does not one?

Perhaps a 14 feet rod is a compromise. It is a rod which you can use single-handed for a few throws, very few with most men, but for any length of time it will call for two hands. It is properly a light two-handed rod, this for those who fancy it. For my part, I stand by my 16 feet rod aforesaid. I have the additional reason that I like to be prepared for all comers, and should a 50 lb. Mahseer, instead of a Carnatic Carp, take my fly,

I could pass the word "ready, aye ready," and should look to making him my own, instead of being anxious to get it out of his mouth, like the thrifty Scot of "Punch":—

DONALD. "E—h, Sir! yons a gran' fesh ye've gotten a haud o'!"
THE LAIRD. "Oo, aye, a gran' fesh eno', but I'd be gay an' glad if I saw my twa and saxpenny flee weel oot o' his mouth!"

I am free to confess that my opportunities have been so few, that I have not had thirty days' fishing altogether for the Carnatic Carp, and ought not, perhaps, to presume to write about it. Still, as it is not a question of presumption at all, but of kindly wishing to help brother sportsmen in the land of their exile to as good sport as I have had myself, and as I have in that brief period been in at the death of a good deal more than my own weight of fish, I suppose even my little experience is better than nothing. Moreover, brother sportsmen ask me for information, and it is easier to me, and more satisfactory to them, to write it fully once for all in a book, than to write and re-write it briefly to every correspondent. Furthermore, it was a case of love at first sight. I got a very nice bag the first day I was out, though I improved upon it afterwards. So I do not think I need further apologise for telling brother fishermen, for their good, not mine, what little I do know, with the frank confession that there is still much more to be found out.

I have killed these fish, for please remember that we are discussing nothing but the Carnatic Carp in this chapter, on flies of many colours, and of pretty nearly all sizes, from a No. 1½ Limerick to a No. 6 Limerick (my scale), and even a No. 5 Sneck bend, which is equivalent to a No. 8 Limerick, and I have killed on a phantom minnow, and tried the spoon, and the spun dead bait; but I have killed both more and larger fish on a No. 6 Limerick hook, and have done more business with a dark, gaudy fly, composed body, legs, and wings entirely of peacock harl, than with anything else; though my old friend the simple black fly seems to be very little less attractive than his more glistening brother. Still, I am bound to confess that there once was an evening, a memorable evening, it was a sorely trying evening, when the fish were rising freely at some natural fly, and would not look at our flies. The natural fly was on only for a brief space at sunset, and I could not catch it, but it seemed as small as an ordinary trout fly, if not smaller. Trout will play you the same trick sometimes, even though you think you have every fly entomologically worked out, and exactly prepared for their acceptance, so that sometimes it really does seem that like the little boy:—

> "Who can thoroughly enjoy
> The pepper when he pleases,
> They only do it to annoy
> Because they know it teases."

Still our flies did their work very well ordinarily, for we got fish running from ¼ lb. to 7¼ lbs.; very seldom, indeed, did we take one under 1 lb., and not often over 5 lbs. or 6 lbs. They generally averaged between 2 lbs. and 4 lbs., and we used to take from three to fifteen fish or thereabouts (I write partly from memory, partly from notes) every morning, and not much less in the evening. Still, I had some thoroughly blank days near Valamhoondy, as experimenters must expect when trying new waters; as even old hands have even amongst their old friends the trout at times.

Supposing that each angler has a boat and boatman to himself, and that not more than two are fishing from the same camp, it is not well to separate; it is a pleasanter way to take the pools alternately. A. commences on the first pool, be it large or small, the luck will right itself before the morning is over, and fishes it down from head to tail. B. meanwhile glides down stream in his boat to the next pool, without even wetting his line in A's pool, though he sees a fish rise. When A. has done his pool, he glides down till he overtakes B., and you ask each other of the sport, as A. passes on to pool No. 3, and so you keep passing and repassing each other, comparing notes, and encouraging each other, while each has the satisfaction of knowing that he is fishing fresh water all the time.

The Indian coracle or basket-boat has no seat in it. It strains the knee joint to sit like a native on the "hunkers," *i.e.*, on your own heels; it is but poor relief to sit cross-legged, and it hurts the knee to kneel; standing is out of the question, so that the Indian coracle is, for any length of time, a very uncomfortable vehicle, so uncomfortable that it does away with half the pleasure of your sport, and prevents your fishing as well as if you were comfortable. You cannot take in a chair, because the legs would find their way through the leather bottom of the boat, which would end in your eventually finding your way to the bottom of the river. You can obviate all this, and make yourself thoroughly comfortable for about 8 annas, say, 1s. Get a bamboo basket, made much the shape of the ordinary basket, that is the shape of half an egg, only have it made much stronger than is usual, strong enough to bear your weight, whatever that may be, and have it made so deep that when turned bottom upwards it will be within an inch of the height of the seat of a chair. On this bottom you are to sit; therefore cover it with stuffed leather. A cushion would slip and trouble you at critical moments, therefore sew the rough leather on to the basket, with a little stuffing under it. This turned mouth downwards in the boat will give you a comfortable, steady seat. Add a slit in one side of your basket seat, and you can then put your fish under you, and have them stowed away out of the sun, and out of the way of your feet, otherwise you may well have the boat so full of fish that you cannot move your feet without treading on and mashing a fish. I add also a basket-work door to the slit, working on a hinge, and fastening with a peg and eye. This keeps the fish in, and enables you to use your chair as a basket when out of the water, and wanting to carry your fish. It comes in handy, then, for you have no one but your boatman with you, and if you go ashore to get round an impassable rapid, the boat, paddle, and landing net is about as much as the boatman can manage, and you will have to carry your rod and fish yourself. Sometimes you will be tempted to wish the basket was not so full of fish, but do not leave them behind, they are very acceptable to the camp servants and to the boatmen. In this respect I always treat the man that shares the toils of the campaign handsomely. Do it yourself, or the camp servants will treat him badly. It is good policy for sport's sake, as well as the right thing to do.

If you have not been at the trouble to have a basket of this sort made beforehand, then two common baskets, which can be picked up ready-made in any bazaar, put one inside the other, strengthen each other, and are better than nothing. But they are not so comfortable as a properly made basket-seat, for they are not high enough, and are rough to sit on. If you go fishing, it is presumed you go for pleasure, and your pleasure will be very much marred if you are sitting all the while in constrained positions which grow more and more trying with time. For a trip such as I am proposing, a comfortable seat is as much a part of your fishing gear as your rod and line, and it should be got ready beforehand and taken with you. You may try ever so much to keep yourself up to the mark, but it is impossible you can keep on fishing nearly as well while increasingly uncomfortable, as if you were thoroughly at ease and enjoying it.

For eating oneself, I do not think the Carnatic Carp are worth keeping, though they are much better than the common English carp (*Cyprinus carpio*), which some people manage to clamber outside somehow. To those about to do so, my advice is, don't.

Our Carnatic friend is not so active a fish as the Mahseer. It does not dash off like the Mahseer, it takes out very little line, but goes down in deep water, and bores about like a log without very much change of place. It is, therefore, not a difficult fish to kill. It never jumps into the air like a trout, nor shakes its mouth in the air like a pike. It has a leathery, toothless mouth, and gives as good a hook hold as the Mahseer. Its teeth are like the Mahseer's, and all carps, pharyngeal or in the throat. Still, do not think otherwise than kindly of him, for is he not a fly taker? And is it not a great thing to get a fish that takes the fly better than anything else?

But it does not take the fly after the manner of the Trout, the Salmon, and the Mahseer, rising to it from its place in the stream, taking it quickly in at a gulp, and then returning to its position. On the contrary, it takes the fly more as the dace does.

It swims leisurely up to it, and just sucks it in. It then does not sink to the bottom so as to oppose its weight to and tauten the line at once. It stops where it is, or continues to swim leisurely about, or it lets itself be carried leisurely down stream to where it was before. And if while doing this it discovers that your fly is a tasteless, uncomfortable-feeling feather, instead of the juicy morsel it had expected, it simply spits it out. It is a pretty little accomplishment commonly practised in polite circles among all fish, and some of them are great adepts at it. *Chelmo rostratus* is a gentleman I would almost back against a Yankee at expectoration. He makes his living by it. He used to be known by the name of *Chætodon rostratus.* I suppose he changed his name because he didn't like the stories told about him. Men do say that when he sees a fly in the air, he, to put it nicely, blows a drop of water at it, with such force as to bring said fly down as dead as Julius Cæsar. Thereon he improves his opportunities, and puts himself outside said fly. He, can make due allowance also for the fly being in motion, and for the wind. *Chelmo rostratus* may have in the formation of his mouth a choke bore, peculiar facilities for forcible and precise expectoration ; but all fish can, and commonly do, perform that interesting operation more or less. The whale takes in a huge gulp of water in its capacious mouth, retains the *medusæ* on which it feeds, and ejects the water in the manner commonly called spouting. Most people will have seen gold fish in an aquarium not only sucking in water, and ejecting it by the gills as mentioned at page 30, but also ejecting it by the mouth when they have taken in any food they do not want to swallow. A grain of rice, for instance, may be seen blown out of the mouth with considerable velocity. Have you never found your worm or your spinning bait blown up your line well clear of the fishes mouth ? How can you account for this except by allowing that the fish has the power of blowing a thing out of its mouth. If you watch very closely you will see how it is done. The mouth having been opened to suck in either the water the fish is to breathe from, or the food it is to feed on, it is closed again while the gills and gill-covers are opened to let the water pass out through the gills, while the oxygen is inhaled, and that the food may be swallowed without water. If, when the water has been thus got rid of, it is found that the substance in the mouth is not the food that is desired, but something to be rejected, the mouth is again filled to the full with water by opening it, and then by closing the gills first, and by compression of all the flexible parts about the mouth, and partial closing of the orifice, the water is violently squirted out. In short, the mouth of a fish is a sort of suction pump capable of working both ways, by alternate dilatation and compression of the mouth, the gills and gill-covers, and the skin under the chin. If it were not so I do not know how fish could apprehend their food. They have no hand in which to take the food and examine it before putting it in their mouth, as briefly alluded to in the chapter on fly-fishing for Mahseer. Their mouth is itself their hand in which they take and examine much that looks like food, but which they are not sure of till they have thus tried it. Only on this principle can we understand a Salmon taking into his mouth all the extraordinary coloured artificial flies he does, not like anything that he has seen in the sea. An extra reason for a fish taking unknown things into its mouth for examination is, that in rivers they are carried past so rapidly, that the fish has not time to trust entirely to the eye. It is this brief interval, then, between sucking in for investigation, in the belief that the artificial fly is or may be food, and the blowing of it out again on the detection of the fraud, that you have for striking your fish. In the case of the Salmon and Mahseer you are helped at the critical moment by the fish's habit of descending to its place at the bottom, and by the weight of the fish tautening your line, so that if your line is thrown and kept straight as it should be, the tautening takes effect at once, you only have to resist and hold on to it, much as you would to a stumbling horse. The Trout helps you just a little by the same habit of descending to his place at the bottom, but the Trout's weight is not enough to tauten your line decidedly, and the trout line is by no means always straight, especially when throwing up and pulling down stream with so light a line, and when throwing across it is often bellied by the force of the stream, and when there is wind to contend with it is impossible to throw a light Trout line quite as straight as a heavier Salmon or Mahseer line. Consequently you need to strike quick for a Trout, as quick as you like, you can't have too quick an eye and wrist. But the hero of this chapter, like the Dace, the *Barbus filamentosus*, and others to whom I shall introduce you, does not descend to take up his place at the bottom; he does not aid you, therefore, the slightest bit in taking the slack out of your line, and the interval left you for hooking him is shorter. In consequence you have to strike if possible still more quickly. On these grounds I hold that you cannot strike too quickly for the Carnatic Carp. With this idea in my head, I have watched these fish. They were taking some small natural fly very freely, and refusing to look at our artificial flies, showing thereby that our flies were not like their natural food then on the water, yet now and again at long intervals, when there was less natural food on the water, some one fish would take our fly out of pure curiosity. Thus the adventurous got taken in. The much-fished Trout has learnt that this spirit of enquiry doesn't pay, and he won't take a fly into his mouth unless its colours and its size and motion are so exactly like the natural fly at that time on the water, that all his hereditary and acquired suspicions about perfidious anglers are disarmed. His motto is *timeo Danaos et dona ferentes.*

There, now, I am always prating about fishing with your brains, and not by rule of thumb, and may be you will be sick and tired of me, and shy the confounded book on one side; but to my mind it is so much more interesting to have an intelligent reason for what you are doing, that I hope you will be graciously pleased to pardon the seeming digression. Suppose, now, that you have been missing rise after rise of our friend of this chapter, the Carnatic Carp, and you cannot make it out, and you vary your tactics and strike a little slower. Instead of there being any improvement in the results your discomfiture is only increased. And then you try back again, and you fish half-heartedly on no fixed principle, but according to your vacillating haphazard mood. Whereas, if you have accepted my reasoning as sound, and have yourself seen that these fish take the fly just as I say they do, then you fish like a man with a purpose. If you miss a rise you do not deviate from your purpose, you only say to yourself my fixed purpose must be still more carefully executed, my line must have been cast just a little carelessly, not quite straight, or it cannot have been kept quite straight as it should have been, or that fellow was one too many for me that time, though my ball was a regular bailer. Try some more of those. The truth is I had not had a rise for some twenty throws or more, and I had got just a little slovenly over it. Never mind, I'll take a pull on myself and see if I can't be even with them next time. Next time you have him.

There are good fishermen that will be angry with me for all this prating, I daresay, because there are good fishermen who lay down points dogmatically, and their dictum is accepted because they are successful. But I maintain that even the successful could be more successful still if they would study the rationale of the thing, and fish at every step on natural history knowledge. The best fishermen do this intuitively, and such would not accept anything on the *ipse dixit* of the writer merely because it is set down in a book. They will want to know the reason why, and to weigh the reasoning for themselves.

But some will say that, when striking very quick, they are in danger of striking too hard and breaking either rod or line when they come across a big fish. There is a simple way of making any such mishap much less likely. Never throw the full length of your line, but just a foot or so under it, so that it is necessary to get the rod out of the same line with the line, to get the rod point just a foot or two elevated before you can quite straighten, or gather up the slack on, your line. Then any sudden pull must come on the top joint of the rod, which being a pliable fly-rod yields till the line runs. Be careful at the same time to grasp your rod underneath the line so that it runs free over your hand. You may then strike without much fear. If you strike a trifle too hard the bending rod and running line will save your tackle from the worst force of the first blow, and after that you have time to regulate the incline of your rod to the pull of the fairly hooked fish.

But this principle is only applicable within certain limits. With a salmon rod you can never strike lightly enough for fine drawn gut, that is, if you strike at all quickly, you must use salmon gut; with a two-handed 14 ft. trout rod you must use coarse or stout gut; with a light one-handed trout rod only can you use the finest drawn gut or even a single hair. To strike quickly and lightly is the finest touch of art in the accomplished trout fisherman, but even he cannot do it with a two-handed 14 ft. rod, much less with a heavy salmon rod. It can only be done lightly enough for the finest tackle with a light rod of from 9 ft. to 11 ft. which you can perfectly command with a single turn of the wrist. I use for such fishing a 10 ft. rod. A 14 ft. rod is just too much for it; you need to take both hands to it, and you use your arms more than your wrist, and directly you have to use your arms you are slower in giving the strike, and slower again in stopping it, in short, you necessarily take longer in overcoming the greater *vis inertiæ* of the heavier rod, whether it be in setting it in motion or in stopping its motion or momentum. Some trout fishermen prefer a 14 ft. rod for trout fishing on the ground that they can cover so much more water and keep further away from the fish. That is true enough, but if they would only consider the above, and try it, they would find that they dare not use nearly such fine tackle, because it is simply impossible even in the most accomplished hands to strike as lightly. As I have insisted elsewhere, under Mahseer fishing, that you must accommodate the strength of your tackle to the pliability of your rod, so here also the converse holds in striking your fish, which is again the converse of your fish striking you, that you must accommodate your rod to the strength of your tackle, accommodate it both in pliability and in lightness, in pliability to allow of the line running readily, in lightness to allow of the wrist having a complete mastery. Of course there is a mean. If the trout rod is too pliable you cannot strike quickly enough. Therefore I prefer in a trout rod that it should be rather too stiff than too limp, trusting to its *lightness* to allow of my wrist giving rapidity. In the salmon rod I prefer greater pliability short of being top-heavy for reasons set forth under Mahseer fishing, in short, because the Mahseer does not lay a light hand on you but a heavy and a sudden one. For our present friend the Carnatic Carp I prefer a light 16 ft. pliable salmon rod. With that you may use single salmon gut on your flies, but not finer with prudence. I have never used a 14 ft. rod for them. I daresay I should like it best of all, provided I had on an ample supply of stout trout Manchester Cotton Twine Spinning Company's 16 plait Egyptian line. An 11 ft. rod is, I think, a mistake for this fishing, for reasons given above. You see thus that your wise selection of a well-made rod has much to do with your success.

I have not had opportunities for fishing for the Carnatic Carp on other rivers than the Bawanny, an affluent of the Cavery, and I have only fished some 16 or 20 miles of the river, half above half below Metapolliam, particulars of which will be found in the chapter on fishing localities. But I have recognised the same fish caught in nets 100 miles or more down the same river in the Tanjore District. I have, therefore, grounds for thinking it is more widespread than Dr. Jerdon was aware of at that time. It is thus clearly not confined to the base of the hills, and it is probably as widely distributed as the Mahseer, which was once thought not to exist south of the Nerbudda.

H——, who is a good fisherman, writes me that he came across very heavy Carnatic Carp at Hoginkal, on the Cavery. 'They would *look* at, but would not take a fly there. They took "a green weed called Pásăm freely," but were as cunning as a fox.

The Carnatic Carp was introduced into the Bilikal Lake, and the Ootakamund Lake, on the Nilagiris. It is known to be flourishing in the former water, and is believed to be so also in the latter. Fishermen should try them with a boat.

The best hours for fishing are, in my view, from dawn till 11, and from 3 to dusk, though just at dusk I could frequently do nothing with them. Fishing for such long hours as from dawn to 11, and often getting up at half-past 3 or 4 in the morning, to get out to your ground by dawn, one gets a little bit hungry before 11, and if you allow yourself to get faint and hungry under a tropical sun, you are simply tempting a sunstroke, and, what is more my business, perhaps, you are not fishing well, but in a slovenly, tired manner. You are not half enjoying it, and you are not killing nearly as many fish as you would be killing if you were feeling quite fit. Now, to think of sitting down to eat while fish are rising is too Gothic. The precious moments cannot possibly be spared for such low uses; so my little plan is to take Abernethy biscuits in the left pocket. They are easily broken with one hand, and eaten without taking your right hand off the rod, or your eye off the line for one moment. Many a one have I eaten while in the act of playing a good fish. In England, where you are at it all day, from morn to eve, and are not going home to breakfast and shelter during the heat of the day, there is nothing like sitting down comfortably to a pleasant meal and chat, and bit of a rest; that's quite another case. Then you should take something for your man as well as for yourself. A gentleman I know of had failed in this little forethought, and was rebuked for it. He had had his snack and was at work again. His man had had none. But no better luck attended the afternoon fishing than had come in the morning; the basket was as empty as the man's inside, and the master broke the silence with—"The fish won't bite." Thereon the man incisively: "Woant boite, woant 'ey. If they was arf as 'ungry as me they'd be boiting as if the divil was in 'em."

I have had insufficient opportunities for arriving at any conclusiveness about the time of spawning, but I noticed that fish caught at the end of September had their roe more than half formed, and that fish caught in December were full of milt; the natives said the fry could be taken in the dry weather (Chitra). Native fishermen say that they feed freely on waterweed, and may be taken with a piece used as a bait. Perhaps this is what the peacock harl body is taken for.

I am inclined to think that the same tactics would suit other small-mouthed carps such as the *Barbus Jerdoni*, a most beautiful fish, not unlike a Rudd, much more highly painted, and running to 5 or 10 lbs. In earlier days I have seen them rising freely, and could not hit it off with them. Would that I had such opportunities now. There are also several other similar fish that I should think might be wooed and won in this fashion, but I have not caught them.

The following description of the Carnatic Carp is extracted from Dr. Day's "Fishes of India":—*

Order. *Physostomi.*
Family. *Cyprinidæ.*
Sub-Family. *Cyprininæ.*
Genus. *Barbus.*
Sub genus. *Barbodes*, with four barbels.
Division *b*. Last undivided dorsal ray osseous aud entire.

BARBUS CARNATICUS.

Jerdon, M. J. L. S., 1849, p. 311; Güuther, Catal VII, p. 128. *Puntius (Barbodes) Carnaticus*, Day, Proc. Zool. Soc., 1867, p. 292. *Pouree candee, Saal candee*,† *Shellee* Tamil. *Giddi-Kaoli*, Hind. *Gid-pakke*, Can.

B. III, D. 12 $(\frac{4}{8})$ P. 15, V. 9, A. 7 $(\frac{2}{5})$ C. 19, L. l. 30–32 L. tr. 5 6.

Length of head $5\frac{3}{4}$, of caudal $4\frac{1}{2}$ to 5, height of body 3 to 4 in the total length. *Eyes*—diameter 3 to 4 in the length of the head, 1 diameter from the end of snout, and $1\frac{1}{2}$ to 2 apart. Inter-orbital space flat. Dorsal profile more convex than that of the abdomen. Upper jaw the longer. Lower labial fold interrupted. *Teeth*—pharyngeal, pointed, curved, 5, 3, 2 2, 3, 5. *Barbels*—thin, both pairs shorter than

* Pub. by Bernard Quaritch, 15, Piccadilly: 4 vols, 4to., £12 12*s*.

† *Sèl-kendài*, pronounced *Shèl-kendài*, is the Tamil of the Coimbatore district for the Carnatic Carp, while the same word stands in the Tamil of the Tanjore district for a Labeo, which again is called in Coimbatore, *Karumula-Kendài*. Such local variations in a single language increase the difficulty of arriving at correct vernacular names, and indicate the need for extreme caution in the understanding of native testimony.

the eye. *Fins*—the dorsal 3/4 as high as the body with a concave upper edge; it commences anterior to the insertion of the ventral, and midway between the snout and the base of the caudal fin; its last undivided ray is a strong, broad, smooth spine, nearly as long as the head in the immature, and sometimes longer in the adult, especially in specimens from Canara. Pectoral as long or rather longer than the head. Anal laid flat reaches the caudal. *Lateral line*—complete, 3½ rows of scales between it and the base of the ventral fin; 12 rows anterior to the dorsal fin. Free portion of the tail as high at its base as it is long. *Colours*—greenish-brown along the back, becoming dull white, glossed with gold on the sides and beneath. Fins greyish. Eyes golden.

Habitat.—Rivers along the bases of the Neilgherries, Wynaad, and South Canara hills. It attains at least 25 lbs. in weight. Some have been introduced into the Ootacamund Lake. The figure is from a young specimen, life size, the dorsal spine not being well-developed, and the snout not so obtuse as in older specimens.

N.B.—The figure which I have introduced is from a mature 7 lb. fish.

Mr. J. E. Welborne (Hatti Shikaree), of Assam, says ("Asian," 10th June, 1879) that the Assam *Bookha* is somewhat similar to the Carnatic Carp. From Dr. Day's description it would seem to be very similar, and I hope the same angling tactics may be found to answer for its capture also. I therefore make a short indicative extract from Dr. Day's work:—

Barbus hexagonolepis, *Bokar* and *Boolooah*, Assam, with 4 barbels (Barbodes) and last undivided ray osseous and entire. B. iii. D. 12 ($\frac{3}{9}$) P. 17, V. 9, A. 7 ($\frac{2}{5}$) C. 19. L. l. 28–31, L. tr. 4½ 4½. *Habitat*, Assam, in the larger rivers, and those from the Himalayas. It attains upwards of 2 ft. in length, and takes a fly or bait freely . . . McClelland considered *Cyprinus putitora* Ham. Buch, as a variety of this species. It is said to attain 9 ft. in length.

CHAPTER XI.

SMALLER FLY TAKERS.

> "Be mindful aye your fly to throw
> Light as falls the flaky snow."—
>
> IZAAK WALTON.

THUS far the weapon of warfare has been the salmon rod. But there is business to be done with the trout rod also, and as it has its devotees, a few pages must be given to smaller fish that rise to a trout fly. Some of them are very small, certainly, but you are not bound to fish for them because they are just mentioned, and why should not ladies and boys have fishing. There are some old boys, too, who will whip away at anything, however small. And quite right, too, when there's nothing bigger to be got. It does them good. It's the only medicine for the mania which is in many of us. Besides some of these fish are easily introducible into any pond, and are otherwise more within every day reach than the mighty rivers which hold the Mahseer and the Carnatic Carp, rivers to which it is not convenient to everybody to make a pilgrimage. Without further apology, therefore, I shall introduce my little friends.

I shall endeavour to call them by simple names. But this is not easy, for the majority of Indian fish are known only to Ichthiologists and native fishermen, and have, consequently, only Ichthiological or vernacular names. Except in the case of the Mahseer, where the Hindustani name has been adopted, the use of vernacular names seems a mistake, as they differ with the language and locality. The full Ichthiological name is frequently too long for common adoption. Where the correct name can be simply anglicised, as in the Carnatic Carp, it seems best to follow it. Where it cannot, and I am not aware of any name ordinarily used

Plate XI

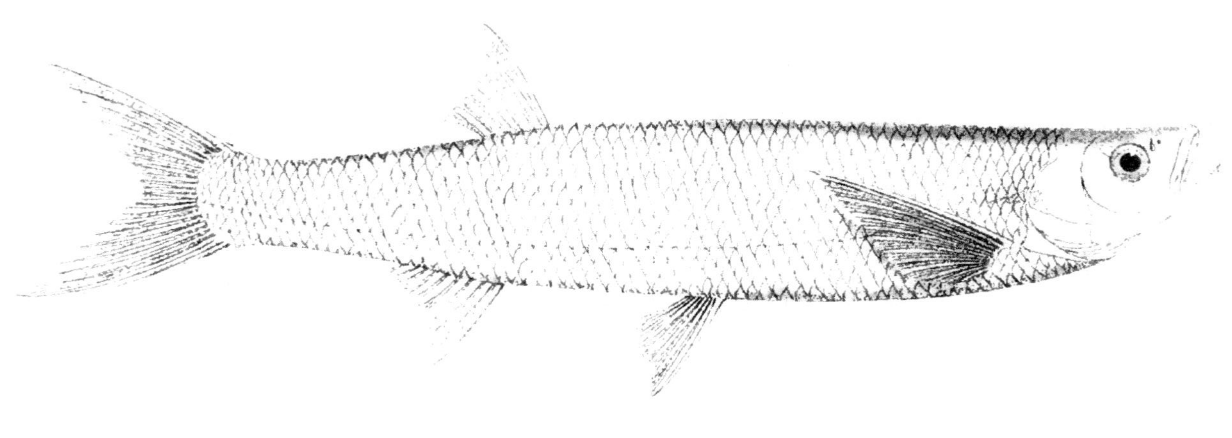

Mintern Bros. lith.

CHELA ARGENTEA

by Englishmen, I hope I may be excused if I propose a simple one for acceptance. Of course the correct Ichthiologists name shall be appended, and, where I can give them, the several vernacular names. Not being a competitive examiner I shall assign no order of merit.

THE CHELA.

Chela argentea.

The Chela is a very common fish. Day gives ten species, some of which are to be found in Northern, some in Southern India. There is a good deal of similarity among them, so that one drawing Plate XI) will probably suffice to help recognition of a fish that must be known to most lovers of the craft. The chief external characteristic of them all is a very flat-sided, thin body, with a stomach running to quite a thin edge, but not a serrated edge, and the dorsal fin set far back just over the anal fin. They are very silvery, some more so than others, and their numerous minute scales come off very easily. They are a delicate fish both to eat and to keep alive, so that it requires care to transport them alive; but, once in, they will live in any pond, and keep its surface alive with rises. They thrive in any still water. In the rivers they are to be found in the still water. One of them is very minute, not attaining more than 2½ inches in length, but the majority run, according to Dr. Day, from 6 to 9 inches in length. I have certainly never caught any over 9 inches in length, but I have seen larger ones, and native fishermen assured me, very positively, and exactly, that some of them, and they particularized a *Chela clupeoides*, ran to 18 inches in length, and to a hand-breadth in depth. Considering the accuracy of their information in other respects, I believe the informants in question to be right. Being such a very thin, narrow fish, with a minimum of depth and breadth, their weight is very disappointing in comparison with their length, and a fish of 6 or 7 inches is flicked out with ease by the lightest trout rod. One of 18 inches in length, however, should be worth catching. They are most game fly takers, springing into the air after the fly. They want striking very quickly, and especially they want the *smallest possible fly*. Any black or dun fly will do for them; but if it is not small enough you may have rises, but you will keep on missing them most provokingly. If they are in the rising humour they will cover the surface of the water with rises, and you may have rises at every throw. But you won't catch them unless your fly is very small, and your fly top inclined to be stiff rather than over pliant, so that you may strike quickly.

Ordinary trout flies on No. 9 to 12 Sneck bend hooks are scarcely small enough, and it would be better to have black flies and light duns tied on No. 14, the smallest size of Sneck-bends and fine drawn gut. Fish with three such flies on a light collar.

They do not seem to rise till 1 or 1½ hours before sunset, and to rise best just before and just after sunset. They rise in the morning also, but not so well as in the evening. I do not think they attain the same size in ponds as they do in rivers, though they become very numerous. In rivers they are to be found all over the deepest, largest pools, pools that hold Mahseer and Fresh-water Shark. They seem to be most numerous along the shore edge and near bushes, but the bigger ones seemed to be mostly in the deep mid water, but always near the surface.

They may also be taken easily with a float, if they are thought worth fishing for in that way. The bait, a single grain of boiled rice, or a small pellet of rice on a minute hook, say No. 14 Sneck bend, should hang within about a foot of the surface, and the float must be very sensitive, and the rod short and light so that you can strike quickly. Natives use with advantage the merest little bit of pith or quill less than an inch long, and a straight bit of small bamboo tip. I have seen them, thus armed, catching them by the dozen, to eat. Perhaps they were having an unusually good time of it; but they spoke as if it could be done whenever they liked. Still they seemed abnormally jolly over it.

I have caught three sorts myself with a fly—*Chela argentea*, *C. boopis*, and *C. clupeoides*,—and I have caught them on the west coast of Southern India, in other parts of the Madras Presidency, and in Mysore.

The Tamil name is *Vellāchī*; the Canarese, *Bellāchī*. Day says, "Generally termed *Vellachee-candee* in Tamil: *Bay-ree-saie* and "*Baarsee*, Tel.: *Bounce-putti*, Ooriah: *Took*, Punjab."

They are evidently the fish commonly spoken of by sportsmen in Northern India as *Chilwa*.

Apropos of these little fish, which are caught as much in ponds as in rivers, I should not omit to mention an absurd little adventure. As we rode into camp we found the tents pitched close to a large pond, and the pond covered with circles. "Just "look there," I cried, before I was well out of the saddle, "we will "have a dish for breakfast," and the trout line was very soon put together, and two expectant friends watched the line fly deftly out, and light with fairy grace among the circles, and lo and behold they were only frogs that were rising so freely at the small flies on the surface! Dear reader, *don't* tell any one.

The Chela is scarcely worthy of my devoting to it the number of pages that would be required if, as in other cases, the full description was extracted from Dr. Day's work. The general characteristics of the genus may suffice, with an epitome for each species.

Body rather elongate and compressed; abdominal edge cutting. Pseudo-branchiæ present. Mouth directed somewhat upwards with the lower jaw prominent, and generally with a knob above the symphasis. Barbels absent. Pharyngeal teeth hooked and slender, in two or three rows. Dorsal fin short, without any osseous ray, situated principally or entirely opposite the anal, which latter has an elongated base. Pectorals long. Caudal forked. Scales of moderate or small size. Lateral line concave.

Order. PHYSOSTOMI.

Family. CYPRINIDÆ.

Sub-Family. CYPRININA.

Genus. *Chela*.

1. *Chela gora*. B iii., D 9–10 ($\frac{2}{7-8}$), P. 15, V. 8, A. 15–16 ($\frac{2}{13-14}$) C. 19, L.l. 140–160. L. tr. 18–20/18. Vert. 46. *Ghora chela*, Beng. *Chel-hul*, Hind. *Habitat*: Sind, Punjab, North West Provinces, Bengal, Orissa, and Assam. It attains at least 9 inches in length.

2. *C. Sladoni*. B. iii, D. 10 ($\frac{2}{8}$), P. 11, V. 8, A. 20–21 ($\frac{2}{18-19}$) C. 21. L.l. 65–68, L. tr. 10/8. *Habitat*: Irawaddy, in Burma, extending northwards as far as Mandalay.

3. *C. sardinella*. B. iii, D. 9 ($\frac{2}{7}$), P. 13, V. 8, A. 21 ($\frac{2}{19}$), L.l. 48, L. tr. 7½/4. *Habitat*: Irawaddy river at Rangoon. Also the Salwein at Moulmein. It attains to at least 6 inches in length.

4. *C. untrahi*. B. iii, D. 9 ($\frac{2}{7}$), P. 13, V. 7, A. 17–19 ($\frac{2-3}{14-17}$), C. 17, L.l. 55–65. L. tr. 7–9/5. *Untrahi*, Ooriah. *Habitat*: Mahanuddi river in Orissa. Also the Cauvery and Coleroon in Southern India. It attains at least 8 inches in length.

5. *C. argentea.* B. iii, D. 9–10 ($\frac{2-3}{7-8}$), P. 15, V. 8, A. 17–19 ($\frac{3}{14-16}$), C. 19, L.l. 43–45, L. tr. $6\frac{1}{2}$–7/3. *Habitat:* Bawanny river at the base of the Neilgherries, Cavery river, and Mysore; attaining 6 inches in length.

6. *C. Punjabensis.* B. iii, D. 9 ($\frac{2}{7}$), P. 11, V. 6, A. 16–17 ($\frac{2-3}{14-15}$), C. 19, L.l. 90–110, L. tr. 12/9. *Took,* Punj. *Habitat:* Lahore, in the Ravi river: also the Indus, in Sind. It attains at least $2\frac{1}{2}$ inches in length.

7. *C. phulo.* B. iii, D. 9 ($\frac{2}{7}$) P. 13, V. 9, A. 18–19 ($\frac{2-3}{16-18}$), C. 19, L.l. 80–87, L. tr. 12–15/6. *Habitat:* Assam, Bengal, Orissa, Central India, and the Deccan as far south as the Toombudra and Kistna rivers; attaining 5 inches or more in length.

8. *C. boopis.* B. iii, D. 9–10 ($\frac{2-3}{7}$), P. 15, V. 9, A. 14–15 ($\frac{2-3}{12-13}$), C. 21, L.l. 38–40, L. tr. 6–$6\frac{1}{2}$/3. *Habitat:* S. Canara and (?) Mysore; attaining at least 5 inches in length.

9. *C. clupeoides.* B. iii, D. 9 ($\frac{2}{7}$), P. 13, V. 9, A. 13–15 ($\frac{2}{11-13}$) C. 19, L.l. 80–93, L. tr. 12–15/6. *Habitat:* Cutch, Jubbulpore, Mysore, the Deccan, Madras Presidency, and Burmah. It attains at least 6 inches in length, and is very good eating.

10. *C. bacaila.* B. iii, D. 9 ($\frac{2}{7}$), P. 13, V. 9, A. 13–15 ($\frac{2}{11-13}$), C. 19, L.l. 86–110, L. tr. 17–19/6–10. *Habitat:* Throughout India, except Malabar, Mysore, and Madras, and parts of the Deccan. Dr. Günther gives Moulmein as one of its localities. It attains at least 7 inches in length.

THE BLACK-SPOT.

Barbus filamentosus and *Barbus Maheeola.*

These two fish differ from each other only in the filaments attached to the dorsal fin in *B. filamentosus* (Plate XII), and in *Maheeola* having two barbels and *filamentosus* wanting them. Their most marked characteristic is the singular black spot on the lateral line near the tail. They frequent the same waters, run to the same size, about six in the pound, and are to be fished for in the same way. They unfortunately seem to be confined to somewhat limited localities. I have only met with them on the West Coast; but Dr. Day adds the base of the Nielgherries, and Southern India, and Ceylon. In any case, the area is wide enough to allow of their being mentioned; very much wider than the area occupied by the Grayling. They affect the smaller tributary streams, and especially, if, indeed, they are not confined

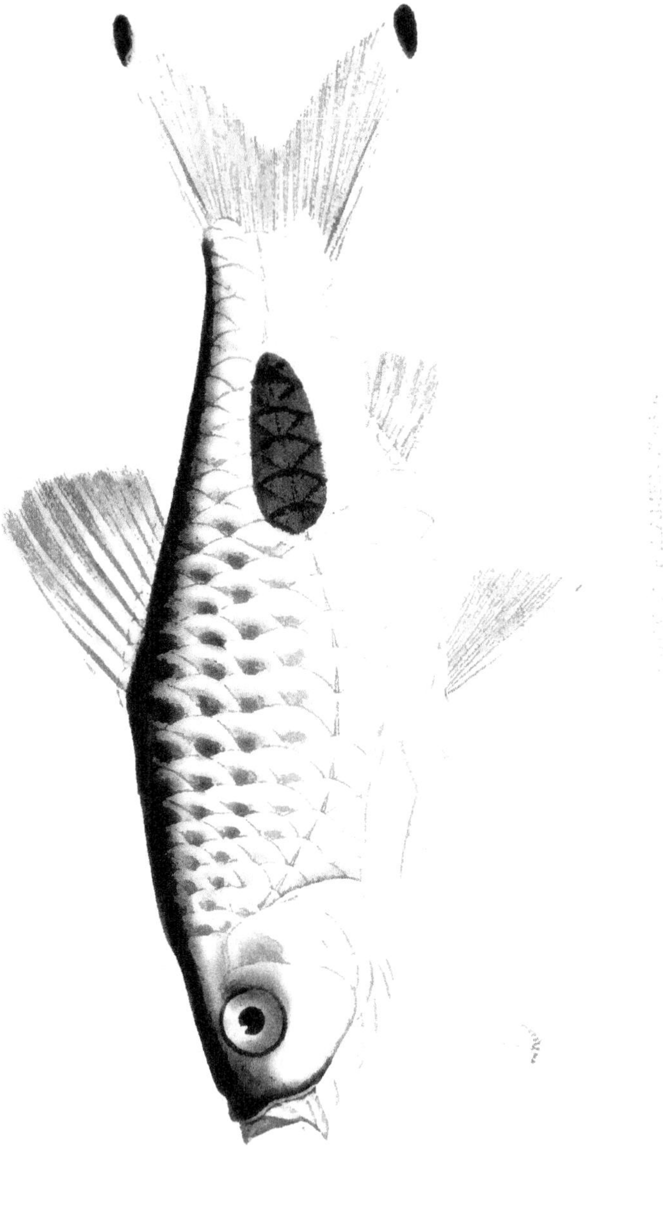

to, those which are rich in water-weed, on the seeds of which, as well as on the weeds themselves, and the insect life therein, they feed largely. They are not to be found in the runs, but where the water flows more gently, and even in the still water. There they congregate in shoals like dace, and take the fly with a very gentle suck like dace.

To make anything of a bag of them they require right good fishing. I have a note of having at Mála, in the South Canara District, caught 30 one afternoon. Up they came, a fish at each fly, and out they came, one or two at a time. In one throw I took three fish the size of the plate, one on each fly. But, aye, there's a but, and it must be admitted I have a note also that runs thus: "Had I taken all that rose that afternoon, I suppose I "should have killed 300 fish, weighing from 35 lbs. to 50 lbs." Of course I write, not from memory, but from notes made at the time. They are very shy and the water very bright, so you must fish very fine. Their mouth is leathery, but small, so that I think a fly on No. 14 Sneck bend is preferable to one on No. 12. You miss fewer rises with a small hook. The above note will show I found this out to my cost. Any light dun or black fly will kill, but I saw on the water a deep purple little fly, and imitating it did best with it. It is coloured on Plate XII, and mentioned among other flies in the remarks on the lesser Barils. Because of their shyness, throw as long a line as you can *perfectly command*, both to fall straight and to strike quickly with, for they frequently rise as the fly touches the water, though a sunk fly will suit them also. Do not draw the fly too close to you, because they will also follow the fly, and if they follow it too close to you they see you, and there'll be an end of your fun. Remember they swim in shoals like dace, so that if you get on a shoal you had better not move from it as long as they keep rising. Out they come, one after another, with a quaint look of unutterable surprise in their faces. "Now, who would 'a thought it!" You may go on throwing in exactly the same place. Draw your fly very slowly. They are deep and thick for their length, so that the full-sized ones are just a little too heavy to flick out. Any fish that cannot be flicked out, but has to be struck fine, with a light, quick hand, and then brought out quietly, contents me if there are enough of them; and I think it is likely to be the same with many of my readers. For the "straight tip" on quick striking with a very fine line, I must refer to the close of the chapter on the Carnatic Carp.

These fish have the further recommendation that they breed well in ponds, but there they seem, though numerous, to run smaller than in the rivers, presumably from inferior feeding. In the rivers they may be seen rooting busily among the water-weeds, where they find shrimps in abundance, just half-an-inch long, and prawns from $1\frac{1}{4}$ to $1\frac{1}{2}$ of an inch in length, and numerous larvæ, from just $\frac{2}{16}$ to $\frac{3}{16}$ of an inch long, and little stinging beetles; and the weed and its seed may be found in their stomachs.

In the rivers they do not seem to take so well in the mornings as in the evenings, at least not till 8 or 9. Whether they go on rising from that hour through the heat of the day I never had the leisure to find out. From 2 P.M. I know they take well, and keep at it till after sunset, till it is quite dark. They seem to sit up late, and be heavy in the morning. Bad habits those. In a pond where they were small and hungry, a friend and I got sixty-six before 11 A.M. This was at Warranga, near Mudradi. I have had *capital* fun with these little chaps.

Order. PHYSOSTOMI.
Family. CYPRINIDÆ.
Sub-Family. CYPRININA.
Genus. *Barbus.*
Sub-Genus. *Capoeta*, with two barbels.
Barbus Mahecola. B. iii. D. 11. ($\frac{3}{8}$). P. 15. V. 9. A. 7 ($\frac{2}{5}$). C. 19. L.l. 21. L. tr. 5 4.
Sub-genus. *Puntius*, without barbels.
Barbus filamentosus. B. iii. D. 11 ($\frac{3}{8}$). P. 15. V. 9. A. 7 ($\frac{2}{5}$). C. 19, L.l. 21. L. tr. 4 4.

THE OLIVE CARP.

Barbus chrysopoma.

I do not know much of this fish, having caught very few. I introduce him rather as a fish to be worked at, for as he will take a fly, and will live in ponds, he can be used to stock ponds where it is proposed to do so to make sport. I have taken them about $\frac{3}{4}$ lb. and slightly under with a black fly on a No. 6 Sneck bend hook.

Plate XI.

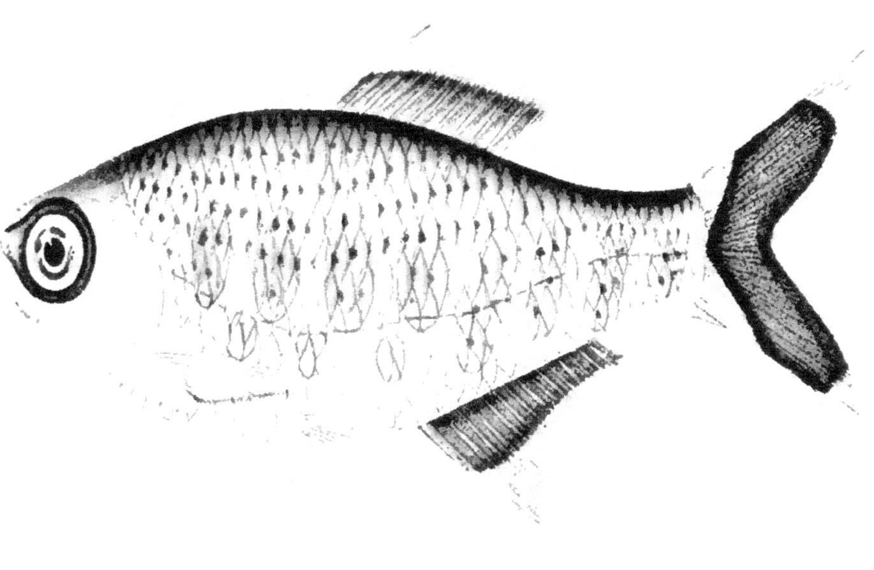

and I have also taken them and seen them taken with a float and paste bait. But I have seen them taken over $\frac{1}{2}$ lb. with a net. I have only seen them in the Adyar river above the anicut, and in the Red Hill Reservoir, both near Madras. From what little I know of them I cannot call them a sporting fish, but may be that is my fault for not yet knowing enough about them. I have never been at the trouble to try roving or bottom fishing with a gentil in India. I should think it ought to just suit fish of this sort. I found these fish always in still water. I see Day says they are to be found in the fresh waters along the coast of India from Cutch to Bengal, also in the Deccan, Mysore, and Madras; he also received a specimen from Darjeeling. Tamulians call it Shâni Kendâe, or cow-dung carp, from its colour, but olive carp is to the same effect, and prettier.

Barbels iv. D. 12 ($\frac{4}{8}$) P. 17, V. 9, A 8 ($\frac{3}{5}$) C. 19, Ll. 28–30. L. tr. 6/6.

THE LESSER BARILS.

Barilius Canarensis.

Of the genus *Barilius*, there are fourteen species in India. They are so widely distributed that every Indian angler must come across them. One of them, *Barilius bola*, attains some size, and is commonly known as the Indian trout; under that name, therefore, it will be treated of a little further on. The others run more or less to 6 inches in length. I shall therefore call them the lesser Barils. Plate XIV is a life-size representation of a full-sized fish. I have given *Barilius Canarensis* because of its colouring being so beautiful; but *B. Bakeri* and *B. gatensis* are to my knowledge so similar in their habits that, for angling purposes, they are practically the same fish. The colouring of the *Barilius Canarensis* is so very brilliant that I cannot do it justice; every colour, also, should shine like burnished metal. The Barils are a very game little fish, rising to a fly with a quick dart just as a burn trout does. They are an active fish, and are to be found where the stream runs briskly among the rocks, to be found in the stickles, and all about the edges of the deep runs. They are in large rivers frequented by Mahseer, and in the very same water. In fact, I was fishing for them once, and the moment I had hooked one, a Mahseer, recognizing that it was a fish in distress, went for it. They are also to be found in the smaller streams inhabited by the Black Spot, but not in the same water. Where the river runs lazily among the weeds you will find the Black Spot, where it runs rapidly among rocks, the Baril.

They are small, not running larger than a hungry beck trout of $3\frac{1}{2}$ ounces and under. They are, however, plentiful, and free fly takers, and to be fished for just as for a trout. They will rise to any small trout fly, and I have had on simultaneously one red, one dun, and one black, and they have taken kindly to them all, and sometimes two and three have been pulled out at once, just as little beck trout are at home. But the trout flies should be of the smallest, for though the fish will rise, they will not be readily hooked, unless the fly is on a hook as small as No. 14 Sneck or Kirby bend.

For choice, black seems to be the favourite colour for these little fellows, as well as for Mahseer, perhaps because it is most quickly seen against the light; and a friend, who is a good fisherman, so far believes in it, that he mounts his collar with all three black, such as the black gnat, small black palmer, and like flies black or nearly black.

Why it should be so fancied I do not know, for I do not remember to have ever seen black natural flies on the water in India, except it be little bits of black flies very little bigger than a well fed mosquito. These I have seen in countless numbers, but they are too small to imitate, and are only fitting food for fry, and minnows, and chelas.

I have noticed and painted red flies and yellow flies which were evidently water-born flies, but they were not in any numbers, and the fish were not sporting at them, so why should I trouble my reader with them? They must remain among the useless notes taken in my endeavour to work out the rationale of fly fishing in India in preference to the rule of thumb. The subject is too big a one to be mastered without very much more leisure at the water's side in all months of the year than I am ever likely to have at command. Will any one else work up the ephemera of India in connection with fly fishing? One fly, however, I have shown on Plate XII, because it is a practically useful fly, the Black Spots taking it freely. I saw it on the water in great numbers both morning and evening, but for want of opportunities of observing sufficiently I am, of course, in no position to say for how many days or months it lasts out, and on what rivers it is to be found. I can only say it is in full force in the northern parts of South Canara in December and January. But of what avail is such very limited information in the direction of the entomology of Indian fly fishing!

I have also observed the overhanging bamboos covered with light dun flies that were clearly land flies, and remained on the bamboo till disturbed, not seeming ever to fall into the water for the fish. Such flies, of course, are useless.

There is no doubt that fly fishing, if worth anything as a science and a sport, should be reduced to its entomological basis, and each artificial fly should be a close imitation of some known natural fly in the habit of living on or near the water, and thus becoming the common food of fish. But if we cannot ascertain the natural flies, we can only do as our fathers pretty generally did in England, and as not a few are still well content to do, namely, to make arbitrary guesses at the sort of fly to be used at certain times and places, with very little reference to entomology, preferring to it, indeed, such crude regulators as the colour of the water, and the brightness or otherwise of the day, to guide our preferences, and after all coming back to this, that if one man has killed with a certain fly, another may. For the *Barilius Bakeri*, then, any small trout fly will do, and the black, perhaps, for preference, the size being No. 14 Sneck or Kirby.

It must not be presumed that, because fish are small, they are not shy. There is no sequence at all in the argument. It may be that some small fish are not so shy as the bigger ones, but some sorts again are; and you may be very sure that none bite the better for seeing a biped making demonstrations at them from the shore. None but those which have been fed by hand will be sociable. Therefore, if you go and stand bolt upright at the very edge of the stream, and don't get sport, don't blame me, that is all. Do not you remember how even the little burn trout in Scotland dart away directly they see a Saxon on the bank?

You will very much improve your sport if you will condescend to be careful in this matter, even with small fish, and notably with the Barils. They should be fished for just as carefully as a trout. It is well to remember that fish ordinarily lie with their noses up stream, looking in front of them, and, more or less, on each side of them, for what may be brought down to them by the stream, but not behind them; and as you know that their backs are consequently all turned the same way, that is down stream, and they cannot see with their tails, it stands to reason that if you want to approach them unobserved, your best chance of doing so is from below them in the stream; and this is why the most successful fly-fishermen endeavour always to approach a bit of water from below, and take the best fish throwing up stream, and pulling down towards them, or rather just keeping the line taut while the stream brings their fly down to them. The most convenient plan is to fish a river upwards, that is, to commence fishing at the lowest part of the river you mean to fish over, and to walk upwards as you fish. This saves retracing steps, as you stalk to the foot of each pool or run your fish. The simplest way to fish any particular bit of water with a fly is to approach crouching, and, kneeling on one knee so far off from the bank that you can only just see and command a little bit of the water, throw your fly straight across, keep your line just taut and no more, and let the stream carry it down and round towards you as quietly as it will, without any pulling from you, and you thus fish first the water where you are most likely to be seen; repeat the process a yard or two higher each time, carefully edging nearer and nearer the while, till you find yourself throwing straight up the stream close under your own bank. These are, of course, only general instructions for thoroughly fishing over water, and cannot be held applicable in all cases; for differently exposed, differently running, waters require to be fished differently, and not a little depends on the generalship displayed in properly availing yourself of every advantage of ground in approaching the enemy's position.

Another argument against fly-fishing from above is, that if you throw your fly downwards, and pull it towards you, you will pull it in the most unnatural way, for no natural fly ever floated up stream. I know that fish *are* caught in this way sometimes, but it is not good fishing, and will not pay as a rule.

Fly fishing, it will be observed, is in this respect the contrary to spinning, the rule in the latter case being to pull the bait more or less against the stream. And the same rule obtains more or less in salmon fly-fishing, but then that is not properly fly-fishing, though commonly so called, because no mortal can tell you the entomological specimen of which a salmon fly is a representation.

Perhaps you may say the fish are too small, and not worth all this trouble. So be it. In such case let them alone, and don't fish for them at all. But if you *will* fish for any of these smaller fish just for a change, you may as well catch them while you are about it. This I tell you, therefore, you will not do unless you condescend to take the pains to fish for a Baril as carefully as for a trout. If you are a good fisherman all this painstaking will come to you naturally, as a matter of course, and be no pains.

Flies draw, and rust, and get moth eaten, quickly in India, and should consequently be got from England in small quantities from time to time. They are light, and can easily travel in a letter. Do not buy any that have been kept some time in store in a shop in this country. But if you tie your own flies, so much the better.

It is decidedly a point to put on your drop flies neatly, so that there shall be no large knot to make a ripple in the water. Some put on the drop by a loop, but this is a clumsy, bungling way, that shows a great deal too much for a wary fish. Some tie their collar with two knots slipping together, so as to be able to pull them asunder and insert the drop, after having tied a knot at the end of it, and then pull the collar together. But I do not like this plan, not only because all collars are not made up so as to allow of its being done, but also because the pulling asunder of tight knots soon frays the gut, and weakens the collar at those points. Better than these knots is the one recommended by Francis Francis. Tie a simple knot at the end of your drop, and then with the drop gut tie a simple knot round the gut of the collar, and let it slip down the collar till just over a knot or join in it, and then pull tight. This is very neat and strong and simple, and I confess I generally use it on a fresh collar. But it is not quite without an objection. As you must always tie your drop over a knot you must always tie it just over a join in the line, or you must make a knot in your collar on purpose for it, and practically it ends in this, that you almost always tie on your drop over the same knot, and if you change often, you fray that spot in the collar and weaken it. I would therefore suggest the knot shown in Figure 4, Plate XXV. Wherever in your collar you wish to place your drop fly, tie, in the collar, the knot there shown, being careful only that E. is the end near the rod; A. the end near the tail fly.

It is very easily done by making the loop C. and doubling the bit B. through it. The line has not to be taken off the rod for the purpose, or the ends passed through at all. It is done in a couple of seconds by two turns. Having done this, and taking care that your gut is thoroughly soft from soaking, so that you may be sure it will not crack in knotting, pull A. and B. so that loop C. becomes a tight knot. Put your drop fly, with a simple knot at the end, through the loop D., and then pull E. till D. also is absorbed into a tight knot. Then pull your drop fly close up to its own knot, and you are ready for action.

What I consider the advantages of this knot are, that it is tied as quickly, if not more quickly, than any other; is as neat as the neatest of them; can be tied in any part of the collar you like, so that you can have your drop fly at the precise distance you fancy from the tail fly; and if a breakage or any thing has somewhat curtailed that distance, you can hit it off again to a nicety. This is no small point to my fancy, for it makes one unhappy to have the drops crowded together. To move your first drop a length further up will, perhaps, bring it too near the other drop, whereas you had rather it were not *quite* so near the tail fly. This is the dilemma in which you are placed, if you are dependent on the knots at the joins, whereas by my plan you can locate your drop fly just where you have a mind, to an inch. Again it is superior I think to other knots in the ease with which you can remove your fly. Pull the end A. and the drop, and the knot will open, with a little aid of the nails on the knot. Or if you are not handy at this work, or will not be troubled, nothing is easier than to nip the fly off close up to the gut. You lose next to nothing of the length of the drop thereby; you lose considerably less than you do when nipping off one of Francis Francis' drops. As soon as the drop is removed, the whole knot easily straightens, and a fresh knot is tied, for a fresh drop in a fresh place, an inch or so higher or lower.

I have said be careful in tying the knot that the end E. is the end nearest to the rod; the reason is obvious. The knot is a slip knot, and therefore a heavy fish on the drop might open it, if it were not so placed that the more the fish pulls, the more he tightens the knot. The end that tightens up the loop B. and keeps the knot at the head of the drop from coming through that loop, is the end E.; E. being the made end connected with the rod, it follows that the more the fish pulls against you, the more he tightens E., and the more secure he consequently makes the knot. I showed this knot to a friend, who tied it with A. towards the rod, lost his fish and fly, and said it was *my fault!*

The following brief extract from Dr. Day's "Fishes of India," may be useful for reference:—

Order. PHYSOSTOMI.
Family. CYPRINIDÆ.
Sub-family. CYPRININA.
Genus. BARILIUS.

SYNOPSIS OF SPECIES.

A.—*With four barbels* (*Pachystomus*).

1. *Barilius vagra.* D. 9, A. 13–15, L.l. 42–44. With 10 vertical bars. Sind Hills, Himalayas, Ganges, Jumna, and Brahmaputra.
2. *Barilius modestus.* D. 9, A. 12–13, L.l. 43. Back dark, sides silvery. Sind and Panjab.
3. *Barilius radiolatus.* D. 9, A. 12, L.l. 56–62. Silvery. Central India.
4. *Barilius shacra.* D. 9, A. 10, L.l. 60–70. Twelve vertical bars. Bengal, N.W. Provinces, and Assam.
5. *Barilius bendelisis.* D. 9, A. 9–10, L.l. 40–43. Short vertical bars: each scale with a black spot in adults. From Western Ghauts throughout India (not Sind) to Assam.

B.—*With two barbels* (*Bendilisis*).

6. *Barilius barila.* D. 9, A. 13–14, L.l. 43–46. With 14 or 15 vertical bars. Bengal, Orissa, and Lower Assam.

C.—*Without or with only rudimentary barbels* (*Barilius*).

7. *Barilius Bakeri.* D. 13, A. 16–17, L.l. 38. A row of large spots. Travancore.
8. *Barilius gatensis.* D. 10–12, A. 15–17, L.l. 40. With 15 vertical bars. Western Ghauts and Neilgherries.
9. *Barilius Canarensis.* D. 12–13, A. 14–16, L.l. 38. Two rows of spots. Canara.
10. *Barilius barna.* D. 9, A. 13–14, L.l. 39–42. Nine vertical bands. Orissa, Bengal, Assam.

11. *Barilius guttatus*, D. 9, A. 14, L.l. 44–48. Two rows of spots. Burma.
12. *Barilius tileo*, D. 9, A. 13, L.l. 70–75. Two rows of spots. Bengal and Assam.
13. *Barilius Evezardi*, D. 9, A. 14-15, L.l. 40. Silvery. Poona.
14. *Barilius bola*, D. 10–11, A. 13, L.l. 88–94. Two rows of blotches. Orissa, Bengal, Assam.

THE INDIAN TROUT.

Barilius bola.

Of this fish I have no personal knowledge at all. But it is too important a sporting fish to be omitted on that account. In the interests of brother anglers my deficiency has been most kindly supplemented by a paper from the pen of Colonel J. Parsons; and while I express my own indebtedness therefor, I know I may add that of my readers. Most kindly has been the response to the invitation thrown out in my first edition, and repeated at page 6 of this.

I have called this fish the Indian trout, because it is commonly thus called in Northern India. Other competitors there are for the name; but *Barilius bola* seems to have the best title to be called the Indian trout. To avoid confusion, therefore, we will commence by deposing the other fish which seem to have less right to the honourable distinction. *Oreinus Richardsonii* has, according to Day, been called the "Kemaon Trout." "In some specimens there "are black spots on the sides and head." Of *Oreinus sinuatus* Dr. Day writes, in his "Fishes of India," "Some have scattered black "and occasionally red spots, and these have been termed Trout." But this fish has a sucker with which it adheres to rocks, which is most untroutlike, and Dr. Day tells me it will not take a fly at any price, a piece of wrong-headedness for which, with your concurrence, it should be shorn of its brevet-rank, in spite of its red spots. *Oh formose puer nimium ne crede colori*—we will degrade you in spite of your looks. "Handsome is that handsome does" is the better rule, and as *Barilius bola* sports like a trout, as we shall see from Colonel Parsons, let us allow his claim, though he has no adipose dorsal fin like the true trouts (salmonidæ). We may have

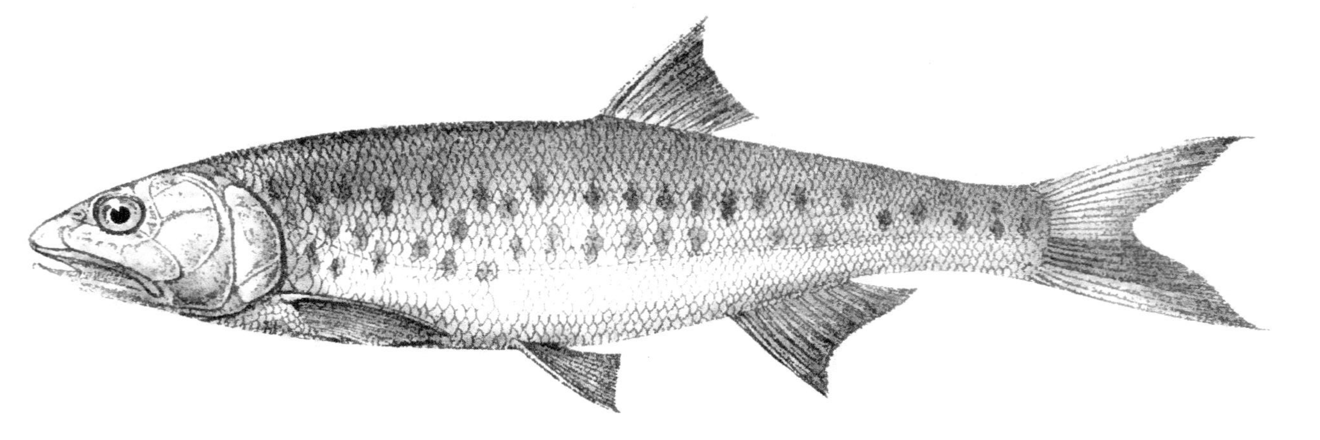

BARILIUS BOLA

the less hesitation in confirming the honorific as there are no indigenous trout in India.

The plate is taken by permission from Dr. Day's "Fishes of "India," the mouth only being a little opened to show the peculiarly beaked and prominent under jaw.

"The *Barilius bola* (vernac. Gulâbi Machli rose-speckled fish) "by Anglo-Indians commonly misnamed Trout," writes Colonel Parsons, "is found in many rivers of India, its chief habitat being "clear streams with stony bed.

"Though not of the Trout genus, it bears some resemblance in "outline to the European Trout, but is of more delicate formation, "and the more brilliant looking fish of the two. Like the Trout, "it is very beautifully spotted."

"The weight of the *Barilius bola* of different rivers varies "greatly, the average weight of mature fish in streams where it "best thrives is probably about ¾ lb., and maximum about 2 lbs. "This may be an estimate under the mark, as the writer merely "notes from his personal experience as a fisherman, as far as it "extends, during periods of fishing recreation that were chiefly "devoted to the capture of Mahseer, and he has never known the "*Barilius bola* to be brought to market by natives of the country, "whereby the quantities coming under observation would afford "data for satisfactorily deciding on the dimensions of this species "of fish.

"The *Bârilius bola* is taken with the fly, and likewise with "small spinning bait; a small sized phantom is a very good bait to "use. They are usually shy, and take the fly best at the close of "day, when a white moth (lake trout fly size) is perhaps the "most suitable lure, the addition of white bead eyes to the fly I "have known to be an improvement. Anglers fishing for Mahseer. "with a good sized spinning bait, occasionally hook a good "specimen of the *Barilius bola*, notably in the 'Sone' or 'Song, a "beautiful stream which joins the Ganges, a few miles above "Hardwar, on its right bank, and which is a grand place for "Mahseer fishing.

"The *Barilius bola* runs large in both the Ganges and the "Jumna in the Doon; I have got them close on 2 lbs at Dâdapur, "the head of the Western Jumna Canal, a few miles from Jagadri on the S. P. and Delhi Railway. This fish is, however, difficult to "catch in most localities where I have tried them, and I attribute "this in a great measure to the frequent presence of Mahseer in "their vicinity. It is a marvel to me how any *Barilius* can "escape at all from the rapid moving Mahseer, which is perhaps "more partial to the *Barilius* than to the young of its own species, "which, by the bye, the Mahseer swallows very freely, as I have "repeatedly proved to my entire satisfaction in live bait fishing "when the devourer has full time afforded to consider the species "of his morsel.

"The native fishermen at the Jumna, on the hills between "Mussoorie and Simla, use scarcely any other bait than the Barilius. "They have a curious way of catching their bait. The trout, "which for convenience sake we may call them, are excessively "keen sighted, and the stream running into the Jumna at this "locality where they are taken is of exquisite brilliancy, conse- "quently they very soon clear out of reach on the appearance of a "net caster. Their capture is effected by means of a weighted line of "horsehair nooses, dextrously slung across stream well ahead of "the fisherman. As he walks up stream, scaring the fish to the "line, the trout shoot along the bottom as if to escape observation, "and the line being weighted, with nooses all along it across the "stream, some of the fish can scarcely fail to run into loops open "to receive them, but which draw tight over their shoulders, "on nearing the dorsal fin. The trout in this stream average "under ½ lb., and are easily held by the noose. I have watched "the performance with interest, and immediately purchased some "of the bait in exchange for English fish-hooks, more prized "than money by the fishermen.

"Speaking of fish hooks, the Limerick and other patterns "would be much improved by the barb being additional, instead "of being, as it were, a slice out of the shank. I have frequently "known hooks of the best makers parted by heavy fish straining "on the narrow bit of metal under the barb; such mishap has "quite recently occurred to me while Mahseer fishing at Tangrot. "If the hook is resting on the point by pressure on bone, "instead of cartilage, of a large fish's mouth, the trial at the above "part of the hook is very severe, and not likely to last!

"The Barilius is numerous in the Morar near Gwalior; it "sometimes takes the fly well, but it is of very small average size "in that stream. In the Seinde, another stream in that territory, "I recollect many years ago, 'when my lines were cast in those "'places,' getting a couple of these fish close on 2 lbs. each.

"When fishing for Mahseer, and hooking a Barilius, there is "little doubt which is hooked from the first, as the spotted one "will jump repeatedly out of the water, and dash about in a "perfect frenzy, and is game to the last; not that I wish in "any way to disparage the noble Mahseer, whose peculiarity is "the truly grand rush he makes when first struck, and woe betide "the line then if all is not clear. This spanking fish, far beyond "the pretty little Barilius, has beguiled many a day of my exile, "and long may he flourish."

And so say all of us.

Turning to Day's "Fishes of India," I extract the following portions:—

"Barbels absent. Branchiostegals iii, D. 10–11 ($\frac{3}{7-8}$), P. 13, V. 9, "A. 13 ($\frac{3}{10}$), C. 19. L.l. 88–94, L. tr. 12-15/9-11. . . . Head "compressed, snout pointed, a well developed knob above symphysis of "the lower jaw. . . . . *Colours:* silvery, with two or more "vertical rows of bluish blotches along the sides, the upper being "about twelve to twenty, and the lower intermediate; some spots also "on the head. Lower half of the dorsal fin slightly gray. Caudal, "orange stained with gray and black. Pectoral, ventral, and anal, "orange, the colours being somewhat similar to those of a trout; it "often goes by that name amongst Europeans."

"*Habitat:* Orissa, Bengal, N.W. Provinces, Assam, and Burma, "attaining at least a foot in length: one killed in Assam by Mr. "Hannay is stated to have weighed 5 lbs. It is a very game fish, "takes the fly well, and is one of those termed *Rajah mas*, or 'chief "'of the fishes' in the Assam rivers.

"*Bugguah*, Ooriah; *Korang*, Assam; *Bola*, Beng.; *Buggarah*, "Hind."

CHAPTER XII.

BOTTOM FISHING FOR LABEO.

"Bait the hook well, and the fish will bite."—MUCH ADO.

SUPPOSE we try a little bottom fishing just for a change. "Variety's charming:" we have it on the old indisputable authority of the copybook. And the swan-quill is not without its charm. There it sits elegant and upright in the water, like a sprightly little water-nymph in its element, on the very tip-toe of expectation, and ready to give you the earliest hint of the slightest flirtation going on with your bait down below. You feel you have a friend in that quill, it will tell you faithfully of every move made against you in the dark depths below, and you have a conviction you may trust it implicity. In cautious silence your little nymph makes mute gestures to you, by a code of her own, like the signs of the needle speaking to you of the man at the other end of the wire. Mind you are quick to read her aright, for your nymph is true as steel, and will tell you all, if you can only follow her signals. There! she made the slightest shade of a bow; some one has entered the room, shall we say just smelt your bait. Again she bows, courtseys, now more and more rapidly, now she is quite excited over it. They're off, and she has disappeared after them. Strike instanter, not roughly, but rapidly. Ha! it's you is it? I thought as much. But mind, mind what you are about, you have only fine-drawn gut, and a light rod, and seemingly a stout party at the other end. Out goes the line off the reel, not very fast certainly, nor very far, still the old alderman will have it, and there's no denying him. He fights long and persistently though not furiously. Stick to him, keep bearing on him all you dare, but gingerly, gingerly. What, no signs of my poor little faithful nymph, yet still down in the depths keeping an eye on that fat fellow? Ah, up she shows at last, one is quite glad to see her little face again.

She tells you that the old alderman is getting pumped. His every instinct is to keep down at the bottom in deep water, so keep pressing on him upwards and shorewards. At last you have him in the landing net, a 3 lb. fish with a funny little fringed mouth. What is he? He is a Labeo, one of twenty-five, of which eight run large, attaining respectively to 1½ feet, 2 feet, 3 feet, and in one case to nearly 5 feet in length, according to Dr. Day. I have only the pleasure of a personal acquaintance with four of them, and they are all similarly thick-built fish, and to be taken in one and the same way.

The Plate which I have given does not exactly correspond with any one of Dr. Day's Labeos, but it is none the less correct, having been taken from life from a 5 lb. fish under my own careful superintendence. I did not choose it because it differed, but because, as I meant to give colours, I was bound to have the very fish to which the colours belonged. I have not named it as a new fish because the difference is slight, and because I could not keep the specimen, and there are difficulties* about the Labeos, arising, seemingly, from varieties rather than from separate species. I have thought best, therefore, to apply the name I have in the Plate in spite of the very slight variation from Dr. Day's fish of the same name. In short, I have preferred to follow his nomenclature.

These fish being of the sizes above-mentioned, and all, as far as I know them, thick-built heavy fish for their length, anglers will see that they are worth fishing for. I have no note of having caught them over 3 lbs. with a line myself, but I have of having seen them 5 lbs. 14 oz. and am assured that they run very much larger, and I have a *memory*, perhaps poetic, of having caught them 7 lbs. They are as cunning a fish as the roach, and to be fished for in the same manner. Good roach fishing is the glory of the Londoner, and here is just the same for you with the fish seldom under 1 lb. and averaging 2 lbs.

I am afraid of want of sympathy for float fishing, so I must transgress my rule promised in the preface, and mention a little bag made one day just to draw the reader on. A friend and self caught in a pond 21 lbs. weight in one hour. Some of them were 3 lbs. each, but the majority were about 2 lbs. each. Another day I got

* For the difficulties, see the discussions under various Labeos in Dr. Day's "Fishes of India," and the differing opinions of different authors.

25 lbs. weight of these fish, besides two freshwater tortoises, weighing together 6½ lbs. There were two more good fish also that a new hand broke off my hook in his clumsy hurry with the landing net (bad luck to him), and another that fairly broke me after a long fight. I suppose I thought it was about time he gave in, and he thought otherwise, for they fight long and steadily, and the tackle has to be very fine. Another tortoise also was hooked foul, brought to the top and lost. This fishing was from 7·10 A.M. to 10·50 A.M. During the first hour I took nothing; during the remaining two hours and 40 minutes I landed the above 31½ lbs., on a light single-handed 10 feet trout rod. When I left they were still biting, but I had to tear myself away. Other similar bags I have made alone or with friends, but of these two days only did I keep a note, because, dear reader, I was thinking of you even then, thinking that you would not believe in bottom fishing unless I gave you particulars from notes taken at the time, thinking what you would lose by such incredulity. As we are on pond fishing one more bag I must give you. Fishing all day H. caught 52 lbs., of which two were freshwater sharks, weighing respectively 10 lbs. and 22 lbs.; the rest were the fish I am introducing to you. A friend fishing with him that day caught about 30 lbs. weight, but of this I speak roughly from hearsay and estimate, not having seen his bag. Thus the two rods took about 80 lbs. weight of fish out of a pond near Negapatam.

Is this enough to draw you with me bottom fishing? In the hope that it is I will continue.

My acquaintance with these fish has been made chiefly in ponds. I have seen them in rivers, but there I confess they have been one too many for me, mainly because I gave them but secondary attention where I could get Mahseer, or was experimenting with the fly, catching Barils and Chelas, and hoping to make new discoveries. In rivers they seem to be very wary. I notice that on this account the natives fish as far from themselves as they can cast the line. They ground-bait freely for two or three days, and attaching a lead, about the weight of a bullet, a little above the bait of dough of millet, and coiling up the line of sago palm fibre at their feet, whirl and fling out the weighted line as far as they can, which is about 40 yards, and, when it has settled, gather in the slack so that they can feel any bite. They have one such line in

14

each hand without any rod. Even with these precautions they do better by night than by day, and prefer the night fishing accordingly. But such fishing will not suit us rod fishermen, for we could not throw so far, nor could we feel a bite through the rod, nor see a float if it were allowed. From a sporting point of view, therefore, I look upon these fish as gentry whose acquaintance is to be cultivated in ponds rather than in rivers, though I am told there are places in rivers where Europeans have good sport with them with rods.

The ponds* in which I have caught them have been fed by channels coming from a river, which channels brought down the fry in flood time; and the natives informed me that the spawn would not vivify except in running water. I have, however, proved the contrary by inserting fry into a rain fed pond, that was certainly bare of them, and watching them till they reproduced fry. Of this pond at Vallam the reader will hear again hereafter in the Chapter on Stocking Ponds. This was before Dr. Day's "Fishes of India" was published, in which I see he says of *Labeo rohita*: "It attains 3 "feet or more in length. It is esteemed excellent as food, and "propagated with care in ponds in Bengal;" and of *Labeo gonius* he writes that it is extensively used for the purpose of stocking tanks in northern India, and attains nearly 5 feet in length, and *Labeo bata* attaining 2 feet is mentioned similarly.

Very quick striking being necessary, a light rod is a *sine quâ non*. If you have a roach rod, so much the better. I am content with my little light single-handed trout fly rod, substituting a short stiff spinning top for the fly top. This shortening and stiffening quickens the stroke, but strike as quickly as you may they will still steal a great quantity of your bait. A reel and fine running line are indispensable. The collar should be of fine drawn gut, and the hook at least must be on such gut. The float should be of the lightest, so as to be sensitive and indicative of the slightest touches of these adepts at bait stealing. Weight it so that when the weight of the bait is added, about one-third only of the float is visible above water. The handiest thing for weighting is the soft drawn lead wire made by the Manchester Cotton Twine Spinning Company, of 51, Corporation Street, Manchester, and sold by them

* About six miles' drive from Tanjore. I speak roughly from memory. They are the private property of a wealthy native, who used to prohibit netting therein.

at 15 yards for a shilling. It is so easily accommodated to the exact weight you want, and with these thievish fish you should weight to a nicety. An inch or so of the lead wire is sufficient, so that it will take you two or three lifetimes to use up 15 yards unless you are philanthrophic to your brother anglers, whether white or black, as a fisherman should be. For hook I have preferred No. 6 Kirby or Sneck bend.

You will find it advantageous to ground-bait beforehand, and a little while fishing, just to keep them together.

Before you begin, plumb the depth carefully by putting a weight on your hook, and arrange your float so that your bait shall lie an inch or two off the ground, not more.

Bait with paste or dough such as you fancy. Dough made up of wheat flour and water kneaded together cold will do, but it is easily stolen. Cheese mashed very fine with a fork and mixed with the above dough, gives it additional consistency, and what is of much more importance, smell. The natives scent their paste with the most offensive, untouchable, unmentionable matters. I daresay asafœtida would answer the same purpose; I never tried. It is undoubtedly right to trust much to the sense of smell in fish when you wish them to find your stationary bait as in bottom fishing; and their preferences are the reverse of Rimmel's. Newly baked bread may also be kneaded up and used. It is not so liable to be stolen as paste, but I think it is a little too hard, offering, therefore, a little too much resistance to the passage of the hook through it when you want to strike the fish. I found the cocoanut rice-flour cakes commonly made by old women at corners of streets, and called by Madrassees hoppers (Tamil, àppăm) to be very convenient and effective when kneaded up. Did'nt I say old women, they have never been known to be made by young women, that's a peculiarity of them. I have used a bait the size of a man's little finger nail; the natives use it as big as a thumb nail. They use also paste madé of the flour of rági (Tamil, kèvaru or kèvaragu, the botanical name would'nt help you) mixed with rice bran, not paddy husk, and boiled up with a little water, stirring the whole till it thickens; and they ground-bait with the same. It is doubtless of a very suitable consistency, and has a strong smell about it, and is as cheap as anything they could use.

When to strike is a very important point. These fish bite very slowly and cautiously like a carp, and it is of no manner of use to strike at the first bob of the float as for gudgeon. If they have not been much fished for, and are biting freely, it is a very simple matter. There will be a very slight movement of the float, then six or eight quick bobs, and then the float will go right under and away; when it disappears strike. If they are more wary or less on the feed, the almost imperceptible quivers of the float will continue longer and stop at times, till you almost think the fish have deserted you; the subsequent perceptible bobs will be less vigorous and will cease at intervals; eventually your float will move away quietly on the surface. When it moves off, strike immediately. If still more wary they will not move your float off at all, and if you look at your bait when the bobs cease you will find it has all been successfully stolen. When it comes to this you must strike on the chance when the bobs are a little more vigorous and rapid than usual. But do not be in such a hurry as that till you find they have stolen your bait several times. Your bait is often stolen by the little fish of other sorts that scramble for it if you have scared away the Labeos. Sometimes you will see your float tilt up and lie down flat on the top of the water. What is to be done then? That indicates that a fish has taken your bait from above it, and has raised it so much that both it and the lead are lifted, and the weight being taken off, the float it is no longer partially immersed, but floats flat on the surface of the water. Strike immediately.

Fish frequently suck up bait from below them, as you may have seen in an aquarium or globe of gold fish. If bottom feeders could not do so, they would be at a loss how to get at such of their food as lies on the bottom. Some protrude their lips in cup-like fashion over the object to be drawn up by suction, notably *Barbus curmuca*. The mouth of the Labeo is ordinarily placed below the snout, not at the end of it, so that it must often have to suck its food upwards. The mouth is frequently fimbricated or fringed with short tendrils, and looking like a frill.

Always make preparations for striking by gathering in stealthily all the slack line between the rod top and the float, so that when the critical moment for striking arrives, you may take instantaneous advantage of it. You will need all the quickness of which you are master, and still they will steal much of your bait.

The stroke is made with a quick turn of the wrist, any blow

from the arm would break your fine tackle, for a fish of over a pound weight will not yield to it at all. You will have to play him before you can get him out, and they make a stubborn well sustained resistance. Only once have I had one of these fish fling itself a little into the air; the rule is that they keep down, and make for the deeper water of the centre of the pond, and fight, not vigorously nor furiously, but very steadily for a good long time. In this their slow way they are very game.

They ascend and descend rivers in floods and low water; and are consequently caught in cruives as Mahseer are. They do not go to sea.

The Tamil name of Tanjore is *Shĕl-Kendai*; but the Tamil of Coimbatore is *Kărŭmŭlă-Kendai.* The Mysore Canarese for the *Labio kontius* is *Kemmin*, or red fish. Which again is particularized in Tamil as *Gundămăni-Shel Kendai.*

They *seem* to take flies, but I think it is only in play that they come to the surface.

They frequent the deep, still parts of rivers.

They are not a delicate fish to transport. For stocking purposes the young bear carriage well.

The various sorts are between them distributed all over India, Ceylon, Burma, and Assam.

THE WHITE CARP.

There are other fish that may be taken bottom fishing with a paste bait. The mighty Mahseer sometimes takes the bait meant for the Labeo, and when tendered on native lines commonly breaks them. There is a silvery fish much like a Labeo in general shape, but having the mouth at the end of, and not under the snout, that takes the same bait and hook, and is taken freely with the Labeos. It is *Cirrhina cirrhosa*, called in Tamil *Veng kendai*, or White Carp, which anglicised name may be fairly given it. Some of my native informants said it ran to $2\frac{1}{2}$ feet in length; others said $1\frac{1}{2}$ feet. We may accept the latter, which tallies, I see, with Dr. Day's information.

I well remember (and find in my notes) catching one of $2\frac{1}{2}$ lbs. that came up with fresh, only very slightly healed, marks of a bite which seemed to say he had been half-way into the mouth of a freshwater shark. These fish formed part of the kills above-mentioned as Labeos, and gave more vigorous play than the Labeos. If I remember rightly, I have no note, I got some of them up to 5 lbs.

The freshwater tortoise mentioned in the above mixed bag bit just like fish, and you could not tell it was a tortoise that was biting till you had hooked your friend, when he proved less active than a Labeo, only clinging to the bottom without any travelling about there. They seemed to scare away the fish by their presence. For this reason, and because I believe I am right in saying they are sad spawn and fry eaters, never fling them back or let them crawl away to the water.

Your native attendants will sometimes be glad of them, and they say they know which tortoises are edible and which are not. I cannot say I have studied them gastronomically. I only observed that some emitted an almost overpoweringly offensive odour, and that was more than enough for me. Mind their bite. It is not easy to kill them. Their tenacity of life is extraordinary to a degree. It is recorded that they have lived for months with the brain removed, and for twelve days without a head. I had the pleasure of recognizing one inside a crocodile, and they in their turn are said to eat young crocodiles and crocodiles' eggs. But they are reptiles, not fish, so we will have no more of them here.

The following epitomized extracts from Dr. Day's "Fishes of India" may be useful for reference:—

Order. *Physostomi.*
Family. *Cyprinidæ.*
Sub-family. *Cyprinina.*
Genus. *Labeo.*

2. *Labeo fimbriatus.* Barbels 4. B. iii, D. 19–22, ($\frac{3-4}{15-18}$), P. 17, V. 9, A. 7 ($\frac{2}{5}$), C. 19, L.l. 44–47, L.tr. 9–10/8. Sind, Punjab, the Deccan, and probably N.E. Bengal; also Southern India, at least to Orissa. Attains a foot and a half in length.

3. *L. nigrescens.* Barbels 4. B. iii, D. 17-18 ($\frac{2-3}{14-15}$), P. 19, A. 7 ($\frac{2}{5}$), C. 19-21, L.l. 36, L.tr. 6,7. South Canara. 15 inches.

4. *L. calbasu.* Barbels 4. B. iii, D. 16–18 ($\frac{3}{13-15}$), P. 19, V. 9, A. 7 ($\frac{2}{5}$), C. 19, L.l. 40–44, L.tr. 7½/8. Punjab, Sind, Cutch, Deccan. Southern India and Malabar, from the Kistna through Orissa, Bengal, and Burma. 3 feet.

6. *L. gonius.* Barbels 4. B. iii, D. 16–18 ($\frac{2-3}{13-14}$), P. 17, V. 9, A. 7 ($\frac{2}{5}$), C. 19, L.l. 74–84, L.tr. 16/17. Indus, in Sind, N.W. Provinces, Bengal, Orissa, Ganjam, as low as Kistna. Assam aud Burma. Attains nearly 5 feet in length.

7. *L. dussumieri.* 13 inches.

8. *L. rohita.* Barbels 4. B. iii, D. 15–16 ($\frac{3}{12-13}$), P. 17, V. 9, A. 7 ($\frac{2}{5}$), C. 19, L.l. 40–42, L.tr. 6½/9. Sind, from Punjab through India and Assam to Burma. Not found in Madras, or on the West Coast. 3 feet or more in length. *Ruhu*, Ooriah; *Ruee*, Bengal.

11. *L. kontius.* Barbels 4. B. iii, D. 15–16 ($\frac{3-4}{12-13}$), P. 15, V. 10, A. 7 ($\frac{2}{5}$), C. 19, L.l. 38–41, L.tr. 7/8. Base of the Nilagiris, Cavery, and Coleroon in all their branches down to the coast. 2 feet.

14. *L. dyocheilus.* Barbels 2. B. iii, D. 13 ($\frac{3}{10}$), P. 17, V. 9, A. 7 ($\frac{2}{5}$), C. 19, L.l. 43, L.tr. 8½/7½. Sind hills and along the Himalayas to Sikkim and Assam. Common in Assam. 3 feet.

17. *L. bata.* Barbels 2. B. iii, D. 11–12 ($\frac{2-3}{9-10}$), P. 18, V. 9, A. 7 ($\frac{2}{5}$), C. 19, L.l. 37–40, L.tr. 7/6–7. From the Kistna and Godavery rivers, through Orissa, Bengal, and Assam. 2 feet.

Those which I have omitted are not to my knowledge big enough to be worth recording in a book on angling. They may be bigger than certain fish I have mentioned as fly takers, but fly taking makes a fish more worthy of notice. I am afraid of swelling my book, and therefore omit whatever may seem not likely to interest an intelligent angler.

Cirrhina cirrhosa. Barbels 4. B. iii, D. 17–19 ($\frac{3-4}{14-15}$), P. 19, V. 9, A. 8 ($\frac{3}{5}$), C. 19, L.l. 42–44, L.tr. 8/9. Vert. 21/17. *Habitat:* Godavery, Kistna, and Cavery rivers, and generally in Southern India.

CHAPTER XIII.

FRESHWATER SHARKS.

"I care not I to fish in seas,
Fresh rivers best my mind do please."—
IZAAK WALTON.

THE name freshwater shark seems to have been given to more than one of the Siluridæ, and it is fairly applicable as indicative of their voracity. I propose, therefore, to adopt it; and under this name to present to my readers three different fish of large dimensions that are highly predatory, and may be taken with a rod and line. They are *Wallago attu, Bagarius Yarrellii,* and *Silundia Gangetica.*

I cannot call them sporting fish, for they show no vivacity in their play. Still they take out line after their fashion, and hang their heavy sulking weight on it, and grow to an enormous size. So I suppose we must be content with quantity in lieu of quality. As the panther is to the wild cat, so are these Siluroids of the East to the Pike of the West in respect to size and general similarity of habits.

They are very voracious, preying generally on fish, but they are not particular, and may be termed foul feeders. Still they are esteemed good eating, and why should they not be? The sweetest fruit are the most highly manured; and I hold that with fish, too, any food that is thoroughly assimilated grows healthy meat. Otherwise who would eat prawns, shrimps, lobsters, crabs, crawfish, and other scavengers of the sea. Carrion eaters, indeed, that's nothing. Is not the much esteemed trout a cannibal, in common with the Mahseer and other gentry of the waters? Set aside sentimentalisms, and take the proof of the pudding to be the eating. Dwell not here on entozoa, and other ramifications of the subject. I believe the above general rule to be sound in the main and sufficient for our purposes.

Wallago attu, shown in Plate XVII, is rather a long-shaped fish, fining down from the head to the tail, the head being the broadest part of the fish. The huge mouth is a mass of formidable teeth. The skin is scaleless, as it is with all the Siluridæ. This one attains to 6 feet or more in length. It affects the still deeps in rivers, and is found all along their courses, from the rocky mountain fastnesses of the Mahseer down to the estuaries, and all over India, Ceylon, and Burma, so that small fish in those parts have rather a rough time of it. It thrives well also in ponds; far too well for its companions in such limited areas, witness the 2½ lbs. fish mentioned in the chapter on Labeos as scarred by this fish. The fishing for Labeos in those ponds would have been very much improved if these voracious fish had not been there to thin their ranks.

The *Wallago attu* are to be taken with live bait picketed to the bottom in the manner and in the places mentioned in the chapter on live bait fishing for Mahseer, or by live bait attached to a float large enough to restrain the bait. I have taken them also with a live frog attached to a float; and even with a small paste bait on a small hook with fine gut line when fishing for Labeos. But this last was an accident, their formidable set of teeth indicating very clearly that gimp or wire should be used. I have known them taken with a plantain, with fowls' entrails, or a bunch of worms, and I have caught a good sized one with a spoon.

But I do not think the spoon or phantom or spun dead bait are to be relied on as a rule. I place more reliance for these fish on a stationary live bait. I do so partly because this fish is not as active in its movements as the Mahseer, and not, I think, as quick sighted. I once attributed its slowness to take a spun bait to caution, but I am inclined to think the more correct reason is deficient vision, for it has small eyes, and such long feelers that it must surely be very much dependent on them, and also on the sense of smell, for supplementing its eyesight in search of food. Living and feeding mainly at the bottom, where light is deficient, it is natural that the senses of touch and smell should be more developed than sight. You must therefore give it time, and this is best done with a stationary live bait. At the same time I should mention that I have seen them go

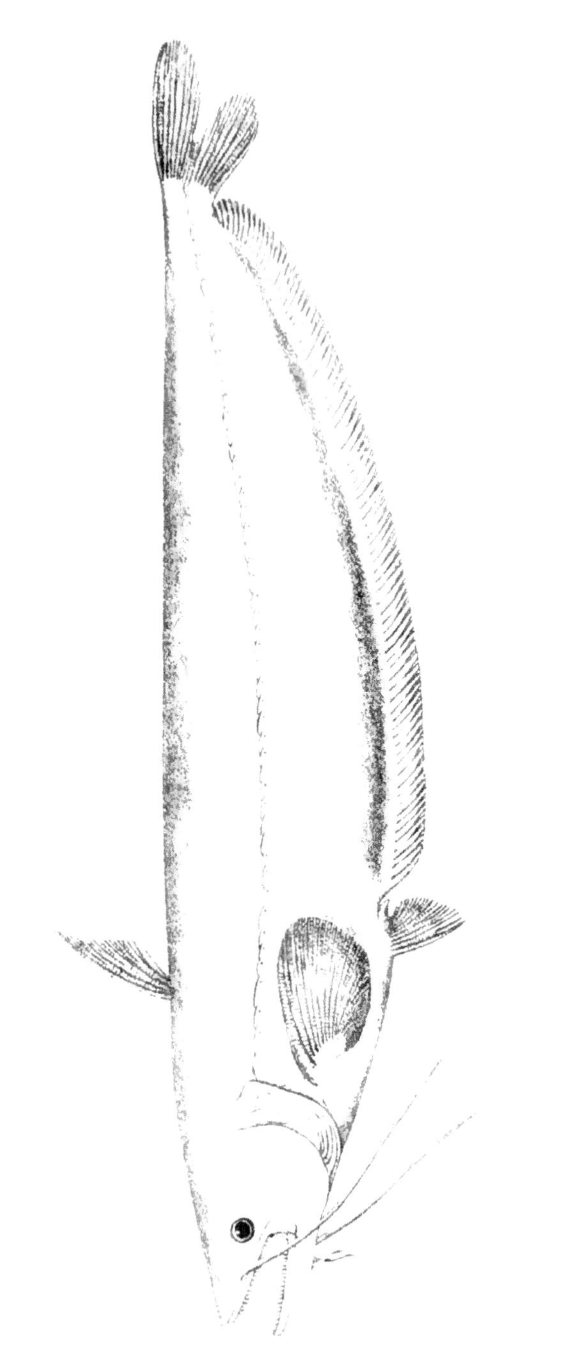

round and round a live bait, inspecting it seemingly, before taking it, and I conclude that you must be a little sparing of big hooks.

Indeed, I think it is always better to err in the direction of fishing too fine than in that of using too obviously large and numerously bristling hooks. Still, in this case, the great size of the fish must not be altogether forgotten, though against that may be set the fact that it is not as strong comparatively as the Mahseer, and cannot compare with it for an instant in the rapidity of its rush, so that you have plenty of time on your side wherewith to ease off strength by play. The terrible array of teeth not only points to the use of gimp or wire, but also indicates that you cannot expect as good a hook-hold as in the leathery-mouthed Mahseer, and had best supplement your chances with a little more hook. Still do not do it wholesale.

They do not take up a position and wait for their food to be brought to them by the stream, like Trout and Mahseer, but they roam about in search of it. I don't say they do not lie in ambush too. They affect still water.

"Doon" speaks of spearing them. Pretty poaching that, says the English salmon fisher, but fair enough, I hold, for such sharks. "Doon's" letter is quoted from the "Asian" of 28th October, 1879, in Chapter XXIV.

The Tamil name for the *Wallago attu* is *Vale*; the Hindustani, seemingly, is *Goonch*.

BAGARIUS YARRELLII.

Bagarius Yarrellii is another predatory monster siluroid, big enough surely to satisfy any one. The one shown in the annexed woodcut scaled 136 lbs., and was 5 feet 8 inches long from the lip to the end of the tail, and 5 feet to the fork of the tail; the circumference of the head being 3 feet 4 inches. The marginal drawing is taken from a photograph kindly given me by Mr. Kirkpatrick, and the fish was caught by his friend Mr. Van Cortland, in the Jumna, at Okhla, at the head works of the Agra canals, on the evening of the 11th May, 1875. The history of the capture is given in the "Field" of 24th July, 1875. It would seem that it took a "young rahoo" or *Labeo rohita*, "of 12 or 14 lbs." which was hooked foul and being played, and ejected it as fish will, in the effort to get rid of the hook, while being played. As it is probably the largest fish yet caught with a rod and line, I must present a plate giving a side view of it. Plate XVIII. The Plate is copied from Dr. Day's work.

The Punjab name seems to be *Goonch.*

SILUNDIA GANGETICA.

The same sportsmen mention in the "Asian" of the 8th of June, 1880, having caught another large Siluroid at the same place, Okhla, near Delhi, while spinning a tin minnow: "It was "very game and fought splendidly, making one magnificent rush "of over 80 yards, and being gaffed cleverly by a friend after "about three-quarters of an hour's anxious play, and before it was "quite done up." It weighed 42 lbs. and was 39 inches long without, and 47 with the tail. The native name is given as *Sinnun.* Day says it attains to 6 feet or more in length, and is

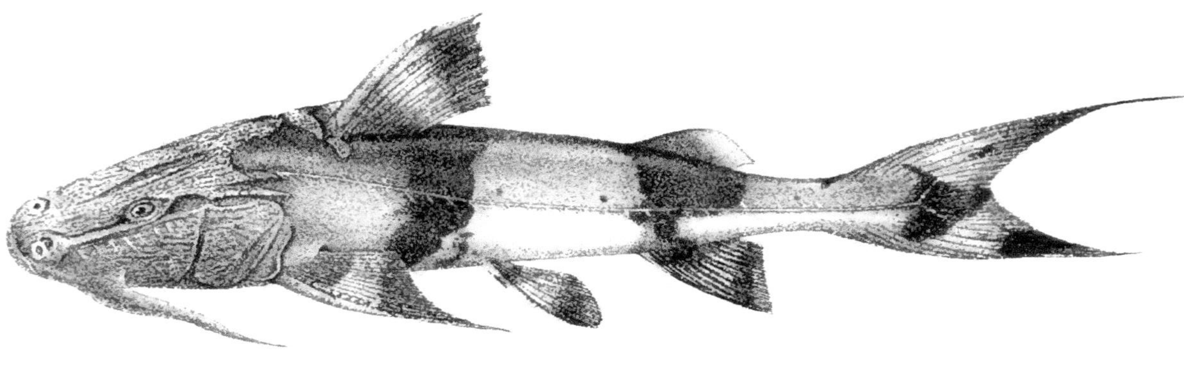

BAGARIUS YARRELLII

to be found in the estuaries to nearly the sources of the rivers of India and Burmah.

In Southern India I have not come across either of these two last fish, but that is only negative evidence, and though *Wallago attu* is much more common in the South, Dr. Day informs us that the other two are also to be found there.

There are smaller Siluroids of many sorts, notably the genus *Callichrous*, that abound in rivers and tanks, and can be taken with a float and worm. They run ordinarily under a pound, and are only fit for small boys and gluttons at fishing.

Order. PHYSOSTOMI.
Family. SILURIDÆ.
Genus. WALLAGO.
Wallago attu. B. xix–xxi, D. 5, P. 1/13–15, V. 8–10, A. 86–93 ($\frac{4}{82-89}$), C. 17, Vert. 13–56.
Genus. BAGARIUS.
Bagarius Yarrellii. B. xii, D. $\frac{1}{6}$/0, P. 1/12, V. 6, A. 13–15 ($\frac{3}{10-12}$), C. 17.
Genus. SILUNDIA.
Silundia Gangetica. B. xi–xii, D. $\frac{1}{7}$/0, P. 1/11–13, V. 6, A. 40–46 ($\frac{4}{36-42}$), C. 17.

The *Kors* (Assamese name) mentioned by Mr. J. E. Welborne, of Assam, as running within his observation to 60 lbs., and his hearsay to 100 lbs., and the *Poongah* (Assamese), seen weighing about 20 lbs., and both to be caught with live bait in the still deep waters of the Assam rivers, are evidently Siluroids, and, perhaps, the very ones above spoken of.

Mr. Welborne's plan is in pools of 30 feet deep, if possible, using for preference a $\frac{1}{4}$ lb. live bait, and even up to $\frac{1}{2}$ lb., with one treble hook beneath the back fin, and one hanging free below the stomach, and an ounce sinker 2 feet from the bait and 3 feet from the bottom, to hang the line, taut from the rod top, over the side, and let the boat be carried down the gentle stream from the head to the tail of the pool; which done, you may work up the edge of the pool and repeat the operation. He has also killed with the spoon. He thought the afternoon fishing the best. ("Asian," 22 July, and 2 September, 1879). Of *Pseudeutropius garua*, Assamese *Basa* or *Bacha*, another fish of the same family (Siluridæ), Mr. Welborne writes, in the "Asian" of 30 March, 1880:—

"The Basa (Assamese) is to be found in all the Assam rivers "towards the plains, but I am inclined to think they do not ascend "the hill streams—at least I have never caught them or seen any "that have been taken so far up. They run up to about 1½ lb., "but the average run of them would be about ½ lb. They are out "and out the finest fish for the table in the Province, and are, "moreover, game to the backbone, hence well worth the attention "of anglers. They will take either a minnow or fly freely, and "for colour, orange; wings and all. Size No. 6.* Fish for them "wherever any water or small stream runs in the main river; "an enquiry, too, from any of the local fishermen will invariably "be successful in determining their whereabouts. They spawn in "April."

The *Puftah* (Assamese *Pabho*) of the same writer is *seemingly* another fish of the same family, viz: *Callichrous bimaculatus*, or *C. pabo*, or both, but it is very uncertain; so I will not quote his letter, though he says, "capital sport" may be had with this fish; but will refer my reader to the "Asian," 10th June, 1879.

His *Sectal*, again, may be Dr. Day's *Seetul*, Assam. *Notopterus chitala*, and probably is. If I was certain I would give a drawing, but the description is not sufficiently exact to justify my doing so. His note is not long, so I will quote it, with the observation that Dr. Day's *Notopterus chitala*, has a small mouth, and silvery sides, and teeth that may have escaped notice from their being villiform or file-like, and Dr. Hamilton Buchanan says of it: "The belly is "uncommonly rich and well flavoured, but the back contains "numerous small bones," etc. Dr. Day says it "attains at least "4 feet in length," and inhabits "the fresh waters of Sind, Lower "Bengal, Orissa, Assam, Burma, and Siam to the Malay Archi-"pelago."

"The Seetal is a very handsome fish ('Asian,' 2nd September, "1879) somewhat resembling the English 'Bream' in shape, but "being much longer in the body; and instead of being a slimy beast "like the Bream, its sides are of the most silvery whiteness. It attains a

* From what scale the No. is quoted, nor of what sort it is, I know not. If from Francis Francis' Limericks, it answers to my No. 2, 0; if from Francis Francis' Sneck bends, or Kirby's, the same No. will answer on my scale.

"weight, I am told, of about 40 lbs., but the average size they are "caught by the Dhooms, in their nets, would be probably about 18 lbs. "It is not usually thought much of for the table by Europeans, but the "natives think highly of it; and I think they are right, for I know "nothing better in the fish line than the thin or belly part of this fish "fried; the back or thick part I will admit to be uneatable. The thin "part, when in condition, is covered with fat, and very rich and tasty. "This fish you will take with the live bait, and in the same kind of "water and manner of fishing as mentioned by me in my last letter;* "but he has a habit, directly he is struck, of running up right under "your boat, and you wind up, and wind up, thinking you have lost "your fish, until you are agreeably astonished with a 'whir,' 'whir,' "of your winch, and a glimpse of his bright silvery side as he goes off "with his grand rush. Take him all in all, he is a gallant fish, and "fights bravely. The only fault I find with him is, that he has such a "small mouth, consequently you strike but few. Probably, however, "with smaller hooks and bait, better sport might be had with them than "I have had; but, as a rule, fishermen naturally use such tackle in "fishing a certain water as is best suited to the majority of the fish they "expect to catch, and therefore the tackle I spoke of in my last is, I "think, the best suited for live bait fishing; and with such tackle, and "in such pools ('Dhoobies') you will probably take three each of "'Kors' and 'Poongha' to one 'Seetal,' for the reasons previously "given. I have never fished for him, so to say, exclusively, but if I "did I should use much lighter tackle, say strong salmon gut trace, "two medium size triangles, and a live bait not exceeding 6 inches; "he has no teeth on his gills to cut your tackle. I have never known "of a 'Seetal' being caught with a spoon."

* Epitomized above under *Kors* and *Poongah*.

CHAPTER XIV.

THE MURRAL.

"Ah me! what perils do environ
The man (? fish) that meddles with cold iron!"—
BUTLER'S HUDIBRAS.

HERE is another gentleman whose acquaintance is worth your cultivating, but how to write his name is the puzzler. In the absence of lucid and authoritative instructions in orthography, such as those volunteered to the judge, "Put it down a wee, my "lord, put it down a wee;" it would seem, like Samuel Weller's name, to have depended "upon the taste and fancy of the "speller."

The Murral, misspelt also marrel, murl, morrul, in the various untutored efforts to transliterate the Hindustani name, is the *Ophiocephalus*, or snake-headed, of Ichthyoligists, and the Viràl, misspelt Verarl of Tamil, *Hal Mars* of Assam, and *Curlu minu*, I am told, of Coorg, and, to make all sure, here's his honour's likeness.

His acquaintance is worth cultivating, for he grows to 2 and 3 feet in length, and is not bad eating. He is as full of bones as a pike, but then he ought to be brought to table as full of stuffing also, so that you may be of a forgiving disposition.

He is very like a pike in more ways than one. He is long-shaped like a pike; has a mouth full of teeth like a pike; like him basks in the sun at the surface, though very tolerant of cold also; and like a pike roams about at times for his food, instead of waiting stationarily behind a rock, for it to be brought down to him by the stream. This is the natural consequence of his living chiefly in ponds, and in the still pools in rivers, where there is little or no stream to bring things past a stationary object; and the consequence also of his food not being such as would naturally

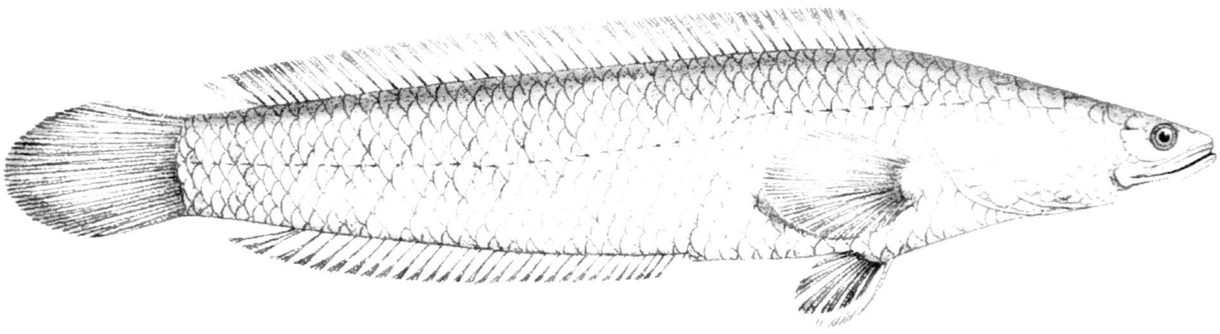

OPHIOCEPHALUS [illegible]

be washed down a stream. At times he lies hidden like a pike, and perfectly motionless behind weeds, under a bank, amongst roots, or in a hole, with just his nose out, watching for unwary little fish to swim by. It is said that they frequently have large holes in the bank in which they live in pairs coiled up. This habit of taking to earth is sometimes very inconvenient to the angler, for if he is not very prompt and very vigorous in keeping them away from the bank when hooked, they will have the line round a corner, and you may then say good-bye to all chances of recovering it, or your fish; you will have to break it. I have had a Murral run into a hole in a rock in this way, and I lost my fish, and my tackle, and my sweet temper, all at a stroke. Of the last two commodities, however, I had more in stock, and soon indented thereon.

It does not make anything like as good a fight as a Mahseer, but bores down to the bottom. When caught, keep your fingers out of his gills as well as out of his mouth.

The Murral feeds much as the pike does, and may be fished for in the same way, and with the same tackle. But whether they require clear water, as the Mahseer does, and the necessary concomitant of fine tackle, or can equally be taken when the water is coloured, I am not prepared to state, though I am *told* coloured water suits them best. The principle on which they surprise their prey is to hide themselves well.

They are, in my experience, very shy fish, and from what has been seen of their habits should be fished for, not in mid stream, but close to the banks, and under them, and in the still pools.

Morning or evening is also the time to take them; in the heat of the day they may be seen basking on the surface or close below it, and can then be shot. I have seen a native doing this very successfully. He walked up the stream like a wise man, so as to approach the basking Murral unobserved from behind, and he used a ball, and aimed always at the head. By making the head your mark, you not only injure your fish less for the table, but you make much more sure of bagging. The one that this native shot for me had the slightest mark on the off side of the head, where the ball had just grazed. Apparently the man had not allowed sufficiently for the refraction, and had very nearly missed his fish in consequence; but just a touch had been sufficient on the head, whereas a flesh wound would not have secured the fish, unless it had been so central as to break the back-bone. If you aim at the head you may even miss your fish, and the concussion of the water will stun him, if you have gone close to him. I am told they sink when killed, or stunned, as I should suppose they would. You must, therefore, have a man ready to go in after them at once.

But if you go in for fish shooting, and I would not call it poaching in India, you must allow for refraction. Refraction makes the fish appear nearer to the surface than it is—you should therefore aim below it; your ball also has a tendency not to pursue a direct course under water, but to glance upwards—another reason for aiming low. Furthermore, your ball will not take to the water kindly at all, will not do business far under the surface. I think a foot under water is the utmost distance at which you can trust it to be effective.

But to return to the rod and line. The Murral may be spun for with the same bait and tackle as has been recommended for Mahseer, except that it is well to substitute gimp for gut, because of his mouth being full of teeth. I have sometimes had my gut provokingly cut by them.

By reason of the Murral keeping mainly to the still deep pools, it can also be fished for with a live bait by those who prefer that mode of fishing. A single gimp hook of about No. 0, 1½, 1, or 2 of Limerick size, shown in my Plate,* will then be the thing; and you had best have also a float, cork, or bung, too big for your bait to take under, and, if you like, a shot or two, as generally recommended to keep your bait down; but as Murral are frequently at the surface I do not think this is necessary. Indeed, I would say fish close to the surface, as Murral feed largely on frogs, for which you may frequently see them roaming about near the surface.

A good reason for fishing near the surface, in preference to fishing deep, is to be found in the position of the Murral's eye, which is placed very high in the head, and is calculated for looking upwards rather than downwards; so that a Murral, even

* When quoting sizes to your tackle-maker, remember the caution given at page 94.

when concealing himself, by lying on the very bottom, can well see what is passing over his head, and between him and the light.

The depressed shape of the head and fore part of the Murral's body, especially of the under half, shows that it is frequently at the bottom; indeed, so depressed is the form, that it seemingly could not swim with its mouth at right angles to the perpendicular, if it was not assisted by an unusual length of dorsal and anal fin.

There are two or three ways of live baiting. There are the ordinary English ways of running the hook just under the back fin, or through the upper lip. Through the lip is unsatisfactory to my mind, both because it gives a very tender hookhold, and is liable to give way when taking your bait in and out of the water; and also because it interferes, I think, with the breathing of the bait, and kills it sooner than it need. Of course you should not adopt the clumsy way I have seen some follow, of hooking the bait right through the body near the tail, for you thereby make its movements in the water unnatural; and, I should think, soon kill it, for I am free to confess I never tried it myself. Then, again, there is the somewhat cruel way not unfrequently used with trimmers in England. Just slit the skin with a penknife, on the side, half-way down the fish, close to the gills, insert a baiting needle, and pass it carefully down the fish only just under the skin till about over the anus, when you bring it out, and draw the loop of the hook after the baiting needle till the hook is home to the entrance, and lying close against the fish. But the natives have a very neat way of baiting a live fish. They insert the hook at the anus, and pass it carefully point foremost towards the back, but only just under the skin; and when they have got it well up to the bend of the hook, they push the shank gently in up to the very head, so that the whole hook is concealed under the skin of the bait, and lies with the back of the hook towards the back of the fish, and the point towards the stomach, for the hook has had a turn given to it in the process of inserting the shank. Lastly, the hook is felt through the skin, and the cord gently pulled, so as just to bring the point through the skin of the bait. This last is a delicate operation, and serves the double object of preventing the hook from slipping out of its concealments, and of being the better prepared for hooking the fish that takes the bait. This sounds a long operation, but is very quickly done, and seems to injure the small fish but slightly. If you have gut attached to your hook there is nothing at all showing, and even if you have thinnish gimp there is very little to be seen in dirty water. The natives use what they call, in Canarese, the Bainy fibre. It is the fibre taken from the network at the base of the fronds of the sago-palm, *Caryota urens Lin.* It is less transparent than gut, but less easy to bite through, and less readily seen, I should think, than gimp. It is very capable of standing great tension, but it is brittle and liable to break across when dry, consequently it should not be coiled up too closely when put away, and should never be used without being well soaked, when it becomes quite flexible. If you will be careful, therefore, of its brittleness, you need not bemoan the absence of gimp, for you will find it a good substitute, and easily procurable for a mere song. Having live baited, you can fish with a rod, or can set trimmers after the English fashion for pike, just as you prefer.

Another way, and a paying one, to fish for Murral is to dap with a dead frog. The common little brown frog (*Rana cyanophlyctis*) is the one they like. Run the hook, No. 0 Limerick in my scale, through the head of the frog, and bring out the point only, not the barb, just through the skin under the chin; extend the legs up the line, and bind them together on it, the frog being dead. Dap the frog on and between the lillies on a pond. A stiff rod and stout line is advisable, because, among a network of lillies, you dare not give any line, but need to lift your fish straight out at once, and as they run large a stiff pole of bamboo is about the best thing you can have. The natives place the butt of the pole in a leather socket at their waist, so as to give them a leverage in using the pole.

Murral are said to take a gaudy salmon fly, and so do pike indifferently. But it is not a natural bait, and I would not recommend it.

The following plan also has been mentioned to me. In repeating it, I speak entirely without personal knowledge, not that my personal knowledge need be any better than any one else's, but that I like to be fair with my reader. Take a hook of about No. 1 Limerick size, by my sizing on Plate VIII, mounted on fine gimp;

select from the common small brown frogs, one of medium size; insert the point of the hook near the centre of the back, and get the whole bend, and as much as possible of the shank, under the skin towards the hind legs, the point remaining under the skin; tie a thread round the frog to keep the hook lying down; put a couple of big shot on, about 3 or 4 inches from the frog, and a float about 1½ feet from the frog, and throw in. My informant says the shot prevents the frog from coming up and sitting on the float, but does not prevent his coming up for air. Set the rod on the bank with a man watching.

I should have thought it would have been better to simply hook through a little skin in the back or thigh, and cast in without shot or tieing. However, I tell the tale as it was told to me. To use such fine tackle, of course, the pond must not be one of those that are completely covered with lillies. Such ponds are best suited to the previous method.

But there is yet another way of fishing for Murral which is the most killing of all. It is the native method of setting a trimmer, and is very simple and very perfect. In your large still pool look for a bush with a bough overhanging the water. You will find plenty of them, and can set an Asiatic trimmer at each. Be prepared with some live frogs in a covered earthen pot. Bait one by passing a hook in and out through a little bit of skin nearer the head than the centre of the back. The way in which a frog sits naturally in the water is not on the flat of its stomach, like a duck, but with just its eyes out, and its hind legs well under water. By inserting the hook a little forward of the centre of the back, you not only give the frog this natural attitude, but you also relieve it of inconvenience by letting its weight be borne by the water, not by the hook. Be careful you do not touch anything but the veriest skin, and bear in mind old Izaak Walton's famous injunction to "treat him tenderly as if you loved him." The skin is easily taken up like the loose skin of a dog. Then reach out, and pass the line over a fork in the overhanging bough, the object of the fork being to keep the line off the shore, and then lower away your frog till he just sits comfortably and naturally on the surface of the water, unsuspended by the hook, his weight really being on the water, and yet without an inch of slack line. Then make fast to any convenient object on the shore, giving, as aforesaid, no slack line at all. You may leave it to do its work while you go away and tie a dozen more, or spin, or smoke the pipe of peace.

The Murral feeds largely on frogs, and sailing quietly about, looking for them, as his habit sometimes is, he comes upon your bait, and, as it is thoroughly natural, of course takes it.

> "Ah me! what perils do environ
> The *fish* that meddles with cold iron."

He has to go through a severe course of steel before he has done with it. As there is no slack line at all, he is struck the moment he has taken the bait; the line is taut on him, and he is seen flapping about, with his head half out of water. You have consequently no need to be constantly examining your trimmers, as you can see, from a quarter of a mile off, a great fish flapping and splashing on the top of the water.

As there is no play whatever given to the fish, but a dead pull from the moment he is hooked, it follows that your line and hook must be strong—must be much stronger than it would be necessary to use on a rod. A single hook of about the size of a No. 4/0 or 3/0 Limerick hook will do very well; but a good strong treble hook is perhaps a trifle better. It should be tied on a piece of the stoutest pike gimp; the natives use a bit of copper or brass wire, which does very well. The line can be any piece of good stout twine. You need not be nervous about its being seen by the fish, for the manner of baiting is such that there is nothing whatever to be seen in the water, and the hook, be it ever so big in reason, cannot be seen, because it is thoroughly screened by the frog, which is in a direct line between your hook and the fish to be taken. Of cord, too, there is only about a foot or two, hanging in a motionless straight line directly down to the frog, by which again it is mainly hidden; it is also generally difficult to see in the shade of the bush.

The whole method of baiting is so simple and so effective, that it might be adopted with advantage for pike in England, for they also have a tooth for frog, though not quite such an one perhaps as the Murral:—

> "But John P.
> Robinson. He
> Sez they did'nt know everything down in Judee."

So the little wrinkle is thrown out.

In shallow edged tanks with no overhanging bushes the same method is adapted by a native wading in nearly up to his armpits, with three thin pieces of bamboo, which he sticks into the mud, with their bases well apart and their tops together, so as to form a tripod; and from the point where they meet he drops his frog just as he did from the fork of the overhanging bough, and the other end of the line is made taut on the shore. One man ordinarily manages three such lines, radiating out from the point where he sits on the shore, to spots 20 or 30 yards apart in the tank. He has one under each foot so as to be able to feel with his bare foot the twitch of a bite, and he has one in one hand. He cannot manage more. Does'nt he just wish he was *centimanus Gyas.* If the tank is covered with weeds, a small clearing is made for the tripod and bait, and though this may disturb the locality while baiting it does not matter. A mole cricket tied to the hook, not impaled, and dapped all alive and kicking, is said to be irresistible. I can quite believe it. But surely it should be among lillies. In rivers I have killed with a spoon also. Cockroaches are also used for such fishing, but in what exact method I cannot say positively, for I have no note; my memory is that they are impaled on the hook, as cockchafers are for chub in England, and cockroaches certainly are wonderfully tenacious of life in a hot climate. I know, however, that you may safely repose confidence in a frog.

Ah me! who would be a frog? To "lead the life of a dog" is nothing to leading the life of a frog. On land mongooses, snakes, kites, crows, rats, larger frogs, and battalions of paddy birds, go in at him greedily. In the water the Murral feeds almost entirely on him, lying *perdu* under the banks for the purpose; while the water-snake follows him in both elements. But the verdict is "serve him right," for he is a fry-eater and a spawn-eater, and he is irrepressible, getting up drunken choruses all over the country directly there is a good fall of rain, and he has had a wet night of it. It is truly disreputable: and then he is so greedy. I had some in a can, together with other bait, when what should I see but one of these "glutinous" ruffians improving his opportunities by endeavouring to swallow a bait longer than his own body. He had the head and shoulders and half the body down his "sarcophagus or elementary canal" and was holding on to it sulkily, while the fish's tail was wagging gaily. I pulled poor fishy out, when froggy straightway went at him, and half swallowed him again. You see what an incorrigible brute he is, so put him into your can, and be off with him to the haunts of the Murral without any compunction.

A frog swallows a frog head foremost, a snake swallows a frog legs foremost, the little frog in both positions calling out lustily the while, and the operation in both cases being a protracted one, the placid impurterbability of the swallower contrasting markedly with the gesticulating vehement oratory of the swallowed. While the big frog, *Rana tigrina*, was swallowing the little frog, *Rana cyanophlyctis*, head foremost, the little brown fellow kicked all he knew, very little more than his hind legs being out, and from cavernous depths shouted in sepulchral tones Police! Police!! Police!!! Being a J. P., I stopped to know what the row was about. *Rana tigrina* had not a word to say for himself, and moved not a muscle of his impassive countenance, much less stirred hand or foot. As in duty bound I eventually interposed and freed the little one. He was not injured in the least, only a little frightened! Considering his character, I think I should have done better had I let the urchin alone.

The Murral lives a long time without water, and can therefore be taken home alive, and consequently fresh.

The reason for this is that, unlike most fish which breathe only the oxygen contained in solution in the water, the *Ophiocephalidæ* inhale the atmospheric air direct. They may be seen coming up to the surface continually, exhaling a bubble and taking in a mouthful of fresh air, and they have an air cavity for the storage of the fresh air. If confined in a globe or other vessel with a net stretched across a little below the surface of the water, so as to prevent them from breathing the atmospheric air direct, they will die from not being able to oxygenate their blood, however fully supplied with oxygen the water may be. Being thus able to breathe our air, and being commonly dependent on it, they do not suffer like other fish on being transferred to it. Indeed, they travel on land of their own accord, and any one allowed to jump out of your can or tub of water will soon be seen to wriggle a considerable distance on land, and to keep it up long after any of the carps would be dead. They are among the fish that have been known to bury themselves in the mud at the bottom of drying rivers and ponds, æstivating there through the drought till the next rains release them. They have been dug alive out of the sun-burnt mud.

The *Ophiocephalus gacua*, which I have mentioned above as a tough bait, is one of this family, therefore easy to keep alive in a can, and not to be picketed to the bottom.

As the Murral can ordinarily be taken home alive, the flesh remains firm.

The Murral will thrive in ponds, and at various altitudes, so you can easily stock a pond if you desire, but they will speedily depopulate it of other sorts. The natives frequently put them into their wells, from which they can take them fresh and fresh as they want them.

The Murral, unlike most fish, exhibits parental affection towards its young, keeping them together in a shoal, and swimming under them, and attacking anything that comes near them. This it does till they are about 3 inches long, when it turns on and eats them itself, if they do not disperse.

The Murral, I have said, is similar in many respects to the pike. I must be allowed, therefore, to tell here a little story of a pike, a story that will bear re-telling, and will serve to enliven the dulness of my page. I quote it from Scrope's "Nights and Days of Salmon Fishing," a work that is, I believe, out of print, hence I snatch the story from oblivion:—

"A friend of mine (sacred be his name) of great repute for his "dexterity with the rod, and celebrated for his agreeable and amiable "qualities, as well as for his intelligence and various accomplishments, "had this poetical facility for seeing what really did not exist in "substance. A curious instance of this popular talent occurred at a "friend's house in the country with whom he was staying. There "was a fine piece of water in the park, well stored with fish, where he "used to spend the greater part of the morning, rod in hand; so that "his perseverance excited considerable admiration from the host, as "well as from his guests. Not having been very successful, his "ardour at length began to flag. It was a pity, for it is a pleasant "thing to be excited. What was to be done? You shall see. A "report was raised that there was an enormous pike seen in the "water, about the length of a decent sized alligator. He was said to "have maimed a full grown swan, and destroyed two cygnets, besides "sundry ducks. At first he was no more believed in than the "great sea-snake, which encloses at least half the world in his folds. "But after the lapse of a few days the keeper came to the private "car of my friend, and told him that a *mortal* large pike was basking "amongst some weeds and could be seen plainly. 'You are sure to "'catch 'im, Sir.' He was rewarded for this intelligence and exhorted "to keep the important secret from the other visitors at the mansion.

"When piscator, cunning fellow! thought that all were out of the "way, employed in hunting, shooting, or some other occupation, "he and John Barnes, the keeper, glided down secretly to the "awful spot, and they there discovered the semblance of a fish so "enormous that it was doubted if anything less than a small rope "could hold him. The sportsman was astounded; the keeper was not, "for the said awful animal was nothing more than a large painted "piece of wood, carved deftly by himself into the shape of a pike, "painted according to order, and stuck in the natural position by "means of a vertical prop, which could not be discovered amongst the "weeds. It was too bad, really a great deal too bad; but tolerably "ingenious and beautifully deceptive. The gentleman approached "with tact and caution, and the eyes of the fish glared upon him; as "well they might, for they were large and dazzling, being made of "glass and originally designed to be inserted in a great horned owl, "which the keeper had stuffed.

"'What a prodigious fish, John!'

"'Very prodigious indeed, Sir.'

"'What eyes he has!'

"'So he has, Sir.'

"'I'll try him with a roach. There, it went in beautifully, but he "'did not move.'

"'No! he won't take it nohow. Give him a frog; he seems a "'difficult fish.' Piscator did tender him a very lively one in vain: "in short, he offered him every bait he could possibly think of, running "through all the devices and temptations he was master of. Cautious "in his approaches, that the supposed fish might not see him, he "always advanced to make his cast upon his knees, to the no small "amusement of his friends who were looking at him with a telescope "from a window of the mansion. Well, thus he spent the whole "evening, waiting, however, at times, for a cloud to intercept the sun-"beams, and a breath of air to ruffle the surface of the lake. When "these came he would set to work with renovated hopes, till at last, "tired and discomfited, he bent his steps homewards. On his arrival "there, he was accosted on the very threshold by some of the guests.

"'Oh! you have been fishing all the morning, I see: but what "could make you stay out so long, and get away so cunningly with "the keeper?'

"'Why, to tell you the truth, Barnes (you know what a good "'creature he is) told me of an immense pike that was lying among "'the weeds at the end of the lake: he must be the same that swallowed "'the cygnets. I never saw so enormous a monster in fresh water.'

"*Omnes.*—'Well, where is he, where is he? let us look at him.'

"*Host.*—'John, tell the cook we will have him for dinner to-day, "'Dutch sauce, remember.'

"*Piscator.*—'You need not be in such a hurry to send to the cook, "'for I am sorry to say I did not catch him.'

"*Host.*—'Not catch him, not catch him? Impossible! with all "'your skill, armed as you are to the teeth with roach, bleak, minnow, "'frogs, kill-devils, and the deuce knows what. Not catch him! Come, "'you're joking.'"

"*Piscator.* 'Serious, I assure you. I never was so beat before, and "'yet I never fished better: but though I did not absolutely hook him, "'*he ran at me several times.*'

"An universal shout of laughter followed this assertion, which "made my friend not a little suspicious: but he never again touched "upon the subject. Sometime afterwards, wandering near the scene "of his operations, he saw an immense carving of a pike, placed upon "a pole, near the margin of the water, and painted beautifully; he "guessed he had seen him before!"

There are nine *Ophiocephali*, of which four attain to about 3ft. long each, and one to 4 ft. These larger *Ophiocephali* are commonly called Murrals. Of these five, then, I will quote abbreviated descriptions from Dr. Day's "Fishes of India," omitting the others, except *O. Gachua*, mentioned above as a good bait.

Order. ACANTHOPTERIGII.

Family. OPHIOCEPHALIDÆ.

GENUS. OPHIOCEPHALUS.

Ophiocephalus marulius. B. V. D. 45–55, P. 18, V. 6, A. 28–36, C. 14, Ll. 60–70, L. tr. $\frac{4\frac{1}{2}-6\frac{1}{2}}{13-11}$ or [illegible] Ceylon and India to China. 4 feet.

O. leucopunctatus. B. V. D. 47–53, P. 18, V. 6, A. 28–35, C. 14, Ll. 50–60, L. tr. $\frac{4\frac{1}{2}-6\frac{1}{2}}{11-13}$ or [illegible] Southern India. 3 feet.

O. barca. B. V. D. 47–52, P. 16, V. 1/5, A 34–36, C. 19, Ll. 60–65, L. tr. [illegible] Bengal, N.W. Provinces, Assam. 3 feet.

O. micropeltes. B. V., D. 43–46, P. 15, V. 1/5, A. 27–30, C. 15. Ll. 95–110, L. tr. $\frac{7\text{-}8}{13\text{-}12}$ Vert. 53 .West Coast of India, Siam to the Malay Archipelago. 3 feet.

O. striatus. B. V., D. 37–45, P. 17, V. 6, A. 23–26, C. 13, Ll. 50–57, L. tr. $\frac{4\frac{1}{2}\text{-}7}{9\text{-}7}$ or $\frac{5\frac{1}{2}\text{-}8}{10\text{-}9}$. Vert. 13/39. India, Ceylon, Burma, China, Phillippines. 3 feet.

O. gachua. B. V., D. 32–37, P. 15, V. 6, A. 21–23, C. 12, Ll. 40–45, L. tr. $\frac{3\frac{1}{2}}{7\text{-}8}$. India, Ceylon, Burma, Andamans. 13 inches.

CHAPTER XV.

EELS.

"The imperious seas breed monsters; for the dish
Poor tributary rivers as sweet fish."—
SHAKESPERE.

THESE fellows are not much in my line. I confess I hate the sight of them; for if ever you see eels lounging about the bottom of a river in England, like so many coastguardsmen expecting foul weather, you may be sure the trout will not rise. How could they be expected to in such low company! And if you have the bad luck to hook one, he just behaves like an excited cork-screw, till he has got your line into so many knots and kinks, that it will take you a month of Sundays to unravel it. And then as to unhooking him. Oh! don't talk of it.

But some think them good eating, and like to catch them, so we will give them a page or so, grudgingly.

Of spined and unspined eels you will find, in Dr. Day's work, 47 species, under the families, *Rhyncobdellidæ*, *Symbranchidæ*, and *Murænidæ*; but many are small and the last-named are almost all marine, and of the others many are tidal. The only ones worthy of the angler's notice seem to be my old friend *Masatcemblus armatus*, which runs, to my knowledge, to about 2 feet in length, and *Anguilor Bengalensis*, which Dr. Day says runs to 4 feet in length, and has been introduced into the Neilgherries. This is probably the fish of which Colonel Parsons caught, by his live bait method, one weighing 18 lbs.

Their flavour is much esteemed by some Europeans, and the natives in your camp are always very glad to get them. It is as well, therefore, to know how to catch them, and as they are easily caught, your servants can be allowed to do this much for themselves, if you will be at the trouble to provide them with the simple tackle necessary, and the bait, which in any case you would have to throw away at the end of the day from its being dead. They will afford *them* a good meal, and *you* beaming countenances to look upon!

The plan is to set night lines with dead fish. Take your dead bait of 4 inches more or less in length, and string one on to a common double eel hook on wire, by passing the baiting needle down the throat and out at the centre of the tail, and drawing your hook after it till the hooks are well home to the mouth of the bait. Then attach the hook to the line, and having tied a bullet or other good sized sinker to the line, throw it well into the middle of any good, large, deep, still pool; make well fast to the shore, and leave it all night. If you have set half-a-dozen of these, you will probably find two or three eels on in the morning.

These common double eel hooks are to be bought in India. Oakes and Co., at Madras, have them, and so doubtless have the tackle shops in Northern India and Bombay. But a neater arrangement is a common pike gorge hook, because there you have the weight neatly stowed away inside your bait; and the hooks are shaped so as to sit closely against the mouth of a bait, and consequently to go comfortably down the throat. *Facilis descensus Averno est.* But as to coming up again, *sed revocare gradum*, that's quite another business.

Your night line must be a good stout one, and well made fast, for the fish is strong, very strong, and has the whole night to himself to work his wicked will.

They are all fish-eaters, so the more your servants catch, the better for the little Mahseer, the youthful *Barils*, and the unsophisticated young of the other sorts of game fly-taking fish. Encourage them, therefore, to go in at them heavily, and show them how to draw the hook home so as to lie neatly against the lips of the bait, and so, in fact, that it shall offer no obstacle to a fish that gradually swallows your bait head foremost.

Be wary how you handle *Mastacembli* because of the sharp spines on their backs. Their fry may be seen in the rice fields. They are widely distributed.

I see no *sport* in this style of fishing.

CHAPTER XVI.

FISHING ON THE NEILGHERRIES.

"We care not who says,
And intends it dispraise,
That an angler to a fool is next neighbour;
Let him prate; what care we?
We're as honest as he;
And so let him take that for his labour." —
COTTON.

THE fishing on the Neilgherries is poor to a degree, while with several such fine lakes it might be very good. It is a thousand pities that, with the exception of Dr. Day's intelligent action, all the admirable energy that has been displayed in stocking the Neilgherries with fish has taken the mistaken direction it has. To go all the way to England for the common carp was truly a sad waste of most laudable enterprise and painstaking perseverance, for the carp is only an imported fish in England, and attains but a slight weight there comparatively, with a very poor flavour, and yields next to no sport; whilst India is itself the very paradise of carps of numerous sorts, from 200 lbs. downwards; carps that are much better eating, that propagate and grow more rapidly, and, moreover, afford excellent sport to the angler with fly, spoon, live bait, or bottom fishing, as may happen to be preferred by the weary health-seeker of the chief sanitarium of Southern India, Ootacamund. How large the carp grow at Ootacamund I do not know, careful netting only could tell us. Fishermen there have told me certainly of lines carried away by them, but then their lines were very frail ones, unsupplemented by reels, and the fish that broke them might quite as well have been the Carnatic Carp put in by Dr. Day. All the fish I have seen taken there, whether by rod or net, were miserable little things, of about 3 ozs. in weight, and I have seen two or three drags made by the authorities, on purpose to try and discover if there were any decent fish. Miserable little carp of this size swarm, and choke the water in the Ootacamund and the Lovedale Lakes. They ought to be kept within bounds by constant netting; and, if sold in the weekly markets, would probably find purchasers enough among the natives to pay for their capture, and to create a fund for the improvement of the fishery; for a little fresh fish diet of any sort would be very highly relished on the Neilgherries, where at present it cannot be had *really fresh* for any price. But the fishing should not be let on contract, but conducted systematically under the superintendence of some trustworthy person or persons deputed by the municipality, or by a committee of gentlemen-residents interested in improving the fishery. All Tench and Carnatic Carp should be carefully replaced, so as not to injure the rod fishing, from which source some slight revenue is now derived by means of rod licences. Anglers would soon find that such systematic netting would improve, not injure, their chances of sport. It would give the Tench a better chance of increasing in size and numbers, but especially in size. At present they seem to be a good deal starved out by the Carp.

The Tench, the only other fish I have *seen* in the Ootacamund Lake, were likewise brought at great pains and expense from England; whereas the Indian rivers teem with fish of a more or less similar nature that far excel it in size, flavour, prolificacy, adaptation to the climate, and sport for the angler. I allude to the Labeos, running to 3 feet and 5 feet in length, and very thick fish for their length. Some of these might have been very easily brought from the river running at the foot of those same hills, and might even now be thus brought and introduced with advantage.

Lochleven Trout are said to have been introduced into the Pykara stream by the late Mr. McIvor. I never saw one alive in India, nor did Dr. Day, and their existence has been very much questioned; but the one fish, said by Mr. McIvor to have been caught with five others by his men near Pykara, and sent by him to me in spirits, just as I was going down the Ghat, on the 12th October, 1875, had bright red spots, as if quite fresh then. I had only just time hurriedly to wrap it in white muslin so as to bear the journey better, and to replace it in the spirits till I should reach the end of my journey. At my first leisure I examined the fish, on the 22nd October, 1875, and found that much of the vermilion in the spots was lost, and on the 25th November none was traceable. This was certainly a Lochleven Trout. It was sent home by me under seal, was examined before the Linnæan Society, and is figured in Dr. Day's "Fishes of India" as a Lochleven Trout. Trout not having been seen alive on the Neilgherries before, or traced since, by any one that was prepared to depose to an adipose fin, and that, too, in spite of much effort, some have suggested that this trout came to me not from Pykara, but from Lochleven. Pennel says, however, that in Lochleven the trout have no red spots, and the presence of red spots in this individual would seem to be the result of its being bred in the clear Pykara stream. The first freshness and subsequent fading of the vermilion spots should also serve to satisfy the sceptical that the specimen was caught where it was said to be caught. These two facts satisfied me. And a friend who saw the fish with the vermilion spots fresh was so satisfied that he backed his belief with coin, the crucial test! Still a Commissioner there, who was a keen fisherman, made every effort to discover more of them, but failed. He wished to put them, a lake trout, into the Ootacamund Lake, for their better protection and growth. If they could be got into a lake, these trout would flourish better and be safer than in the Pykara stream, where they are liable to be poached; and it is the greatest pity that all the energy and pains-taking perseverance which brought out the fry should have ended in putting them into the wrong place. If they had only been put into the Ootacamund Lake to begin with, and had it all to themselves, the carp and tench being pitched into the sea, what fishing we should have had there by this time, and what a source from which to stock the other Neilgherry Lakes with acclimatized trout.

Possibly they were put in the Pykara River under the impression that trout cannot breed except in a stream, running water being necessary to the sufficient oxygenation of the ova. This idea is held, I believe, by not a few. Doubtless trout will not breed except in a stream, if they can help it, but it is not that they cannot. It is only because their instincts tell them to prefer the stream, for the very same reason as a Mahseer's instincts, and we may say a salmon's also, impel it to seek the higher streams, for the deposit of the ova in positions best suited, not only to its hatching, but also to the prosperity of the fry. Whether intentionally, or of what is called instinct, the prudent trout and Mahseer exercise parental forethought how they put their young people out in the world. Lake trout lay their ova in the stream, but then fall back themselves into the lake. Thus the fry have much better chances of escaping being eaten than if they were reared in the lake, in the midst of their own and everybody else's hungry parents. Fancy eating your own children, and not finding it out till all too late, by the peculiar taste, not till

"In those mutton pies,
You do recognise,
The flavour of your old dog Tray."

That is what trout do, and that is why they spawn in the stream in preference to the lake. But that they can breed in a lake there is no room for doubt, witness the hundreds of small tarns and bog-holes fed by no superficial drainage, only by percolation from adjoining morasses. Those places are full of trout that have bred there for ages. In such places more of the fry may be eaten in immaturity, but the extraordinary fertility of fish allows of numbers surviving the extra risks. The Ootacamund Lake has

THE OOTACAMUND LAKE.

enough of shallow, shelving, gravelly bottom to form excellent spawning ground for trout; and that done, the law of chances in so large a lake may well be trusted to for enough of survivals.

If even now the trout could be caught in the Pykara stream, and as many as half a dozen at least put together into the Ootacamund Lake, so as to be pretty sure of having both sexes, there might still be some hope of eventually getting good sport in the Hill Lakes. I am not unaware of the arguments for and against the possibility of trout breeding in such a climate as the Neilgherries, a very different thing from their breeding in the plains of India, which is of course out of the question. But the matter seems now to have passed beyond the region of argument into that of fact. If trout are introduced into the Ootacamund Lake, it will be advisable to make a little elbow room for them, by some netting out of the diminutive carp that choke the lake. It is not that carp would injure trout, but that they breed faster, and would monopolize the available food.

By way of improving the trout struggling for existence in the Pykara stream, a certain gentleman, and he a fisherman too, I will not name him lest anglers should "Boycot" him, was at much pains to introduce into that stream Murral, the Indian Pike!! and was proud of the achievement, and was abetted in it too!!! Ah me! how those poor Hills have suffered from misdirected energies. It is to be hoped no one will be energetic enough to put them or Freshwater Sharks into any of the lakes.

Dr. Day, however, did good work there, as might be expected. He introduced from the rivers at the foot of the Hills, the *Barbus Carnaticus*, my fine fly-taking friend of Chapter X. It is flourishing in the Billikal Lake, the owner of which, Mr. Thomas Kaye, told me, in September, 1875, that he saw the big fish spawning on the shallows of the lake, sixteen at a time, and that they rose best to the fly in the N.E. monsoon, after and in a shower; that they took butterflies, when he threw them in, and tried at swallows. He had shot 3 lb. fish, and had seen them 4 feet long in the water. He heard them splashing from his bungalow, which is two or three hundred yards away from the lake. He preserves well from netting, and is kindly about allowing gentlemen anglers to fish. But alas! alas! he had put in the small English carp from Ootacamund in 1874. The Carnatic Carp are believed to be also in the

Ootacamund Lake, at any rate they are now thoroughly acclimatized in Billikal Lake.

I paid one day's visit to the Billikal Lake, which is about 6 miles from Ootacamund, but could catch none, because the big fish keep to the deep water, and are unapproachable without a boat. Anyone essaying them there should have a basket boat brought up from the low country, or try the deep water near the embankment, bottom fishing if he cares to. The existence there of the Carnatic Carp would seem to say that if they have borne the change of climate to that elevation, and have got acclimatized to it, they will probably bear it on to Ootacamund from thence, even if they do not bear it direct from the plains.

The Billikal Lake swarms with the little indigenous *Rasbora daniconius.* It only attains to 8 inches, but it rises *very freely indeed* to the smallest fly you can use, and may serve excellently to teach schoolboys to throw a fly, and to feed bigger fish. They thrive very well there in company with the Carnatic Carp, but they cannot stand the common carp, seemingly.

There is no doubt that Labeos will thrive on the Neilgherries, for I sent some fry to a friend, and they lived and grew well in his pond, till a clever coolie let off all the water, and they went into the coffee pulper.

If they will live on the hills one might hope that the *Cirrhina cirrhosa*, or White Carp, mentioned in Chapter XII, would also thrive there.

Barils would not thrive in the still water of the lakes, but Chela might. The Gourami, of which more hereafter, has been tried and died from, it is said, the cold.

But with Carnatic Carp, White Carp, several Labeos, Chela, and Tench, very fair fishing might be had in the Lakes at and about Ootacamund. With so many residents at, and so many visitors to, this the largest sanitarium in Southern India, and a fishery act in existence, something surely could be done to improve the fishing, and thus to contribute to the health and amusement of not a few.

As to the fish already there, the manner of capturing them may be dismissed in very few words.

The Carnatic Carp has already been treated of in Chapter X and above. Of *Rasbora daniconius* enough has been said. There remain the English Carp (*Cyprinus carpio*), and Tench (*Tinca vulgaris*).

The English carp are very difficult to take with the rod. They are the fox of the waters for cunning. The plan, however, is to use fine gut and light quill float, with small shot about a foot from the hook, No. 6 or 7 Kirby size, not larger. Let the shot rest on the bottom, just tilting the float. Bait with paste, worms, or gentils, ground-baiting with the same mixed with clay and bran. Keep out of sight and quiet, and strike when the float moves off, not before. Ephemera says they rarely reach 6 lbs. in rivers, and 12 lbs. in ponds in England; while other writers say they grow to twice those weights, and even more in warmer climates than England. Let us *hope*, therefore, that they really do grow to a respectable size on the Neilgherries, with their sub-tropical clime, and that we have seen only little ones because they are the most easily caught. To catch these little ones with a rod and line is a very simple matter for any boy that thinks it worth doing, but to catch the big foxy ones wants ground-baiting and very quiet and very fine fishing. Ground-bait two or three likely holes, and keep ringing the changes on them, moving from one to another to let it quiet down after landing a fish. Rest your rod on a forked twig or otherwise so as to keep quiet.

Tench should be fished for in the same manner, or with the bait just off the ground, the bait being a well-scoured brandling. Though captious feeders, they are much freer biters than carp. They seldom exceed 5 lbs. or 6 lbs. in weight; 2 lbs. is a common weight. I have boyish memories of fair fun with them. They are somewhat more palatable than the common carp. A pond may be full of them, and the existence of a single one never be suspected because they are undemonstrative, and keep about the bottom. I sent some fry to the Shevaroy Hills in June, 1878, and they were safely turned into the smaller lake there. Tench bear carriage remarkably well.

CHAPTER XVII.

FISHING IN ESTUARIES.

"There is a tide in the affairs of men,
Which, taken at the flood, leads on to fortune.
*　　*　　*　　*　　*
And we must take the current when it serves
Or lose our ventures."—
JULIUS CÆSAR.

ALL fishing in estuaries is very much, and I am inclined to think entirely, governed by the tides, except, *perhaps*, when monsoon floods somewhat modify calculations by overpowering the tides, and except in the months when the tides of putrid-smelling sea water set in; then the fish are sickened. But the tides seem to affect different fish differently, so that it is a very difficult matter to work out to a satisfactory conclusion. I have noticed fish taking freely at the very commencement of the flow in an estuary, while not a few fishermen agree that certain fish take best during the latter part of the ebb tide.

I am inclined to think that the former are chiefly the rock-fish *Lutianus roseus*, and *Chrysophris datnia*, and *C. berda*, and sometimes *Lates calcarifer*. The latter are the well-known *Bámin* of the Malabar coast, *Polynemus tetradactylus*. The latter go to sea with every tide, I believe, whereas the former do not leave the estuaries, I think; and this difference in their habits may well account for a difference in their time of feeding.

Watching an estuary I noticed that when I first came to the spot all was quiet, not a fish was moving. Then the tide turned to flow, and I saw all along the edge of the river, between me and the sea, heavy fish rushing at smaller fish, and making great swirls on the surface; when they came opposite me, the place was alive with big fish striking little ones; but it did not last more than a quarter of an hour: with the advancing tide the swirls passed upwards, and I could plainly watch their course into the far distance. It was clear that the text at the head of the chapter was closely applicable, and it came into one's mind at once

> "There is a tide in the affairs of *fish*,
> Which, taken at the flood, leads on to fortune."

It was not the same at the ebb tide. It was only at the commencement of the flood tide that the fish were moving. These fish were, I am inclined to think, the rock-fish mentioned above, and sometimes *Lates calcarifer*.

But why is it, you will want to know, that the big fish in estuaries cannot be content to feed in one place, like the big fish in the rivers above tidal influence? Why is it that they must be for ever advancing with the advancing tide? You want a reason, and I will give you one. If you place yourself on a projecting rock, or stone-jetty, and watch the first flow of the in-coming tide, you will see innumerable shoals of minute fish, from an inch long and upwards, coasting busily up the river.* They are near the surface, and you can see them well. Keep motionless, and as much out of sight as you can, that you may not frighten them or anything else, but may see them pursuing their natural course. How pretty and sociable they look. Dash into them goes a huge open-mouthed ruthless-looking monster, and makes a cruel gap in their closely packed column. It is pitiful to behold. Poor little things, how like they are to soldiers when a great round shot has torn through their ranks. They close up again and press on

> "They fill
> The ranks unthinned though slaughtered still."

* They coast, because there is always a back-draught, or back-flow of water, at the edge of every stream, in the opposite direction to the main current of the stream, and caused by the stream carrying down, by friction, water that must return to fill up the vacuum it left as soon as it is released from the power of the friction that removed it. This backwater (not to be confounded with the common Indian name for an estuary), is constant in all rivers throughout their length, and the tide on entering a river, and while still contending with the current of the stream, takes first advantage of this *backwater*, and accelerates it, till merged in the general inflow of the tide. Small fish wishing to ascend a river take advantage of this backwater, which is always running up each shore, and thus by coasting they get up a river, without having to swim against the stream.

Dash goes another monster, or, perhaps, the same one, and again there is an obvious gap. "Close up, close up," is the word, and so they keep pressing on up stream, apparently very much frightened, but still unwavering in their purpose of pressing on up the river, with all their little strength. What their purpose is in resolutely struggling up stream, and whether they are small fish or fry I am not certain; but I have a strong suspicion that they are the minute fry of mullet, which, I am assured by native fishermen, ascend and descend for the sake of food with every tide, and which I know are caught in large numbers by taking advantage of this their habit as mentioned in para. 122 of Chapter XXV. When they have passed the fish cease taking. Whether it is because the big fish have followed the little ones, or have turned their attention to other food, as trout will when the rise is over, I cannot say; but that it is no use fishing for them I can say.

For the brief period that the small fish are passing, you will have excellent sport. Put on a dead fish, and spin as for jack, with stout hooks on gimp. Gut will not do, it will be cut through in a trice. The gimp, too, must be stout. I have had every available bit of tackle broken by successive fish in twenty minutes. But then I was learning: I was buying my experience a great deal dearer than you will buy this book. But I have made the fish pay for it eventually, for, when a shoal has been passing, I have taken toll of them as fast as ever I could land them and throw in my line. It is "a short life and a merry one." Have good stout gimp and let there be two trebles, besides the lip hook, on your flight of hooks, instead of only one treble as for Mahseer. The fishes' mouths are hard, and closely set with teeth, so that it is as well to have the extra chance of an extra hook.

POLYNEMUS.

But the best fish to be caught in estuaries is the *Polynemus tetradactylus*, Plate XX, well known to sportsmen on the West Coast by its Malayalim name, *Bă-mīn*, pronounced Băr-meen, and all too well known for its tackle-breaking propensities. "They "eat an astonishing lot of phantoms," writes a friend, bemoaning his tackle. The fish I spoke of in my first edition as the Pámban

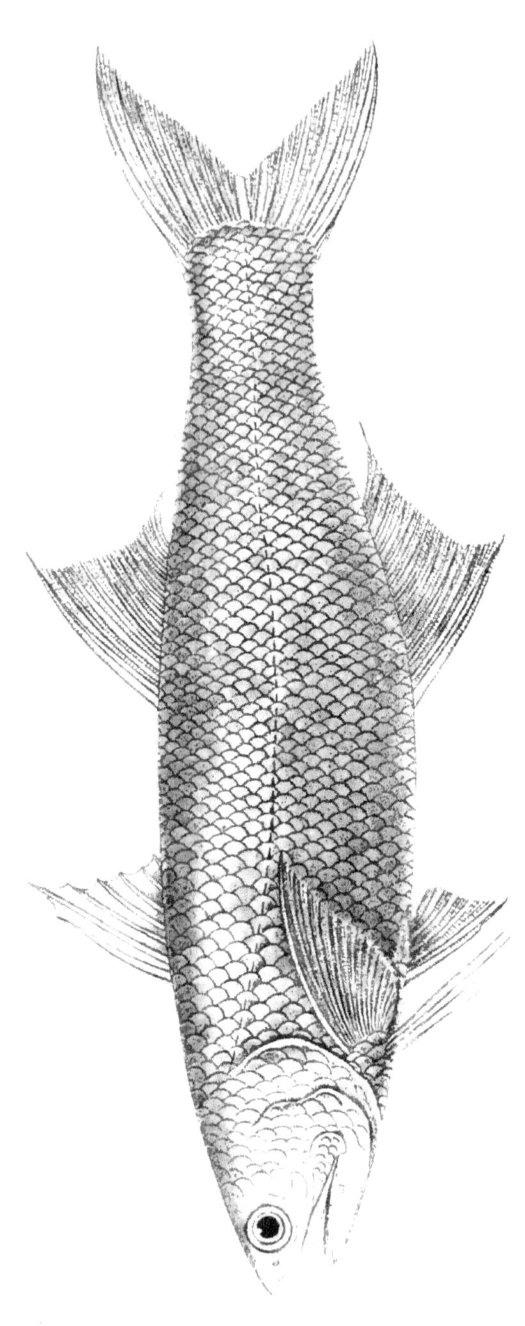

salmon is either this same fish or *Polynemus Indicus.* I have caught and seen them caught with a fly at Pámban, and seen thousands netted at sea, and seen them, unfortunately, only when they were sick and unfishable in the estuaries. So I have indented on my friends for details of their manners and customs in the estuaries. I am chiefly indebted herein to Colonel W. Osborn, Commanding 9th M. N. I., who has most kindly been at much pains to draw up a paper which, it will be seen, forms the body of this chapter.

The mouth of the BÂ-mín is placed well underneath, the nose being very prominent, as may be seen in Plate XX, and the jaws and the inside of the mouth (vomer and palatines) are armed with villiform, or file-like teeth, which not only cut through any tackle, except wire or gimp, but present a hard and bad hook-hold. The eye is covered with a fixed transparent membrane, through which the eye may be clearly seen moving free of it inside it, and which is so tough that Colonel Osborn has twice hooked fish foul by it and landed them. The free rays of the pectoral fins are singularly prolonged.

Dr. Day says that in this species "The free rays reach nearly "to the end of the ventral." The individual from which my drawing was taken was only 1 foot long, and possibly youth may have something to do with their growth. Unfortunately my approaching departure for England prevented my being able to get a larger specimen to draw from. The first dorsal is also wanting, in the drawing, of one short small spine. This *may* have been an oversight of mine, and I cannot positively say it is not, for I have not brought the fish home with me, whereby to re-verify, but I think I took every possible precaution against oversights. It *may* also be a vagary. Dr. Day's footnote shows that other observers have found such divergencies from rule in this fish.

Like the Bass fish, which is sometimes called the Salmon-bass, it has a rough general similitude of shape and silvery colour to the Salmon. All anglers agree that it is much more powerful than the salmon.

Colonel Osborn writes:

"The lying places of the Bahmeen in the tidal backwaters, are "in the swift, deep runs, where the incoming or outgoing tide "produces a quick stream, with a strong ripple, where the stream is "narrowed between submerged rocks, and where, as a consequence, "the run is swift and the surface broken; and where there are side "eddies is a very favourite spot with them: they seem to be attracted "thither by the small fish which abound in the side eddies.

"Bahmeen are also found among the piers and piles of wooden "or iron bridges, such as the bridge across the river at Mahé, or the "three bridges on the Cannanore side of Tellicherry. These are "their haunts, and it is of no use fishing for them until you observe "them on the feed; in fact you will not know that there are any "Bahmeen about, till the tide begins to ebb or flow, bringing up or "down with it shoals of small fish, principally young grey mullet, "and on these latter, while they are running, the Bahmeen prin-"cipally seem to feed. In fishing for Bahmeen, these small grey "mullet form the most attractive bait that the fisherman can use.

"At such times of tide and at such places as I have described, "you will not be long in doubt as to where the fish are, or the "proper spot to fish for them, for as soon as the ebb or flow settles "into a steady stream, you will see the Bahmeen dashing up at the "small mullet every minute, and throwing themselves completely "out of the water. They will continue to feed in this way till slack "water.

"I have heard it discussed whether Bahmeen feed, and take "best on the ebb, or the flood tide; in some waters, possibly at "certain times of the year, these fish seem to take more readily on "the flood, than on the ebb tide: such I found to be the case once "on the Mahé river, when fishing from the bridge there, in the "month of April, but, as a general rule, I think it will be found that "Bahmeen take best on the ebb tide, though it is also possible to "catch them on the flood; but, after a good deal of experience, the "ebb is the tide I recommend, though when the tide is flowing it "should not be neglected, as you are always likely to get a run or "two even on that tide."

This question of the right time of the tide has exercised many great minds, and I have quite a bundle of letters on the subject from observing fishermen kindly wishing to help me to a right decision in the matter. Their views differed from time to time, but the end of it was that certain of them, personal friends, well known to me as good fishermen, met together for a combined Bà-mìn attack, and after putting their own several experiences, and those of their friends together, wrote me what I shall call the report of the Bà-mìn Committee. It entirely confirms Colonel Osborn's view, for though it may seem to limit it somewhat, it will be seen that a subsequent quotation from the same pen qualifies the limitation just as Colonel Osborn has qualified it. After so much diversity of opinion as there has been, a concurrence of opinion is satisfactory. "The reason I had never succeeded before "was that I was always told to go at low tide just at the turn, "whereas the time is two or three hours before the low tide. An "hour before low tide they are quite off the feed, and probably not "there." These views are again confirmed by another fisherman, R., who tells me that not only has he fished for Bà-mìn with advantage during the last quarter of the ebb tide, but has, in a boat, followed them down with the tide, and caught them all the way down to the very sea.

Colonel Osborn continues:

"As with the Mahseer, when he makes his first rush, so with the "Bahmeen, the smallest check and you part company, for he is a "strong and hard-mouthed fish.

"The rod I like best for this kind of fishing is one of Farlow's "Pike spinning-rods, bamboo for choice. Mine is 12 feet long, with "its short top,—for Bahmeen I prefer the short top—as I would, "indeed, for Pike, for the long flexible top joint is only of use in "spinning a minnow for trout. Note the length with short top, "12 feet, because the farther you go beyond this length, the less "line you can throw out, the exertion in throwing will be greater, "your control over the line not so complete, and the cast not nearly "so perfect and artistic as that which can be got out of a 12-foot rod.

"The reel should carry 100 to 120, or 150 yards of 8 plait "smooth running, spinning line, not a corded line, for in spinning "either from a bridge or from the banks for Bahmeen (which latter "you may have a chance of doing), you have to spin in exactly the "same way as you spin for Pike, and a corded line would kink, "and spoil your sport.

"A gimp trace, with two swivels—brass gimp I prefer to silver, "as it shows less, though when silver gimp gets clouded and soiled "it is equally good. In thickness the gimp should be of medium "size; if new and good, it will be quite strong enough, and the finer "you fish for Bahmeen, the greater will be the measure of your "success.

"I now come to the flight of hooks, and for this there cannot be "anything better than the spinning tackle recommended by Mr. "Thomas for Mahseer, in 'The Rod in India' (page 48); but as the "Bahmeen is a hard mouthed fish, and as he sometimes comes short, "I found it best to add to this flight. I consider the following to be "the most serviceable. A snood of medium brass, or silver gimp, with two* trebles instead of the one treble that Mr. Thomas "recommends for Mahseer, and a flying treble, made with a short "loop, to slip over the snood, after the latter has been threaded "through the bait.

"It will save you time and trouble, for you only have one "really good tide to fish on, if you have six or seven of these flights "ready baited.

"Baits are the next thing to speak of, and I will confine my "remarks on this point to natural baits, as I have tried for Bahmeen "with both spoon and phantom, without success, though I have "heard that others have found the spoon and phantom answer."

I may here put in a word to say that not only have others written me of kills made with phantom and spoon, but one used nothing but phantoms, and exhausting his shop supply had to set up a home manufactory thereof. I, too, have killed and seen them killed with a white fly in the Pámban Channel. But a fish bait, as argued above, is doubtless the deception nearest to their natural food; *àpropos* of which remark it was that I was once upbraided in the presence of these very Bá-min, "You have written a book "to teach men how to deceive."

"A young grey mullet about 3, 4, or 5 inches long, is the best "bait that can be used; these small mullet are not difficult to "procure, for they abound in all waters inhabited by the Bahmeen, "and the latter seem chiefly to feed upon them. On the shores of "these waters also, native fishermen and casting nets are always to "be found. Some time before the turn of tide, set one of these "men to work with his net, give him a bait kettle, or an earthen "pot as a substitute, to hold the baits, and bid him be careful to "sink the kettle in the river each time he puts fresh baits into it, "as natives have no idea of the necessity of supplying fish fre-"quently with fresh water to keep them alive. By the time the "tide ebbs or flows, you should have enough small mullet to last

* The last one flying free about on a level with the tail.

"you a day. Other small silvery fish will, of course, do for bait, "but the mullet is decidedly the best, being the favourite food of "the Bahmeen, and being also very tough and lasting, bearing the "same proportion in these latter qualities to other fish, as a "gudgeon does to a bleak or a small dace. Should there be any "difficulty in procuring baits at any particular spot, small mullet "or other fish can be preserved for a short time, in a wide-mouthed "bottle of spirits of wine or methylated spirits. I have several "times used baits thus prepared, while Bahmeen fishing, and found "them answer very well. Baits do not get soft in methylated "spirits, and their toughness is very well preserved.

"Having now mentioned rods, tackle, and baits, I now turn to "the actual capture of the fish.

"As I have already said, when the tide steadies into a regular "stream, you will, if standing on a bridge, soon see the mullet, and "other small fish, darting in different directions, and the Bahmeen "dashing after them. Commence spinning at one end of the bridge, "by throwing out as much line as you can control; let the bait "trail, and spin in the water, and be careful to spin well over those "spots where you have seen fish rising. Hold your rod with both "hands across your chest, with the point rather elevated, and without making another cast, walk at such a pace as will keep the "bait spinning nicely, to the other end of the bridge. And now "comes the question, which is the best side of the bridge to fish "from. This is an important point. The best side of the bridge "is that towards which the stream is running, the reason being that "mullet always work up against the stream, and the Bahmeen "always lie in wait for them, on that side of the bridge towards "which the stream runs, so that as the shoals of young mullet toil "slowly up against the tide, and make their way through the arches "of the bridge, they fall an easy prey to the Bahmeen which "are lying in wait for them, and hiding behind the piers and piles "of the bridge, on the other side. When there are a large number of "fish about, they can be caught on both sides of the bridge; but the "rule I have given as regards what I may call the stream side should "be adhered to."

This is Colonel Osborn's view. I am not prepared to contradict it. But my own idea is that the mullet fry go with the tide both in and out, and that the Bà-min hide or rest behind the piles as

Trout, Salmon, and Mahseer ordinarily do behind rocks (see page 88). However, the fishing rule here given is equally supported by either theory.

" In nearly all of the bridges I have mentioned in these notes, " you will find projecting planks outside of the hand-rail, or balus- " trade, on both sides of the bridge. Climb over the railing and get " on one of these planks, and spin away wherever you see the fish " breaking. This is the best way of all to fish from these bridges, " as you have full command of the water, and of your fish when you " strike him.

" If the Bahmeen are feeding you will not be long without a run, " and should the fish run away from the bridge, into clear water, " get to the nearest end of the bridge as soon as you can, leave " it, and run up the bank as far as possible, so as to prevent " the fish from running through the bridge, or among the piles. " Having got into a safe place, play and land your fish as you " best can.

" It is a good plan to have a canoe with a man or two with it, " moored on the most convenient side of the river, and on striking " a fish, should he run through the bridge below your feet, run " down to the bank letting out line all the time, get into the canoe, " follow, and either play him from the canoe, or from the bank " below. This is the reason why I recommend a long line, it enables " you to do all this. If you are steady, and do not get flurried, and " your tackle is as strong as it ought to be, even if the fish should " run through the bridge, below you, you can often, with careful " management, work him back again gradually to your side, and send " a man down to the nearest pier to gaff him; this only holds good " with a masonry bridge. Should a fish behave in this manner at a " bridge built on piles, a canoe is the only thing to get you out of " your difficulty, and even then you may loose your fish and tackle " by his running three or four times round a pile, as they are some- " times fond of doing.

" You may, if lucky, find a place frequented by Bahmeen, where " you can spin for them from the bank, in which case proceed in " exactly the same way, as if you were spinning for Pike. There " is such a place, about five or six miles from Cannanore, in the " Billipatam backwater, and just at the end of the village on your " right, as you face the water; the tide at the place I mean makes "a deep and swift run between sunken rocks; and at this point "Bahmeen congregate, and sport is to be had.

"The places I know of where Bahmeen fishing is procurable "are Billipatam village, near Cannanore, just mentioned, the three "bridges on the Cannanore side of Tellicherry, of which three the "centre one is the best, Yellatoor bridge near Calicut, the back-"water at Beypoor, Currulhoondy railway bridge near the camp "platform and troop rest house, about a mile and a half down the "line from the Beypoor station, and there is another small bridge, "up the Tellicherry backwater, about three miles from the central "bridge, that I have already spoken of as being a good place for "sport.

Near the mouth of the Kallei River, in Calicut Town, between the mouth and the bar, is mentioned by M. as another place.

"About the best place I know of for Bahmeen is the Mahé river, "where it runs through the little French town of Mahé, about 20 "miles south of Cannanore, from the bridge that spans this river, at "the entrance to the town, capital Bahmeen fishing is to be had, and "you can generally hire a tolerably comfortable bungalow on the "bank of the river, close to the bridge, and from your windows you "can always see when the fish begin to feed, so you only have to "shoulder your rod, and walk a few yards to your sport.

"I don't know the spawning time of the Bahmeen, but I have "had good sport with them all through the monsoon and in the "months of March, April, and May. At the end of, and after the "monsoon, however, the sea at the mouth of these backwaters "becomes almost putrid, and a very unpleasant smell arises from "it. When the incoming tide brings this dirty water up the back-"waters, it seems to poison the Bahmeen, Nair fish, and other large "fish; the water has a brown tinge in it, and, as the tide ebbs, num-"bers of large fish, all dead, float down with it and go out to sea. "At these times the native fishermen wade in, and secure the dead "fish as they pass, with a short harpoon. I need hardly say that, "during the months when the rivers are in this state, it is of little "use attempting to fish.

"In concluding these notes, I think I may say that Bahmeen "fishing is good sport, and quite worth following. In starting on a "fishing trip it is well to be provided with plenty of tackle, as the "fish are strong, and breakages frequent. I don't know what in weight

"Bahmeen run up to, the largest I have landed was one of 9 lbs., "but I have seen many larger than this which have been caught in "nets. Some of the latter having scaled 11 and 12 lbs. A Bah-"meen of this weight would give very good sport."

I have seen thousands of *Polynemus Indicus* brought ashore by a fleet of netting boats: 12 lbs. was quite an outside weight. They averaged 10 lbs., and were all very much of a size. Day gives much larger sizes for *P. tetradactylus* as will be seen below.

"When taking your bait, the Bahmeen does so with a violent "rush, in the most determined manner, and away he goes at his best "pace as soon as he feels the hook. After he has gone a few yards, "and you can safely do so, strike him twice, so as to drive in the "hooks, for he is by no means a leather-mouthed fish, like a Mahseer, "and without some such performance on your part, he is apt to get "rid of the hooks, as soon as the line slackens, which by-the-bye, "you should always endeavour to prevent. Be careful to have your "line clear, and free, for if there is a check of any sort when the "Bahmeen has made up his mind to go, you will probably have to "lament the loss of both fish and tackle."

I never could be persuaded to endorse this striking of any fish after he is hooked, my own belief being that if you will only keep on sufficient pressure his struggles will do all the jerking you can possibly desire, and that it is very dangerous for you to slacken ever so little for the purpose of getting up a jerk.

Before parting with the Bà-mìn, I will quote from M., whom I have already quoted as a member of the Bà-mìn committee: "We "are agreed that they run stronger than Salmon for their size; "but with gimp, and 100 yards on a good reel, the only danger "of being broken is their charging the piles under one's feet. The "first one that tried that broke me, but I find that with judicious "use of stones they can be kept off, and one gets down at last on to "the shore of the river and brings them to the landing net." But the same writer had rather a rough time of it afterwards, as the following letter will show :—

"I had rather a disastrous morning with the Bà-meen the other "day. A peon on watch reported they were feeding at daylight, "though it was then almost high tide, just beginning to run out. A "lot of fry were under the bridge, the Mullet were eating them, and "the Bà-meen the Mullet. This was under the still arches near "one side, instead of, as usual, in the centre where the current is "strongest. The first fish I lost after playing a few minutes. Hold "gave way.

"The next, a very lively fish, drowned me as I was getting off "the bridge, as he ran down stream and got a bush between us. "However, being well hooked, he did not get off, and I got the "slack in, and had nearly tired him out, when, to my horror, I "found the reel running stiff, and his next rush I could not give it "him fast enough, and the bait came back with one of the tail "trebles straightened.

"It turned out that a screw inside the reel had started, and "jammed against the disk, into which it was cutting, and when "opened the box was full of brass filings.

"This was, then, bad luck. I then put on a fresh phantom, "having, luckily, a second reel and line, and had two or three "runs, the fish missing being hooked.

"This I attribute to my having tied the treble on stiff wire, "making the whole bait stiff. I then put on a guttapercha bait, a "great favourite, and had hardly begun when a fish took and bolted "at once round a pile. I make it a rule to break them directly they "get close to a pile, but this one I gave line to, in hopes of saving "my bait, and did so, a large treble breaking I got a boat and "rescued line and bait, but found the casting line all frayed against "the barnacles on the pile. I had now to set to work and tie the "stiff phantom afresh with gimp; and, while doing so, a monster rose "under one of the arches. As soon as I was ready I went at him and "soon hooked him. He went down stream, and after 10 minutes I "began edging off the bridge to get to the bank, when he suddenly "came charging at me to get under the bridge. His power was "enormous; and, in spite of stones and a long bamboo with leaves "tied on the end, he came under and actually got a few yards "above the bridge, I being in an upside down position, and holding "him very tight. At last he made for the piles and broke me. "This was the biggest fish I have hooked, and I think he must "have been from 15 to 20 lbs.

"Had I then had what I have now, a wooden ladder fixed into the "centre piles, and a boat moored with men ready, I could easily have "killed him, by following him on his first rush, and getting below

" him if he tried to make up for the bridge. Next day I went out. " I had hardly begun when a brute came and took me and instantly " went round a pile and broke me. This made seven consecutive " fish that had broken me here. I then hooked and landed a 6- " pounder, using the ladder and boat. I have lost three fish round " piles after they have run away fairly down stream, and this, of " course, is avoidable; but if they go at the pier at once, there is no " remedy. It seems to depend on where one's bait is. The fish " naturally pulls against you; and if your bait has been swept 8 or " 10 feet down stream he runs down; but if he takes almost under " the arch, he runs in.

" In one case I purposely gave a fish line instead of breaking, " to see what he would do, and this was the result."

Here was a sketch of a labyrinth of piles with which, dear reader, you must kindly dispense.

" I unravelled the maze, and finally, after going from pier to " pier in a boat, caught sight of my friend at the eighth pier. The " run I must tell you, was all done in a few seconds. It took ten " minutes or a quarter of an hour to work it out, and I could at " one moment have checked the fish, had I been ready. Seeing me " close to him he took three turns round the pile and broke. The " last few days I have been out fish have not been feeding. I " have a theory that every fish left there has got a phantom in " his gills.

" I think you will admit that they treated me badly that " morning. They seemed to have determined to show me what they " could do. They straightened one treble, broke another, a large " strong one, filed the casting line, pulled off one phantom's head, " demoralized a reel (one of Bowness' best Mahseer reels) by sheer " hard running, and, finally, the big chap tried all he could to break " the rod, and has given it a permanent bend."

In the Pámban channel, just opposite the Superintendent's house, there are, or at least there used to be some twenty years ago, a number of splendid runs. It is to be hoped the Government has not cleared them away for the benefit of the shipping!! Probably not, for they were not in mid channel. There was a fish there that we used to call the Pámban salmon; and were well content with the name, for in those days I had not troubled my head with fish nomenclature and classification. It turns out to be our mutual friend Polynemus. Either *P. tetradactylus* or *P. Indicus*, probably the latter. I only had one hour at them, but it is a day to be remembered in all my lifetime. What splendid sport they gave! We anchored the boat at the head of the run, and fished below us in the middle of it. We used a full sized salmon fly, made of nothing but the white feather of a quill pen, tied palmer-fashion all over it. Much the same fly is used for Bass in England. How freely they rose, and how vigorously they tugged. My companion, who put me up to it, and provided rod and boat, lived there, and used to catch any number of them. But there were certain seasons, he said, in which they would not take at all. Which were the favourable and which the unfavourable months, I cannot at this length of time recall. W., fishing there in October, writes me: "Pamben salmon do "not come on till late in the year." I presume he means later than October.

The natives, in fishing for Bà-min, use a strong cord, with a large sea-hook, on a piece of bell-wire. But they use much direct force in pulling in their fish, because they have very crude ideas about the *suaviter in modo, fortiter in re* principle of running tackle on a reel, which enables you in time to kill a heavy fish on a light line. Don't be alarmed, therefore, at their tremendous preparations, but trust to stout gimp, and a salmon rod, with a good length of line, and making your fish work as hard as you dare for every inch of it. Do not waste a bit of it by giving it too easily. The native fisherman may examine your tackle, and condemn it as too weak, and you may be disposed to believe in him, because he has actually killed the fish, and ought to know. Never mind that; just do with him the very same as you will probably do with this book, namely, listen to all his advice, and then *don't* follow it. Only draw your own conclusions therefrom. At the same time you need not be uncivil, or he will become uncommunicative. Do not rudely disturb his complacent belief that you cannot help yourself, that your tackle is not so good as his, and that you must make the best of a bad job; and then, when you land a fish nevertheless, he will be all astonishment, and doubly anxious to show you there is still "a thing or two" which he knows better than you; and you may pick up many a useful wrinkle from the native fishermen

It is now time I made the usual descriptive quotation from Dr. Day's "Fishes of India," and bid good-bye.

Sub class. TELEOSTEI.

Order. ACANTHOPTERYGII.

Family POLYNEMIDÆ (including eight species).

Polynemus tetradactylus. B. vii, D. 8 $\frac{1}{13 \cdot 15}$, P. 17 + iv, V. 1/5, A. $\frac{2 \cdot 3}{15 \cdot 17}$, C. 17, L. l. 75–85, L. tr. 8/14. *Cæc. pyl. many. Habitat*: Seas of India to the Malay Archipelago and China. Attaining 6 feet and upwards in length. It is excellent eating. This species appears to ascend higher up the river than any others, and the young are numerous in the Hoogly, at Calcutta. Ham. Buchanan observes: "I "have been assured by a credible native that he saw one which was a "load for six men, and which certainly, therefore, exceeded in weight "320 lbs. avoirdupois." (Fish Ganges, p. 225).

P. Indicus. B. vii, D. 8 $\frac{1}{13}\frac{}{14}$, P 15 + v, V. 1/5, A $\frac{2 \cdot 3}{11 \cdot 12}$, C. 17, L. l. 70–75, L. tr. 7/13, Vert. 5/19. *Cæc. pyl. many. Habitat*: Seas of India to the Malay Archipelago and Australia. It attains 4 feet in length, but it is rarely above 20 lbs. weight.

THE COCK-UP, OR NAIR FISH.

Lates calcarifer is said by Dr. Day to be the Cock-up of Europeans, though how it got the name I know not. It is also called the Nair fish by Europeans. The Canarese called it *Kulanji*, when small, *Madàru* when large; just as we use the terms Jack and Pike. The Malayalim name Colonel Osborn writes is "Coollon, the "final *n* being pronounced as the *n* in the French place Dijon." For other vernacular names, Dr. Day shall be quoted hereafter.

I have seen them weighing 30 lbs. on *terra firma*, and Colonel Osborn says he has seen them over 50 lbs. or 60 lbs. in weight. They are a sea fish frequenting the estuaries, and are found in company with the Bàmin. Their mouth is similarly armed with numerous minute file-like (villiform) teeth; their colour is silvery, with a bronzy sheen on the back. Plate XXI will aid recognition. The young have not the humped back seen in the adult fish.

I have done not a little business with these fish myself, but Colonel Osborn seems to have had more opportunities of watching them, so I will quote his kindly contributed paper:—

"When the S.W. monsoon is at its height, and the rivers are "very much discoloured by the floods from the western mountains

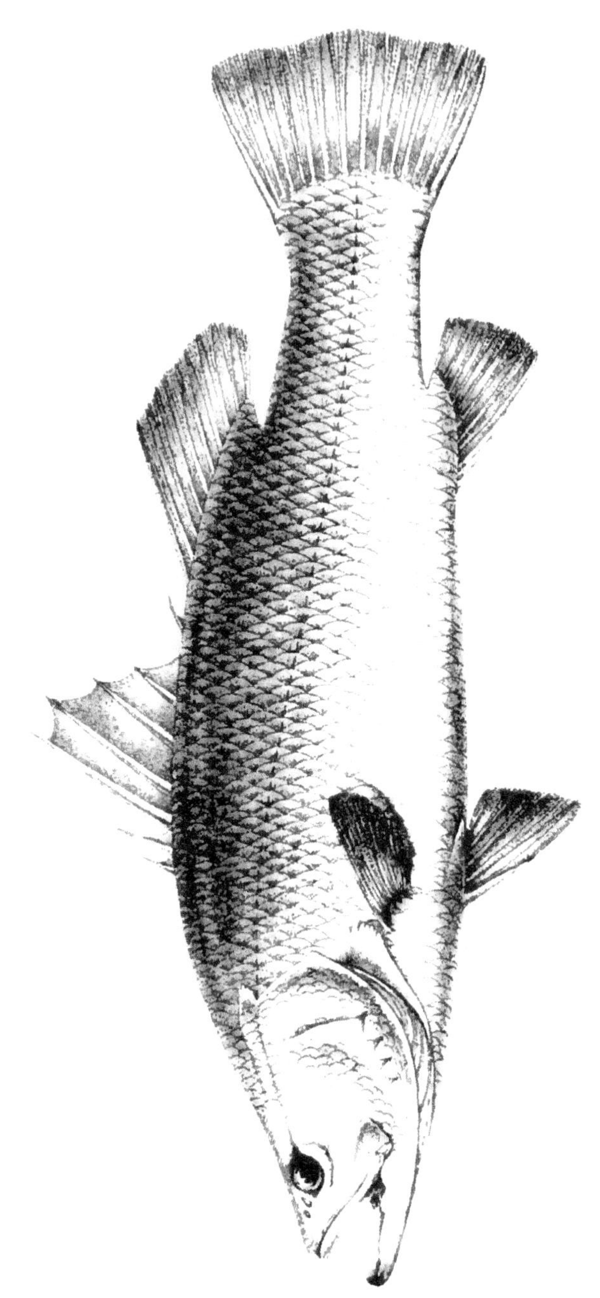

" the Nair fish enter the backwaters, which are then quite thick " from the inland floods, and congregate about the bridges, in company with the Bahmeen; during the day they seem to take best " when the water is most discoloured, coming in with, and feeding " on, the flood tide; they have a large and very brilliant eye, and " possibly can see well in thick water, while they themselves are " concealed from other fish, whose vision is probably not so perfect " in muddy water, and I am strengthened in this opinion by " having noticed the nocturnal habits of the Nair fish, and observed " them feeding during a good portion of the night.

" The tackle to use for these fish is the same as that which I " have recommended for Bahmeen, but the gimp should be the " thickest kind, and the hooks rather larger than those used for " Bahmeen, say a size larger than ordinary Mahseer hooks, as the " larger hooks lie better on thick gimp, and the fish, remember, " runs to a very large size, besides being very powerful. The " bait should also be larger than that used for Bahmeen, as this " fishing is carried on in thick water, and at night. Rod, line, " trace, snood, and hooks, should all be strong, for when the Nair " fish really finds out that he is hooked, he starts off on a journey " which is a pretty long one before he stops. I allude here to the " large sized ones. I once struck one that must have weighed about " 50 lbs., and off he started up the river; I only had a medium sized " gimp trace, and snood, so dare not check him. I managed to jump " into a canoe from the bank, and followed him for about 400 yards " before he stopped. In a subsequent struggle, he broke my snood " and I lost him. A friend of mine followed a fish, of similar size, " for about the same distance up the river, before he came to a " stand-still, a few days before. I mention this incident to show " that, when these fish make their first run, after being struck, they " go far. Let them have their run out, and keep them going afterwards if you can.

" In spinning for the Nair fish, you should spin slowly; he " takes the bait, not with a rush like the Bahmeen, but slowly and " deliberately, as compared to the hurry of the other fish. And " sometimes, while fishing rather deep, as the fish does not always " rush off after taking the bait, I have not known that I had a fish " on, till I felt the check on drawing in the line. I have known a " Nair fish, after taking, move about at a quiet pace as if nothing "had happened, when it suddenly appeared to occur to him that he "was 'on,' and off he went for his run. It does not answer to check "this, or any other fish, while he is running, even if there be danger "ahead; try and let him have his run out, for these strong and "heavy fish have a way of plunging violently when checked, which "is fatal to tackle. As soon as the first run is over, reel up quickly "till you are as close as you can get, and then start him for another "cruise. Continue in this way till you can master him, without "fear of a break. In mentioning these precautions I allude again to "the fish of large size, the smaller ones are easier dealt with, but "the large fish are so heavy, that caution is necessary in handling "them, when they are inclined to plunge and be restive.

"The best time for fishing for the Nair fish is, as I have said, for "daywork, during the monsoon, when the waters are thick. At "other times, when the rivers and backwaters are clear, commence "fishing well after sundown, and go on as far into the night as the "fish are on the feed, for you will hear them feeding, and splashing, "all about you. When they have stopped doing so, it is not much "use trying for them any more.

"The break of a Bahmeen you never can mistake for that of a "Nair fish: the former is a sharp and violent splash, the spray flies "in every direction, and the Bahmeen nearly always shows himself; "that of the Nair fish is a deep-sounding plunge, the sound of which "a practised ear can recognise, even in the night, when you cannot "see the break; there is not much spray, and the water subsides "with a peculiar swirl.

"I have here noted all that I know at present about the Nair "fish, for, compared to the Bahmeen, he is, I may say, a new "acquaintance of mine. I will only add that, for this fish also, a "small grey mullet is the best bait that can be used. I have "mentioned, also as a peculiarity of this fish, that he takes a bait "rather slowly, and in a much quieter style, than the Bahmeen "does. This is what I have observed, during a somewhat limited "experience of the habits of the Nair fish, a period not extending "over a full year. There are times, I believe, when the Nair fish "takes a bait greedily, and goes at it with great eagerness.

"The ways of fish differ so much under various conditions—local "and atmospheric—that it is impossible to find out all about "them, or even to arrive at a correct knowledge of a good many of

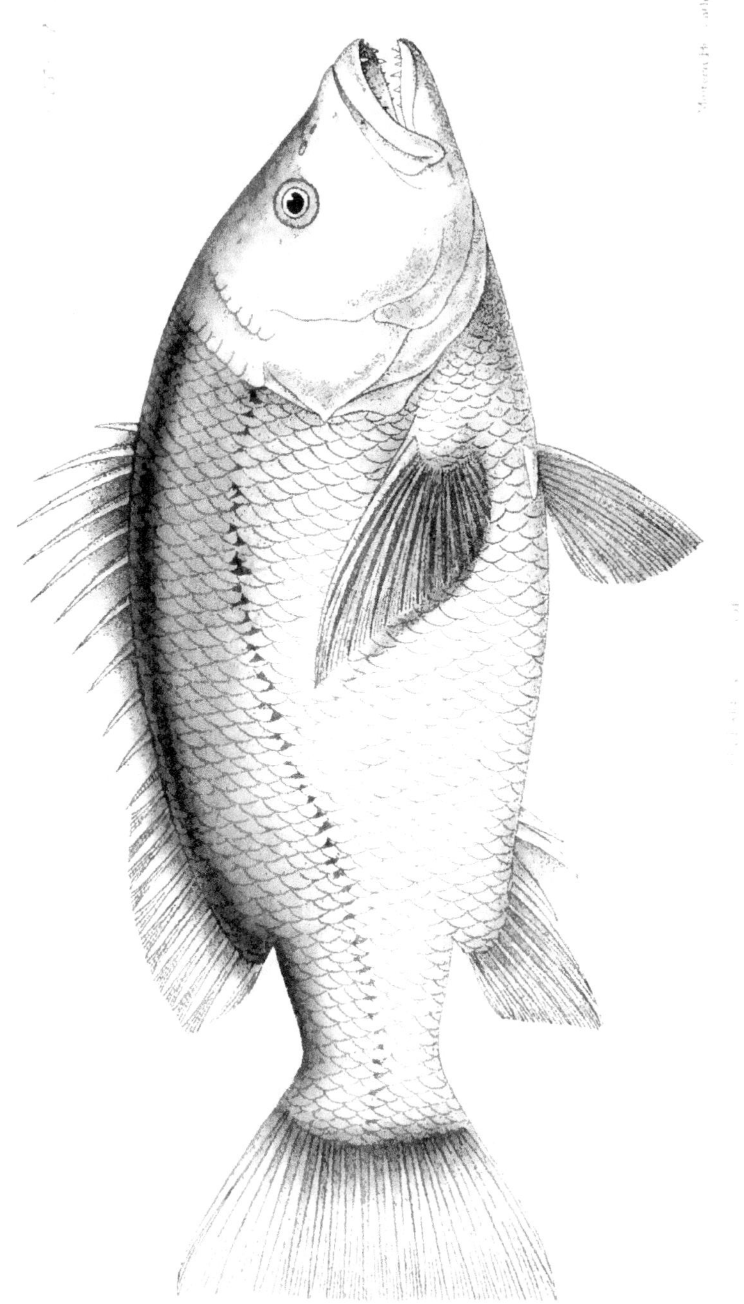

"their habits, without close observation, extending over several "seasons.

"These notes are simply the result of my own observation of "the fish, whose habits, and the method of whose capture, I have "endeavoured to describe. They are intended, not so much for the "use of sportsmen, many of whom are probably better informed on "the subject than I am, but for those to whom a few hints as to "where, and how to obtain sport, may be useful."

I have let Colonel Osborn's opinions stand as they are, but for my part I do not see the advantage of letting a big fish have his run, except it be that you get a belly on the line which acts as a cushion to sudden jerks. I would rather contest every inch with him from the first, trusting to the elasticity of my top joint and fresh tackle to help me over the angry plunges.

The sizes of the treble hooks I would recommend are No. 1 in Plate VII, for the hook embedded in the vent; No. 5 for the other two.

This fish has also been caught in the Fort moat at Madras; they would seem to have got in through the sluices as fry. One of these fish caught there by Mr. Robinson, and now stuffed in the Madras Museum, weighed 33 lbs. 5 ozs.

Sub Class. TELEOSTII.

Order. ACANTHOPTERYGII.

Family. PERCIDÆ.

Lates calcarifer. B. vii, D 7–8 $\frac{1}{11\text{-}12}$, P. 17, V. 1 5, A $\frac{3}{8\text{-}9}$, C. 17, L.l. 52–60, L.tr. 6–7 13, Cæc. pyl. 3.

Dangara, Sind; *Nuddee-meen* or *Nair-meen*, Mal.; *Painnee-meen* or *Koduwa*, Tam; *Pandukopa* or *Pandu-meenu* Tel.; *Durruah* and *Bekkut*, Ooriah; *Begti*, Beng.; *Nga-tha-dyk*, Arrac; *Koral*, or, if large, *Baor*, Chittagong; *Todah*, Andam.; *Cock-up* of Europeans.

THE RED PERCH.

In the Madras Fort ditch I have also caught spinning as for the two previous fish, *Lutianus roseus* of 5 lbs. weight, Plate XXII, and I have caught them in estuaries, and in a pond at Cundapur where they had become acclimatized to nearly fresh water. They are an estuary fish frequenting the rocks. The bait should ordinarily be much smaller than for the two previous fish. The Canarese name is *Kemberi*.

Family. PERCIDÆ.

Lutianus roseus. B vii, D $\frac{10}{14}$, P. 16, V. 1/5, A. $\frac{3}{8}$, C. 17, L.l. 48. L.v. $\frac{57}{50}$, L.tr. 7/18.

There is another fish (*Chrysophrys berda*), and called *Yeri* in Canarese, that may be caught in company with *Lutianus roseus*. A prawn has been recommended as a bait.

MEGALOPS CYPRINOIDES.

Megalops cyprinoides, which it is as easy to call Megalops as anything else, also takes a bait well at times. I have come across them coming up an estuary in a shoal, and it was like hauling in Mackerel; and they run about the same size. There was a fish on as fast as ever you could get your line into the water. But the fun was very short-lived. It was in mid stream, and they were all past the boat in a very little time. I am told they, as well as an *Elops saurus*, have been caught in the Madras Fort ditch with a white fly. My fishing for them was with a small dead-bait. I should think a prawn used like a fly very slowly would suit them to a nicety. They acclimatize very readily to fresh water, and grow fast, as I know, and breed, as I am told, in ponds. But they must be very destructive of the fry of other fish. It is not a prudent thing, therefore, to put them into any pond in which you wish to breed fish. But natives are fond of keeping them in ponds, and in a Fort ditch or any place into which predacious fish have already got it may be added without injury. Plate XXIII will help you to recognize it.

Order. PHYSOSTOMI.

Megalops cyprinoides. B xxiv–xxvi, D. 19–21 ($\frac{2}{17\text{-}19}$), P. 15–16. V. 10, A. 24–27 ($\frac{2}{22\text{-}25}$) C. 19, L.l. 37 42, L.tr. 5–6,6.

Punnikoun and *Naharu*, Ooriah; *Cunnay*, Mal.; *Moran candai*, Tam. *Nga-tan-gouet*, Burmese.

THE SEER.

If you try the same tactics at, or close to, the mouth of a river, as have been recommended for Bâmîn, you may get the Seer fish, which is a splendid fellow. I do not think they ever come far into a river Indeed, I am pretty sure they do not. I

once saw a fine one of 15 lbs. killed in a funny way. A friend and self were spinning for them. I left my friend spinning at a projecting sand spit, at the mouth of the Mangalore harbour, which is cut abruptly away by the current, and is very little above the water level. He threw out his bait, and spun it home to him, and had just pulled it out when, to his astonishment, and I believe alarm, a 15 lb. Seer fish, in dashing after it, sprung clean on shore, at his very feet. There he was, a fine fellow, flopping about, and in imminent danger of getting into the water again. All hands punched his head, with the butt of the rod, with boots, for we had been bathing, and anything handy, and with any amount of excitement. Meanwhile, others of us were in a boat trying the mid stream, and coming back we were shown the fish, as if it had been a legitimate bag, with a long yarn about the line it had taken out, etc. But I had happened to get a glimpse of it in the distance, and joined in, therefore, with their story, saying, "I saw you *showing him the butt*."

I am inclined to think much fun might be got out of the Seer fish. The matter wants developing.

H. writes: "I caught a couple at Ponany, and I never saw finer "running. I do not think I exaggerate in saying they leaped 8 feet "out of the water at times. They were 15-pounders." The writer, be it remembered, is no tyro, easily exhilarated, but an old salmon fisher, and otherwise a mighty hunter.

The Seer fish is *Cybium*, of which there are five species in the Indian Seas, attaining some of them 3 and 4 feet in length. They are excellent eating. Their mouth is full of very formidable teeth. They are a sea, not an estuary fish.

It should be remembered that Seer are not always present. They do not make their appearance till a month or so after the close of the monsoon, when they follow up the little fish frequenting the rivers. The simplest way to ascertain when they are in, is by having them for breakfast from the fish market, for the natives net them as soon as they come.

Seer, and, I believe, other fish, are caught off the Indian coasts much after the manner of mackerel in England. A crude imitation of a fish is made out of the white kernel of the cocoanut cut to shape, and placed on a big hook, about the size of No. 10/0 Limerick, or out of white rag; and three long lines thus baited are trailed well behind the vessel as she sails, one from each arm of the yard, and one from the mast head. They are thus kept well apart out of danger of tangling. A bridle or connecting line, one from each of these lines to the deck, makes it easy to tell if there is a fish on, and to pull the line in so as to have it and the fish on deck. This style of fishing wants a good breeze. "It's the pace "that kills" fish. This I give from hearsay, not personal trial, for my "soul does sicken o'er the heaving wave."

Friends going home by P. and O. tell me that they have caught fish in this way from the steamer. They did nothing in the deep sea, but in those parts of the Red Sea where they ran near land or rocky shallows they killed big fish in spite of the jeers of incredulous fellow passengers. The hook about the size of No. 10/0 Limerick was on thick wire, the body weighted with lead and covered with white rag, the wings and tail being of the same.

But splendid sport though estuary fish give you at times, I cannot but say that, in my estimation, estuary fishing is highly unsatisfactory, for the simple reasons that the fish, whose habits are governed by the tides, will not take except at the right time of the tide. If the tide would always turn conveniently, just half an hour after one got out of Cutchery, I would not complain. But as it is, the chances are just about twenty-three to one against your hitting off the right time. If your time is your own like a native fisherman's, and you do not mind a little sun, and can study the tides, and be on the spot at the right time, then you may have excellent sport. But how few Europeans there are in India who have the necessary leisure. If you have the leisure, and have come to know their times, this very periodicity of their taking is in your favour. The fish are all on the feed at the same time, and to be able to predict this beforehand, and to arrange to meet them at dinner, is a very great point indeed. What lucky and uncertain hours are those when the tro[illegible] are fairly on the feed, in a taking humour at home. How one fis[illegible]s on, hour after hour, in England, in spite of indifferent sport, in the expectancy that at any time in the day there may be a change, with the air full of flies, and the water covered with circles. But there is not such an amount of uncertainty about the estuary fish. He takes his meals at regular intervals, and you can tell his dinner hour as well as he can himself, for his clock is in the heavens, to wit the moon; only it is a little like Captain Cuttle's famous watch, about which he gave the advice and testimony—"Put it back half-an-hour every morning, and about another "quarter towards the afternoon, and it's a watch that'll do you "credit." Similarly your fishing clock, the moon, is irregular, and you must remember that it is not exactly 12 hours between high tide and high tide, but nearer 12 hours and 20 minutes; though even this odd 20 minutes is sometimes nearer 15, sometimes nearly 25. But you will not be far wrong if you bear in mind that each high tide, after an interval of 12 hours, is about 20 minutes later than its predecessor, and as there is one in the night as well as in the day, the day high tide recurs, more or less, about 40 minutes later than it did the day before.

On the whole, therefore, the estuary fish is no lunatic for not sitting down to table till the cloth is laid, and his dinner ready in the shape of passing shoals of little fish; and, though his punctilious punctuality, and his lunar time, may be inconvenient to me, there may be others to whom it may be no bar to the closer cultivation of his acquaintance. To them, therefore, I introduce him with this caution about punctuality. He will not wait a minute for you.

Sea-fish are to be caught in India, as elsewhere, by bottom fishing from a boat, and for those who fancy this style of fishing, good sport may sometimes be had. With a view to tell them about it, I commenced collecting the information from the native fishermen. But it strikes me there will be very little practical use in my swelling my book with what anyone can learn just as well direct from them. Moreover, it is difficult for any book to make a man independent of local aid in sea-fishing; for there are certain places in the sea that hold certain fish, while other places hold none, and he will still want the local fishermen, who know the spots, and the guiding landmarks, to anchor him immediately over these favoured spots. Being *perforce* reliant, therefore, on the native fishermen for locality, he may as well leave them to supply bait, lines, and everything else.

CHANOS SALMONEUS.

One sea-fish, however, I will mention briefly, because, though not to be caught with rod and line that I know of, it, in its own way, shows really exciting sport. Acclimatized to water that is very slightly brackish, it runs to 20 or 30 lbs. in a pond at Cundapur, and having the repute of having been reserved by Hyder for his own use, it has ever since been protected, and going by the name of Hyder's fish, is believed to be a freshwater fish, imported and put there by Hyder. I entertain no doubt, however, that the fry introduced themselves through a breached sluice from the adjoining estuary, and that, on the sluice being permanently closed, they gradually got acclimatized to the water growing less and less salt. Now they breed there freely. Being satisfied this must be the explanation, I showed a peon a stuffed specimen, and, impressing every detail of its form on him, and making him repeat them with his back to the fish, and selecting the month in which I thought it most probable that the *Chanos salmoneus* would enter the estuaries to spawn, and allowing time for the fry to hatch and grow before going to sea, I sent the peon to the estuary, not the pond, to catch some fry and take them to another lake, the bigger Karkal Lake. He found them as predicted, and introduced fifty in the Karkal Lake, bringing me back specimens in spirits that I might be satisfied there had been no mistake.

The full grown fish are caught in the pond in a singular manner.

Ordinary drag nets are connected till they are together long enough to stretch right across the pond; but not a single fish of this description is by any chance ever caught in this net; its sole use is to frighten them. Behind this net comes a long row of small canoes tied to the drag net at short intervals, so that the hauling of the drag net shall keep them in their places close behind the drag net. On the thwarts in these canoes stand men extending a similar net in the air, at about the angle of 45° from the water, to the greatest height they can reach. Thus arranged, the line proceeds, and the fish, frightened by the drag net in the water, endeavour to leap over it, and in so doing fall into the net spread in the air. It is a sight to see a silvery salmon-like fish of 20 pounds or thereabouts face the line with a spring that clears boats and standing men and up-raised nets. Sometimes he leaps against the net close to the boatman, or even hits him and brings him down like a nine-pin, a sort of tumbling that the fishermen seem to enjoy if the fish is secured, and the eventual victory lies with them. Altogether it is a pretty and somewhat exciting scene to witness, especially if the spectator be himself under fire.

They are such magnificent fish that it is a thousand pities they cannot be taken with a rod and line. I have tried spinning and fly in vain. They have a mouth like a grey mullet and might, perhaps, be similarly tempted with a rag worm. But I should not be hopeful, for the grey mullet also are very difficult to take with a bait, as is well known.

It may be noticed in passing that the acclimatization of salt water fish to fresh water is no uncommon occurrence. There are ponds in the sand strip between the sea and river at Mangalore in which the water is fresh, and yet they contain several distinct species of purely sea fish that have lived and spawned there for more than eight years. The salmon, shad, and hilsa, for instance, change every year from sea to fresh water, and trout are found at sea. So there is nothing extraordinary in the *Chanos salmoneus* taking kindly to fresh water.

CHAPTER XVIII.

ROD AND TACKLE.

"Away to the brook,
All your tackle out-look,
Here's a day that is worth a year's wishing;
See that all things be right,
For 'twould be a spite
To want tools when a man goes a-fishing."—
COTTON.

I BEGAN my fishing in India with rough and ready self-made articles; accordingly, in my first edition, I began this Chapter with instructions how any brother fishermen in like distress might set himself up with an impromptu self-made kit. I think it was a mistake. Such a kit is sure to be a bad one, sure to lead only to terrible disasters and disappointments in any but the most skilful hands, and not unfrequently even in those. Practised hands will know how to make up makeshifts without my telling them; others should not venture on using them. Rather let them be careful to buy the best implements to aid them in their first efforts.

Hooks.

The hooks required for Mahseer fishing will, as far as the fly fishing is concerned, be the same as for Salmon fishing, to wit, Limerick hooks, but in ordering them you will please not forget the caution given at page 94, and will refer your tackle-maker to my Plate VIII.

But for spinning you will require a very different style of treble hook to the sort ordinarily used for spinning in England, you will require one made specially for Mahseer. The sizes of Mahseer trebles are the same as those of other treble hooks as given in Plate VII, but Mahseer trebles are made of very much stouter wire.

A tackle-maker accustomed to supply Indian tackle will know what you mean if you call them Mahseer trebles; but from ordinary tackle-makers you might just as well ask for the man in the moon.

and expect to get him out by the next overland parcel post. You will have to tell them that it is the treble hook called by the hook makers extra-stout. The ordinary tackle-maker, who is not educated to the supply of Indian tackle, is sure to have none of these hooks in his shop. He never deals in them, has probably never seen them, and does not know how to order them of the hook maker, even if he sees them. Tell him they are called extra stout, as I said above, and that such hooks you must have. It will shock his sensibilities doubtless, his refined eye recoiling from anything so clumsy.

Moreover, he considers it no compliment to offer such a hook to a sportsman, as if he had not fine enough hand to kill a fish on an ordinary hook; and, indeed, it might be considered an insult, if the pull of the fish was the only thing to be afraid of. But that is not the difficulty at all, it is the very unusual power of compression exercised by the Mahseer, the violent chop with which he seizes his fish, that crushes an ordinary treble hook before you feel your fish at all, as explained at length in Chapter IV.

Tackle shops.

My readers being mainly Indians, some of whom had come out to India without being innoculated with the fishing virus, I felt in my former edition that they, some of them, might not know where to look for tackle shops; and in those days, the days of my first edition, few tackle-makers knew anything about Mahseer, and the special hooks needed for them. It was specially due to my readers, therefore, that I should mention shops in which these hooks were kept. I mentioned, therefore, C. Farlow, 191, Strand; and Bowness, 230, Strand, as the only ones I knew. Since then, however, letters to the "Field" have been frequent, and much more is known to tackle-makers generally about Mahseer, and perhaps my little book itself has added its mite to spread the knowledge; and anglers have talked to their tackle-makers so that it would seem invidious at this date to single out and mention any particular shops, as if they were the only ones that could supply the proper articles. Any tackle-maker that you are accustomed to deal with can equally supply you, if only you will be at the pains, in ordering, to sufficiently particularize the tackle, and especially the hooks, as I have set them down for you. Of course I am writing only for such as need such aid. It is of no use your simply referring your tackle-maker to this book, unless you are going to lend or give him a copy; for unless he has a large Indian trade, it will not pay him to buy it. But if you will only particularize carefully, and I have done all I can to help you, you can continue to deal with your old friends. But if you will not be troubled to particularize, perhaps, you had better go to those who are likely to be in the way of supplying Mahseer tackle, always warning them, however, that you *don't* want a "Mahseer rod" for Mahseer, but a Salmon rod as particularized. There may be a hundred such shops that I know nothing of. I can only mention such as I know, that the reader who happens to know none may be helped as far as I can help him. In so doing, however, I don't want to tamper with your love if your affections are already centred. My love was plighted long ago to Farlow. He first hooked me with a proper Mahseer hook, and then stole my heart with one of his rods. It is the special confidant spoken of among rods. But I have poked about in other shops picking up tackle lore, and paying for it by purchases. Bowness above-mentioned understands Mahseer tackle. So does G. Little and Co., 15, Fetter Lane, Fleet Street. He is employed to supply the Civil Service Co-operative Society of 28, Haymarket, and also the Army and Navy Co-operative Stores Society, 117, Victoria Street, Westminster, London, S.W., so that if you are in the habit of going to them for other things, I suppose they, too, could get you the proper tackle. They profess to do so in their Price Lists. In Madras, there is the shop of Messrs. Oakes and Co., Exchange Hall, Blacktown. They have some excellent tackle supplied by Bowness, and some that must have been made up for Methusaleh, "or his uncles or his aunts," and unless you go and pick for yourself, they don't know which to give you. In Bengal, I am told, there are three men who know how to supply the right article:—

R. B. Rodda and Co., 7 and 8, Dalhousie Square, Calcutta.

Manton and Co., 13, Old Court House Street, Calcutta.

Biswas, whose address I do not know.

Presuming presumptously that *some few* of my readers will be converted to my ideas of tackle, and will wish their tackle shop to supply them with the things particularized, to lighten the labour of the tackle-maker, I have gathered together in one place in the index all the references that will be useful to him.

Phantom minnows should be dressed with hooks of the same

Phantoms.

strength, the size of the phantom being from 6 inches in length, tail included, with hooks of No. 4 size. I think the best phantom for general use is 4 inches long, dressed with No. 4 hooks, and that you want no other. For Mahseer they should be mounted on stout treble gut; for Bà-mìn, on medium gimp; for Cock-up, on stout gimp.

Spoons.

Spoon baits also should be mounted with the same hooks specially for India, and should, for the reason already given (page 43), be made of thicker metal than fishing spoons ordinarily are. I like them as thick as a good teaspoon, and gilt on one side, silvered on the other. The sizes for Mahseer spoons are from two to three inches in length in the bowl. The smallest may be used when the river is very small, and the fish run small; indeed, I have killed well in such rivers with a spoon one and a quarter inch long. The largest size may be used when you expect particularly big fish. But the best spoon for general use is, I think, two and a half inches long, which is just the size of an ordinary dessert spoon.

For the reasons given below in connection with rust-eaten gut, it is desirable that the ring in the spoon to which the gut trace is attached should be of some material that does not rust like the steel split ring ordinarily used. Electro-plated iron or brass might be substituted with advantage.

Split rings.

And split rings must unquestionably be abhorred. They are an abomination. No matter how stout they may be, they are utterly untrustworthy, and are sure to fail you with your first big fish. Tackle-makers, even the best of them, *will* use split rings, because they are so easily put on, look so neat, and are supposed to be so convenient for the angler. I enter against split rings the most uncompromising protest. Oh, the magnificent fish they have lost me! I cannot bear the sight of them. I take them off and break them up the moment I see them, for I wouldn't trust one for a single day, even when perfectly new. I substitute a bit of brass wire a little less than the thickness of the hook. One end goes through the eye in the point of the spoon, and through the eye of one treble, and being brought back just loose enough to allow the treble to play, is given with the pliers three turns round the wire, as neatly and as close to the spoon as possible; the other end goes through an eye of the swivel, and is similarly doubled and given three turns—a double swivel is best. The hook at the thick end of the spoon is similarly fastened on with wire and the hook not unfrequently added at one side of the spoon is dispensed with, because two trebles are quite enough to ensure the hooking of any fish that is fool enough to take the spoon into his mouth, and more than two hooks unduly impede the spinning of the spoon. Tackle-makers ought not to give you the trouble of doing all this, but should send out your spoons mounted in this trustworthy manner, or on *soldered* solid rings, which is a very easy matter. In this matter of split rings I do hope, dear reader, that you will be content to be guided by me. It is not a matter for compromise, not a matter for argument. It is *aut Cæsar aut nullus.*

Double loop-knot.

Any one who baits with a fish on one treble hook, or on a single hook drawn home to the anus, should have a loop at the end of his spinning trace big enough to allow of the bait being passed through it; for the simplest way of attaching this bait to the trace is to put the large loop of the trace through the loop of the snood,* and then pass the bait through the large loop. But traces are not always made with large loops, and then the only alternative is to unhitch the collar from the running line every time you fresh bait, and passing the loop of the snood through one loop of the trace, then to pass the whole trace through the loop of the snood, and hitch on to the running line again. This is a tedious operation, and time is too precious when fish are taking. I have, therefore, a little knot of my own for getting over this difficulty. It is a double loop, made of a single length of good stout salmon gut.

Commence by thoroughly well soaking your gut for a quarter of an hour or more. Then arrange it as in Figure I, Plate XXV, and tie a simple whip knot or common knot in it, such as is commonly tied at the end of a whip; a single knot, not a blood knot. The gut will then be disposed as shown in Figure 2. If in this stage you take the trouble to see that the guts fall evenly side by side, and not across each other, your knot will be both tighter and neater than if clumsily tied. Pull the two loops, and the two ends, till you get all quite taut; and then cut off the ends, and you will

* The snood is the length of gut, or other material, with loop, which is attached to the hook.

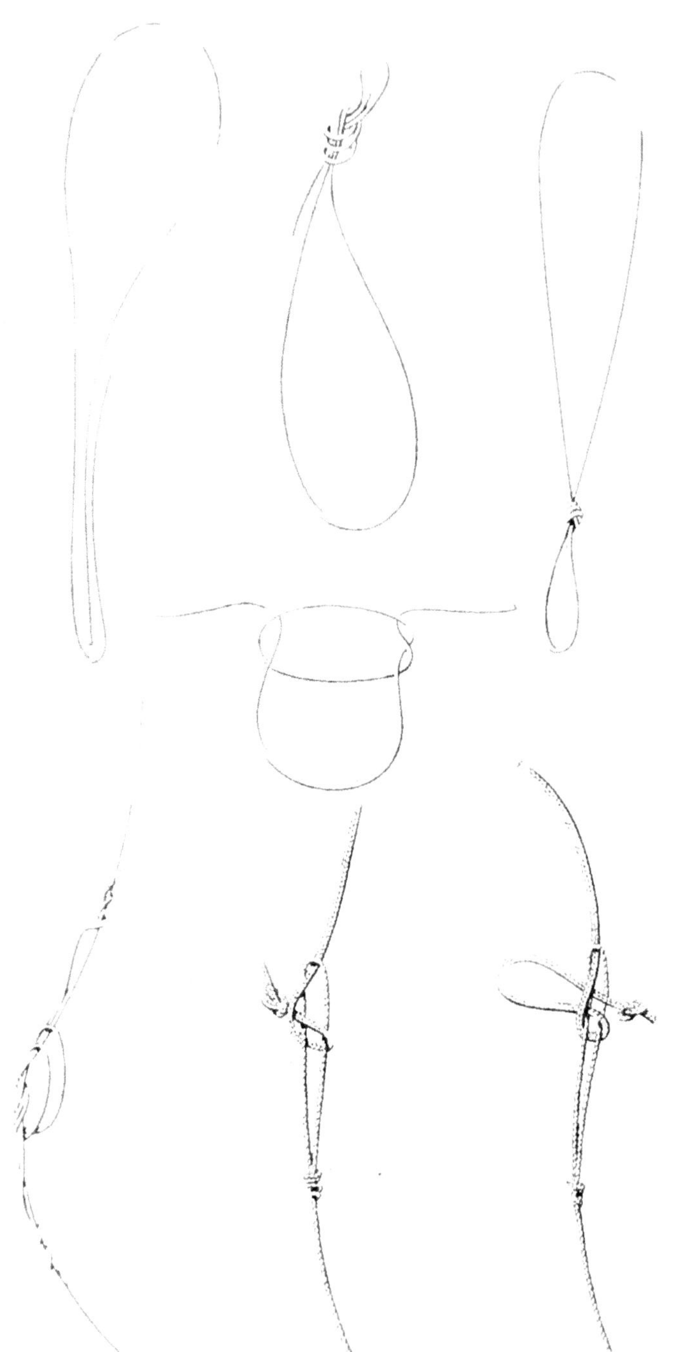

have a neat knot as in Figure 3. When neatly tied and well pulled together, in well soaked gut, the knot is a very neat and strong one indeed. Of course you will arrange to have a large loop at one end, and a small at the other. A very little manipulation is sufficient for this.

Put the end of your trace through the small loop, and then pass the big loop through the trace loop, and you have then furnished your trace with a large loop of double salmon gut big enough to pass any bait, and strong enough to hold any fish; stronger, probably, than your spinning trace, which is seldom made of such strong gut.

Soaking gut.

Thoroughly soaking your gut, before tying any knots in it, is a precaution inculcated in all books on angling; but it is very much more important to attend to this in India than it is in England, because in a tropical clime the gut is much more dry and brittle, and consequently cracks more easily. But if the gut is soaked in cold water till it is quite soft and limp, there is no fear.

If your trace, your phantom, or fly collar, has been much doubled up in your book or case, I would suggest well wetting and straightening it in the river, before trusting it with a heavy fish. Indeed, I would suggest well wetting it whether it has been so doubled up or not, for the fish may give it an uncanny turn, and I have lost two good fish in an evening, and that on treble gut fresh from England, solely from the gut being dry and brittle and easily broken. Always soak your gut thoroughly, therefore, both before tying, and before fishing, Do not trust to your not getting a run the first half dozen casts, and your line being by that time well soaked and pliable, but soak before endangering it at all. And if you have a man with you, as elsewhere recommended, always keeping a second hook ready baited for you, take care that that snood is well soaked. Do not let him hang it out to dry in his hand or keep it in his pocket, but have him drop it into the bait-can when ready, and let it soak there till wanted. I always put my spinning trace and two flights of hooks into the bait-can before starting for the river side, so that, by the time I reach the fishing-ground, they are soft from having been well soaked, and I can begin fishing with them without delay. Another simple plan is to steep a pocket-handkerchief in water, half wring it out, and wrap your tackle in it before starting.

A constant source of disappointment in India is the swivels rusting, and eating into the gut to which they are tied, and the gut consequently giving there when you get a heavy fish. If they have been put by for a fortnight, always try them in your hand before risking them. Don't be afraid of breaking them, it is much better that you should do so yourself and re-tie, than that a fish should break it for you, and carry away your phantom, or spoon into the bargain. But well soak before testing, or you do not give the gut fair play, and it may crack from brittleness at the double, though it would be strong enough after being soaked. Test with an even strain, not a jerk.

Rust-eaten gut.

Why on earth swivels, which are meant to be amphibious, are almost always made of a material that will not stand the water without rusting, is a thing I never could make out. The only excuse for it is that they can be made finer of such a hard material as steel, than of anything else. This is all very fine, but it is an advantage which is more than counterbalanced in India, and the sea, by their rapidly rusting; and if brass swivels cannot be made small enough, or galvanized iron is too soft a material to run well in a swivel, then I would suggest swivels made of steel in the centre bit, and of brass at each end; so that the two eyes to which the gut is tied should be of a material that does not rust and corrode the gut. At any rate it is an easy plan to have your swivels electro-plated, the gut at each end is then tied to silver, not iron, and is saved from being rust-eaten, that is, if the plating is thick enough. I had such from Farlow; they looked beautiful, and were so for a time, but from thinness in the plating it was soon worn through, and the rust commenced doing its work again. They should be liberally electro-plated, at least at the two ends; a little wax over the centre would easily prevent the plating from settling on and clogging the working centre. My idea is that the action of rust is more rapid in a tropical country than in England; at any rate it is much more provoking and remarked in a country where you cannot replenish for want of a tackle shop, and consequently it should be the better provided against. Brass in steel, or *vice versâ*, run better than any other metals. The ordinary plan is to use two swivels on a trace, with a length of gut between; but swivels are now made double, and such a double swivel immediately over your spoon or phantom,

Swivels.

close home to the *origo mali*, in short, should thoroughly prevent your line from twisting.

The sizes of swivels are as follow :—

No.	1/0	single	swivel is	$\frac{21}{16}$	of an inch	long.
,,	1	,,	,,	$\frac{19}{16}$	,,	,,
,,	2	,,	,,	$\frac{17}{16}$	,,	,,
,,	3	,,	,,	$\frac{16}{16}$	,,	,,
,,	4	,,	,,	$\frac{15}{16}$	,,	,,
,,	5	,,	,,	$\frac{13}{16}$	,,	,,
,,	6	,,	,,	$\frac{12}{16}$	,,	,,
,,	7	,,	,,	$\frac{11}{16}$	,,	,,
,,	8	,,	,,	$\frac{10}{16}$	,,	,,
,,	9	,,	,,	$\frac{9}{16}$	,,	,,
,,	10	,,	,,	$\frac{7}{16}$	,,	,,

The double swivels, being made of two swivels linked together, are nearly double these lengths, and are similarly numbered from 1/0 to 9. The sizes most convenient for Mahseer are, in my opinion Nos. 3 and 4.

Hooks drawing.

Hooks draw dreadfully in India, from the great heat drying up and shrinking the gut, as well as slackening the silk tying, and making the wax as brittle as resin. Every fisherman in India should be ready to re-tie his hooks afresh after any length of time; and every tackle-maker should take precautions in making up Indian tackle, which he does not condescend to do with English tackle. Two hundred years ago, careful old Izaak Walton advised one to singe the end of the gut before tying a fly, and this should always be done with trout flies for Indian use. It is neglected because flies are tied in the daylight, when a candle is not at hand, and because it is considered unnecessary. But for India it is necessary, however good the fly tyer, and should never be neglected, or at least the gut should be flattened between the teeth.

For salmon flies for Indian use, the same precaution should be taken; or the simpler one of tying a common knot in the gut. There is so much thickness of body in a salmon fly that this knot is concealed under it, and is not noticeable, as it would be in a small trout fly.

With a treble hook, the obvious plan is to double the gut, and bring it half way up the other side of the hook. It is impossible for it to slip then. All flights of spinning tackle, and all minnows mounted with treble hooks, should invariably be tied with this care for a tropical clime. But, except where one treble is placed below another in a flight, it is best to have eyed trebles.

Winch.

"K.," in his interesting letter ("Field," 9 October, 1869, and copied below) on Mahseer fishing on the Poonch, says the winch should be capable of holding 200 yards of running line. And "Barkis," writing to the "Field," 6 July, 1878, is not content with less than 250 yards; but I find Colonel Parsons agrees with me that 120 yards is ample, and he speaks of 50 lb. fish. And K.'s biggest fish, see Chapter XXIV, in the Poonch did not run out more than 100 yards. There may be singular occasions when a big fish wants more than 120 yards, and you are not in a boat, so that you can follow, or are hemmed in by forest, so that you cannot move after him along the shore, and the home he is making for is far from where you hooked him; but such are very singular occasions I am satisfied. Much of your enjoyment in fishing depends on having in your hands a rod you can work with comfortable ease. The winch is not the least part of the weight, and if you enlarge your reel, and double the length and weight of your running line, fishing becomes a labour instead of a pleasure. I do not see the wisdom of making all your sport a labour for the possible chance of falling in with a fish that, in very exceptional circumstances, might want a most exceptionable amount of line. I would rather fall out with such an exceptionable character. I would rather break my line with one such fish in 1,000, or, perhaps, it would be nearer the mark to say there is only one such fish in several thousands. I would rather deliberately break with such a fish than take the cream off all my sport with the other 999. I have never had to do it yet. Of course I have been broken again and again, who has not, but it has always been in the first violent rush, never for want of running line, and I use, and commend to your use, 120 yards.

Will you consider for a moment; a fish does not ordinarily set out for the next county the moment he is hooked, his object on such occasions is not foreign travel but his own village. He is frightened at the novel feeling of restraint, exerts all his strength to rush from it, and his object is to seek shelter in his home, which, with a Mahseer, is ordinarily the deepest part of the very pool in or near which you have hooked him. He has left that shelter for the shallow, or the run, in search of food, and only aims at returning to it; or, perhaps, he has not left it, and it is there you hooked him, and he has no definite ideas of where to go; he just wants to make a short rush to shake off the restraint, the thing that is holding him, and then he will return to his home.

Consequently a fish does not usually take out all your line, and expend all his strength, in one rush. No one has told him that your line is only so many yards in length, and that if he will only persevere, he must come to the end of it, and break it; on that subject his mind is a blank, so he ordinarily confines himself to the limits of the pool in which you have hooked him, and rushes up and down that; so that you lose and recover and re-use the same length of line many times in the course of one fight. And if by any chance he does come to the end of your line, the course is simple. I confess I once had a fish take me so very near the end of my 120 yards of line that I kept anxiously watching the reel to see if it would hold out, and had to make up my mind what I would do if it didn't. If something must be broken, the choice is obvious, let it be the line, not the rod. The course, then, is simple; lower the top of your rod till it is in a straight line with your line, till all the strain is taken off the rod, and goes through the ring straight from the reel to the fish. There hold on, but don't despair yet. Of course you then have on the very utmost strain you can possibly put on, and it is death or victory. After running out 120 yards of well contested line, the odds are it will be victory; you will turn him, and if he will only go in any direction but straight away from you you are saved. I hope I am not romancing, but citing from the tables of real memory, I think I am, that either I or one of my friends have thus been victors at the last tug. At any rate, I know there's a firm conviction in my mind that the die-hards in life not unfrequently live through it. But if the worst comes to the worst, and you are broken, it is pretty certain that the break will be in the snood or trace—most probably in the snood that has seen most wear. There is also another view of the position, the unpractical perhaps, but the romantic one. The existence, or idea of the existence, of a remote possibility of a tug as a last hope, remote though the bare possibility be, is just the little risk that adds spice to your sport. Sport reduced to a certainty is sport robbed of its essence. H., whom I have quoted elsewhere, was such a thorough sportsman that he would never keep a head, however fine, that was not shot with what he called "the toy," the other rifles, which were the usual weapons of ordinary mortals, were never used by him, except at elephant and bison, and, in cases of emergency, with bear, &c.; but any deer shot unadvisedly with what he was pleased to term scornfully a "blunderbus" was a head to be given away, got out of sight as an unsportsmanlike thing to be ashamed of. The chances are your 120 yards will never be run clean out and broken, and, even if they are, it is certainly very much more enjoyable, and perhaps just a trifle more sportsman-like to run those remote chances.

The amount of line a winch will hold, depends very much on the description of line you use. The same reel will hold nearly twice as much of the cotton twine recommended for Mahseer fishing as it will of the india-rubber coated plaited silk, which is both more expensive and more bulky. To avoid repetition, therefore, it is perhaps better that I should give the sizes of winches when speaking of running line.

I would recommend the invariable use of a check reel in preference to an old-fashioned simple reel. When you have just the length of cast you wish to throw, the check on the reel keeps the line at the same length; whereas, without the check, it is liable to run out a few inches each cast, and thus throw you out, and trouble you. The noise of the check gives you immediate notice of your having a fish on, and, what is of more importance than anything, it makes the reel cease to revolve directly the fish ceases to pull; whereas, if it goes on revolving as a wheel or common reel from the impetus given to it, it will take a turn or two more after the fish has ceased running, and your running line will get wound the wrong way, and the chances are that if your fish makes another dart of it, there will be a hitch in the line, and your fish will break away. The best winches are termed revolving plate winches. In them the handle has no separate elbow round which the line is apt to get hitched, but is let into the plate which revolves. Winches are made of all sizes, increasing by a quarter of an inch in each size from 2 inches to 5 inches in diameter, and after that the breadth is increased, and I have seen a specially made one very much bigger than 5 inches in depth. If you *will* have a mile of line in a weighty winch it can be arranged that the winch shall be fitted into a belt, so that the weight may come on the waist, not the hands. But a winch with a plate of 5 inches in diameter, and a breadth widened to $2\frac{1}{4}$ inches, will hold 250 yards of Manchester Cotton Twine Spinning Company's *thick* line, and you surely cannot want more than that. But I see beautiful lines a trifle, if anything, cheaper are also made by the Manchester Cotton Twine Spinning Company. One that I have of 60 yards tapered at both ends looks perfection, and I see them highly spoken of in the "Field" by correspondents, but I have not yet tested mine. For such a line a winch of $2\frac{3}{4}$ inches in diameter, and 1 inch broad, inside measurement, will suffice. For heavy fish, such as Salmon or Mahseer, I find nothing to compare with the lines of the above Company; though they are objected to as too stiff, and liable, if badly packed, to break like a wire. They make lines of all sorts, and the one they recommend for Mahseer is their No. 5 "16 plait Egyptian enamel waterproof" at 2*s.* per score of yards. They make this No. 5 of six sizes, to wit, 5, 4, 63, 64, 84, and 600, which, for brevity sake, I will term No. $\frac{5}{5}$, No. $\frac{5}{4}$, No. $\frac{5}{63}$, No. $\frac{5}{64}$, No. $\frac{5}{84}$, and No. $\frac{5}{600}$. Of these—

No. $\frac{5}{5}$ is so thick that no one would think of using it except when in very rough weather he wanted a specially weighty line to enable him to cast against a strong wind.

No. $\frac{5}{4}$ is the next thickest, and is the thickest ordinary size. In their letter to me the Company call it "heavy Salmon."

No. $\frac{5}{63}$ is the next in thickness, it is what many use for Salmon and Mahseer. I suppose we may call it ordinary Salmon line.

No. $\frac{5}{64}$, the next size, which is a trifle, only a trifle, finer must, I suppose, be called light Salmon, though it is very little lighter than No. $\frac{5}{63}$. This is the line I have used, and prefer. It is strong enough to kill any Mahseer in Hindustan on a rod, and 120 yards of it will just go comfortably into a $3\frac{1}{2}$-inch reel; whereas, if you take the line before it, No. $\frac{5}{63}$, you will want to increase your reel to 4 inches. No. $\frac{5}{64}$ is the line I have in view in my recommendations for winches at the close of this chapter.

No. $\frac{5}{84}$, their next size of this style of "16 plait Egyptian enamel waterproof" is called by the Company "strong trout." And—

No. $\frac{1}{000}$ is finest plait trout.

Of these last two I can say nothing from experience after practical trial; but from the samples sent, what they are pleased to term "strong trout" seems to me strong enough, as far as strength goes, to kill Mahseer, but perhaps not the best weight for throwing a treble gut cast. If your habit is to use a single gut cast, as "Doon" does, it would be heavy enough and strong enough, and of course you could get more yards on a reasonably sized winch. These 16 plait lines cost 2*s.* per score of yards.

There is no getting anything out of them without *previously* paid cash, which it is difficult to manage in India, when you do not know the exact price. Your tackle-maker ought, however, to arrange this for you.

Running Line.

In the way of running line there is nothing nicer for light fly-fishing than plaited silk, coated with india-rubber, and use 30 yards.

Of all your lines be careful that they do not rot from being put away wet.

Gut.

For gut, too, I could wish that some fisherman, who has time on his hands, would give the tussa silkworm (*Antheraa Paphia*) a trial. It is more than twice the size of the ordinary silkworm; and the Atlas moth (*Attacus Atlas*) is still larger. I am inclined to think a thicker and stronger piece of gut, for Salmon and Mahseer fishing, might be got out of them. The process of manufacture is simple enough, apparently, for, if what one reads be true, you have only to take the worm, when, from a piece of silk hanging from his nose, you see he meditates spinning, and put him into a closed jar of vinegar, and let him pickle therein, for some six hours in a tropical climate, more in a colder; then break him open, and taking one of the two guts, stretch it between finger and thumb, and keep it stretched across a plank, by hitching the ends into niches, or round pins or tacks, and put it into the sun to dry.

From "Shifts and Expedients of Camp Life, Travel, and Exploration," by W. B. Lord and T. Bains, I quote the following:—

"Silkworm gut can also be obtained wherever silk-spinning worms "are met with. To make it, a number of the caterpillars are to be "collected just prior to their time of spinning. These are to be "placed in a pot or other convenient vessel, containing a mixture of "vinegar and water in equal quantities: they are then to be covered "down and allowed to stand for about twelve hours. A worm may "then be taken out, opened, and tested as to its fitness for drawing. "If, in pulling the yellowish green coils which will be found within "it to their full extent and extreme, they break from softness of "texture, the worm must be allowed to remain in the vessel some time "longer, the temperature having much to do with the condition of "the pickled insects. When the coils are found to be tough, and "stand stretching fully out, one end of the strand must be placed in "a slit made in the end of a thin board or sheet of bark prepared for "the purpose. This strand is now to be drawn and stretched to the "other end of the board, in which corresponding slits have been made, "when the extremity of the gut is secured in one of them. When all "the worms have been thus treated, the stretching board is to be "placed in the sun, in order that the gut may dry, which it usually "does in about twelve hours. It will now be found that a considerable "quantity of yellow substance will remain adhering to the gut. This "must be removed, and in order to do so dissolve a common piece of "soap, about the size of a musket-ball, in a gallon of rain-water. "Place this, with the gut in it, in a boiler, and boil it for ten minutes, "when the gut must be turned out in a cloth to drain. Before "cooling, each strand must be lightly and smartly drawn through a "pledge of cotton held between the finger and thumb, which will "at once strip off the yellow coating: but great care must be taken "not to press the softened strand hard enough to make it flat or "curled. As fast as the strands are run through the cotton they "must be replaced on the board, and again dried in the sun, after "which they can be selected as to size, quality, length, etc., and "packed up in banks by twisting cotton or any other kind of thread "round them."

The advantages which I suppose these worms to possess over the ordinary silkworm are, that they are larger, and will probably yield much larger guts; also that they are indigenous to the country, and do not require to be fed on mulberry leaves, or other choice food, but on the wild tree leaves on which they are found.

More or less objection is taken by silk-spinners to both these worms, on the ground that the silk is difficult to reel, by reason of its being stuck together by such a strong gummy substance, that diluted sulphuric acid is recommended for mixing with water in which the cocoon of the tussa silkworm is boiled; and of the *Attacus Atlas* it is said "the silk is difficult to reel, though it yields partially if boiled in vinegar." But this very objection becomes a decided recommendation from a fisherman's point of view, for the stronger the gluten the less likely the gut is to fray in water, as ordinary silkworm gut will when worn.

To aid recognition by those who do not know the tussa silk-moth, I quote an extract from a description by Dr. Shortt, F.L.S., F.Z.S., etc., of Madras:—"The male and female moths differ "in size, the male measuring from the tip of one wing to the other "between 4 and 5 inches, whilst the female measures from 6 to "7 inches in expanse of wing; both are of a uniform yellowish "brown, having a couple of lunated transparent talc-like spots on "each wing, and it is chiefly in the form of these spots that they "differ from other moths of the same kind."

An exhaustive history of these and other silkworms, their food and culture, will be found in an official report on "Silk in India," by J. Geoghegen, Under-Secretary to the Government in India, Department of Agriculture, Revenue, and Commerce, and published at the Office of the Superintendent of Government Printing, Calcutta.

Rod.

For fly fishing for the smaller fish a light single-handed rod of 10 feet in length is the luxury. You should have an extra top in case of accidents, and a short stout spinning top is an advantage; not that you will use it for spinning in India, but for bottom fishing for Labeos, as stated in Chapter XII.

For Mahseer, however, you want a double-handed salmon rod, and 16 feet is quite long enough. I have had 17 feet and 19 feet, and prefer 16 feet.

The Irish rods, with splices instead of ferrules, play the best from end to end, if you will be troubled with putting them together, and if you will also do so thoroughly tightly, so that they are like one piece; but most fishermen will not be so bothered in spite of their proverbial patience.

On no account buy a rod with a screw inside the ferrule; the screw always wears, and then the rings do not come in line, and the joints are always stiff and unbending.

An ordinary ferruled rod is the general favourite, and though glue dissolves in the damp, and wood shrinks in the drought, of a climate which runs to extremes, still, if the ferrules are all rivetted inside and outside, as a good rod should be, they will stand. Mine have had a pretty lively experience, in as much as 135 inches of rainfall in two months, and have consequently had a constant glue-melting atmosphere, besides a very bone-drying one at other times.

But be very careful how you choose your rod, for it is to be your best friend in Mahseer fishing. On no account buy one of those stiff, almost pike, rods ordinarily advertised as Mahseer rods. I know there are those who commend them, and that it is on that account that they are so made and so styled. I suppose, also, that the commenders thereof are held to be law-givers in the matter of rods, or the trade would not follow them. One such writes to the "Field," under the name of "Barkis," and I will not do his view of the case the unjustice not to state it fully. I will also give you the opinions of another writer, equally unknown to me, a writer to the "Asian," under the name of "Doon," one, however, whom I gauge from his writings to be an expert. He entirely disagrees with "Barkis," and goes further even than myself in the opposite direction. While you read what "Barkis" says about rods, complete his argument by noting also what fearfully heavy tackle he has to use on his stiff rod, nine strand gut traces! His rods are, in my humble opinion, specially designed to smash any ordinary tackle. I argue as I have argued above, that it is not the heavy fish, but the heavy rod, the barge pole, that smashes the tackle. But I will not repeat the argument, I will rather beg your re-reading of it in this connection, and the tackle-makers reading of it as set forth on page 45. I will only add to those remarks that all the experience and talent of England, Scotland, Ireland, Norway, and Canada has devised for the capture of a fish, the salmon, that shows much activity, and runs up to 70 lbs. or thereabouts in weight, a thing called a salmon rod, certainly not a so-called Mahseer rod ; and no proper reason has been shown to my thinking why a fish, the Mahseer, that exhibits the selfsame qualities, in a somewhat higher degree, should be best captured by an implement devised on opposite principles. I hold that the principle adopted by all the salmon fishing skill of the world is the right principle, the one to be adopted also for the Mahseer; in other words, that there is no better implement for the capture of Mahseer than a salmon rod. But as the activity and strength of the salmon is somewhat intensified in the first violent rush of the Mahseer, so the principle of the salmon rod, its pliability, should be somewhat intensified in the Mahseer rod.

In brief, I hold that the best Mahseer rod is a pliable, but not top-heavy, salmon rod of 16 feet in length. For portability, I like it in the usual four joints, and of my two, I very much prefer the *lighter* one, by Farlow. You should have an extra top in case of accidents.

Fish that are less active than the Salmon and the Mahseer may, like the pike, be safely killed on a stiff pike top. Such fish are the Marral and the Freshwater Sharks of Chapter XIII, and the Cock-up. If you want a shorter and stiffer rod for the throwing out of a heavy bait in pike trolling fashion, it is easily managed by having a third extra and very short top to your pliable salmon rod. With such a top your 16 feet pliable salmon rod will become a 12½ feet trolling rod.

For the *Barilius bola*, or Indian trout, may be a 14 feet fly rod is the most enjoyable.

My complement of rods is two pliable 16 feet salmon rods for Mahseer, one of them very light for its length, two in case of accidents, and one 10 feet trout rod. The complement is doubtless incomplete without a 14 feet fly rod, only somehow I have always been thinking some one might possibly give me one on my birth-day!!

I will now quote "Barkis" as promised. The "Field," 6th July, 1878:—

"Avoid the ordinary black salmon rod of the London maker; it is "a delusion and a snare. I broke five of them in a fortnight, all by "good makers. The fact is the wood won't stand the climate, and "gets as brittle as sealing-wax. After many trials of rods of every "description, I decided in my own mind what was the best rod to get "for Mahseer, and I came home and got it. I took it out, used it last "season, and handed it over to a friend, who wrote to me last mail "and said it was 'the best rod in Asia;' and I think he was about "right. My friends in Crooked Lane made it for me, an 18 feet "greenheart, in two joints, with a splice and a spare top (the latter

" much stouter than that of an ordinary salmon rod), and standing " rings all the way up both joints.

* * * *

" I shall now recapitulate the various articles I have mentioned, " with a few additions:—

" One 18 feet spinning rod.
" One 18 feet fly rod.
" Two 5-inch metal reels (a spare one is always necessary), " one smaller reel for fly.
" Two 250 yards plaited silk lines.
" One 150 yards silk and hair line.
" Four nine-strand traces.
" Four treble gut traces.
" Twelve gilt spoons, of sizes varying from 1½ inch to " 2½ inches.
" Six phantoms from 3 inches to 6 inches, ordinary trout " colour, or blue and silver for choice.
" Six natural bait traces.
" A casting net.
" Two hanks of gut, one salmon, one strongish trout gut.
" A reel of copper wire.
" A box of spare triangles of sizes.
" A few spare swivels.
" Some cobbler's wax.
" Some leads of sizes.
" Some split shot.
" Some whipping silk.
" Some small hooks for bottom fishing.
" A 10 feet trout rod, a reel, and some 80 yards of line for " the same purpose.
" A landing net.
" A baiting needle.
" Some spare standing rings.
" Small bottle of linseed oil.
" Small bottle of Rangoon oil.
" A scale, up to 60 lbs.
" A japanned tin box, with trays for holding tackle."

Against the above, I now quote "Doon's" views ("Asian," 30 September, 1879), with the principle of which I cannot but entirely agree. His principles and mine are fully in unison, and it is a matter of choice whether you prefer his 14 feet or my 16 feet pliable fly rod for Mahseer :—

" You will easily understand that advice as to kit, etc., must vary, " not only to suit means, but for many other reasons.

" A strongly-made man could wield a rod for hours, which would " be a simple nuisance to a light frame, and some may go in only for " 'big' fish, and consider it almost waste of time to be hooking 6 or " 7 lbs.

" No special rule, therefore, can possibly be given. Keep in " mind your means and your strength, and buy your rods and tackle " accordingly.

" I give my 'turn out' for the benefit of what I termed light-" framed men.

" 1. A double-handed trout rod, by Farlow, one I can just use for " half a dozen throws single-handed.

" 2. A single-handed trout rod, by Farlow, rather a long rod, " and one that it is pleasanter to use with both hands than with one.

" 3. A light single trout rod.

" I doubt if the above will suit every one. In tackle, too, there " will be a difference of opinion—some holding with me that *light* " tackle, and plenty of line will land almost any fish in almost any " water; others preferring treble, and even 'six-strand' casts; the " latter I term 'cables.' No fish ought to break such things, but I " know they do! Woe to me for my presumption! but I put the " blame entirely on the holder of the rod!

" For rod No. 1, I have some 80 to 90 yards of good 'Tussa' silk " line. *Almost* always a good single gut salmon cast, and with that " rarely lose a fish. The 'Tussa' line is a grand line. It will not do " for spinning, but for 'fly' it is splendid. Not only is it strong, but " it has a quality little known probably, and still less appreciated— " *stretching power*. Try a bit and see how beautifully it yields.*

" This quality is a grand gain in hooking a fish. The sudden " 'jerk' on the rod with a line that will not give is entirely avoided, " and many a rod-top and trace saved, and many a valuable fly, and " the fish too! I may say here, to show the double-handed trout rod " *is* capable of good sound work, that a 44 lbs., 36 lbs., two fish over " 30 lbs., and several hundred (I can safely say, for I have had the " rod over 12 years) lesser fish confirm its capabilities. Therefore, for " a light-framed man, what we call a 'salmon rod' is simply a " burden. *Could* he wield it comfortably, he would land his fish sooner,

* I wish I knew the Tussa line, it sounds excellent

"but your humble servant prefers the lighter rod, and the lighter "tackle, not only because it gives more *play*, but because it is more "—what shall I say?—'scientific.' It is a *real* pleasure to land a big "fish on light tackle. I know nothing more exciting, bar the charge "of a 'devil' boar or a fighting tiger.

"On rod No. 2 there are fully 70 yards of good 'Cotton Twine "Spinning Co.'s' line, and a cast of 'lake trout' gut, and you can "laugh, if you are careful, at the efforts of a 10 to 12 lbs.

"The little rod has not, of course, pretensions to much, but a 6 or "7-pounder has a bad time of it, and generally comes to grief.

"This you may say is all 'egotism,' 'boasting,' etc., but let it not "be taken as such. I simply show you what I believe *any* fairly good "fisherman will do; simply what *any* man, with a fairly light hand, "and patience and 'head' can accomplish, and the satisfaction "when you once reach this stage is a recompense for all one's "troubles."

* * * *

Doon, "Asian," 1st October, 1879.

"Use also, always, as flexible a rod as you can throw with. It "saves a lot of 'breakages' in rough waters, and is generally lighter, "pleasanter to handle, and throws a fly far more neatly than any-"thing stiff."

One or two extra eyes (brass, not glass), and two or three dozen rings, will not come amiss for repairs in this distant land.

Sinkers.

I want a word or two on sinkers, insignificant though the subject may be. They are generally sold with a little brass wire loop, jutting out from the lead in which the rest is embedded when the mould is cast. So far so good. But then tackle-makers always insert into this loop an iron split ring, whereas if they would simply knot on a small loop of gut, it would be much better; it would not be so awkward in baiting, for it would bend on one side as desired; and it would not stick stiffly out of the bait's mouth and show, as an iron ring frequently does. And what if it does wear out a little sooner than iron, nothing is simpler than to knot a fresh loop. But in practice I do not think it does wear, because there is very little strain on it.

If you have not the time to wait for sinkers from home, many a native blacksmith will turn out a thing like a bullet mould, for casting three sizes of sinkers, and that is all you want.

These sizes may be $\frac{7}{8}$ of an inch long in the lead, by $\frac{3}{16}$ thick in the broadest place, and $\frac{9}{8} \times \frac{2}{8}$ and $\frac{12}{8} \times \frac{3}{8}$, but the medium size will be found most useful, and next to that the smallest size.

But you cannot get more than a limited amount of lead stowed away in a bait's inside, and for still further weighting your line very convenient sinkers are sold in English tackle shops, consisting of a long shaped piece of lead strung on to a short bit of line with a loop at either end, so that it can be attached to, or detached from the trace at pleasure. I am not sure that I would advocate the use of this except as an additional sinker, and after having stowed away all you can in the bait's hold; for it is there out of sight, and makes no splash, and is in the best position for throwing. Still, on the other hand, the lead in the bait soon tears its way out of the bait's stomach, breaking through the skin of it, and when your bait is not very fresh and tough, it will be found less trouble in the end to have the weight outside and well away from the fish. It adds much, however, to the difficulty of throwing lightly. It thus becomes a question, I think, for individual choice. When fishing deep pools for heavy fish you should have it, but in the shallower runs it is not necessary, and is trying to your top joint.

Whipping.

I have one more complaint against the tackle-makers. It is the fashion with them to bind the gut loops in the snood and collar with silk, whereas the fastening would be both tighter and less visible, besides lasting longer, if in single gut it were simply knotted after well soaking the gut. In India particularly, where whip fastenings are so liable to come undone, from the extreme dryness of the air shrinking the gut, spoiling the wax, and slackening the silk binding, it would be more satisfactory to have plain gut knots. Knots also are not liable to fray as silk is from wear. With treble gut collars, of course, the best fastening is the whipping with gut, which is exceedingly neat, and durable.

Flight of hooks.

In Chapter V. I have, for special reasons there given, recommended two sorts of spinning tackle for Mahseer, one a solitary treble hook, which any one can tie, the other a lip hook and one treble, which is tied as follows. Take the lip hook first, and with silk whip a small piece of very fine gimp on to it, so as to leave a loop at the head not more than an eighth of an inch long, and another similar loop where the tail of a fly would come, that is, at the end of the shank and at the back of the hook. I have tried loops of salmon gut instead as being less easily seen than gimp; but I was not satisfied with them, because the gut, when well soaked from fishing, becomes so limp that it readily bends, and the result is that the snood is not kept in position, loses one of its turns in the yielding gut loops, ceases to have two turns round the shank of the hook, and, as a consequence, slips. For the same reason the fine gimp loops should not be a bit bigger than I have said. Having thus disposed of your lip hook, take the snood of salmon gut or treble gut, on which you are going to tie your treble hook, and pass what is to be the treble hook end through the loop at the head; give it two turns round the shank of the lip hook, or, if you like, three turns, but certainly not less than two complete turns, and pass it through the tail loop, and then on to the end tie your one No. 7 Mahseer treble hook, after the fashion recommended for tying treble hooks in India. Knot the usual loop at the other end of your snood, and your flight of spinning hooks is complete. Your lip hook will, of course, hang the same way as your treble.

You will find that, when pulled taut, the two turns round the lip hook keep it effectually from slipping when spinning; and even should you chance to hook your fish on that hook instead of the treble, it will still hold without slipping. At the same time it is easy enough for you to adjust the length intervening between the lip hook and the treble, by pushing the snood together, so as to slacken the double turn round the lip hook, and you can then work the lip hook either way. The lip hook should thus be adjusted so as to suit the varying size of your bait, by making the intervening space just long enough to bring the treble hook even with the vent, when the lip hook is in the lip; but care should be taken to do this when the gut is limp after having been well soaked, or it is liable to crack, because of the sharp turns given to it round the shank of the lip hook.

The lip hook will be very much the better for being an eyed lip hook, for whipping is so untrustworthy in India. I have had the whipping rip right up from having got rotten, and lost a good fish at the last moment which I should have landed if I had had the metal eye in the lip hook to fall back upon.

If you are spinning for murral or sea-fish, however, you cannot be quite so sure of hooking with one treble, and can either add another treble to my flight of hooks as above described, or can adopt Francis Francis' or Pennel's flights of pike hooks, which, if quoted by the inventors' names, will be sufficiently described for recognition by tackle-makers. I, however, would rather recommend the use of small stout Mahseer hooks, because Indian waters are generally so bright, and pike hooks are so large and formidable. For these fish, however, they should be tied on gimp, not gut.

When I am fishing with at all a large bait, so large that it carries the hooks well without showing, I do not mind adding a second treble hook, so as to have one treble hook half-way up the fish, and another near about the region of the tail, but I never have one trailing all unconcealed behind the bait, and I do not know that this second treble is really of any use. It is more fancy, I think, than anything else, the remains of an old creed still clinging about one, though all reason in connection with the material of the Mahseer's mouth, and the manner in which it seizes its bait, argue that one treble hook is really all that is wanted; and if more than one is superfluous, then it is objectionable, for it certainly cannot tend to make the bait look more tempting to the fish. Keep then, as a rule, to no more hooks for our bright waters than are absolutely necessary, to wit, one lip hook and one treble.

Preserving Tackle.

In consequence of hooks rusting so quickly in India, and the difficulty of replenishing your stock, the prudent man will perhaps take extra precautions which I confess I never had the time for. A thin coating of shellac varnish put over your hooks, swivels, traces, and flights of hooks, and heads of flies, will exclude the air, and thus preserve them from rust. It is recommended that the same should be done again on putting away used tackle. I believe the way to do it is to dip your hooks and tackle in the varnish, and then hang them on a thread stretched crosswise. If laid on the table, of course they will stick to it.

My flies I always kept in a tin box of sandalwood sawdust. The oil in the sawdust kept the hooks from rusting; the smell preserved the feathers from being moth-eaten.

Shellac varnish is easily made. Lac is procurable in any

native bazaar in India. Put it in a tightly corked bottle with spirits. Time does the rest. Made thick, it is liquid glue; thin, it is varnish. Naphtha is the spirit ordinarily used in England as the cheapest, but spirits of wine, or any highly rectified spirit, will do as well.

Your running line must be scrupulously dried every day you use it. *Never* put it away damp, unless you want it "rotten as "pears," to fail you with the first run-away fish. This I never neglected to see to myself. Dry it after morning fishing; dry it again after evening fishing. There are things sold for this purpose, but I always found the backs of two chairs, or the eves of the verandahs, or something else handy enough.

Wax.

Wax you must have. Cobbler's wax you can get from any boot-maker, but now-a-days you must be careful to call it shoemaker's wax, or you may be told he has not got any. If you are living in the wilds beyond the pale of shoemaking, and are compelled to make your cobbler's wax yourself, the following recipe may be useful:—

"Take 4 ounces of resin, grind it to a fine powder between two "stones, ¼ oz. of bees' wax chopped up small, and 2 ozs. of common "pitch; mix these substances with the resin, and place the whole in a "small native chatty pot. Then put the pot in a bed of hot wood "ashes, and with a long, flat-pointed stick work and stir the mass "about until thoroughly melted; then add ¾ oz. of good clean fat, "and keep the whole in solution for about a quarter of an hour or "twenty minutes. Grease the bottom of a calabash or bowl, half fill "it with cold water; take your pot off the water with a twisted stick, "and pour the molten material into the water. When cold enough "to handle, grease your hands and work the wax about, pull it out "into long strips, double these back on themselves, and so proceed "until all the materials are well amalgamated; then work it out into a "long stick or rod, take a greased knife and divide it up into pieces. "large enough to make convenient balls for use. These are best kept "floating in water until wanted."—"Shifts and Expedients of Camp "Life, Travel, and Exploration," by W. B. Lord, Royal Artillery, and T. Baines, F.R.G.S.: Horace Cox, 346, Strand

For white fly-making wax here is a recipe: "Two ounces of best yellow resin, one drachm of bees' wax; put them into a

" pipkin over a slow fire till completely melted. Then add a " quarter of an ounce of spermaceti; and let the whole simmer, " constantly stirring it for a quarter of an hour longer. Pour the " melted mass into a basin of clear cold water. It will instantly " become thick. In this state, and while yet warm, work it by " pulling it through the fingers till cold. This last operation is " necessary to make the wax tough, and to give it that silvery hue " it has when made in perfection."—(" The Angler and his Friend," by John Davy, M.D., F.R.S.) Francis Francis substitutes tallow, I see, for spermaceti.

Lead Wire.

For weighing lines for float fishing, split shot are ordinarily used, but a much handier thing is the soft-drawn lead wire of the Manchester Cotton Twine Spinning Co. It is so easily put on, and can without the least difficulty be exactly accommodated to the finest float, whereas it is troublesome sometimes to exactly hit it off with shot. It is cheap enough, 15 yards for 1s.

Copper Wire

The same Company supply also fine soft copper wire, as fine as fly tyers' silk, in knots of 40 yards for 1s. It is nice for whipping, and fishermen should not be without it.

Whipping Cord.

While you are sending to this company for running line, &c., you will do well to get their " waterproof cable whipping cord, 100 yards for 1s." It is excellent for repairs of breakages. Their silk for whipping hooks, flies, &c., is also good. They supply also all sorts of excellent lines for sea-fishing. But, as I said before, their transactions are all for prepaid cash, a little difficulty which your tackle-maker will arrange for you.

Bait Kettle.

A common earthen pot makes a very good bait-can. Arrange a string by which to carry it by one hand, tie a cloth over the mouth to prevent the bait jumping out, and punch small holes round the neck of it with a nail; in doing so use caution to prevent breakage. When fishing, keep it well under water in the river, having first poured out all the old water. Your bait will keep alive the longer for thus having fresh water. Do not bore holes lower than the neck, or you will have no water in your earthen pot, when carrying it from place to place. This is as good a bait kettle as you can desire, and is to be had for between one and three pies, say, at the very outside, for the vast sum of two farthings. If your bait are *Ophiocephalus gachua*, less care is necessary about the changing of the water, but more that they are not suffocated by being cut off from the air; for them the earthen pot must be left out of water, not immersed and the cloth kept carefully over the mouth for they jump out more than any fish.

Otter.

An artificial otter is not unfrequently used in lakes in Ireland; and as some may like to use it in India, where the competition amongst anglers is not so great as to bring down on you from your neighbours the charge of poaching, I will supply instructions for making one.

I should add that it has this to be said for it in India, and that it is on this account solely that I mention it, or ever deigned to give it a thought, that here we do not know definitely by the experience of ten thousand anglers exactly how to fish. We are all more or less explorers, trying to find what fish there are in India that will take a bait, which will take a minnow, which a fly, and what fly is preferred. For this purpose the otter covers a larger field of experiment, it searches more water, and it allows of one man trying twenty or thirty flies at one time, instead of three at the most.

Take a light plank, ¾ inch or an inch in thickness, of 2 feet in length, by 7 or 8 inches in depth, and lead it so that the water-line shall be about 1 inch from the top. Insert a brass ring, or light staple, exactly half-way up in the centre of the stern of the plank, and two more like staples, two-thirds forward, one in the top edge of the plank, and one in the bottom edge, or exactly opposite each other. To each of these staples tie a cord about 2 feet long, and bring the ends together, so that when suspended the plank shall hang quite even crosswise, but lengthwise shall have the stern slightly lowered, say 6 or 7 inches, for it is on the principle of the inclined plane that the otter acts. Then to the point where the three cords are knotted together tie a long cord, push the otter out from the shore, nose foremost, in the direction you mean to walk along, keeping the line taut, and try it. If the otter acts properly, it should keep parallel with you, keeping the line taut all the while. But if the top and bottom cords are not of exactly equal length, it will not sit true, and consequently will not have so good a hold of the water. If the cord from the stern is too short, the otter will have a tendency to yield to your tension and to come in to you, and will not keep away enough to keep the line taut. In such case let out the stern cord a little, and try again. If you lengthen the stern cord too much, the angle of the plank will be too great, and the otter will pull away from you too much, and in consequence will not keep pace with you, but will lag behind. You must therefore humour this stern cord till you have got it to work nicely; and, that attained, knot all three cords together in one simple knot, such as is usually tied at the end of the lash of a whip by non-whip makers, so that they may not slip; and leave a loop over to which to attach your towing line with the hooks on it. This adjusting of the stern line of the otter is rather a nice operation, but, once done, it lasts for ever.

The towing line can be used with flies or spinning bait, just as you like. To lead the otter so as to sink it to the desired depth, drive in small screws all along the bottom edge of the plank, one every inch, say, so as to stand out a little in continuation of the plank and give the lead something to hold by. Then paste brown paper on both sides of the plank, near the bottom edge and let it dry and stiffen. Stand the plank bottom edge upwards and pour molten lead into the trough thus made all round the line of jutting out screw heads along the bottom edge of the plank. You will need at least half an inch of lead, and it is better to pour too much than too little, for it is easy to plane off what is extra with a common jack plane, whereas it is not so easy to add lead with a second moulting, for it does not make a good joint with the previous cold lead; there is always a crack left with a want of firm hold. Remove the paper wall, and trying the otter in the water, plane down the lead till the plank sits evenly in the water, with just about an inch or an inch and a half above the water level.

The usual way is to attach the tow line to the loop, where the three otter plank cords are knotted together, which three cords we will call the bridle; but another plan, as suggested by Mr. Wilcocks, in his "Sea Fisherman," is to tie the tow line primarily to the staple at the stern of the otter plank, and connect it with the bridle by a piece of fine twine. When a fish is hooked you will then, by the act of striking the fish, break the thin connecting twine, and the strain coming on the stern of the otter, you will easily haul it on shore end-on; whereas it is not so easy when the otter remains broadside-on, and more or less interfering with the playing of your fish. The better way when it remains broadside on is to stand still, or retrace your steps, so as to get the otter in, and keep on pulling in the line till the otter describes a semicircle and runs in to shore.

But against Mr. Wilcocks' plan it is argued, again, that the otter does not interfere with the playing of your fish, but more or less aids it by yielding to violent tugs, and coming up and going on again as you proceed, and thus helping you in the drowning of your fish. Moreover, it is urged that you do not want to be compelled to pull in your otter with every individual fish, because it saves a great deal of trouble to keep moving on, the fish is soon killed, and trails quietly, and it is time enough to pull in when you have five or six fish on.

Still it may be that Mr. Wilcocks' plan is preferable, with heavy sea fish, of 10, 20 or 30 lbs. each, and it is about sea-fishing that he writes.

The tow line should be prepared as follows:—Get a number of small brass rings just big enough to run easily on the tow line, but so small that a knot tied in the tow line will not pass through them. Put twenty or thirty of these rings on the tow line, each 6 or 8 feet apart, say 8 for preference, with a common whip knot on each side of it, so as to prevent its shifting. The ring is to prevent the drop lines from twisting round the tow line. To these rings attach your drop lines, which must not be more than 2½ feet to the hook; so that by no means can they reach each other, and entangle in the water, even when the drops are only 6 feet apart.

But I think 8 feet is a fairer distance at which to place the drops, so as to be secure against entanglements, even in the event of the tow line sagging, or a heavy fish behaving badly. These drop lines will be the better, in the case of spinning fish, for having one or two swivels each. I would recommend the drop lines having two brass swivels each, and being not more than 2 feet long, with a large loop at the end. To this loop your spinning bait snood can then be easily attached, and re-attached, when fresh baiting. But the whole drop should be removable, because you want no swivels with flies, and will be the better for having nothing but gut, 2½ to 3 feet of gut to your fly.

The otter can be made larger if you like, maintaining the same proportions, which are that it should be about three times as long as it is deep, and always sunk with lead so that the water-line shall be within an inch of the top. I have one, 4 feet long, which nearly pulls me into the sea. It was made for fishing broad estuaries for heavy sea-fish, and for fishing the seashore outside the waves on calm days; but I have had very little opportunity for trying it. Still I have seen what it can do in the lakes in Ireland, and have seen also that Indian sea-fish, the seer, for instance, will take a small fish readily enough. I wonder if a porpoise would take it. If he did you would have caught a tartar.

The otter can be used whenever you have a good extent of uninterrupted shore or beach to walk along, without interposing trees, etc.; and it can also be used from the stern of a rowing boat, for as you move on rowing it will move parallel with you; and if you are very avaricious, you can have one on each side of a boat. But remember, that weeds have a strong affinity for tow-lines and drop flies, especially when there is a fish on.

I will confess, however, that I have not had the patience to experiment with the otter half as much as I purposed to do. It went against my grain, and in golden moments of leisure I found myself fingering my old friends the rods in preference.

The simpler way, however, is to have two small otters as above; if you like to use them singly you can do so, one on each side of a boat. If you wish to have one of double the power, so as to take out a very long line from the shore, drive a small staple into one of the otters, midway in the plank perpendicularly, and a little forward of midway longitudinally. The staple may be easily made of a piece of strong brass wire, with the eye protruding on the off-side and the ends on the near-side doubled down. To this eye attach the bridle of the second otter. The two otters will be thus coupled, and will walk side by side, together bringing just twice the tension to bear on the tow-line that either does singly. If you always worked your otter one way, say from right to left, nothing more would be wanted; but as you sometimes require to work from left to right, drive in another staple close alongside of the first one, and, as before, in the centre of the perpendicular of the plank, but with the eye protruding on the opposite side. You have thus an eye on either side to which to attach your off otter. To reverse an otter, turn the nose in the direction in which you wish it to run, and bring the bridle between you and the plank. To hitch on and unhitch the second otter, it is convenient to have a thing like a "nursery pin," only shorter, and made much stronger of thick brass wire. A pair of pincers will twist one up in a minute.

How to Order.

Friends wishing to set themselves up in tackle have come to me to advise them what to order, and to help them how to describe what they want, so that the English tackle-maker may not misunderstand them, and have asked me to give them some idea also of prices; I wish to sit down similarly by the side of my reader, and help him to indite his order. This may seem a work of supererogation to some, but to others I am convinced from experience that it will be a practical assistance, because they have not a tackle shop into which they can walk, and point out this thing and that thing, without knowing its name, and take the shopkeepers' advice about other things.

For such, then, I add a good comfortable outfit, the prices being taken from a good tackle-shop's list, and when three prices are named, the medium price being ordinarily taken. Inferior articles can, of course, be got at cheaper rates, but it is most unsatisfactory to buy such. Those who think my order too big can easily omit what they do not want.

FOR MAHSEER.

	£	s.	d.
1 Pliable, but not top-heavy, rather light, salmon rod (not what is commonly called a Mahseer rod), four-joint, greenheart, double brazed, winch fittings, with button-ended butt, partition bag, and extra fly top, 16 ft.	3	10	0
1 Extra spinning top	0	5	0
1 Superior bronzed revolving plate check winch, of 3½ inches in diameter	1	8	0
120 Yards Manchester Cotton Twine Spinning Company's No. $\frac{5}{63}$, 16-plait Egyptian enamel waterproof running line, at 2*s.* a score yards	0	12	0
4 Treble gut salmon spinning traces, stout, at 2*s.*	0	8	0
1 Treble gut salmon fly collar	0	2	6
1 Salmon fly collar, half treble, half single, extra stout, salmon gut ..	0	2	6
3 Single, extra stout, salmon gut fly collars, at 2*s.* 6*d.*	0	7	6
2 Stout spoons of 2½ inches, silvered and gilt, mounted without split rings, but with wire or solid soldered rings, with one No. 1 Mahseer treble hook at head, and one like hook at tail, and none at the side, and on a double No. 4 swivel, as given at page 227, on stout treble gut at 2*s.*	0	4	0

	£	s.	d.
4 Like spoons of 2½ inches	0	8	0
1 ,, ,, 3 ,, ...	0	2	0
3 Phantom minnows of 4 inches in length, including the tail, mounted with No. 4 Mahseer treble hooks, and on stout treble gut, with one double No. 4 swivel at 2*s*. 6*d*.	0	7	6
1 Hank of stout salmon gut	1	0	0
12 Lengths stout treble twisted gut..	0	4	0
3 Dozen Mahseer treble braized hooks, No. 1, at 2*s*. a dozen	0	6	0
3 ,, ,, ,, ,, No. 4, ,, ,, ...	0	6	0
3 Flights of my hooks (page 50), tied on extra stout single salmon gut	0	1	6
3 ,, ,, ,, ,, on stout treble gut	0	2	0
6 Snoods on stout treble gut of my one-treble spinning tackle (page 48),	0	1	0
3 Baiting needles	0	0	3
3 Sinkers with loop at each end of stout treble gut for fitting on trace..	0	1	6
1 Dozen sinkers, medium size, page 239, for putting in the mouth of bait	0	0	6
1 Dozen double swivels, silver plated, No. 4	0	2	0
3 Blackamoor flies on No. 2/0 Limerick hooks, my sizes	0	3	0
6 ,, ,, No. 2	0	6	0
1 Fly book, 7 × 4 inches	0	9	6
1 Pair fly scissors	0	2	6
1 ,, pliers	0	0	6
1 Skein of silk for tying flies, and 2 skeins of silk, stouter, for rod repairs	0	0	6
100 Yards Manchester Cotton Twine Spinning Company's waterproof cable whipping cord	0	1	6
1 Dozen bare Limerick hooks, No. 2/0	0	0	3
2 ,, ,, ,, No. 2	0	0	6
1 ,, peculiar eyed No. 6/0	0	0	3
1 ,, ,, ,, No. 4/0	0	0	3
1 Gut twister	0	10	0
An extra rod, winch, and running line as above	5	15	0

FOR CARNATIC CARP, Extra.

	£	s.	d.
2 Dozen Blackamoor flies on No. 6 Limerick hook, my size, with gut eye	1	4	0
1 ,, ,, ,, No. 5 Kirby, on stout single salmon gut ..	0	3	0
1 Landing net, 14 inch diameter, folding ring and handle	0	9	6
3 Dozen No. 6 Limerick bare hooks	0	0	9
1 ,, No. 5 Kirby ,, ,, ...	0	0	3

FOR FRESHWATER SHARKS, &C., Extra.

	£	s.	d.
3 Yards stoutest gimp	0	1	6
3 ,, medium ,, ...	0	1	0
3 Phantoms, 4 inches, including tail, on stoutest gimp, with No. 4 Mahseer treble hooks, and double swivel attached by wire, not split-ring, at 2*s*. 6*d*...	0	7	6

	£	s.	d.
3 Flights, as at page 202, on stoutest gimp, with No. 4 Mahseer treble hooks, at 6*d.*	0	1	6
3 Flights as at page 202, on medium gimp	0	1	6
3, My flights (page 50), on medium gimp..	0	1	6
1 Disgorger	0	0	2
1 Stoutest gimp trace..	0	1	0

FOR SMALL FLY TAKERS.

1 Single-handed trout rod, not top-heavy or too limp, 10 feet, three joint, greenheart, double braized, winch fittings, with screw spike, partition bag, extra fly top, and short spinning top	1	10	0
1 Superior bronzed revolving plate check winch 2¼ inches	0	18	6
30 Yards waterproof plaited silk taper trout running line	0	6	3
1 Dozen black flies on No. 14 sneck-bend hooks	0	2	0
2 Dozen light duns of various shades on No. 14 sneck-bend hooks ..	0	4	0
½ Dozen black flies on No. 6 sneck-bend hook	0	1	0
3 Fine drawn trout fly collars or casting lines	0	3	0
1 Ordinary trout fly collar	0	0	9
1 Hank trout gut	0	3	0
2 Dozen bare No. 14 sneck-bend hooks	0	0	6

FOR LABEOS, EXTRA.

2 Lines of medium trout gut, furnished with fine quill floats, with No. 6 Kirby hooks on wooden reels..	0	4	0
2 Spare fine quill floats with caps complete	0	1	6
2 Dozen No. 6 Kirby hooks on medium trout gut..	0	2	0
3 Yards soft drawn lead wire	0	0	1

FOR LUXURY. *See page 236.*

1 Two-handed trout rod, 14 feet, 4 joints, greenheart, double braized, winch fittings, with extra fly top, and partition bag	1	15	0
1 Superior bronzed revolving plate check winch of 3 inches in diameter	1	4	0
60 Yards Manchester Cotton Twine Spinning Company's trout line, with taper at both ends	0	10	0
Total ..	27	14	3
Add 25 per cent. for freight, insurance, loss by exchange..	7	0	0
	34	14	3

Say, 340 rupees, and order the whole to be sent out in one stoutly-made hinged and locked box with your name painted on it. You will find such a box very convenient for keeping your tackle in, and for transporting it on your trips to the fishing grounds, occasions on which you will sometimes find a good lock an advantage.

For those who prefer "barge poles" and "cables," as "Doon" calls them, I have quoted above a list taken from "Barkis'" letter to the "Field," dated 6th July, 1878; only let me be allowed to say, I disapprove of its principles quite as much as "Doon" does. Still, there are those who are wedded to "Barkis'" views, and I cannot convert them, so for their benefit the list is introduced. One last effort, however, I will make,—compromise by having a long line, 250 yards long if you will, and stick to my pliable rod, and you still may avoid "barge poles, cables, and meat-hooks."

For 250 yards of thick Manchester Cotton Twine Spinning Company's line, the winch will need to be 5 inches in diameter, and $2\frac{1}{4}$ inches broad in the bar. For plaited silk it will probably have to be broader still. Be careful to particularize the line your reel is to hold, for the guidance of your tackle-shop, for even the Manchester cotton lines differ much in thickness, and at an Indian distance you cannot easily remedy mistakes.

In India, one commonly makes up a party for distant fishing and shooting, and several rods are apt to get thrown together in a corner of the tent, and when coming from the same makers, and ordered after one pattern, as they would be if two or three chums ordered from this book, it will be found that they are very much alike, and that it is no easy job to tell the several joints one from another, when starting, perhaps somewhat hurriedly, for the day. It will save you some trouble, and cost nothing comparatively, to have your initials cut small, at twopence a letter, on every joint of every rod, and on every winch you possess, and marked pretty large on the rod partition bag. Thus you will always be able to pick out your own property at a glance, and will not get in exchange a carelessly put away rotten line, or your friend's top with a bad warp in it from ill-usage; or, still worse, give him yours, or exchange tops, that when you are a mile apart, and putting them up at the river's side, are found not to fit into the second joint!

For those who wish me to indicate a minimum economical kit, I will extract from the larger order the following:—

For Mahseer.

	£	s.	d.
1 Salmon rod as in the larger order..	3	10	0
1 3½-inch winch	1	8	0
120 Yards running line	0	12	0
2 Spinning traces	0	1	0
1 Treble gut fly collar	0	2	6
2 Spoons of 2¼ inches..	0	1	0
1 Phantom	0	2	6
1 Dozen No. 1 treble hooks	0	2	0
6 Lengths stout treble gut	0	2	0
2 Snoods of my one treble spinning tackle	0	0	2
1 Baiting needle	0	0	1
2 Sinkers on treble gut	0	1	0
3 Blackamoor flies on No. 2	0	3	0
1 Skein silk	0	0	6

For Carnatic Carp.

	£	s.	d.
6 Blackamoor flies on No. 6 Limerick	0	6	0
3 ,, ,, 5 Kirby..	0	1	6

For Freshwater Sharks, &c.

	£	s.	d.
Gimp as in the larger order..	0	2	6
1 Gimp phantom	0	2	6
2 Flights on stoutest gimp, as in larger order	0	1	0
1 Stoutest gimp trace..	0	1	0

For Small Fly Takers.

	£	s.	d.
1 Fly rod	1	10	0
1 2½-inch winch	0	18	6
30 Yards running line	0	6	3
½ Dozen black flies on No. 14 snecks	0	1	0
½ Dozen dun ,, ,, ,,	0	1	0
2 Ordinary fly collars..	0	1	6

For Labeos.

	£	s.	d.
1 Furnished line	0	2	0
½ Dozen No. 6 Kirby hooks on gut..	0	0	6
3 Yards soft drawn lead	0	0	1
	10	7	1
Adding 25 per cent. as above	2	14	0
	13	1	1

Say, 130 rupees; and of this any of the parts for different fish that are not desired can be omitted. But this is a highly limited order.

CHAPTER XIX.

FISHING GEAR AND OTHER SMALL BEER.

"The apparel oft proclaims the man."—SHAKESPEARE.

JUST a few short words on the clothes most convenient to wear when fishing in India, will add to the comfort of those that will be troubled to read them.

As you have already seen, you will have to do a good deal of wading if you are at all keen about sport. But on no account get waterproof wading stockings. First rate things though they are in England, they are not at all wanted in India. I doubt if they would keep good in India. I am quite sure they would be unbearably hot in this climate, and, much though I have waded, I never felt the want of any such protection in India; for the water is not perishingly cold, as in England, but comfortably tepid, so that, if you make a rule never to be tempted to go in over the fork, you will not be the worse for it. If you walk in deeper, and stand in the water up to your stomach and vitals, I will not be responsible for congestion of the liver, dysentery, and all the rest of it.

Remembering that you will be often in water up to the fork, shorten your coat tails accordingly; and have your pockets high and dry, or you will find, after landing a fish you have been very intent on, and waded in to get at, that your fly book, or some other valuable, has been thoroughly soaked the while.

The stony bottom, with its rounded boulders, is often very slippery, and, as you see the native naked foot slips less than a shoe, you may be tempted to wear thin shoes, so as to give you the better foot-hold. I tried thin racket shoes, but was very soon convinced of my mistake. Under water you cannot always see where you put your foot, and you are watching your fly, etc., and have to feel the bottom with the foot, and you are sometimes in a little hurry, for life is not long enough for dawdling, and then you bring your unprotected foot against a rock, and generally right on the top of your pet corn. "I never knew a dear gazelle," etc. But what is worst of all is when you get your unprotected foot jammed by the weight of your body between two rocks—that will decide you in favour of thick boots.

Have good heavy boots, then, with the sole a trifle broader than the foot, and of a good thickness. I mean the boots commonly made with a sort of open verandah all round the foot. Ankle-boots are a protection to the ankle from being bruised, and also from being turned and sprained; laced boots best protect the ankle. In short "the Alpine boot" is about the most comfortable you can have.

Walking amongst the rocks in, and on the edge of, a river is a galloping consumption of boots. Nails are an antidote. But too many nails make the sole slippery, make it almost as bad as one without any at all. Have the sole studded all over with large nails an inch apart. These will improve your foot-hold.

After being so soaked your boots will get uncomfortably hard if not greased. If you dry them first and then grease them they will shrink, but if you grease them when wet and put them in the sun the grease will take the place of the moisture, and the boots will remain comfortably soft and unshrunk. Jones' Gloucestershire paste is much used for shooting-boots in England, but in India my servants used common mutton fat, and my boots were always comfortable.

Braces are a mistake, for when exerting the arms by making a long stretch in clambering round a rock, for instance, they give, or, more likely, a button flies. The trousers should be supported from the waist.

Good thick socks are not only a wise precaution for health's sake, but a comfortable protection more or less against the sand, which, however, *will* get in when stirred up from the bottom in wading, and which proves a nuisance when walking home again.

The forest-clad riversides often swarm with leeches, which bite better than the fish. Tuck the trouser into the sock, and tie round tightly with a string in lieu of leech gaiters.

I have been told that the after itching, which is the worst part of their bites, may be prevented by rubbing gunpowder into the bite immediately on your return home, and that no mark is left by the gunpowder, but I am satisfied the amount of after itching is entirely dependent on your then state of health, and that nothing you can do affects the matter.

It is better to get them to let go their hold themselves, than to risk the leaving of a broken tooth in your leg by pulling them off. If you should happen to be so far behind the age as to have a flask of powder in your pocket, a little of that sprinkled on the leech will effect the desired release. They cannot stand the saltpetre in it any more than common salt. Tobacco juice or a hot cheroot end will get rid of them.

But all this is a somewhat luxurious method of being leech-bitten. The usual recipe is grin and bear it, but *never* scratch the annoyingly itching bites, or you will rue it in their long continuance.

As to the material of your clothes, you need not "fash" yourself, though woollen, of course, is most comfortable. But as to the colour you should be careful. White turbans, white coats, and white trousers, are all to be eschewed; "for the apparel oft "proclaims the man" in more senses than Shakespeare meant. Common shikar clothes are the things.

Wading not only enables you to get at many a pretty bit of water otherwise unapproachable, but when up to the fork in water you are lower down, and consequently less likely to be seen by the fish, than when standing out in fine relief on the bank, with the sky for a back-ground.

I do not think fish see any great distance laterally in the water, and I am inclined to think this is why you find preying, and preyed on, fish living so near each other in the same stream, without clashing half as much as one would expect them to do. It is also a reason in my mind for spinning in the right places, close to where you conclude preying fish to be lying. The case is very different with the fly, for that shows against the light; and the nearer it is to the surface, the further it is seen by a fish on the bottom; for conceiving a fly and the angle of radiation, or vision in the water, are represented by an isosceles triangle, of which the apex is the fly, the two legs the angle of vision, and the base the bottom of the river, it follows that an extension of the two legs extends the base, or, in other words, that the fly which is further off, from being at the surface, is visible over a greater breadth of bottom, than the fly which, from being sunk, is nearer the bottom.

An objection to wading is said to be that you are now and then swallowed by a crocodile. But I have not experienced that sensation yet, and though there are crocodiles enough, I do not think there is really anything to be feared from them. I have again and again waded in just where I have seen a crocodile disappear, or have noticed fresh footmarks and basking places. Mr. Sanderson, in his "Thirteen Years among the Wild Beasts "of India," writes the following:—

"The few crocodiles that are found in the Mysore rivers very rarely "attack people; and fishermen—who pay no heed to them—have told "me that, if they come upon a crocodile whilst following their employ-"ment, it will skulk at the bottom, and not move though handled, "apparently believing it escapes observation. Crocodiles are, like all "wild creatures, very timid where not encouraged, as is sometimes "done by superstitious natives. Incredible though it may seem to "readers with no knowledge of the saurians but that derived from "stories of their boldness elsewhere, I may instance having seen several "'bestas' (the professional boatmen, divers, and fishermen of Mysore) "dive time after time into water 12 feet deep, and bring to the surface "by the tail a crocodile 7 feet long which I had wounded. The "creature was not in any way crippled, but seemed overcome with fear. "It offered no resistance till dragged near a rock, where I stood with "a rope, when it would turn and snap at the man pulling it, always "sinking, however, the moment this demonstration made him let go its "tail. Different divers went down successively, one at a time, and "brought it to the surface. I at last killed it with a charge of shot.

Still they did kill women and children groping for shell-fish in Malabar.

Whether or not it was under a mistake on this head, the Government sanctioned a reward for killing them in Malabar, at so much a yard, and the result was that seven miles of them were killed in a very short time.

I think it must be the American alligator that is the basis of all the beliefs in the dangerousness of saurians, and that the Indian crocodile is an inoffensive coward. The Canara crocodile is *Crocodilus palustris*; the Malabar, Mysore, and Madras one, *C. porous.*

Trousers hang about the legs, and are not only cold and clammy when walking, but are also heavy with water. A more comfortable costume is knee-breeches and worsted stockings.

CHAPTER XX.

THE TAME OTTER.

"Oh! the gallant fisher's life,
It is the best of any;
'Tis full of pleasure, void of strife,
And 'tis beloved by many."—
Jo. CHALKHILL.

ONE can imagine the above song being jovially rolled out by a rollicking otter, after a good day's hunting, just as well as by Isaak Walton's old friend John Chalkhill; for the otter is as fond of hunting in the water as any hound is on land. He evidently hunts from the love of it, and not for the pot, for he eats a mere snack out of each fish he catches, leaves it, and hunts for another. Any one who has been much on the banks of rivers where otters abound, will have seen many a fine fish little more than tasted and left on the bank. Having watched five full sized wild otters hunting together, calling cheerily to each other in the water, gambolling on the sand together for a minute or so, and then in again at a call, and going on calling cheerily again, shall I say laughing, chaffing, and singing "jolly dogs are we," as they went hunting down the river together, I could not doubt they were thoroughly enjoying themselves, and following a propensity, a sport, rather than working for their living.

The otter picks up and follows the scent of a fish under water, just as a dog does that of game on land. You may think a fresh live fish has little or no odour. Perhaps not to man, and you may be surprised at a scent being left in water. But water retains a scent well, as may be seen from dogs readily recognizing the scent of deer, and following it across a stream. And as to the powerfulness of different smells, it evidently depends on the capacity of differently formed olfactory nerves for appreciating them. It is astonishing how a dog will follow at speed the scent of his master's foot, left, through a sock, and through a thick boot, on the gravel path on which it has been only momentarily placed while walking, and detect it also from other footsteps. A man might sniff away for ever, and never recognize the presence of any odour whatever on that pathway, except perhaps the smell of earth. At the same time a man is struck offensively at several yards distance by the stench of certain things which the dog almost touches with its nose, and very deliberately examines, before it seems to have made up its mind. If this last example were not enough to show that different olfactory nerves appreciate different odours very differently, we all know the conclusive dictum of the huntsman that his checked hounds had lost the scent "all along o' them stinking violets." And so we say the olfactory nerves of the otter are endowed with the power of recognizing the scent left by a live fish in the water?

The otter (*Lutra nair**) is the nìrnài, or water-dog of the Dravidian languages of Southern India, the pànika-kutha, or water-dog, again, of Hindustani; and the different names applied to it in Sanscrit mean water-cat, water-rat, and water-animal (udrah†) from which last our word otter is probably derived. And why should he not be utilized as a water-dog, instead of being exterminated before his uses are discovered? Why should he not be domesticated and bred for the chase in the water, just as the wild dog has been on land?

The wild dog is very destructive to game, and so is the otter to fish, it being estimated in England that each otter destroys a ton of fish a year. But the domesticated dog under man's control is very useful to his master, and the following extracts will show that the otter can be readily domesticated, much more readily I imagine than the wild dog, and affords both sport and business-like profit to his master. If the same attention were paid to the breeding and training of otters as has been paid to dogs, there seems no reason why similar marked results should not be obtained in varying size and power; at any rate you can very soon get a retriever otter, and that is about all that is wanted. I have now, as I write, three little otter pups dili-

* The common English otter is *Lutra vulgaris*.

† For the Sanscrit, my authority is A. C. Burnell, Esq., of the Madras Civil Service, whose scholarly attainments are well known.

gently sucking away at a pariah bitch, though they made difficulties at first on the score of the dog's teats being not so fine as an otter's nipple. When their eyes open, I trust that they will awake to the fact that they are dogs after all, and should comport themselves as such. They are not "unlicked cubs," for the pariah takes to them in this respect, and it is hoped that the educational career that is before them will form their minds, and make them morally all that can be desired. And now I will let the following extracts from "Land and Water" speak for themselves:—

FIGHT BETWEEN A JACK AND AN OTTER.

"Sir,—Much having been lately said in 'Land and Water' about "Otters, I beg to offer a contribution.

"Many of your readers may not be aware that these very sagacious "animals are capable of being tamed, indeed I may say domesticated, "or, in other words, that they can be trusted to go free about the "premises, to which they become quite attached, like cats or dogs. "In some parts of India they have long been used, not only for "fishing for their masters, but for driving fish into nets. Having had "such interesting pets, and having been instrumental in others "keeping them, I could give quite a curious history of them; but at "present this is not my object, which is to try and describe a glorious "battle, which came off on the 21st instant, between a trained otter "and a very large pike. I was summoned to the scene of action by "the otter's master, Mr. Hulse, of the Rifle Brigade, who brought it "from India about a year since. The pond where the fish was is a "small but deepish one in Stoke Park, near Guildford. The otter, "following its master to the place, entered the water and immediately "dived, when we could follow his track as he hunted below by the "long string of bubbles ('bells,' as otter hunters term them), which, "coming from his nose, marked his passage. In a short time there "was no doubt as to 'a find,' as the rush and troubled state of the "surface too plainly indicated, for it was like two express trains in "full chase of each other. All this lasted but a short time, say, about "half a minute, and the exertion and coldness of the water, etc., seemed "to take a good deal out of the animal, for he not only came up to "breathe, but landed, and after rolling himself, which they delight in "doing, 'time being up,' in he went again at the word of command. "Many rounds like this took place, the pike always breaking away, "until it was varied by the capture of a carp, the head of which he "was allowed to eat. His appetite seemed whetted by this, for he "became very eager, and, whenever he came across the pike, a great "struggle took place, but the big fish seemed such a monster that he "could not worry him, yet, by the aid of his feet, he turned him over "once, but never brought him to the top, though the otter's tail often "waved above water. Up to this time behind the fish's head was the "part attacked, his great and powerfully armed jaws being avoided, "but now the fish was evidently growing weaker, and the otter "changing his tactics by attacking the enemy in the rear. Each "round told in favour of the otter, and, finally, 'the sponge was thrown "'up' by the beaten fish being towed to land by its tail, amidst the "loud and hearty whoo-whoo-ops! of all present, the doubtful battle "having lasted above half an hour. The fish, which proved to be a "female, weighed 20 lbs. 11 ozs., and the weight of the otter (a female) "and very like an English otter, is only 18 lbs. Thus ended as well-"contested a battle as I ever witnessed, and a sight I would have "gone any distance to have seen. Surely all true Englishmen must "admire the bull-dog pluck of this animal, and endorse Mr. Benson's "sentiments, as given in your last impression, which clearly is that it "is a disgrace in this enlightened age of progress and civilization to "allow ignorant keepers and watchers to exterminate the poor otter. "Otters will travel any distance, and I have no doubt that some of those "which have lately been so cruelly murdered are from the Wey, in my "neighbourhood, and consequently I particularly regret their loss, for "I know they do much more good than harm, and this knowledge I "have gained by studying their habits for years, both in the wild and "tame state. I have plenty of fish, and I cannot see that they "diminish; and yet I am seldom without an otter or two, and some-"times a brood of them, for they are sacred here, as well as all rare "birds, etc. Occasionally I find the remains of a small jack or an eel "which they have caught and partly eaten. I know *they scent these* "*under water*, and bring them up from the mud: indeed, they prefer "them to every thing. Then they are very fond of frogs, and they "will kill water-rats, water-hens, and even rabbits occasionally. "They certainly seldom kill large fish in the wild state when they "can get smaller more easily. Otters appear to grow for about two "years, and they seem to differ considerably in weight. I once saw "one killed in the Lune, near Lancaster, by Mr. Lomax's otter hounds, "which was 28 lbs., and that excellent sportsman told me that the "largest he had ever seen was a male, which weighed 30 lbs. It was "found in a hollow willow, in Warwickshire, and was evidently a "patriarch, from its teeth. I hope some day to hear of a salmon being "presented to Mr. Buckland's Museum of Economic Fish Culture, "killed by Mr. H's. otter."—F. H. SALVIN.

The more thoroughly to convince my reader of the practicability of utilizing the otter for sport, I add still another extract, which is taken from "The English Cyclopaedia."

"But it must not be supposed that the common otter is, as it has "been asserted, confined to the fresh waters.

"That the common otter is capable of domestication and attachment "we have ample testimony. Albertus Magnus, Aldrovandus, Gesner, "and others attest this. Every angler will remember the passage in "Walton, where good Mr. Piscator is anxious to possess himself of "one of the young otters which the huntsman, after the death of the "'bitch otter' had found :—'Look you,' says the huntsman, 'here-"'abouts it was she kennelled ; look you, here it was, indeed, for here's "'her young ones, no less than five : come, let's kill them all.' 'No,' "exclaims Piscator, 'I pray, Sir, save me one, and I'll try if I can "'make her tame, as I know an ingenious gentleman in Leicester-"'shire, Mr. Nich. Seagrave, has done ; who hath not only made "'her tame, but to catch fish, and do many other things at pleasure.' "Buffon, who could be as hard of belief in some points as he was "credulous in others, disbelieves the otter's capability for domesti-"cation. The testimony above noticed has been confirmed by a cloud "of modern witnesses. Goldsmith mentions an otter which went "into a gentleman's pond at the word of command, drove the fish "up into a corner, and having seized on the largest, brought it out "of the water to its master. Daniel, Bewik, Shaw record instances "of the animal's docility in this way. Mr. Bell and Mr. Macgillvray "both corroborate the fact. The latter has collected the following "anecdotes :—'Mr. M'Diarmid, in his amusing "Sketches from "'Nature," gives an account of several domesticated otters, one of "'which, belonging to a poor widow, when led forth plunged into the "'Urr, or the neighbouring burns, and brought out all the fish it could "'find. Another, kept at Corsbie house, Wigtonshire, evinced a great "'fondness for gooseberries, fondled about her keeper's feet like a pup "'or kitten, and even seemed inclined to salute her cheek, when per-"'mitted to carry her freedoms so far. A third, belonging to Mr. "'Monteith of Carstairs, was also very tame, and though he frequently "'stole away at night to fish by the pale light of the moon, and "'associate with his kindred by the riverside, his master, of course, "'was too generous to find any fault with his peculiar mode of "'spending his evening hours. In the morning he was always at "'his post in the kennel, and no animal understood better the secret "'of keeping his own side of the house. Indeed, his pugnacity in "'this respect gave him a great lift in the favour of the game- "'keeper, who talked of his feats wherever he went, and avowed, "'besides, that if the best cur that ever ran "only daured to girn" "'at his protégé, he would soon "mak his teeth meet through him." "'To mankind, however, he was much more civil, and allowed himself "'to be gently lifted by the tail, though he objected to any inter- "'ferance with his snout, which is probably with him the seat of "'honour.' They are, however, dangerous pets, for, if offended, they "will bite grievously.

* * * * *

"*L. Nair*,* has the fur deep-chesnut, lightest on the sides; lower "part of the neck and cheeks, as well as the throat, reddish bright- "brown; above the eye a ruddy yellow or yellowish-white spot.

"This is the *Nir-nagie* of the people of Pondicherry, and is probably "the species seen by Bishop Heber, who passed a row of nine or ten "large and very beautiful otters, tethered with straw collars and long "strings to bamboo stakes on the banks of the Matta Colly. 'Some "'were swimming about at the full extent of their strings, or laying "'half in and half out of the water; others were rolling themselves "'in the sun on the sandy bank, uttering a shrill whistling noise as if "'in play. I was told that most of the fishermen in this neighbourhood "'kept one or more of these animals, who were almost as tame as dogs, "'and of great use in fishing, sometimes driving the shoals into the "'nets, sometimes bringing out the larger fish with their teeth.' "Another proof, if any were wanting, of the feasibility of taming these "animals and rendering them useful to man."

Of a different species of otter the writer of this article continues:—

"D'Azara further states that a neighbour of his purchased a young "whelp, which at six months old was 34 inches long. It was "permitted to run loose about the house, and was fed with fish, flesh, "bread, mandioca, and other food, but it preferred fish. It would "walk into the street and return, knew the people of the house, came "when called by name, and would follow them like a dog, but its short

* The common otter of Europe is *Lutra vulgaris*.

"legs soon failed it, and it soon grew weary. It would amuse itself "with dogs and cats as well as with their masters; but it was a rough "play-fellow, and required to be treated cautiously, for it bit sharply. "It never harmed poultry or any other animal excepting sucking-pigs, "which were not safe within its reach, and it would have killed them "if it had not been prevented. It entered all the rooms, and slept "always below the bed, was very very cleanly, and always visited one "particular spot for the deposit of its excrements."

Lastly, I must give the reader an extract from our eminent Indian Naturalist Jerdon's work on "The Mammals of India," where he treats of "The common Indian Otter" which he calls *Lutra nair*:—

"Accepting the synonymy as above,* then, this otter is found "throughout all India, from the extreme South and Ceylon, to the "foot of the Himalayas, and from the Indus to Burmah and Malayana, "frequenting alike rivers and salt water inlets, and from the level of "the sea to a considerable elevation. It has its lair under large rocks, "among boulders; and, in alluvial countries, excavates extensive "burrows, generally in some elevated spot close to the river, "with numerous entrances. It is almost always found in parties of "five, six, or more, and, though partly nocturnal in its habits, may "often be seen hunting after the sun is high, and some time before sun- "set. I have seen a party out in the sea, on the Malabar coast, "probably making their way from one backwater to another, but as

* *Fam. Mustelidæ, Weasels and Martens. Lutra Nair.*

F. Cuvier—*L. chinensis* and *L. indica*: Gray—*L. tarayensis*: Hodgson—Elliot, Cat 15. Blyth, Cat 214. *Pani-kuta*, H.; *Nir-nâi*, Can.; *Neeru-kuka*, Tel.;—all signifying water-dog.—*Jal Manjer*, Mahr., *i.e.*, water-cat. *Ud* or *Hud*, *Udni Udbillau*, Hindi.

The Common Indian Otter.

"Description.—Above hair brown, or light chestnut-brown, in some grizzled "with hoary tips, in others with a tinge of isabella yellow; beneath yellowish-white, "or reddish-white; upper lips, sides of head and neck, chin, and throat, whitish, "the line of separation between the two colours more or less distinctly marked; in "some the throat tinged with orange brown; paws, albescent in some, simply of a "lighter shade in others; tail, brown beneath. F. Cuvier, in his description, "mentions some pale facial spots, but these are indistinct, though there is some- "times a faint pale eyebrow.

"Total length up to 46 inches, of which the tail is 17, and 3 inches wide at the "base.

"I have followed Blyth in joining *L. Nair* and *L. Indica*, though at one time I

" they are very numerous on this coast, they may now and then hunt " in the sea. This otter is trained in some parts of Bengal to assist in " fishing, by driving the fish into the nets. Young ones are not " unusually caught in the fishermen's nets, and are very easily tamed. " I had one brought me when very young, whilst at Tellicherry, on the " Malabar Coast, which I brought up with a terrier dog, with whom " it became very friendly. This otter would follow me in my walks " like a dog, and amuse itself by a few gambols in the water when it " had the opportunity, and now and then caught frogs and small fish. " As it grew older it took to going about by itself, and one day found " its way to the bazaar, and seized a large fish from a Moplah. When " resisted, it showed such fight that the rightful owner was fain to " drop it. Afterwards it took regularly to this highway style of " living, and I had on several occasions to pay for my pet's dinner " rather more than was necessary, so I resolved to get rid of it. I " put it in a closed box, and having kept it without food for some time, " I conveyed it myself in a boat some seven or eight miles off, up some " of the numerous backwaters on this coast. I then liberated it, and " when it had wandered out of sight among some inundated paddy " fields, I returned by boat by a different route. That same evening, " about 9 P.M., whilst in the town, about one and a half miles from my " own house, witnessing some of the ceremonials connected with the " Mohurrum festival, the otter entered the temporary shed, walked " across the floor, and came and lay down at my feet!"

The peculiar formation of the otter's tail is not without interest. It is not round like that of a dog, cat, or rat, but flattened, and specially at the base, where it is 3 inches broad. It is flattened horizontally, too, as in the Cetaceans (whales and porpoises, etc.), and not perpendicularly as in true fish. Were it meant only for a propeller in swimming it would have been most useful had it been put on like a true fish's, but the advantage of having it flattened horizontally is that the otter, like the whale and the porpoise, is thereby enabled to come rapidly to the surface for air. Ordinarily

" was strongly inclined to believe them distinct. My impression was that the com- " mon otter of most of the rivers of Southern India, at all events, was distinct from " the generally larger, and more robust otter found in such numbers along the " Malabar coast, and in Lower Bengal; and that the latter, besides being larger, had " the fur more reddish or yellowish-brown, and with the two colours much more " distinctly divided; in fact, more resembling *Lutra vulgaris*; but in the absence " of authentic specimens, I can only draw the attention of observers for future " verification."

it is used like the whale's tail or "flukes" to bring it to the surface head foremost, but from Captain Salvin's letter above quoted, it would seem that when the head of an otter is forcibly kept down by a struggling fish, the tail of the otter is still a power to bring the otter to the surface tail formost, and it is readily intelligible that when holding on to a fleeing fish, the otter can put on a very heavy drag by simply curving its tail. On the few occasions which I have as yet had of being near a swimming otter, since I wished to observe it with this view, I have never seen it use its tail in swimming; the tail trailed idly behind, while the otter swam with its feet only. I can understand the horizontal compression of the tail being very useful and necessary to the animal in diving, as well as in rapidly coming to the service. In a long-continued dive, when giving chase to a fish, how could the otter regulate the depth of its dive sufficiently rapidly, without its horizontally flattened tail.

The otter always comes to the shore or a rock to eat its prey, or to shallow water in which it can stand, and sits up and looks about it like a dog, and, when eating, holds the fish down with its sharply clawed feet just as a dog holds a bone on land, and growls over it in somewhat the same fashion; but when standing in shallow water it holds the fish up in air between its two fore paws, and every wild otter that I have noticed always commenced eating the fish by the tail, like a wise general cutting off the retreat. When wishing to travel with its capture, however, it always retakes it in its mouth, so as to have the use of the fore paws for swimming. When lapping milk, however, it is much more like a dainty cat, and it spits much like a cat. How neatly it picks up or catches a fleeing frog! Active minded though it be, and taking quick and long leaps, and more slippery than any cricket ball, the frog is fielded in the best style of "Lord's" and is "well held" too, and no mistake. And then what a quantity of them an otter eats. My babes, which have grown while this Chapter has been with the printer, require a regular commissariat of frogs, and my major-domo complains that frogs are more expensive than sardines!! But then veracity compels me to admit that the price of fresh sardines is here from 300 to 600 for an anna, say Anglice from 200 to 400 for a penny. For the present I confine my little otters to frogs, as the only meat diet besides their cunjee or pap; for I lost an otter by letting them take too early to fish. When they are old enough to cost me no more anxiety *in re* diet, I must try to find out by experiment whether they prefer fishes or frogs, and how much of each they voluntarily eat. It is beyond a doubt that otters are useful, in destroying frogs, which are again great eaters of fry certainly, and I think of spawn too; but the question is whether the good they do in this way preponderates over the havoc they commit on fish. The weight of general opinion is against the otter; but what of that, who has not been misjudged? He has a staunch friend above quoted, and he is certainly entitled to an impartial trial.

I have been asked to say what became of my otters. They grew, and their numbers were added to, and they had a dog-boy all to themselves, and went out walking with him, answering to his call and following him, and playing round him, the admiration and amusement of many, as they went out for their daily walks. But I could not give them as much personal attention as an experiment of this sort requires, and I had to be away on circuit for months at a time, and coming back, found my personal intervention resented, and the dog-boy's authority lapsing. In an evil moment I added to their number an otter puppy that had been weaned by its own mother, and had thus seen a little too much of the world. This one went about with a collar and chain trailing to prevent its escape. But it taught my little innocents bad ways, till, having established the leadership of age, it one day gave a shrill whistle, which was a call to the others to follow, and dashed into a well. All followed, and all were entangled in the chain, and all were drowned together. It would have been better if I had tried a single otter, with only dog companions to help in its education; and it is useless to attempt such a task by native proxy as I did; you must be able to give much personal attention, and to bring up the animal almost entirely in your own company, and have him much alone with you. Numbers are against you.

CHAPTER XXI.

SPAWNING.

"I marvel how the fish live in the sea.
Why, as men do a land; the great ones eat up the little ones."
PERICLES.

A FEW general words will suffice to show how much room there is for interesting enquiry in connection with the reproduction of fishes, and to what good use information on the subject can and has been turned. Most readers will be aware that in the case of salmon and trout the female produces eggs without any connection with the male, and when they are ripe within her, scoops out a hollow in the gravel to receive them, and as she exudes them the male or cock salmon, who waits upon her, ejects over them a milk-like fluid called milt, which fertilizes them, and in which the spermatazoa can be detected by the microscope. It has lately been ascertained* that the ova of trout are covered with an adhesive matter which makes them keep more or less together, and therefore more within the influence of the milt, than if they were separated, and which makes them adhere to stones, so that they are not in danger of being washed down, even by a strong stream, and do not need to be covered as was formerly thought. Again the spermatazoa are observed under the microscope to radiate in the most regular order, so that nothing escapes them. This manner of breeding makes it comparatively easy for man to capture male and female fish, express the ova of the latter when ripe into a bucket of water by very gentle pressure of the stomach, and then similarly cause the male to emit milt, and stirring the two up together to fertilize the eggs, and hatch and rear them under protection. It has been calculated that, when exposed to the ordinary vicissitudes of nature, only one in a thousand salmon ova ever

* C. C. Capel, in "The Field" of 15th January, 1881; and, previously, Dr Frank Buckland.

becomes a fish fit for the table; whereas man has learnt by artificial means to bring about three quarters to maturity.

The Mahseer and many other fish breed in the same way, with this difference, that the Mahseer appears, as already shown (page 27), to lay its eggs not all at one time, but in several batches. The Mahseer might, therefore, be artificially multiplied in the same way as the salmon and the trout.

In India, however, we have another means of culture in the rice-fields, which are filled at times with the fry of all sorts of fish, the Mahseer, I believe, amongst others. As it is the instinct of some mature fish to ascend the rivers for the purpose of spawning in small waters calculated to suit the puny strength of their tiny fry, and by their shallowness to afford them protection from predatory fish, so is it the instinct of their fry to descend, as they grow, to deeper, wider waters. In India, moreover, they are compelled to do this by the decreasing in the hot weather of the rivers. Down the river these fry dawdle, therefore, feeding as they go. But as the rivers are frequently dammed up and turned off for irrigation purposes, they naturally go with the stream down the irrigation channel, and consequently find themselves in a rice-field. In the shallow water of the rice field, and under the shadow of the growing rice, they would do very well, were it not that death awaits them at every turn, in basket traps placed at every drop from rice-field to rice-field, into which they fall by still following their natural instinct of descending the stream. It is hoped the day is coming when these rice fields will, some of them, be utilized for the preservation, instead of the destruction of fry, and others have their connection with the river guarded with gratings.

While some fish, like the Salmon, the Trout, and the Mahseer, lay their eggs in hollows worked out in the gravel, others lay them in the sand, where it is pretty to see the tiny fry still nestled together after birth, so closely that they look like one black spot, in a hollow like an inverted cone of one or two inches in diameter, with their umbilical sacks still unabsorbed. Other fish, again, like the perch, lay their eggs in long strings like beads, and adhering by a glutinous matter to bushes. The stickle-back builds a nest among the reeds and keeps fierce guard over it. It is the male stickle-back that builds the nest, and that unaided by the female, for in due conformity to the rules of modern society he makes no matrimonial overtures till he has provided for the becoming maintenance of a wife, and no girl stickle-back with any self-respect would think of accepting him without a furnished house. The murral takes up its quarters in a hollow in the bank, and protects its young by keeping them in a crowd, and swimming under them till about 2 inches long, when, like other predatory animals, it kills them if they do not separate. Some sharks bring forth young alive, some deposit them in a purse with tendrils for attachment to seaweeds, and their young flee for refuge into their mouths. Certain cat-fish, *Arius*, I have observed, hatch their ova in their mouths, and keep them there even after being hatched. Dr. Day and I examined over 500 of these fish in company on one occasion, besides the observations we had each made at other times separately. The conclusions we came to were that the female seemingly holds the eggs as she extrudes them in her two large cup-like ventral fins, where apparently they are fecundated, and whence they are taken by the male, who thenceforward keeps them in his mouth, never eating till they are hatched. The eggs sink in water, and are about half (·5 and ·6) an inch in diameter, consequently the males were found on an average to carry not more than 16 ova each; and the female laying about 50, she seemingly occupies three husbands. Some friends were going over my little museum with me one day, and a lady, hearing how the bringing up of the children was, in this case, left unreservedly to the devoted husbands, turned reproachfully to her husband, "A very "*proper* arrangement." Thus was the poor hen-pecked *Arius* held up as an example. Some sea-fish spawn in the open sea, leaving their ova, which float, to be hatched on the surface, some in the sand, some among the rocks and seaweed.

As a *general* rule the ova of fresh-water fish sink to the bottom, and the ova of sea-fish float. It is a wise provision that it is so. The ova of river-fish require to reach the bottom to prevent their being washed down by the stream, that would otherwise soon carry them to the salt water and destruction. If the ova of sea-fish similarly sank, they would, at the bottom of the deep sea, lose the life-giving influences of that heat and light which they gain by floating on or near the surface.

Remembering this great leading fact, and remembering, also, another matter in connection with the sea which, though well known, we are apt to lose sight of in connection with sea-fisheries, I think we are in a fair way to discover the causes which govern the migrations of certain sea-fish. We are accustomed to look upon the sea as one vast pond of still water, differing only from other ponds in being salt, in having tides, and in being more moved by winds than other ponds or lakes, by reason of its having a larger surface exposed to their influence. We are not ignorant, by the way, that there are currents also, and that there is one mighty one called the Gulf-stream, and we can understand mariners having to know something about them; but that they should affect fisheries is not, I think, commonly considered. So many and various, however, are the sea currents, that it would be a much more accurate starting point for thought, if we looked upon the ocean as an agglomeration of vast salt-water rivers of varying depths and velocity, of greatly varying temperatures, with banks and courses as well defined as fresh-water rivers, with counter currents or back sets along those watery banks, some of them flowing on the surface, some at the bottom. From their widely varying circumstances, these vast sea rivers naturally support different sorts of insect life, or, in other words, different sorts of food for fishes. These currents or sea rivers, their strength, their length, their depth, their breadth, their course, their temperature, their saltness, have been laboriously ascertained; the mariner has them all well laid down in charts, and studies them carefully. The sea pisciculturist should do likewise. I hold that he can expect to make little progress in his science till he studies it from this point of view. What should we know about the salmon and its propagation if we had always watched it in one particular pool, and not taken into consideration the flow of the river, and its varying circumstances in different parts of its course? The same remark applies equally to the Mahseer, which is migratory only in fresh water. Similarly, how can we expect to understand the migrations of herrings, mackerel, pilchard, etc., unless we study them with special reference to their rivers, the salt-water rivers of the sea.

Having then floating spawn and flowing rivers in the sea, it is easy to conceive that the former is carried great distances by the latter, and frequently taken out of our ken. But if we identified the sea rivers in which particular spawn was shed, we might, by referring to their known courses, have a clue to where that spawn was carried; and be in a better position to trace out why the mature fish sought certain portions of certain sea rivers wherein to spawn at certain times, where the fry are hatched and reared, and by what counter currents, and wherefore, they return. Mackerel, herring, and pilchards are usually in spawn when caught in England; it was, therefore, thought that they sought our shores for the purpose of spawning. But as it has been concluded that the ova of all these fish float, I believe the shore itself has no connection whatever with their spawning, except in so far as the land affects the sea currents; and my impression is, that it is the character of the sea current or sea river that must be looked to for an explanation of their wanderings. Taking this clue, it would seem feasible, after sufficient research, to map out the journeyings of a mackerel or a herring, as particularly as that of a salmon. If there were not salt-water rivers in the sea with well defined courses and banks, how could fish know their way about it. They would be liable, one would think, to lose themselves in the trackless vast expanse, instead of coming back year after year with punctuality to certain shores at certain seasons. There are reasons for concluding that a salmon knows his way about his own particular river, knows every snag, and stone, and pool, and run, in it from mouth to source, just as well as an old fox knows his own beat. And I can readily believe that a herring knows his way about his sea rivers just as well, and has a regular round which he goes every year of his life. The thing is for us to ascertain it and make use of it, both for fishing and piscicultural purposes.

In the hope that this book will fall into the hands of some few who are not only fishermen, but naturalists also and pisciculturists, I take the opportunity of repeating an idea thrown out by me in 1868, but which, from being in an official report, never got any further than the Government shelves, and the few newspaper columns in which it was reprinted; and I repeat the idea in the hope that it may be worked out, and brought if possible to some practical use, not only in India, but also in Australia, Burmah, and the warmer parts of China and America, in short, in any tropical clime in which there is more of sun than ice. I quote, therefore, from my own report: "Long before the commencement "of pisciculture as a science, Aristotle, and subsequently Mr.

"Yarrel, and Sir J. Emerson Tennent,* had observed that 'the "'impregnated ova of the fish of one rainy season are left un- "'hatched in the mud through the dry season, and from their low "'state of organisation as ova, the vitality is preserved till the "'recurrence and contact of the rain and oxygen in the next wet "'season, when vivification takes place from their joint influence.' "It would seem, therefore, that we need not be disheartened at "being met with the objection that ice and moss are not as easily "procured in India for the transportation of ova as in England. "We have at least reasonable ground for entertaining the hope "that in the tropical heat of India there is placed readily at our "command an equally potent, much more simple, and much less "expensive, means of suspending the animation of ova encased "in sun-dried mire. There are numerous instances on record of "vivified fish also (of particular sorts) both as fry and as mature "fish, being thus kept alive in the drought, and the crocodile "æstivates in the sun-burnt clay of a Ceylon tank in the same "way as the alligator of the Mississippi hybernates in the frost. "This interesting fact in Natural History may be made of "practical use in pisciculture, and the experiment would seem to "be at least worth a trial." If the suggestion prove practical, pisciculturists of tropical climes will be at no disadvantage, but rather the contrary as compared in this respect with the pisciculturists of Europe.

It may be that this manner of treatment will only suit certain sorts of fish ova, it may be that it will suit more than we find ordinarily using it in nature, for the manner in which the animation of various insects is suspended, when encased in mud by the carpenter wasps, and by certain ichneumon flies, is somewhat analogous and suggestive.

* And I since find Buchanan also.

CHAPTER XXII.

STOCKING PONDS.

"But we'll take no care when the weather proves fair;
Nor will we vex though it rain;
We'll banish all sorrow, and sing till to-morrow,
And angle, and angle again."—
IZAAK WALTON.

EXCELLENT fishing might frequently be had in ponds close to one's own residence, ponds to which you need make no expensive pilgrimage, as for the mountain-loving Mahseer, ponds to which you might easily resort any morning or evening that you had an hour or so to spare. Golden opportunities for creating excellent sport are thrown away through want of knowledge, so I shall venture a few words on stocking ponds in India.

First, I will tell you of a little experiment which I made myself. Close to my house at Vallam, in the Tanjore District, was a rain-fed pond of some three to five acres of waterspread, as my memory runs. It ran very dry in the famine, and the opportunity was taken to clear it out for sanitary purposes. Thus it had been cleared of all predatory fish, and this was my opportunity. When it refilled with water, I put in about 2 lbs. weight of well selected fry of non-predatory fish. Their intrinsic value was about 2 annas, say, 3*d.*, but, by reason of my living 7 miles from the river, I actually paid 2 rupees, say 4*s.*, for them. I threw in a handful of small snails, and I prohibited any sort of fishing for eighteen months. I soon saw the banks lined with young snails, and observed that the fish were doing well. At the close of the eighteen months' rest, I made it known that any one might fish with rod and line as much as ever they liked for nothing. The banks soon showed increasing numbers of native anglers. When they had got well accustomed to it, and were thoroughly happy about their takes, I said, one day, "you get all this good "fishing for nothing, because the watchman prevents netting." (He was the municipal watchman whose business it was to see that the drinking water was not befouled or stolen, and nothing extra had to be paid him on account of the fish). "Will it be a "great thing for you all to give him one fish in ten of what you "take, so as to keep alive his interest in being your protector?" "Not at all," they answered, with willingness; and so it was arranged that the watchman was to take tithes, and henceforward I called him the "Rector" in my notes. I gave him a few days to fall into grooves, and then I told him to keep an account of what he got daily. He did so, but he complained that the anglers stood very rigidly to their one in ten, never giving him one in nine or two in nineteen, and never giving him a good sized fish when they got one, but always the smaller ones. I thought this was better than encouraging him to be grasping, so joined with him in deploring the depravity of mankind, but did not interpose in his behalf. The result, you will see, was that his tithe was very much less than a real tenth, was probably much nearer one-sixteenth or one-eighteenth of the real weight of fish caught. This was more satisfactory for my calculations than over-estimating. He kept this account for a month in an average sporting period. I frequently weighed his tithes to arrive at a fair average of the weight corresponding to his numbers, and here, again, I erred on the side opposite to exaggeration. I found that anglers were taking fish out of that one pond at a rate which amounted to 4,000 lbs. weight of fish a year. As time went on, anglers rather grew in numbers than otherwise, and some of them took to it, not as a pastime, but as a profession, selling their takes; and as the fish grew bigger, they started country-made reels and running line, as I taught them, and always met me with a pleased look as I strolled round to ask what sport, and look at their bags; and after more than a year had passed, they declared that not only had all the fishing made no impression on the fish, but the total takes were continuing to increase. As there was no netting, only angling, I let them fish all the year round without any close time.

Among the fry that I put in were some Labeos. The natives were very positive that they never bred in ponds, but needed running water. I thought they might be induced to try breeding in a pond when they found it impossible to get to a river, and the event proved I was right. After a time, Labeo fry were caught very much smaller and more numerous than I had put in. When these fish began to grow in size and multiply, the total weight of the takes increased very much, and this did not take place within the eighteen months, when I took my fish census.

From the above little story I think I may fairly be allowed to say that my 2 lbs. weight of fry yielded, after 18 months, 4,000 lbs. weight a year, and in subsequent years yielded at a much greater rate.

This was the result of careful selection of species, species that would not prey on each other, and that would more or less feed differently. The native fishermen brought me pots full of fry, the majority of them dead as usual, and, pouring them out on the ground, I cast the predaceous ones on one side, and saw them killed, and the desirable sorts I selected with my own hand, and put them into the pond myself. Some people, in stocking a pond, put in any fish the natives recommend for size and flavour. Foremost among their recommendations are the Murral and the Freshwater Shark. As well might you expect to raise a flock of sheep successfully by turning wolves and wild dogs into your fold along with your lambs.

The first thing to be done in stocking a pond is to be sure you have no predatory fish in it. It is very hard to be sure of this, while there is a drop of water there. The Murral also is one of those fish that can live in the mud of a sun-dried reservoir. It is best, therefore, to dry your pond, and clean it out, using the silt for manure, for good manure it is, and raising a crop in the bed of the reservoir. This cultivation of the bed of the pond should not only consummate the destruction of any fish fry or ova left in the mud, but leave the bottom more full of insect life to form good feeding for fish when the water is turned in.

Then water turned in should not be brought by a channel from a river, or by overflow from another reservoir, so that fry of all sorts of fish might indiscriminately find their way in. You should be able to be certain that no fish can get into your pond, but such as you select and put there. If your source of water-supply is at all doubtful in these respects, you must be very careful with gratings.

First, throw in a few water snails to make food for your coming fish ; the small black one, Tamil, *Ummachi,* is the most common and the most useful. They will soon multiply astoundingly, and the minute young snails, smaller than any pin's head, form excellent food for fry, while the full grown ones are taken by the mature fish. If you like to take the opportunity of breeding some in a glass tank, it is very pretty to see how they feed. Crumble some biscuit powder very fine between your fingers, and let it drop quietly on the water, and it will cover the surface like scum. You will then see how the stationary snail feeds itself thereon. Remaining quite stationary on the glass, it creates a current which draws the fine biscuit powder to and past it in a continuous stream ; and if you watch closely, you will observe that there is much less biscuit powder in the stream that leaves it than in the stream that comes to it. I thought to breed snails for my fish, and put some in a large bathing tub in my garden. They did famously, till an observant old Turkey cock went his rounds one morning and ate them. *Similia similibus curantur,* so I ate him. I should think it would not be a bad plan if you are preserving fish very closely, so closely that you want to feed them for the table, as in stews, to have a separate very small pond in which to breed snails free from being preyed on when minute, so as to have a constant and large supply of mature ones wherewith to feed your fish. Snails are excellent scavengers, and rapidly clarify water.

A few water-weeds will help to clarify your water, will give food and harbour to both fish and snails, as well as numerous larvæ which make fish food ; and some fish will lay their ova on them. But if your pond is frequented by bathers, you must be careful what you put in. I have known a poor fellow drowned by having his legs caught by weeds, and I had a most narrow escape of it myself, when swimming home after snipe shooting, in preference to walking a long way round a long tank. There is a weed which grows from the bottom by a long stem, about the thickness of your Mahseer running line, with small hairs at long intervals on each side of the stem. It is very brittle, and easily breaks away from the swimmer, and it is beloved by the fish, and snails, and larvæ, and easily removeable when excessive, and it does not die down and make the water offensive at times, as some other weeds do. In Tamil, it is indifferently called *perumpáshi, kedipáshi,* and *ilaipáshi.*

Plate [illegible]

[illegible]   Mintern Bros. lith.

[illegible]

Then, as to the fish to put in. This must depend on your object. If you are stocking for native fishing, you may put in any number of the small carps that never grow beyond 6 or 8 inches in length, for they will multiply more rapidly than any others, and natives like catching those little fish fast with their small rods, which break with a big fish. But if you are stocking for European fishing, exclude them, or they will monopolise the food supply. The several Labeos, the White Carp, and the Olive Carp, all introduced to you above, may be put in in any numbers. The two first are bottom feeders, the last more a mid-water feeder. The Chelas may be added as surface feeders. The Gourami should be added if possible, as a chiefly weed-feeder. These will not conflict with each other, in eating each other, or in eating each others' food to any great extent.

The Gourami, *Osphromenus olfax*, Plate XXIV,* is a most desirable fish to breed in ponds. It is a native of China, where it affects the still places in rivers. It attains 20 lbs. in weight, is said to take a fly and a paste bait, and is so highly esteemed for flavour, and is so easily cultivated in tropical climes, that it has been naturalized in Mauritius, Cayenne, and Australia. In Batavia, the Dutch rear Gourami for the table in earthen pots. Commerson said that nothing that he had tasted amongst fish, whether marine or freshwater, was more exquisite. They are said to feed chiefly on water-weeds, particularly the *Pistia nutans*. They were introduced into the Calcutta Botanical Gardens, but I am told that they were so neglected that, in 1841, only one was found to be still existing. I am not sure that I did not hear that they had been re-introduced there. Sir William Denison, when Governor of Madras, introduced them there, at his own private cost, and the following record of their subsequent existence is worth preserving:—

"I beg to give you the following information obtained from "Mr. Thompson, respecting the Gourami fish:—

"The fish, 20 in number, were imported from the Mauritius, "and arrived here in the early part of Lord Napier's stay. They "were taken to Guindy, and half of the number put into each

* This plate is copied, by kind permission, from Dr. Day's "Fishes of India." The scales are incorrect in number, because Dr. Day's plate was blurred, and too indistinct to follow them, and I had no natural specimen.

"of the two tanks in the garden, about 18 months after they "were captured by nets, and ten put into the tank at Madras, and "ten sent to the hills. Of the latter number, three died in transit.

"About 20 months ago eight young fish were caught in a "bucket when drawing water, and these were taken to Guindy "and put into the tank in which you saw them lately.

"There must be a good many in the Madras tank, unless "they found their way out through the sluice running out of "Government House during the heavy rains.

"*Government House, Madras,* (Signed) J. COOMBES.
"*8th September,* 1875."

It will be a thousand pities if the Gourami in Madras are from neglect or any other cause allowed to share the same fate as the Calcutta ones. I am told that one of the ponds in which they are holds Murral also, which, of course, is against their propagation. They should be put out without delay in suitable waters, where they will be free from natural enemies, protected from poachers, and secured against floods by gratings. There, carefully propagated, the fry could very soon be spread all over the country. The Tanjore District particularly abounds in thousands of perennial ponds set aside for drinking and bathing purposes and attached to temples. More than a million of similarly suitable ponds are doubtless to be found in Southern India, and the amount of highly palatable fish that might be added to our food supply by means of these Gourami is incalculable.

For commencing the experiment, Madras has excellent facilities. Attached to the Government Central Museum there are two good sized ponds, fed by a pipe from the Red Hill reservoir, and free from any other supply except local rainfall. In these ponds there are now unfortunately some Freshwater Sharks and Murral, besides other fish, so that they would have to be cleared of them first. But by the aid of the Railway Company's steam-pump this would be no difficulty, and the water and the mud clearing might be spread over the adjoining grass with profit to it. With watchmen to prevent night netting, these ponds in Government grounds might easily be made the nucleus of a supply for the Presidency. Considering the value of the culture to the Presidency, the Government might well sanction the few pounds necessary to carry to completion the undertaking commenced by Sir William Denison, and forwarded by Lord Napier.

In the People's Park at Madras is a most perfect system of numerous ponds of all sizes, fed by pipe from the Red Hill reservoir, and connected by slight overflow through long channels. Similarly treated, with the connecting channels carefully guarded by gratings, they afford opportunity for the most perfect breeding system that could possibly be desired. Something was thought of in this direction at one time, but all sorts, wolves and lambs, tigers and calves, as fish go, being turned in together indiscriminately, with pelicans, swans, and such like birds by way of encouragement, of course the results are as barren as might have been easily anticipated. Those who have mainly benefited by the arrangement have been the Freshwater Sharks. The ponds are so many that one might be allotted to gold fish for ornamental and sale purposes, others for native fishing for the smaller carps, which they specially affect, and for bait, others for the larger non-predaceous fish particularized above, one for Gourami alone, and the large one at the end of the system for all sorts of fish, the larger predaceous fish included. In that you might have Indian pike fishing without injury to the fly fishing and bottom fishing in the other ponds. The connecting channels, if protected from birds by a little bamboo work or wire netting, would make excellent breeding places for snails. From the Gourami pond or ponds, the whole country might be supplied, not only the Presidency, but as far north as they were found to flourish. With sign-boards attached it would be easy to know what fish were in each pond, and thereby how to assay them. Excellent fishing might thus be had for all classes in the midst of the town of Madras, and a small fee for fishing in certain ponds, a larger one in others, while others were left free, would go far to remunerate outlay, and the fishing would afford healthy amusement to the soldiers by whom the park is largely frequented, as well as the numerous "poor whites" and East Indians who have little enough to solace their exile in India. Amongst the natives, fishing is generally confined to the poorer classes, who fish for their dinner or for sale, except in a native regiment, where they not unfrequently take to it kindly enough.

In these ponds very much greater results could be obtained than in my Vallam pond above-mentioned. If my 2 lbs. of fry there became 4,000 lbs. of fish a year at the very lowest calculation, and more probably 6,000 lbs., or 7,000 lbs., what might not a fair start with some 20 lbs. weight of fry do? and greater results might also be expected from ponds that are so much larger.

But any pond well stocked with fish is a standing temptation to professional poachers with nets. Such gentry have a way of coming by night when honest men are in bed. They have ways, too, of intimidating and buying up your watchman, especially in India, where your watchman is of their creed, colour, and language, not yours at all. I do not see any reliable way of preventing netting in India, but covering old casks or boxes with strong tenter-hooks, and sinking them all over the pond by half filling them with stones. Let it be known that you have done so, and no fishermen will adventure their nets in your ponds. Anglers tackle may sometimes be caught in them, but not often, and it cannot be helped. Pyrimidal stones used in England for keeping nets off the bottom, and thus letting the fish escape, without endangering tackle, would be perfectly useless in India, where the native fishermen are accustomed to dive and follow their nets under water, helping them over every rock and snag. Such tenter-hook armed boxes would, of course, be against your own netting of your own ponds when you wanted to supply fry. But you would have to throw a casting net in the spaces between the boxes, which spaces would in the daylight be well known to you.

I ought to have mentioned that the Gourami bears transport excellently, and that all fry are best transported when about 4 inches long. At night they do not suffer from the sun. The water in which they are should be changed occasionally, and constantly aerated by taking a little water out, and pouring it in from a height, or by blowing air in with a bellows or syringe.

If you protect your pond against netting it is obvious that you must put in no sorts that are to be caught only with nets, as they will have perfect immunity from capture, and will be likely in the end to outbalance the other sorts.

I have spoken of fish as predaceous and non-predaceous, whereas almost all Indian carps of any size are, to a certain extent, prone to prey on fish, but they are so only with reference to fry; they do not destroy the parent fish as do Pike in England, and Freshwater Shark and Murral in India. The destruction of a few fry, more or less, in this manner does no practical harm, for their name is legion.

A point on behalf of the fry, which is by no means to be neglected, is, however, the overflow. The tendency of fry is to go down stream; when, therefore, you have a heavy rainfall, and a decided overflow, their natural instincts will impel them all to follow it out of your pond, and so you will lose them. They will stream out in shoals. The first idea that occurs to one is to bar their way with a grating. But a grating that will prevent the passage of fry must be very fine indeed, and such a grating on the surface is liable to be very soon choked with the débris that always floats down with a flood. Let A B be a section of your bank, and A the point of overflow, A H the outfall. You will, of course, be guided by circumstances in the amount of height you allow at A C for overflow, and in diminishing its height and force by lengthening it. Run out a plank C D E F one foot or more, continuing E F 2 feet or more below the surface of the water, at the lowest level of the outfall. At F G have a fine wire grating. Then any débris floating down towards the overflow must necessarily come against the plank at the surface of the water at E, and the grating F G is left clear and unchoked for the flow of water, and F G being well below the surface, the draught of water is not enough to overcome the buoyancy of the débris, and draw it down so far. Similarly the instinct of the fry is to escape by the surface, never by the unnatural course of the arrow, and if any stray curious one should accidentally find the unusual outlet, you have a fine wire grating F G. If the pond be a small one, and the overflow slight, A G B, instead of representing the bank, may be a pipe let through the bank as a syphon, and lead anywhere into the pond, and surrounded by a box, K I H F, as shown in dotted line. If the overflow be considerable, the strength of it may be minimized by extending its breadth, and C D E F may be formed of masonry, and at any slope, and turfed over for appearance sake.

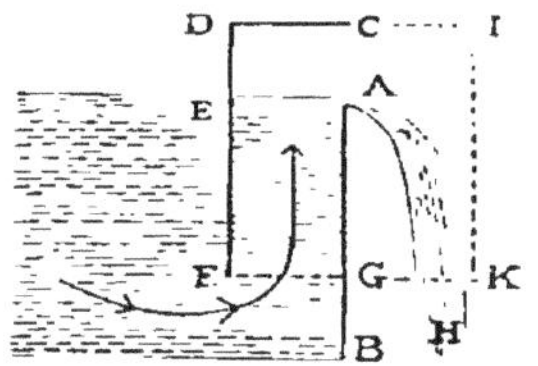

Fish breed much more rapidly in India than in England; they come to maturity sooner, and the young commence breeding sooner. Insect life in some forms is, I think, more rife than in England, though one does not see so many flies on the water as in an English trout stream. Fish are preyed on by more and larger animals in India than in England, which indicates that it is necessary to make greater provision to prevent their over increasing; in other words, the scale against them has to be more heavily weighted to maintain Nature's balance. The greater, then, is the advantage to man when, by excluding predatory animals, he monopolises the preying. Both countries have otters, but England has no crocodiles, and its Pike and Perch can bear no comparison to the numerous and large sized species of predatory fish from Freshwater Sharks, of sorts, of 136 lbs. downwards through *Ophiocepali, Macrones, Callichrous, Arius,* and many others, down to the little *Ophiocepalus gachua,* and the very legion of frogs that prey upon fry, all which run riot in Indian waters. Salmon, it is true, despoil a river when they take possession of it, but even they are a trifle beside the armies of predatory fish to be found in Indian rivers. Even its very carp run in the Mahseer to as big as a man, and live largely on other fish.

CHAPTER XXIII.

MISCELLANEOUS.

"HAMLET.—A man may fish with the worm that hath eat of a king; and eat of the fish that hath fed of that worm.
KING.—What do'st thou mean by this?
HAMLET.—Nothing but to show you how a king may go a progress through the guts of a beggar."—SHAKESPEARE.

DID you ever watch amadavats going to bed? It is a provoking sight, because they take such a long time tucking themselves in. Yes, they tuck themselves in, it is a fact; and they do it in a very provoking way, provoking to their neighbours as well as to spectators. They all perch huddled together in a row, and seem to be arranging it comfortably enough for all parties when just as

"Tired nature's sweet restorer 'balmy sleep,'
* * * his ready visit pays,
Where fortune smiles,"

the unfortunate amadavat at the outside awakes to a sense of his weather side, which is exposed, being colder than his lea side, which is against his neighbour's ribs, and suddenly jumping up runs along the backs of his sleeping neighbours, and wriggles himself in, in the middle. This half wakes and annoys every one, and they all look cross about, but shortly get over it, and are just comfortably off to sleep again, when amadavat No. 2 at each end discovers that the absence of an outside neighbour, and consequent exposure to the elements, have similarly seduced his weather side of its caloric, and convinced him that amadavat No. 1 was not such a fool as he looked after all, so he, too, jumps up impulsively, scuttles along the backs of his fellows, and tucks himself in, in the middle. And so the tucking-in process goes on as one outsider after another cools down, and wants a warm place in the middle of the row, till it is too provoking to look at any longer. Fancy fellows with long claws running over your head all night long at intervals of a quarter of an hour, and your being blandly asked the next morning if you "had passed a pleasant night!" It would be too exasperating. But that is just what these amadavats do every night of their lives. And that is just what several of my ideas want to do, they keep on wanting to tuck themselves in, in the wrong places. But I cannot stand that, so these amadavatish ideas are allotted a perch to themselves, whereon to jostle, and wriggle, and tuck themselves in higgledly-piggledly, just as they like. Between ourselves, I verily believe that, even after they have been arranged for the night by the printer, they will fidget about and change their places. I therefore disclaim all responsibility for their order.

Crocodiles are very shy, and not to be caught, except by night line. A simple way of setting this is to get a bamboo of full thickness, and 10 or 12 feet in length. To one end of it tie a hook with only a foot of line between hook and bamboo. The line should not be a single cord, which the crocodile can bite in two, but fifteen or twenty pieces of common twine tied together at the ends, but not twisted at all. These will get between his teeth, and escape being bitten, and their united strength will hold him fast enough. Bait the hook, which must be a large and very strong one, with a bull frog, or a fowl's entrails, or a couple of crows, or any meat, and push the whole out into the lake, pool, or ditch in which the crocodiles are, and leave it for the night. If there is a slight current, it is easy enough to attach a stone, by way of anchor, by a long string to the other end of the bamboo, and to drop it in. The line between the bamboo and the hook being so short, the bait is kept near the surface, and is not liable to be concealed amongst weeds, etc., at the bottom; when the crocodile takes the bait and turns down with it, the shortness of the line, and the ready opposition of the floating bamboo, quickly strikes the hook into him, and the more he tries to get down the more stoutly the bamboo resists him, for it is full of air from end to end, and is a very powerful buoy. As long as he keeps to the water the bamboo plays him well, and if he tries the land he will soon be brought up with a round turn by the bamboo getting hitched amongst bushes. As far as my experience goes they always take to the land eventually.

I have been told that good fun can be had out of the crocodile by baiting as above in the day time, and setting a man to watch from a distance in concealment. The man must be very still, and well concealed, and at a distance, or not a crocodile will be hooked, for they are very wary. Directly one is hooked he gives the information. Then into small boats quick, one man in each prow with a hog spear, start fair, and "ride" or "off" for first spear. As he sees the boats coming, down goes the crocodile, and up stands the bamboo, more and more upright the deeper he goes, so that the more he tries to avoid you, the more conspicuous becomes his course. Follow him up, for if the bamboo is a big one, as it should be, it will be so strongly buoyant that he must come to the top soon. There, now, the bamboo is beginning to slope, showing that he is coming to the surface. Now is your time for a spear. But look out for his tail—it is very powerful. If he upsets you, he has big brothers about, and they may reverse the sport.

What is the difference between a crocodile and an alligator? Sir J. Emerson Tennent, in his interesting sketches of the Natural History of Ceylon, makes it clear enough:—

"The Portuguese in India, like the Spaniards in South America, "affixed their name of *lagarto* to the huge reptiles that infested "the rivers and estuaries of both continents; and to the present "day the Europeans in Ceylon apply the term *alligator* to what "are in reality *crocodiles*, which literally swarm in the still "waters and tanks in the low country, but rarely frequent rapid "streams, and have never been found in the marshes among "the hills. The differences, however, between the two, when "once ascertained, are sufficiently marked, to prevent their being "afterwards confounded. The head of the alligator is broader, "and the snout less prolonged, and the canine teeth of the under "jaw, instead of being received into foramina in the upper, as "in the crocodile, fit into furrows on each side of it. The legs "of the alligator, too, are not denticulated, and the feet are only "semipalmate."

The Gangetic Gavial has a lengthened beak which marks him unmistakably.

Do not deem crocodiles to be unmitigated evils. They have redeeming points like the rest of us. I have found in the stomach of one, beetles which eat spawn, tortoises which eat fry, otters which eat fish, besides fish which it had taken itself. Doubtless their chief use is to keep down the larger predatory fish till man comes in and dispenses with their services.

Have you ever had a porpoise in a boat or net? He is like a bull in a china shop, is difficult to kill, and will stand a good deal of cudgelling. The natives have a very simple way of disposing of him. They just plug up the blow-hole with a lump of clay, and he is soon suffocated.

I once had a young whale on shore. What brought her ashore, whether mistake, or fright of enemies, I know not. She was in full health and vigour. We got hold of every rope and every man we could muster, and tried to pull her further up, but we might as well have pulled at Regent Street. Ropes broke like pack-thread, and the tail, pardon me, the flukes, kept banging on the rising tide, and making reports like a pistol. Men produced knives and made great incisions in the poor thing's sides, so that the whole arm passed in after the knife right up to the shoulder. Every wave that came up went back dyed with blood. But to no purpose, the tide was gaining on us faster than the whale would die. It was clear she would soon have water enough to float her, and then she would laugh us all to scorn. The above-mentioned way of killing porpoises occurred to me. Sea-sand was the only thing available. I took up handful after handful, and reached up and poured them into the blow-hole faster than she could blow them out. The effect was very rapid, and the approaching tide, instead of helping her, helped us to get her huge carcase higher up the shelving shore, and secure.

Have you ever been in a boat that leaks in the bows, or in any particular spot, and noticed the ready means by which the native boatmen confine the leak to its own locality, and thereby keep the rest of the boat dry, till such time as they can conveniently get it caulked. Just fore and aft of the leak they run up a little wall of dabbled clay as high as the water-mark. The consequence is that the leak cannot spread. If you want a well for live bait it is easy to apply this cheap and ready plan. Bore in the bottom of the boat a hole or two of a size that you can easily plug with a cork at other times: and fore and aft of this leak run up your mud walls, making your well just as large or as small as you like.

But if you want to keep bait alive at your house for any time, and have not a running stream, you must oxygenate the water by growing water-lilies in it; by having a fountain playing in it, which is very easily arranged; by blowing into it with a bellows from time to time; or even by taking up some of the water in a tumbler, and pouring it in again from a height.

If you turn a fish belly upwards, he loses his power in the water. It is like putting salt on a bird's tail, but natives can do it.

Has it never surprised the angler that he seldom catches a fish with a single scale wanting in its whole coat, though those scales come off all too readily in his hands. It is because scales are renewed like feathers; and it is believed that a salmon exfoliates its whole coat of scales every year, in the same way as a bird moults, and that this is the reason why a foul salmon looks so dull and dirty with its skin minus scales; while a clean run salmon is resplendent with a brand new set of silvery scales.

Fish have a marked line, somewhat like a pencil mark, on each side. This is called the lateral line, and its position and course is very carefully noted by naturalists. It is formed by minute perforations in each scale, and it is supposed by some that its use is to allow of the exuding of the slime, or mucous matter, with which a fish's scales are covered; by others for allowing the escape of a fluid which lubricates the skin beneath; by others to be organs of sense, connected with nerves, and sensible of several forms of vibration.

It is not commonly known that sea-fish can be acclimatized to fresh water, but it has been done again and again. The salmon is an instance of a sea-fish taking kindly to fresh water of its own accord. The Sable or Hilsa (*Clupea ilisah*) is another, and instances might be multiplied. But besides those fish that by nature resort at times to fresh water, those also that never go of their own accord into fresh water, have been acclimatized to it.

Fish, like the tench, which are bred in muddy water are improved for the table by being kept a few days in stone troughs, in bright spring water.

"Like a fish out of water" is a common saying, the drift of which needs no expounding. I venture to question its accuracy in its full acceptation. I venture to think a fish out of water is not quite so much abroad but that it has still a sense of where the water is, and that it makes as good efforts to regain it as a man that cannot swim does to gain the shore; makes as good efforts, in short, as could be made by an animal of its formation. Crocodiles travel long distances to water. Eels, too, are well known to cross meadows in the night, and not to fail to find their way back to the water. The climbing perch (*Anabas scandens*) intelligently retraces its way to its own element.

Why should not all fish have a sense of knowing, by smell or otherwise, where the water is, and making their best endeavour to regain it? It is true they are generally aided in their efforts by the shore ordinarily shelving down to the water, and it is thence concluded an accident that their jumping about resulted in bringing them nearer to their own element. But the shore does not always so shelve, and yet the same result has taken place so often with me, that I could not help observing it. When considered without prejudice, it is more natural that the fish should have this sense than that it should not. Savages and other animals seem to have an intuitive knowledge of the points of the compass to aid them in selecting their direction. Why should not fish have a similar power adapted to their needs?

I do not believe that a fish suffers more pain from being caught by a hook than from being caught by a net. We all know the well-worn story of the angler, who, hooking a perch foul by the eye, so that the eye came out and he lost the fish, would not be troubled to rebait his hook, as the fish were taking so fast, but cast it in just as it was, with the eye on the hook, and immediately caught the owner of the eye on that very hook. That perch cannot have suffered much ophthalmically, his appetite must have been his chief trouble. I have myself seen a shark hauled half out of water, when his weight was such that the chain attached to the hook broke; within a very few minutes, however, he was again following the ship, and in the clear ocean water we could see the chain hanging out of his mouth. A new hook was rigged, and on his being hooked and pulled partially out of water, a sailor swarmed down the rope, and slipped a noose over him, because of his great size. We soon had him on deck, and recovered the old hook and chain. That shark cannot have suffered much pain, even from the hauling of several sailors. How do you account then, you will ask, for a fish dashing away directly it feels it is hooked. I say it is not from pain, but from fright at the sense of restraint. If it were from pain it would give in sooner. Fish are equally frightened at the same feeling of restraint in a net, and struggle hard to break through the meshes. They will do the same from your hand. Fish were created for capture and food, and I do not suppose that it is as unpleasant to be caught with a hook as to be masticated by a Freshwater Shark. We have no records of the sensations undergone in being masticated, whereas we do know that drowning and hanging, forms of suffocation, are rather pleasant than otherwise; so those say who have tried, and I suppose you would rather take their word for it than try yourself. There is a vision of green fields. True, they didn't complete the experience, but they liked it well enough "as far as they'd got" as Brigham Young said of matrimony. And fish are killed by suffocation. They begin by being out of breath as mentioned above, those which are hooked in the mouth more so than those that are hooked foul, because you interfere more or less with their respiration. It is said, too, that a fish is drowned by water entering through the gills. When out of water they are still more suffocated unless, as some do, you kill them with a blow.

Mr. Henderson, in his "My Life as an Angler," writes that he had just lost a fish with more than half the casting line, and immediately after caught a 9 lb. salmon in the same lie:—

"What was our surprise," he adds, "to see hanging from its mouth "the lost line with a long array of heavy shot attached to it. On "examination we found that the first set of hooks was planted far "down in the stomach; and yet though the long heavily weighted line "was hanging in a strong stream, and therefore tugging at that most "sensitive organ, our salmon's appetite was equal to a second break-"fast. Surely this bears out the comfortable theory that fish have "little feeling."

In "The Moor and the Loch," by John Colquhoun, London, John Murray, Albemarle Street, there is the following further testimony to the same effect:—

"Having tied a cast rather hurriedly in the morning, I hooked a "good fish upon my bob . . . . when the single knot slipped. "Two days after, when fishing the same place, I again hooked and "killed a fine trout, upwards of a pound weight, and to my astonish-

"ment my own handiwork, with two inches of gut, was sticking in his lip. "One of the fraternity, sedulously employed on the opposite bank, "remarked, that 'it must have been an honest trout, for it was not "'for want of temptation that he kept the hook for the right owner.' " . . . . The insensibility to pain, which an angler can scarcely "fail to notice in these cold-blooded creatures, is a point which happily "redeems from cruelty the necessary inflictions of his craft. I re-"collect catching three fine trout one evening when trolling on Loch "Lomond with a friend, and we discovered hanging out of the mouth of "one of them a strong hair line. On opening the fish we found a large "bait-hook fixed firmly in its stomach, the wicker and part of the "hook being nearly digested. The creature had evidently been caught "and broke away from a set line, and though hooked in so vital a part, "not only took our bait greedily, made a most capital fight for a "quarter of an hour, but was in the very finest condition, having "fattened on his hard fare instead of wasting from torture."

In connection with the power of language, vocal or non-vocal, in fishes (pages 62 to 65) I omitted to mention that I have had trout emit distinctly audible sounds in my hand, perhaps mechanically produced by the unavoidable pressure of the hand, but seemingly not so. I grant that it is very rare to hear a trout make a noise with its mouth, but that is no argument, for it is equally rare, if not more so, to hear a fox utter a sound when run into; only once out of hundreds of kills have I heard a Deccan fox cry when picked by the silent greyhounds. The fact that sound is uttered at all, if, as it seems, it was voluntarily not mechanically produced, is a strong argument for the general power of utterance, and that, again, is an argument for the concomitant power of hearing, which some have denied, though, without an external orifice, the ear is internally traceable in fishes.

Do fish sleep? If you can solve the enigma you will be clever. It is a question worthy of a competitive examiner of most malignant type.

A fish's means of progression has interested me much, and may similarly interest some of my readers. I therefore make the following extract, and copy the drawing from the English Cyclopaedia:—

"The whole of the fins are more or less employed in certain kinds "of movements. In order to ascertain the true use of the fins in "swimming, Borelli, having cut off the ventral fins of a living fish, put "it back again into the pond. It then rolled from side to side like a "drunken man, and could not keep an upright position. When the "fish move with great velocity the pectoral fins are laid close to the "body, in order that they may not retard its motion; and in rapid "motion the tail becomes the great propelling organ. We shall "therefore now investigate its mode of action. The first move-"ment of a fish from a state of rest is produced by a flexion of the "tail (as seen in Fig. at *a*); during this movement the centre of "gravity (*c*) is drawn slightly backwards. When the tail has arrived "at *a* it is forcibly extended by its "muscles in the direction *a i*, per-"pendicular to its plane; the force "of its action upon the water in *a i* "is translated to the fish in the direc-"tion of *i a*, causing the centre of "gravity (*c*) to move obliquely for-"wards, in the direction *c h* parallel "to *i a*. The tail having reached the "central line *c d*, its power of urging "the body forwards not only ceases, "but during its flexion on the opposite "side in the line *a o*, it tends to draw "the body backward in the direc-"tion *o e*. Having reached the point "*o* it is again rapidly extended in "the line *o e* causing an impulse "on the centre of gravity in *c b* "parallel to *o e*. If the two forces "*c h* and *c b* acted simultaneously "we should obtain the resultant *c f*; "but as they do not, the point (*c*) "will not move exactly in the right "line *c f*, but in a curved line "which lies evenly between *d c f* and a line drawn parallel to it "through *h*. The fish being in motion while the tail moves from side "to side, according to Borelli, it describes an ellipse instead of a "circular arc which would be the case if the body were stationary "and the tail only moving. The velocity with which fishes move, and "the continuance of their movements, are enough to give us an idea of "the great strength of their muscles especially when we reflect on the "density of the fluid which is opposed to their speed."

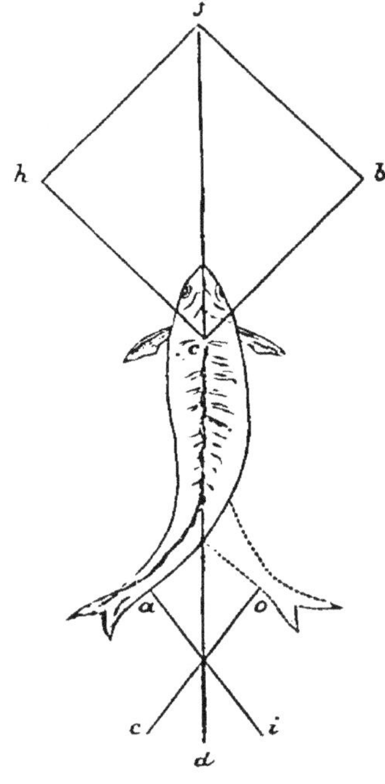

This is doubtless the manner in which the tail is used when the fish swims rapidly forwards in a straight line. When it wishes to turn abruptly to any side, successive strokes of the tail are made on one side only, and the body curled round as much as possible, and the pectoral fin on the inside of the curve is, I think, thrust out, and the one on the outside of the curve worked. The pectoral fins are certainly used for turning slowly, but the tail seems to be the great motive power when turning rapidly, as, for instance, when passing a fleeing fish and turning round so as to take it in head foremost. Every ray in the tail, and in any other fin, is under as much separate command as each toe in a duck's foot, and in drawing up the tail for a blow, the fish can contract the tail as a duck does its webbed foot, expanding it again for the blow; or it can shape and use it like the cross-fanned screw of a steam vessel. As the ventral fins enable fish to maintain a horizontal position in the water, so does the dorsal fin. I have noticed a gold-fish which had no dorsal fin, and though it had been hatched thus it could not well command its position in the water, but rolled slightly. Gold-fish are unusually subject to deformity, not unfrequently having two heads or two tails. The pectoral fins are used to swim slowly backwards. The anal fin also seems to be used in maintaining the horizontal. It and the dorsal fin are much prolonged in the Murral, which, in accordance with its bottom-seeking habits, has not so much of the ordinary compressed shape of a fish, but being more than ordinarily depressed seems to need this additional provision. It is the same with the extensive anal fin of the bottom feeding *Wallago attu* (Freshwater Shark).

We may stay pleasurably for a moment to note a peculiarity in the locomotion of fishes. It is based on principles markedly different from those which govern the locomotion of birds and beasts. The flight of birds is in the midst of a highly elastic element, the progression of beasts on the outside of an inelastic, immobile substance, the swimming of fishes is conducted in the midst of an inelastic but easily-displaced element. Again, the locomotion of both birds and beasts is dependent on the law of gravitation, whereas fish may be almost said to dispense with it, at any rate relatively to the element in which they move. It is not so with a bird; it could not move in the air if its superior weight therein did not supply it with a fulcrum whence to apply power, and with the means of utilizing in some the principle of the inclined plane. The fish, however, is suspended in the midst of an element of very nearly the same weight as itself, so nearly the same weight that the dilation or contraction of the little air bladder, which most fishes possess, suffices to make it heavier or lighter than water, and consequently to fall or rise quickly therein. To solve the problem of locomotion in such widely different circumstances would have sorely puzzled man surely. Even with the secret laid bare before him, and availed of in steamers, what a very poor approach has he made to the rapidity of the motion of fish, a progression so rapid that the eye can scarcely follow the trout that has darted up stream like a vanishing shadow. What is 16 or 20 knots an hour to 160 or 200? And why should not the latter speed be attained in vessels by following more closely the fish's method of swimming, and utilizing the unlimited powers of stored electricity. Surely the "open secret" of the locomotion of birds and fishes may serve, and be meant to serve, to show us how to utilize like powers, and, with stored electricity as a motor, we may well vie with them both in their own elements.

To some this may seem grandly chimerical; but to them we will say that stranger things have happened; such, for instance, as this little book coming to a Second Edition! With such extended means of communication the widely scattered and divided Empire of Britain could be consolidated into far the most powerful nation in the world. But I beg pardon that a follower of "the contemplative man's recreation" should have dared to be contemplative. Those fishes set me on.

Kingfishers do not eat fish and fry only. I have seen them doing good work in killing tadpoles, and when the rivers are discoloured with monsoon floods, in which they can see nothing, they desert the rivers and go miles inland, feeding on young frogs and other things.

When the *Bassia*, the tree called in Tamil *illippe*, and in Telugu and Canarese *ippe*, sheds its flowers on the water I have seen the *Barbus Jerdoni* and the *B. Chrysopoma*, and I suspect others, feeding on it with avidity.

Riding at a foot's pace after a guide on foot is tedious. If you press him you only lose time in the end by his getting out of breath, and it is cruel. Send a peon that understands it with him overnight, with instructions to lay a paper scent. With posted horses, G. and I did 30 miles across unknown country, in this way, country in which it was easy to lose one's way, and got in comfortably for breakfast. With guides at a foot's pace it would have taken us all day.

When white ants are on the water, they are said to be like the May fly in that the fish will look at nothing else. I can well believe it. But their flight is very short lived.

I tried white elephant's hair as a substitute for gut. When dry it seemed as tough as a wire, but when well soaked it became very elastic, and broke at a tension of 6 lbs.

Size in a river affects both the feeding and the lifetime of fish. Regarding the feeding we may say that size in a river ordinarily implies a greater quantity and a greater variety of food; and in India, where rivers are so liable to suffer from drought and from the supply of irrigation, it implies also greater constancy of food supply. Each one of these three items of quantity, quality, constancy in the food supply has a marked influence on the growth of fish; all three combined have necessarily a much greater effect. As to quantity it is marvellous what an amount a fish will eat, and the rapidity of its digestion is extraordinary. You may see trout quite poor in condition after a long drought, and a single flood in the afternoon leaves them markedly improved in condition the very next day. Their food sticks to their ribs in no time. It is a good thing it is not the same with you and me. And then the quantity they take. I have caught trout full to the very mouth of food, at one time of flies, at another of small slugs, at another of young eels. There was no necessity to apply pressure to make them disgorge. Their stomachs were distended, and their last food still unswallowed. And yet they showed no signs of surfeit, for they took my bait and made a much more active fight than a fish in lower condition. I expect a fish with a surfeit is as hard to find as a contented man. I know it is *said* that over feeding on sewage makes the roach at places in the Thames so gross that they lose their fertility, but I should think it was highly questionable. All other experience is in favour of rapid growth accompanying liberal feeding in fish, and of maturity and fertility being proportioned to the size of the fish. The best fed salmon-par return to the sea and come back as salmon a whole year before others. As to quality of food, it may be noted that three batches of trout having been fed experimentally, one batch exclusively on flies, another on worms, and another on minnows, it was found that the trout fed exclusively on flies showed the most growth and weight, those dieted on worms the next, and those on minnows the least of all. The Loch Leven and other trout might be instanced as profiting by the quality of their food. Constancy of food supply means freedom from periods of starvation, and my belief is that such periods permanently stunt growth in fish as they do in everything else that has to keep awake and in active existence the while. I put out of the question hybernating bears, and æstivating crocodiles.

If you have a particularly fine fish, or a new specimen, and want to preserve it by stuffing, it is not a difficult matter, but you must then be more careful about getting it home uninjured. Having washed it clean outside, commence by entirely covering both sides with a piece of paper each, pasted on, and allowed to dry. The object of this is to secure the fish from losing any scales in the manipulation of skinning and stuffing. With a knife and stout pair of scissors cut from the top of the gill-opening down to the tail, keeping about half-way between the lateral line and the back. Arrived at the tail, or rather within a quarter of an inch of it, cut down at right angles. Turn down the flap thus made, and thoroughly clean out the fish, not neglecting the head. Remove all the bones except those of the head. Paint the inside freely with arsenical soap. Stuff tightly but shapely with cotton, remembering that fish shrink dreadfully. Sew up the opening with needle and thread. Wash off the paper; spread out the tail and the fins on the good side and back, with pins and cardboard, so that the rays may be easily counted. Paint over outside with spirits of turpentine, dry in the shade and finally give two coats of varnish.

For arsenical soap the following recipe may be relied on. Take—

36 Tolas of bar soap.
30 ,, white arsenic in powder.
12 ,, camphor.
4 ,, carbonate of potash.

Put the soap in one pint of water, and let it simmer slowly for a quarter of an hour. Then add the arsenic flour and well mix it. Avoid the fumes, they are baneful. Pound the camphor in a little spirits of wine, and add it when the soap mixture is lukewarm, and the carbonate of potash when it is cold.

This recipe is in a convenient form for Indians, if it is remembered that the unit of weight, a tola, is exactly the weight of a rupee. It is equivalent to 180 grains.

I add another recipe, however, in English terms :—

Arsenic..	2 pounds.
English bar soap	2 ,,
Salt of tartar	12 ounces.
Camphor	12 ,,

Cut the soap into thin slices; put it, with a pint of water, into a pot over a gentle fire, stir it with a wooden spatula; when the soap is dissolved, add the salts of tartar, take them off the fire, add the arsenic, and, when lukewarm, the powdered camphor, mixing the whole well together.

Put the compound into a conveniently wide mouthed jar, or glazed earthen pot, taking care to secure it well with bladder and twine.

I have given the above recipes for making arsenical soap, because it is what I was taught to use as the only and accepted preparation for preserving fish. I should not, however, fail to add a caution about its use, which I may as well give in the words of that eminent naturalist Waterton, as they have frightened me into trying his solution of corrosive sublimate. He has evidently found it answer with snakes; I conclude, therefore, that it ought to be equally successful with fish. In the cases in which I have already tried it I have, as yet, no fault to find.

"A preparation of arsenic is frequently used; but it is very "dangerous, and sometimes attended with lamentable conse- "quences. I knew a naturalist, by name Howe, in Cayenne, in "French Guiana, who had lost sixteen of his teeth. He kept them "in a box, and showed them to me. On opening the lid, 'these "'fine teeth' said he 'once belonged to my jaws, they all dropped "'out by my making use of the *savon arsenitique* for preserving "'the skins of animals.'"

I, too, have sacrificed sound teeth on this shrine, and lately came across a gamekeeper who was, of course, strong, and active, and healthy, as such men have to be. His sound teeth were dropping out. The cause was found to be the same. He was stuffing birds, and using arsenical soap. If you take my advice you will have nothing to do with it.

With reference to a long and thorough trial of the solution of corrosive sublimate, Waterton says:—"The result has been aston-"ishing success, and a perfect conviction that there is no absolute and "lasting safety for prepared specimens in zoology, from the depre-"dations of insects, except by poisoning every part of them with a "solution of corrosive sublimate in alcohol. I put a good large "tea-spoonful of well pounded corrosive sublimate into a wine-"bottle full of alcohol. I let it stand over night, and the next "morning draw it off into a clean bottle. When I apply it to "black substances, and perceive that it leaves little particles on "them, I then make it weaker by adding alcohol. A black feather, "dipped into the solution, and then dried, will be a very good test "of the state of the solution. If it be too strong it will leave a "whiteness upon the feather."

Once more I will quote Waterton:—"You must not use "arsenical soap, for two reasons. First, as it cannot be applied to "every part of the skin, *inside and out*, it is not efficient. Secondly, "the frequent use of it would injure your health. Last year, "seeing poor Mr. Johnson, of the Royal Liverpool Institution, "broken down in health, I asked him to Walton Hall, and he "accepted the invitation. On questioning him what had brought "him to his present state, he said, he had been for weeks preparing "skins of lions, etc., and that he had been working up to the elbows "in arsenical soap. He returned to Liverpool and died. Now "there is no danger whatever in using the dilution of corrosive "sublimate in alcohol, because, being liquid, no dust or small "particles can be taken into your system through the medium of "breathing. Moreover, although corrosive sublimate be the most "deadly poison known to *insects*, it is not so deadly to other "animals, and I can assure you that, although I have used it most "copiously for above forty years, I have never experienced the "smallest inconvenience from it. I once read of a Turk who was "in the habit of taking sixty grains of corrosive sublimate per "diem. But do not misunderstand me. I never use the sublimate "in paste or powder.

"Alcohol is cheap and plentiful abroad. The corrosive subli-
"mate must be very finely pounded. Highly rectified spirit of
"wine may be diluted with water equal in quantity. Thus, to one
"quart bottle of alcohol, I would add one quart bottle of water.
"Into this, I would put a table-spoonful of corrosive sublimate, and
"nothing more is required."

Here in India I use the country arrack.

With reference to preserving in spirits, I can hardly do better than add the following:—

REPRINTED FROM THE "NATURAL HISTORY REVIEW," APRIL 1862.

Directions for Collecting and Preserving Fishes.

1. Collect fishes of every size. The eel-like fishes ought not to exceed 36 inches in length; the broad kinds not 18. Six specimens of each species will be quite sufficient.

2. Tie to each specimen a label of parchment or of tin foil, on which the name of the exact locality where the specimen is procured is written, or a number referring to a list of localities.

3. Cut a small slit in the belly of the specimens, so as to admit the spirit, but do not remove the intestines.*

4. Put the specimens into a large jar or tub containing spirit to extract the water, mucous, etc. This spirit may be used for any number of specimens as long as it is strong enough to preserve them from *early* putrefaction. Leave the specimens in this spirit for from 8 to 10 days.

5. Transfer the specimens into other spirit, stronger than the former, and leave them there for another fortnight.

6. Pack, finally, the specimens in spirit which is strong enough to be inflammable with a lighted match. In spirit like this the specimens may be shipped, and will keep for six or eight months. Rum or arrack of the strength indicated, answer very well for this purpose, but spirits of wine, if procurable pure, are best.

7. The best way of sending specimens is in a tin box fitted into a wooden case. Wrap each specimen in a piece of fine linen to prevent the rubbing off of the scales and other injuries. Pack the

* In tropical climes, decomposition sets in so soon that I think it is better to remove the intestines, notwithstanding the loss.

specimens as close as herrings, and do not leave any free space at the top or on the sides of the box. Fill the box with spirit, taking care to drive out the air which may remain between the specimens, and close it hermetically by soldering down the cover. The best way of closing the box is to make a small round hole in the cover of the box. First fix down the cover of the box, then pour spirit through the small hole, until the box is quite full. This hole may then be easily closed by another small square lid of tin.

8. Turn the box upside down and see whether it keeps in the spirit perfectly.

9. Reptiles of every description may be preserved in the same way. However, as they naturally contain less fluid, it will be sufficient to change the spirits once.

10. The list should be prepared in duplicate, one copy being retained till the receipt of the other is acknowledged. The list should contain the native names of the fish, and any information of their habits, qualities, etc., that may be procurable. It should state in particular whether the fish was caught in a tank or river.

In India I have found it an advantage to add 1 in 40 of carbolic acid to the spirit, and on one occasion on which I could not get any spirit in the forest, the same solution in water preserved the fish till I could get them to head-quarters, and put them in spirits. Too great a strength of carbolic acid will shrivel the scales. Any of it is objected to by some as injurious to the colour; but as the colour of a dead fish is no guide at all to the colour of the live fish, but rather misleads, I do not consider that objection a weighty one as regards fish. Your spirit may be as strong as you like, there is no fear of overdoing that for either your first, second or third bath. In tropical India it is safer to have it strong enough and to spare.

CHAPTER XXIV.

FISHING LOCALITIES.

"I am, Sir, a brother of the angle."—
IZAAK WALTON.

In my first edition I wrote:—"This appendix is necessarily a mere "skeleton, because it is unavoidably the result of only one "individual's knowledge, and public officers in India have not "leisure and express trains in all directions to aid them in explor- "ing different fishing localities. In full knowledge, however, of its "meagreness, it is, nevertheless, introduced more as a provocation "than any thing else, for other fishermen to throw together their "local knowledge, and perhaps some day make up a useful com- "pilation like 'The Angler's Diary.'" And recently I sought the aid of the "Asian," the editor of which was good enough to support my request to anglers most cordially. Kindly have anglers responded, some in its columns, some direct to myself. I must commence this Chapter, therefore, with acknowledgments, especially to "Doon," and the editor of the "Asian," and I would mention others, but that I am not quite sure that I am free to publish names. With the kind permission of the editor of the "Field" I have gleaned also in those pages. The list of fishing localities, though much amplified by these means, is doubtless capable of being more than doubled in so vast a continent as India, and if anglers will continue to help, and my book lives to a Third Edition, they shall find the advantage of it in an ampler record of localities. I shall be glad, too, to be set right wherever I have made any errors in spelling, etc., through want of local knowledge.

The best maps that a stranger can buy for his guidance as to whereabouts are the Government Survey Maps, always procurable at very cheap rates from the offices of the Surveyor-General of India, at Dehra Dhun and at Calcutta; and probably through any bookseller, but—

The following are named as agents:—

Calcutta. Messrs. Thacker, Spink and Co.
Allahabad. Curator of Government Books, N.W. Provinces.
Nagpore. Curator of Government Books, Central Provinces.
Lahore. Curator of Government Central Book Depôt.
Madras. Messrs. Higginbotham and Co.
Poona. Superintendent Government Photozincographic Department.
London. Messrs. Allen & Co., Waterloo Place.
" Mr. Edward Stanford, 6, Charing Cross.

India No. 2, is a sheet about 2 feet square, neatly doubled up, of course, giving in one view the principal places and rivers of all India, Burmah, and Afghanistan. The price is 1½ rupees, uncoloured, 2 rupees coloured.

For more detail, a stranger should have also the same on a sheet about 3 feet 6 inches square, entitled "India without Hills." It is a good clear map. Uncoloured, 3 rupees; coloured, 4 rupees.

When he has fixed his locality, if he wants to know his immediate surroundings, and every bend in the river, and the cross cuts, etc., he can get a sheet of "The Indian Atlas," on a scale of 4 miles to the inch, at 12 annas a quarter sheet, the sheets being 3 feet 4½ inches by 2 feet 3½ inches. An index to the sheets of "The Atlas of India," on a scale of 128 miles to an inch, may be had for 1 rupee, and will enable him to decide what sheets he wants.

MADRAS PRESIDENCY.

Bellary District.

It is as well to know sometimes where not to go when places look tempting on the map. The Toongabadra runs within 40 miles of Bellary. W. H. went by rail from Bellary to Toombadra Station, and worked up the river nearly to Hampee, and in the whole of that portion of the river there is not a single good run, or likely place for Mahseer. There are one or two deep pools in which there are probably fish, though these are netted constantly; but the bed of the river for the whole of that distance is simply a broad, flat, sandy plain, with some half dozen small streams winding through it. It is nearly a mile broad in many places. Hardly a tree to shelter a goat all the way. N.B.—The writer, W. H., is a good fisherman.

From the *map*, I should think that the hilly part of the river above the junction near the corner of the Bellary District should show good water. Will any one stationed in Bellary have the energy to try?

South Canara District.

All the fish were comparatively small, that is, ordinarily under 15 lbs. I have never known one taken over 20 lbs.

Chàrmàdy.—Here there is a District Officers' Bungalow. This place is only good early in the fishing season, as the stream here soon gets too small. Mahseer may be killed exactly opposite the bungalow; but I would recommend walking down the stream to where the hills close in on it, and then fishing downwards. Take a guide, as there are short cuts from which you can ride home. Time, September, October, and November, and probably later also, till the fever sets in in January and February. Here are bison, spotted deer, and an odd snipe or two. Otters too.

Neriya.—Near Chàrmàdi, and good for Mahseer similarly early only. Fish the larger of the two streams and below the junction. No accommodation. Fish very plentiful, but small, running from 5 lbs. to 7 lbs.

Kàrkal.—There is a good stream about 2 miles' walk from hence. It is the river into which runs the tank surplusage. It is good early in the season only, say September and October. You will want a guide.

Kirebày.—A very good place early in the season. Shooting also good. But difficult of access, and no accommodation. Mahseer.

Sampaje.—There is a travellers' bungalow here. Do not fish the stream in front of it; it is too small to do much in for Mahseer. Take the road to the coast for about a quarter of a mile beyond the bridge, and with a guide strike through the wood on your left to the main river. There used to be tigers, but I think they are pretty well thinned now.

Siràdi.—There is a travellers' bungalow here at present, but supplies are somewhat scanty, so go provided. The river may be fished from the shore, both above and below the bungalow. From close above the bungalow there is a long gap of still water which can only be got at by a boat. Above this the river is full of runs. There are fine pools below the bungalow. The Cubbinàli stream may also be ridden to, and fished. Time, September to end of December. Beware of fever in February till 15th June, and then of monsoon floods till September. I never could do anything with the fish in the cold east winds of January. There are other fish besides Mahseer. *Barbus Jerdoni* is very numerous. There are Bison and Sambre about. The place is densely forest-clad, and a great favourite with me.

Uppinangady.—The place was praised to me, but I did no good there, that is with the fishes, but much in the way of business doubtless !!!

Subramani.—Good till December or January. The Subramani river, which is the Comàrdàri, may be fished both above and below the ferry and ford; and its affluent the Yennakal-holle may be ridden out to. There is no accommodation. Avoid the time of the Jatra, a lunar festival occurring about the middle of November, because the thousands (50,000) of cattle brought for sale discolour the water by their trampling, and the pilgrims befoul the approaches, and are everywhere washing at the river's side. Mahseer.

Wondse.—Not far from Coondapur by road or river. There is a District Officer's empty bungalow, about the use of which no objection is ever made; but no supplies. There are no Mahseer here, but the river holds some lesser Barils and Chela, and is full of "Black spots" (*Barbus filamentosus* and *B. mahecola*), which give excellent sport by their numbers. Leave the road a little south of the police station, and ride by foot-path about a mile up the river. Time from October to January inclusive. Being so near the sea, the place is probably free from fever, even in March and April. Nowhere in South Canara can you go far from the coast later than the end of January without getting malarious fever, of which, however, there is no danger whatever from within a month, say 1st July, of the commencement of the monsoon, about 5th June. But the monsoon makes travelling quite out of the question till September, and the rivers are in high flood and discoloured.

Jadkall.—A similar bungalow, only "Black Spot" fishing, but that is very pretty.

Mála.—No accommodation. Capital Black Spot fishing.

Cooloor.—Stream very small indeed, and fishing even for small fish indifferent. No Mahseer. A rough bungalow like that at Wondse.

Nágawadi.—A bungalow. *Hannar,* none. Only small *Chela boopis.* Good snipe at the latter.

Biranthadaka and *Biramangalam.*—Not easy of access. No accommodation. Some fair Mahseer water.

Dharmastala.—No accommodation, but a very good station for Mahseer. Try the river, both above and below the ford from the shore. Also take a guide and walk, it is unrideable, through the forest, etc., down to the junction of the two rivers. Try them both from the shore. Also try the grand pools below the junction from a boat. There is plenty of excellent water. Time, September, October, November, December.

Mangalore.—The only place is the Salt Kotars, and the fish the Cock-up, with an occasional Red Perch. I had excellent sport at times, but numerous disappointments. I never could make out their times. I expect Colonel Osborn is right about their being taken only in coloured water. Never saw any Bà-min there.

Cicilly.—Do not touch the tame Mahseer. You will find plenty more further down the river.

Cundapoor.—Close to the sea. A beautiful spot. There are plenty of estuary fish close to the bungalow, if you can catch them. They beat me. Others have done better with prawns. In the pond within a ride, the peculiar fishing for *Chanos salmoneus* is worth seeing. The Red Perch is also to be taken in that pond. Also a Horse-mackerel (*Caranx*).

Mudràdi.—In a pond attached to a Jain temple at a place called Warranga, near Mudràdi, there is excellent Black Spot fishing. At Mudràdi there is a District Officer's bungalow.

Coimbatore District.

The Bawanny and the Càvèry rivers, which run through and skirt much of this district, afford excellent sport, and at many places heavy game can simultaneously be got.

Metapolliam is well known from being on the way to the

Nilagiris. There are bungalows and supplies here. You can do some fishing from the bungalow, by riding out, but not much, for it is so netted. There is an easy bridle-path to Nellatorai, 4 miles, whence I have fished down to the Metapolliam bridge, killing all the way down to the junction of the Kallàr River, which was so muddy that I took no more below that point. The Coonoor and Kàrteri stream gets muddy very rapidly under very slight rainfall because it is so steep, and comes through so much cultivation, carrying its wash. There was plenty of excellent water. The fish were the Carnatic Carp, but they run small, none being over 3 lbs., doubtless on account of the netting.

You may also fish from the bungalow as your head-quarters, by fishing down stream from the bridge, and sending your horse down the Erode road to ride back on. Nothing can be done without a boat. Basket-boats are plentiful.

But it is far better to camp higher up the river at Tèkàmpatti, where is a forester's hut, available, I daresay, if you can make love to the Forest Officer. Tèkàmpatti is the highest place up the river at which it is safe to sleep. It is well situated half a mile away from the river and malaria, and on the plain side. From thence fish the river, the Bawanny, above and below the Puthùr ford. What we concluded was the best way of doing it, was to be up in the dark, and ride down to the river, across the ford, and along the bridle-path up the other side, the Neilgherry side of the river till dawn, taking our basket-boats with us at a foot's pace. It is too rough a road to ride any faster in the dark. Directly it dawned, we called a halt, and put the boats in, and fished alternate pools downwards to the ford, to which our horses meanwhile walked, ready to carry us thence to a late breakfast about twelve. In the afternoon we fished the river downwards from the ford till dusk, and rode home. In December, the river is fordable in one place near the Tèkàmpatti camp, and that is the Puthùr ford, but you must take it circuitously the way you are shown.

The distances, as nearly as we could ascertain and judge by timing ourselves, were :—

From Mètapolliam		to	Nellatorai,	4	miles.
,,	,,	,,	Puthùr,	4½	,,
,,	,,	,,	Chengal,	8	,,
,,	,,	,,	Shittugunie,	9	,,

From Mètapolliam	to	Pillur stream,	9¾	miles.
,,	,,	,,	Kadukai,	10¼	,,
,,	,,	,,	Nìrali stream,	12	,,
,,	,,	,,	Nìrali Hill,	12¾	,,
,,	,,	,,	Pèrali village,	13½	,,

The Taimalai brook is crossed just below Pèrali, on the Nìrali side. Thence the road ascends a steep incline, and crosses cultivation at the top of the hill, which belongs to Pèrali. Thence the road strikes down by an easy path to the most magnificent pools and runs you may wish to set eyes on. They are in the midst of the wildest, forest-clad, rocky country, and the water is crowded with grand Mahseer, as Paddy would say, "the "wathur's *stiff* with 'em." But don't dream of sleeping there. I slept as high up as Sittuguni, we being a jolly Christmas party of five Europeans, but every man John of us, black and white, got a thorough going fever, some being very seriously ill indeed, and we lost one poor fellow of our number from it, in spite of all the good doctor could do for him at Madras. We had been told it was safe at that season. Don't you be tempted to sleep higher up than Tèkàmpatti; there friends and self, and natives, have slept again and again with immunity.

Just a little above Kadukai or Kadavu, which means a ford, is the lowest large pool, just below a waterfall, where you will find Mahseer. Above that pool they swarm, below it you will get splendid pools in abundance, but only Carnatic Carp. At least the Mahseer below it seem to be so comparatively few, and the Carnatic Carp so many, that below that point we always put aside our spinning tackle, and took the fly. If you want to fish for Mahseer, therefore, you had better go on past Pèrali; though I have struck the river at Kadavu, struggled up the river to this pool—an awful struggle,—fished it for Mahseer, and then fished the river down to the Puthùr ford, and so back for breakfast at Tèkàmpatti. The natives were very reluctant indeed to show us the river above this pool. We only found it by most persistent clambering, and that is why I have put it down so particularly for you. Below Pèrali you can do nothing without a boat, above it you can do a little from the shore, but to do the river justice, you ought to have a boat. The Mahseer here are, as nearly as I can tell you, "as big "as a portmanteau."

Higher up the same river are Attapàdi, Shermangundi, Gopaneri, found mentioned in the Malabar District. From Karamadi railway station carts can go, a native of the locality told me, to Gopaneri, 15 miles, which is 15 miles from Attapàdi, the straight road being by Tholampolliam.

Sirumugi.—There is a public bungalow here, within a ride or drive, 10 miles, of Metapolliam. Between it and the Kanayampaliam anicut, 5 miles, there is nice water, in which you will find Carnatic Carp, but not nearly so many as at Tèkàmpatti. A boat is necessary.

The Bawanny ordinarily clears from the monsoon floods in September.

Animalais.—M. tells me he has caught a 5 lb. fish with paste in the river at Animalai, and that the river is full of runs and rapids higher up, but that falls prevent the fish getting to the higher river. Beware of fever.

Madura District.

The Vygay being generally a dry sandy bed only, you cannot expect any Mahseer in that; but you may get sport at the Pâmben channel with the Bà-min, which *see*.

Periàr.—M., an R.E., tells me he caught any number of fish with a fly in the Periàr, near the site of the Periàr project. My note does not say what fish, unfortunately.

On the Pulney hills in this district is a lake. I believe some pains has been taken with the stocking of it, and much might be done as suggested for the Nielgherries. I have never heard of anything being caught in the Kodikânal Lake yet but a small sort of Murral, under 1 foot in length, *Ophiocephalus punctatus*, and *O. gachua*, and in Tamil, I think, *Korare*. Of course they are not worth catching. They are only fit for small native boys with a worm and a pin.

Malabar District.

For this district I have had a memorandum kindly prepared for me by W. L. I should premise that the Mahseer are seemingly small, like the Canara Mahseer, and that the country, being subject to the same monsoon, the time is the same. The country being flatter than Canara, the lengths of tidal estuary are greater.

"MALABAR RIVERS.

"*Ordnance Survey Map, Sheet No.* 44.

"1. *Tullipurmbu River*, tidal as far as Chuparapadu. West of "75° 30′ east longitude. Small Moplah village, above which there "is a moderate sized stream with pools.

"2. *Billipatam River*, the largest river in North Malabar, tidal "as far as a mile above Sukukundapuram on the branch joining at "Kogem, and as far as Eroocur on the main stream. At Eroocur, "a considerable Moplah village, there is a good road running up "the right bank to Iratti bridge, when the Perambadi Ghat road "into Coorg (not shown in the map) crosses the stream immediately "below the junction of the two main branches a little to the north-"east of Kishur. Above Eroocur, and on both branches joining at "the Iritty bridge, there are fine deep pools and streams swarming "with fish. At Eroocur there is a D. P. W. hut: at Iritty bridge "there are a native travellers' choultry and a good Amshom "cutchery, used also as a police station; and at Gamoth there is a "good travellers' bungalow close to the river.

"3. *Anjeracundy River*, tidal as far as Anjeracundy, a cinnamon "plantation, belonging to Mr. W. Brown, above which it is a "moderate sized stream with pools. At Canooth there is a "travellers' bungalow.

"4. *Mahe River*, tidal as far as Parakudu, above which it is a "considerable stream.

"5. *Cootyaddy River*, tidal as far as Cootyaddy, where there is a "travellers' bungalow near the foot of the ghat of the same name "leading into Wynaad. This is a large river in the monsoon, but "in the dry season there is very little water.

"6. Between the Cootyaddy and Beypoor rivers, there are a "number of streams of inconsiderable size, except in the rains.

"7. *Beypoor River*.—The mouth of this stream appears on sheet "No. 44, at lat. 11° 10′ W. Turning to sheet No. 61, it will be "seen that in length of course, this is the largest of the Malabar "rivers proper It is a tidal stream as far as Areacode, but in most "seasons small boats can go up as far as Edda, Mummah, and "Maumbat. The whole of the upper branches of this river, which "spread out like a fan from the Government teak plantations at

"Nellambur, are interesting from an angler's point of view. "There are bungalows at Areacode, Eddamunnah, Nellambur, and "Yeddakura, all on the main road leading from south-east Wy-"naad by the Careoor Ghat to the coast.

"8. *Tiruangady River*, a considerable stream, the upper waters "of which would repay investigation. There are bungalows at "Mallapuram, where a detachment of European troops is stationed "in the heart of the Moplah country: and at Munjary and "Angadipuram, and there used to be another at Alanaloor. The "country in this stream and its branches to the west of Alanaloor "and Pandekàd, is highly cultivated, theré is therefore little likeli-"hood of good fishing, except in the upper waters.

"9. *Ponany River*, which runs parallel to the railway from "Pàlgàt westward, is a large stream with a broad shallow sandy "course. At Cudalloor a large stream comes in from the north-"west. The head waters of this branch can be reached from "Meonaur, where there is a bungalow on the main road from "Pàlgàt to Calicut *viâ* Angadypuram. Another branch comes in "from south-east of Cottompally, and, turning to sheet No. 62, it will "be seen that the head waters of one branch can be reached from "Wurraecunchairy, where there is a bungalow, and of the other "branch Colungodi,—neither of these streams can, however, be "considered promising.

"10. The upper streams of the Cubbany, Noogoo, and Moyaur, "feeders of the Càvèry, lie in the Wynaad Taluk, and those of the "Bawanny also in the Wallawanàd Taluk (all in sheet No. 61). The "former can be reached from Manantoddy, Bawally, Caukancotta, in "Mysore, Gunnapaddyvattam (Sultan's battery) and Guddaloor, at "each of which places there is either a bungalow or other accom-"modation. The latter can be reached from Munaur (No. 9) by "ascending the Attapàdi (misspelt as Allapady in sheet No. 61) "ghaut, but this is an out-of-the-way place with no local supplies."

Of Attapàdi, which means the hamlet of leeches, H. writes that he saw fine fish there. I can well understand that there should be, for it is on the head waters of the Bawanny, in fact above Pèrali, mentioned in Coimbatore district. H. writes that Attapàdi was healthy in the monsoon, and the water clear even in July and August, evidently because it came through grass and forest, whence there was no befouling wash. All the Mahseer in the river seemed to have gathered up there, and he caught two Carnatic Carp of about 1 lb. each, that were scarred from fish bites, probably bites from Freshwater Sharks, for I do not think a Mahseer bite would leave a scar.

Shermangundi is on the Bawanny; the river is clear there in the monsoon, and holds Mahseer. H. will answer for it. Gopaneri is on a feeder only.

Eddavarra, on the Nilambur River. D. saw a 5 lb. Mahseer and Murral and Freshwater Shark caught with live frog suspended on the surface from 5 feet springy bamboos stuck in the bank, 20 such baits being simultaneously set by the natives.

Nadghàny.—D. writes again, there are no fish in the pretty river one mile below the bungalow, but following down stream one mile another river joins and the Mahseer commence there from the waterfall at the junction. The fish we got were small, 1 lb. and under; they took your small sized fly (*i.e.*, the smallest one I have mentioned for Carnatic Carp) and were greedy and violent. He and L. got eight Mahseer.

In the Malabar District is also the Bà-mìn (*Polynemus*) fishing of which the localities are given in the Chapter on Estuary Fishing.

K. G. had sport with Bà-mìn at Mahe in November and December.

Nellore District.

The Muri.—E. got some good sport, writes C., in the Muri with Freshwater Sharks.

Kistnapatam Estuary.—C. had tackle broken. Thus there is not much to be said for poor Nellore.

Salem District.

Hoginkal, or the Smoking Rock, which is about 5 miles' ride from Pennàgaram, mis-spelt Pengugaram in the Ordnance map, is a very picturesque spot, on the Càvèry. Its grand falls and rocks are well worth a visit. Tents are required. No supplies except from Pennàgaram.

H. writes me the water is 65 feet deep. About March the fishermen drive the fish for 20 miles up the river to the long pool below the falls, which are impassable, and block the river below with nets. They cannot net the pool because the water is too deep, and the bottom too rocky, but they fish with lines and catch "tons." There are Carnatic Carp, Freshwater Sharks, and Murral, but no Mahseer he thinks. I should think there *must* be Mahseer there.

Sholapádi, 30 miles from Salem. H. writes the river is so beautiful for fishing, such rapids and pools, and all open, but he chronicles no bags.

Tanjore District.

There is not a ghost of a Mahseer in the district, but I have had good fun with Labeos in a pond about 6 miles out of Tanjore, on the Combuconum road; in fact, the 31½ lbs. mentioned in the Chapter on Bottom-fishing.

Also in a pond attached to a small temple, half a mile off the road, at a point about a mile from Negapatam, on the Karekal road, one rod got 52 lbs. weight of Labeos and Freshwater Shark in a day.

The Tanjore District abounds in Temple tanks, and tanks kept for bathing and drinking, and washing clothes promiscuously. These are mostly fed by small channels from the Cavèry and Coleroon, and as their supply comes to them only when the rivers are in flood, it generally brings them fry of all sorts of fish, notably the Labeo, the Freshwater Shark, the White Carp (*Cirrhina cirrhosa*), the Chela, and sometimes the Hilsa. The last-named is a sea fish, *Clupea ilisha*, vainly endeavouring to regain the sea. Some of these ponds cover several acres, and are never netted. Fates, and very little soul for bottom fishing, and the publicity of most of these tanks, combined to prevent my investigating them; but any one so inclined might doubtless get much fun out of them.

Tinnevelly District.

Courtallum, the sanitarium of the district, has water near it.

A writer in the "Madras Mail," 31st August, 1874, says:—

"The milk falls are situated in the Pulliary Pass, and about 14 "miles of an easy road to the north of Courtallum. . . . The "Pulliary Pass is a charming place when it does not rain hard, but "during the Courtallum season the rain is almost incessant, and in "the dry weather the place is hot and feverish. The pass connects "Tinnevelly with Travancore. The road runs for a long way by the "side of a babbling picturesque mountain torrent, in which there are "places for good fishing. The Mahseer is among the fish found. "Comfortable bungalows, situated at convenient distances, are met "with throughout the pass. The vegetation is luxurious, and any one "delighting in ferns, orchids, etc., game, and scenery, will find the "pass a very paradise of pleasure."

This has been confirmed to me on many hands.

B. caught small Mahseer of 5 lbs. at Paupanassam, and in the Arienkavu Pass. The season is June, after the monsoon has set in, July, and August, and others declare it healthy till the end of January, as I can well imagine.

Paupanassam (properly Pàpavinàsam—the forgiveness of sins; there are many places bearing the same name). B. writes:—Paupanassam, where the Tamberapoorny, the irrigator of Tinnevelly, debouches from the hills by a splendid fall. There are charming streams, pools, etc., about there, and lots of fish.

Travancore.

With its good rivers, ought to be as good for sport as Malabar and Canara.

Anglicoorchi.—H. writes, November, 1875, that in the river Toracàdu he has caught ¾ lb. Mahseer with a fly, but did not stir a Carnatic Carp.

Trichinopoly District.

There is business to be done at the Anicut, I am told.

B. . . . . . y writes, that at the Anicut the Freshwater Shark (*Wallago attu*) run very large; that he had good fun with *Kilathays* (Tamil for *Macrones*), things with feelers, flat under jaw, forked tail. He caught them 5 lbs. and over, with a small fish live bait, and they gave very good sport, being very strong for their size. He stood on the rock when the stream was running slightly through the shutters of the Anicut and making the water just as it should be for trout fishing. They required fine tackle.

He caught Labeos also there.

Mysore.

Somewhat recently I have had an opportunity of giving the Toongabadra a trial, and was grievously disappointed, for though the water was in the places named below all that could be desired, and though I did run a few really big fish, the fishing was very poor indeed. Not only did I see the rivers very thoroughly netted by men who understood their business right well, and travelled in gangs netting all the rivers all their lengths, but I saw also cruives set for fry, and was told that poisoning was practised. This seems to be the fate of all rivers in much inhabited or easily accessible localities. Only in out-of-the-way jungly tracts do the fish get a chance. I tried the following places in Mysore, which I may, perhaps, most fairly describe by calling them worth wetting a line in by those on the spot, but not worth making a pilgrimage to as I did :—

Tirthahalle.
Mâlur.
Mandagadde.
Sacrabyle.
Shimoga.
Bâlehannur.

The last place is not very far from Calasa, where, in former years, I had excellent fishing.

Mr. Sanderson, author of "Thirteen Years among the Wild "Beasts of India," also gave me the following list of likely places in Mysore, but it was in 1873, when he was not so great with the rod as the rifle, and I should attach more weight to it if I could send it to him to be revised with his present knowledge. I should think the forest-clad Cubbany should be good, negotiated in a boat.

Hoonsoor should be your first place; from there you can go to Chunchincuttay, on the Cavery, about 16 miles, where there are considerable falls in the river. There is lots of accommodation in the temple, and a Channel Department hut; but take supplies for a day or two, till you can get into swing from Hoonsoor. There is a good cart road.

About 500 yards below the fall there is a small pool with *big* fish. You will probably see them *rolling* in the evening. From the fall to this point are several grand runs, but rocky. All this holds fish.

Mundegherry on the Hemavutty, about 12 miles across country from Chunchincuttay, you might try if you find Chunchincuttay answer; there are fish; lots of fine water.

Hansoyee and Ramnathpoor, 9 and 18 miles respectively up stream from Chunchincuttay, with a good road, and accommodation at both places, might be visited. The first has lots of big fish, but only pools. At Ramnathpoor you would see the temple fish. They don't mind your fishing 100 yards or so above the temple bathing steps, where there is good water.

Returning to Hoonsoor you could run down to the Cubbany, near Heggadevencottah, 20 miles; there is a fair road. Should you do so, you should camp at a village near the mouth of a tributary river called, I think, the "Sartee," which you will see on the map; there are *fish*, and Moormen who know their whereabouts well. I caught my 150-pounder there.

There is nothing in the river at Hoonsoor, the Lutchmenteert.

I have always had a great opinion of the chances of good sport in the Cubbany, but have never had proper appliances. It is a treat to see the fish rising and feeding about in the runs near Carkencottah.

The rivers I now have fishing on, are the Cavery and Hemavutty. I do not know the Toongabudra from personal experience, but have heard from natives that it is inferior to the former two. But *the* river for monsters, and lots of them, is the Cubbany. This comes from about Manantoddy. It is A 1 for all kinds of fish from Caukencottah, in Mysore, downwards to its junction with the Cavery. The fishing is varied and handy. It is certainly the best place, and for 20 miles down, in this part of the country. I presume your most convenient way of getting there, would be *viâ* Mercara and Manantoddy. Caukencottah is about 12 miles from Manantoddy, with good shooting if you care for it.

Coorg.

Coorg has, I am told, good fishing grounds in the Cavery, near Verajendrapet; and Sampaje is easily accessible from Mercara.

Sport may also be had before the coffee pulping begins at Wottakuli, half way down the Sampaje ghaut, but at Wottakuli the Mahseer are very small, running to about 2 lbs. or 3 lbs.

Manzerabad.—S. writes of a lovely little golden brown Mahseer, being taken with a black palmer fly, about the size of a No. 5 Kirby hook, in a rocky little stream at the top of the Manzerabad Ghât. Also at a tank somewhere about Manzerabad, J. writes that he killed, with a black palmer, and subsequently with gaudy flies, on No. 6 Limerick hook, my sizes, fish of some sort, averaging ¼ lb., but sometimes running to ½ lb. and 1 lb.

Maranhally.—I caught fish of some sort, description not given, of 3 lbs. and 4 lbs., roving with a dough bait.

BOMBAY PRESIDENCY.

North Canara District.

Gairsoppa.—This far-famed fall, which beggars all description, ought to be visited by every lover of the grand and beautiful, but *not without a salmon rod.* There is fair fishing above the falls.

Keep the road from the bungalow towards Mysore till you come to the bridge and stream at the bottom of the hill. Just past the bridge a bridle-path will conduct you about mile to the head of the big pool. Thence upwards there is one succession of pools and runs. But the fish are not plentiful or large. I never tried the big pool, but towards the tail of the big pool above the falls, where it first begins to have eddies on it among the rocks, fish are said to have been caught. The water below the falls is recommended by some wag in the bungalow book, but do not you go on such a fool's errand. I have struggled barefoot where natives would not follow, and could not get to any decent water there.

I also waded through the bungalow book, and though "fine "fish" are talked of therein, nothing definite is recorded over 5 lbs. In the rapids far above I saw S. kill one of 20 lbs. weight, and we got others of 6 lbs. and 8 lbs., but the majority of the Mahseer were very small, say 1 lb. and 1½ lbs., and the river seemed very bare of fry and of all sorts of small fish. I fancy the river must be very much poisoned, netted, and cruived like the rest of the rivers in Mysore of which I have seen anything; for the river rises in Mysore.

The Kálanaddi.—W. says that A. (a dark horse) fishes much in the Kálanaddi from Bommanhalli down to about Ancholi, and he thinks for Mahseer.

BENGAL.

An Extract from the "The Field" of 9th October, 1869.

"HAVING had some excellent sport, Mahseer fishing, in the previous "years, A. and I determined upon seeing what the capabilities of the "Poonch river really were. A trip of this kind of course requires "considerable preparation in a country away from tackle-makers, and "where gut rots almost as soon as it arrives. Strong lines also are "absolutely necessary; they must be 200 yards long, and have a reel "capable of holding that length. We knew by experience how fatal "these monsters were to tackle—even treble gut—and to hooks, which "they managed to break, bend, or straighten in a most mysterious* "way.

"We were prepared and equipped for a start on March 1st, 1867, "and had our Murree cart at the door for our 60 mile drive, which we "accomplished in five hours. These carts reflect great credit on Mr. "Faichnie, Inspector of H.M.'s Mail at Rawul Pindee, who invented "them. They have four seats, back to back, fore and aft, placed just "above the axle-tree. The shafts run through the whole length of the "cart, which is substantially built, and has the centre of gravity so low "that it would be next to an impossibility to overturn it. Two horses "are always used, one in the shafts, and the other attached to an out-"rigger; and keeping the horses at full gallop is by far the most "comfortable motion for passengers. Nothing can be simpler than the "harness. One horse carries a saddle to support the shafts, a crupper, "and a padded chest strap, to which are fastened the traces; and the "other has merely the chest strap. Horses are changed every 6 miles, "and, as the coachman blows his horn as soon as he gets within earshot "of the changing place, two fresh horses are ready by the time the cart "is brought to a standstill. Two minutes effect the change, and off the "cart is again at a hand gallop. A 15 mile ride from the trunk road, "where we left the cart, took us to our destination, the junction "of the Poonch and Jhelum, about 20 miles north of the town of "Jhelum.

"The Poonch rises in the Pir Punjal, a Himalayan range to the

* See remarks on compression, page 36.

"south of the Kashmir Valley, and after a course of 120 miles or so, "falls into the Jhelum. In spring time, the Poonch is about the size of "the Tweed at Coldstream, but the pools are deeper, and the streams "more rapid; I fancy they run about a mile an hour quicker than in the "Tweed. We reached our camp about five in the evening, in high "spirits, the weather looking very promising, though the water was "lower than we quite liked. Our tents were pitched close to the "junction. Our servants had all arrived, and were busily preparing "dinner; so we employed our time in putting our rods together (Irish "rods, preferable to all other, when ready, but troublesome to put "together), and strolled up the river to view the scene of our exploits "of the previous year. As fishing from a boat was more effective than "wading, we were made a little anxious by the non-arrival of a native "boat from some 6 miles up the river, as we had sent a man for it several "days before.

"Early to bed and early to rise was the order of the day, and next "morning we were both up by daylight. A. commenced fishing in a "grand deep pool, with a high bank on one side, and I began at the "junction a quarter of a mile below him. Neither of us had even a "rise; so at nine we returned to breakfast, and after our meal, to our "great delight, the boat appeared in sight. It was a huge, cumbersome, "flat-bottomed, square ended machine, with two enormous oars, roughly "hewn out of a tree. We had two men for each oar, besides a steerer. "We were soon on board and at work. My third try with spoon in the "pool was successful, hooking a fish of 30 lbs. or so; but after playing "him for some minutes, and just as I was about to land him, a swivel "broke, and he was seen no more. When I had somewhat recovered "my equanimity, I began again with a phantom minnow, about the size "of a ½ lb. fish, hooked another, and had him a short time, when after a "vigorous run, the rod straightened, the line slacked, and I discovered "the hooks drawn, an instance of how silk and cobbler's wax dry up in "India. No sooner had I put on another phantom than I lost it, and a "whole casting line, by fouling a rock. This last disaster most effectu-"ally disgusted me, for our supplies of phantoms, lines, etc., though "very ample, could never last at my rate of expenditure. However, I "persevered, and our bag for the day consisted of five fish, of 35 lbs., "29 lbs., 17 lbs., 7 lbs., and 3 lbs., respectively, which was not bad, as "we had not a rise before three in the afternoon, and it was dark by "six. The water was rather thick, especially in the pool. At dinner, "we discussed the failures and successes of the day, repaired our "damaged tackle, devised fresh schemes for capturing the wily Mahseer, "and then turned in, so as to be up and ready by daylight.

"Our custom was to fish from daylight (about half-past five o'clock) "till nine or ten, and not start again till between two and three, when "we fished till dark. Our time between breakfast and our start in the "afternoon was always fully occupied in repairing tackle, whipping "fresh hooks, or making entirely new lines, so that the time never hung "heavy on our hands.

"Next morning, A. tried the junction with fly, as the water was "somewhat clearer, but without success. At times, however, Mahseer "rise well; by far the most deadly fly—indeed, the only one that "appears to tempt them—was Madras jungle-cock feathers in the wings, "if with silver body all the better. While A. was wading at the "junction, I fished from the boat in the pool, and landed one of 18 lbs. "Shortly afterwards we changed places—A. fished from the boat, and I "waded. I first tried fly, but not getting a rise, put on a phantom. "Hooked one, played him for some time, and lost him; so then, as it "was quite breakfast time, I walked back to camp, where I found A. in "great glee, having just brought home a splendid fish of 40 lbs. In "addition to this monster he had hooked five others, all of which got "away. As the day turned out cloudy, and our keenness was redoubled "by the sight of the 40-pounder, off we started soon after breakfast, and "made a brilliant beginning by landing a 36 lbs. and 40 lbs. between "us. Then came a lull, and we did nothing till the afternoon was "well advanced; then we had sport indeed. On our return to camp "there was laid out before our admiring gaze, as the result of our "day's sport, seven fish, of 44 lbs., 40 lbs., 36 lbs., 18 lbs., and 14 lbs., "making a total of 210 lbs.—a feat as regards actual weight for num- "ber of fish seldom, if ever, surpassed in rod fishing, and as regards sport "certainly unequalled. I have never seen salmon run as vigorously or "as long as these fish; they are game to the backbone; and, bearing in "mind that we were fishing with treble gut, it will be seen that their "powers of endurance are very great, for I never spare my fish—in "fact, I fear, I lost some by being over-severe with them. During "their run they take out the line so very quickly, that one has the "greatest difficulty in preventing it from hanking on the reel, in "consequence of the bar on which the line is wound revolving after "the fish stops running. At first I fished with reel and rings under "the rod, but I found that did not answer, as some of the rings "were cut through in a couple of days by the friction of the line; "so I was speedily converted to the Irish fashion of reversing the "rod as soon as a fish was hooked, thereby having the reel and "rings uppermost, and so placing all the strain and friction on the "rod itself. Another advantage was, that by so doing one was "enabled to prevent the line hanking in the reel by pressing one's "fingers against the line. This plan was effective, but not always "agreeable, as I found to my cost, occasionally having had the tips "of my fingers blistered. While on the subject of reels, I might "mention that no reels of English manufacture that I have ever seen "have hard enough metal in the cog or cog-wheel of the check. I "was using on this fishing expedition a new reel of Farlow's, and in "six days the teeth of the cog-wheel had almost disappeared, the "space between the plates being filled with brass filings. In a reel "intended for Mahseer fishing, all the parts that have to bear friction "should be made of well-tempered steel.

"At sunrise next day I again tried the pool, but did not even get an "offer; so I strolled up the river, attended by my shikāri—who, by-the-"bye, was quite new at this kind of sport. He took to it very keenly, "however, and soon became very handy at landing fish, which was "done in a way rather surprising to a man accustomed only to the gaff "or landing net. When the fish is nearly exhausted, the man walks "quietly into the water, gets behind the fish, gently runs his hands "along his back until they reach his gills, then slips his thumbs into the "gills, and lifts the fish out of the water. This mode of capture sounds "very simple, and it is so if the fish does not see the man; but if he "does, off he goes for another run. Mahseer have no dread of being "handled; they keep perfectly quiet during the time the man runs his "fingers along their back, and even remain motionless while the hook "is being taken out, as long as they are held up; but no sooner are they "placed on the ground than they commence kicking and jumping in the "most violent manner.

"When I had walked two miles I came upon a very likely-looking "piece of water by some mills, which I fished diligently with fly, spoon, "and phantom, till I was pretty well tired out by the exertion and the "sun, which was well up by this time; and the day promised to be very "hot. So I turned homewards; and when I had finished my two-mile "walk over boulders and deep sand, I was quite prepared for my break-"fast, which I found all ready, and A. very anxious to begin. His "morning bag was but little better than mine, for he had only succeeded "in landing an 18-pounder. In the afternoon, when the day had got a "little cooler, we set to work again. I took a few casts in the pool, but "stirred nothing, so went down to the junction. Here the Poonch "divides itself into four or five very tolerable streams. I fished them all "with every conceivable bait, but the only result was a miserable "3 pounder, and that I hooked by the stomach. A., however, was much "more successful. He had resolved to persevere in the pool, and by so "doing was rewarded by landing two, of 14 lbs. and 33 lbs., but, with "his usual bad luck, lost an enormous one. He had played him for "more than half an hour up and down the deep water, when he lost him "by the hooks drawing.

"Though, for some mysterious reason, I never had good sport in the "early morning fishing, still I was up again next morning by sunrise, "and we both tried the pool from the boat; I literally did nothing—did "not even stir a fish; but A. landed one of 19 lbs. At 3 P. M. I went up "the river and fished the head of a small pool, with a glorious stream "running into it, close by some jutting rocks. Here I landed a 4 "pounder and a 22 pounder with phantom and spoon. I then tried a "stream a little higher up. I suspect the water was rather too heavy— "at least, I stirred nothing; so, having given the lower stream an hour's "rest, I returned to it, and put on a natural bait. I soon hooked and "landed one of 14 lbs., when I put on a fresh bait, intending to have a "few more casts before it got dark, it being then a quarter to six, and "rather cloudy. The bait had just come across the stream and was "entering the backwater, when I felt a vigorous tug, and a monster "rushed off down stream, with nearly 100 yards of line before I "managed to stop him.* Then he tried a run up stream to nearly "opposite where I was standing, then down again, then opposite me "again, but on quite the further side of the river, and there he sulked for "the best part of an hour, all of which time I was keeping a very severe "pull on him. Unfortunately, I was fishing from a point of rock, and "on my left hand, down stream, was what is best described as 'a long "'bay' of dead water, 50 yards or so across, and between it and the "stream was a bar, consisting of huge rocks rising to within 2 feet or "3 feet of the surface, but with intervals varying from 2 feet to 6 feet "between them, so that getting below the fish was quite out of the "question. At last I managed to move him, and he dashed down "stream 70 or 80 yards, and sulked there. Now commenced my task. "I soon found that merely keeping a steady pull on him had no effect, "especially as he was now below me. The pressure I kept on him was "so great that attempting to wind up line simply caused the line to sink "between the coils already on the reel; so my only plan was to draw in "an inch or so of line with my hand, and then wind it up on the reel. "By dint of perseverance I succeeded in getting him up to within "20 yards or so, and then not another inch could I gain; but I managed "to rile him apparently, for off he rushed to the bottom of the stream "again. Of course by this time it was pitch dark, or else I should have

* This goes to support my idea that 120 yards is enough. *See* Winch, in Chapter XVIII.

"been tempted to try and effect a passage across the bar, with the "almost certainty of going in over head and ears. As it was, prudence "carried the day, and I sat down on a rock, put the butt of my rod "between my legs, and lit a pipe. I then sent my fisherman off to camp, "about 2½ miles over very rough ground, to order some dinner to be "brought out, besides dry shoes and socks, and a great coat. By the "time the welcome sight of a lantern appeared it was near ten o'clock, "and all the time I had been fighting for every inch of line. There was "a splice in my line, and the struggle I had to get it on the reel is "almost incredible. Time after time I felt it pass through my fingers "and just reach the reel, when the fish would shake his head, and pull it "half-way down the rod again.

"After some little delay in collecting sticks and lighting the fire, I "managed to make a very tolerable meal, keeping a tight hold on the "line with one hand while I used the other for dinner purposes. Feel-"ing much refreshed by my hasty repast, I devoted all my energies to "my enemy with redoubled ardour. After one or two runs, I fancied "there appeared to be something wrong with the reel, so, calling for a "light, I examined it, and found to my discomfort that the two screws "which connect the reel with the bar that was tied on to the rod were "gone, and, of course, on the same side as the handle; the consequence "was that the mere act of winding up caused the reel to gape very "considerably at this opening. I tried various methods for remedying "this mishap, such as getting my fisherman to hold it as firmly as "possible in his hands while I wound up line, etc.; but I found none of "them so satisfactory as crossing my legs as I sat on the rock, and "pressing the reel against my left knee. This answered tolerably well, "but it was a somewhat awkward position to remain in for long. To "make a long story short, however, about 2 A. M. I prevailed on my fish "to cross the bar and have a swim in the deep, still pool. He gave two "furious runs up and down, I luckily just preventing him from return-"ing to the stream, and then I hauled him into a nice little shallow "creek. The fisherman carefully handled him, and he was secured. I "made my man carry the captive some yards from the water, and "deposit him in a safe place, and then a most pleasant sensation of "triumph filled my heart, as by the light of the lantern I gloated over "the splendid fish which had fought so bravely and pluckily for eight "hours and a half. By this time it was 2.30 A.M., so my servants "shouldered the fish, pots, and pans, and we started off home, flounder-"ing about over the two miles and a half of boulders and shingle in "pitch darkness, as the lantern had burned out. On arrival I, of course, "routed up A., and we weighed the fish. He just turned the scale at

"52 lbs., and was 4 feet 5 inches in length, which I must confess rather "disappointed me, as I had landed in the previous year one of 57 lbs. "that had not given anything like the sport of this one.

"A. had most patiently waited three hours for dinner, and then in "despair sat down to his solitary meal. My fisherman's appearance with "my dinner order was a great relief to his mind, as he was on the point "of sending out natives with lanterns to search the banks and pools of "the river, fearing that I had been carried down a rapid and stranded "in some uncomfortable place, even if nothing worse had occurred.

"On the following day we did not start till twelve, and had very "poor sport, only catching one of 7 lbs. each—attributable, I think, to "there having been a thunderstorm in the hills during the night. We "had serious thoughts of moving our camp a few miles up the river.

"Two friends arrived next morning in time for breakfast; though "we had fished in the early morning, we had bagged nothing. In the "afternoon I went 3 miles up the river, and caught three in a beautiful "rocky stream, losing a phantom; then, finding that a small boat we "had ordered from higher up the river had arrived, I tried a deep "narrow pool from it. I soon hooked a fine fellow, certainly over 14 lbs., "played him for nearly an hour, when he sulked; and, as no amount of "stone throwing or pulling would move him from his position behind a "big rock, I got into the boat to go across. That started him, but un-"luckily he passed a sharp rock, and cut the line. This drove me "nearly frantic—not only losing the fish after having played him for so "long, but on account of its being the second phantom I had lost that "day; and besides, if I had only had a little more patience, and not "crossed the river, I probably would have bagged him. Afterwards I "caught four small ones with spoon. A. had a blank day, but one "of our friends, M., landed a 24 pounder.

"Our next five days' fishing was much in the same style as I have "described. We moved our camp some 3 miles up the river, between "two pools. Every day we made good bags, averaging about 100 lbs. "a day. A. was always very unlucky with big fish; somehow, they "invariably came to me. Once a 43 pounder that I had hooked, after a "good deal of play, sulked in the most determined way; nothing would "move him. Bearing in mind how my line had been cut a few days "previous, I was very patient with him, but it struck me as being "rather odd that I could not stir him at all. So at last A. went over "the place in the boat; and, finding that the line was round a rock, he "very cleverly cleared the line. Luckily, the fish was nearly drowned, "and became an easy capture; but, from the amount of slack line that "flew back in my face the moment the line was freed, though I was "running back from the shore and winding up as fast as I could, that "very disagreeable sensation of 'He's off,' which every fisherman must "know, came over me. In this instance, however, my alarm was "groundless, as the fish still proved to be on. Another day I lost a fine "fish, that I had played for the best part of an hour, and had completely "tired out, by a swivel breaking, making the second good fish lost in "that way.

"The accompanying table shows the particulars of each day's "sport:

March.	Respective weights of fish in pounds.	Number of fish caught.	Total weight. lbs.
2nd.	35, 29, 17, 7, 3 (lost 3 fish)	5	91
3rd.	44, 40, 40, 36, 18, 18, 14 (lost 6 fish) ..	7	210
4th.	38, 18, 14, 3 (lost 3 fish)	4	73
5th.	52, 22, 19, 14, 4 (lost 2 fish)	5	111
6th.	7, 7 (lost 2 fish)	2	14
7th.	17, 16, 10, 8, 3, 2 (lost 3 fish)	6	56
8th.	30, 18, 10, 8, 5½, 3, 3, 2, 2, 2, 1 (lost 3 fish)	11	84
9th.	25, 24, 18, 16, 11, 10, 8, 8, 8, 7, 7, 5, 4, 3 (lost 2 fish)..	14	154
10th.	43, 28, 24, 18, 11, 9, 8, 8, 7, 7, 5, 14, 4, 3, 3, 2, 2, 2 (lost 4 fish)..	18	221
11th.	33, 13, 10, 7, 5, 5, 5, 1½, 1, 3½, 3½, 2½ 2 (lost 3 fish)	13	98
12th.	30, 3	2	33

"In eleven days 87 fish were caught, weighing 1,145 lbs.; being an "average of rather more than 13 lbs. 2½ oz. each.

"I hope I have been able to convey to your readers some idea of "what splendid sport Mahseer fishing is in India, especially in a good "river. For gameness and vigour the Mahseer, to my thinking, is "superior to any salmon; his rushes are grand. His not taking fly as "readily as bait is, of course, a drawback. A friend has landed a 63 "pounder in splendid condition with fly; but still it is undeniable that "a man fishing with bait, natural or artificial, will make a heavier bag "than one fishing with fly only. As far as my experience goes, "phantom minnows, natural bait, and spoon are all equally good, and I "invariably gave them all a try over the same water. I used to weight "my line very heavily, putting on at least the weight of an Enfield "bullet, and to that* I attribute my catching heavier fish than A. The

* Because the Mahseer is mainly a bottom feeder, and a great fish eater. *See* page 29, *et seq.*

"phantoms we used were at least 6 inches long. Big fish, however, "have been landed with much smaller ones. The principal objection to "the small phantoms is the difficulty* of being able to use hooks strong "enough. My favourite spoon was the size of a dessert spoon.

"The sun in the day time in March is powerful, the nights are very "cool—almost cold. The previous year we fished in April; even then "living under canvas is bearable; but the great objection is not so "much the actual heat as the constant dread of the snows melting, for "when that happens an end is of course put to all sport for the "season †

"Our two friends landed 339 lbs. of fish, but caught none of any very "great size. They were fishing five days. In the previous year three "rods (of which I was one) caught 700 lbs. in five days, averaging over "$18\frac{1}{2}$ lbs. each, in this same river, the Poonch. In one day we landed "358 lbs.—K."

An Extract from "The Asian," of 2nd September, 1879.

"In most localities, it is quite out of the question going out in July, "August, and September. The rain is one hindrance, muddy‡ water "another, fever, etc., a good third. The consequence is, no one ventures "out, except perhaps once or twice during what should be 'close' "time. The only true fishing months may, therefore, be confined to "October and November, and from February to the rains.

* * * * *

"First, then, Mirzapore is the railway station, and thence some "25 miles down the Rewah road is a dak, or rather a road bungalow, "to which, whilst I was stationed at Mirzapore, the courteous engineer "never refused entry; supplies and servants must be taken, as no estab-"lishment is kept; permission to occupy the bungalow must be obtained. "In the hotter months and rains the shelter is a necessity; and in the "cold weather tents are preferable. The river, the Beylun, is about "300 yards from the bungalow, and the best fishing is just above and "just below the bridge, an 'Irish' one. Here, on 11th October, my "diary reminds me of the capture of a full 12 lb. fish, and with the

* This difficulty is got over by a hook made specially for Mahseer.—*See* page 220.

† Colonel Parsons has now shown us that we may still continue fishing by his method. Chapter IX.

‡ This difficulty is now overcome. *See* Chapter IX.

"recital I give the description of two flies used before the Mahseer was "landed.

"It is four years ago now since I first camped at Buroundah, where "the road bungalow is. The river had just cleared, and my bag with "a medium-sized fly, yellow all round except a black feather tail, was "three good fish, the largest scaling $3\frac{1}{2}$ lbs. This was $3\frac{1}{2}$ lbs. This was "encouraging, because I have been told I should get no fishing in the "district. I changed my fly for one of a larger size, with a dark blue "body, broad silver tinsel, no hackle, wing of peacock harl and 'ruffed' "with buff-coloured silk. Three pools below the bridge I was into a "good fish, but after the first rush the line came away slack. He had "gone, quite a yard of good stout salmon gut and a good fly lost. It "was late, so we (a friend had joined me) went back to camp.

"Next morning we shot. In the evening my double-handed trout "rod, a beauty, with treble gut, was sailing a fly over the first pool under "the bridge. The fly was a large one, as I now knew heavy fish were to "be got, but until close on dusk there had not been a rise. Three good "pools fished from both banks resulted in blanks, but I sat down and "chose a fly as nearly as possible similar to the one I had lost, and soon "felt myself safe in something good. I shouted with joy, and my chum "S. soon came up. We had to light a lantern, and by its aid at last I "landed my first, and, alas, my last 12 lbs. in the Beylun. Unhooking "him, we found the fly he had carried off the day before firmly fast in "him, and the gut trailing. I have never seen such a thing happen "before. It was rather curious, too, that a fish should, after being "struck the day before, remain about the same rapids; but I am one of "those who do not believe the finny tribe are very sensitive about the "mouth. I wish I could give coloured plates of the flies that are "killing, but I cannot even draw. From Buroundah we returned to "Lallgunj, and here a pretty fair bag of trout rewarded us. The little "stream is 'little indeed.' Sometimes almost running dry, but half "pound trout on a very light Castle Connel rod was not bad fun, and "over six brace was our reward.

"Let us return to Buroundah. The rapids below the bridge end in "a very deep pool and long one, full of alligators, but if you have time "follow it down and you enter the Allahabad district,—famous for pig "sticking, good for gaiety, and noted for a charming club and a "charming secretary. Many runs have I had with him. I would they "could be multiplied indefinitely. But in those days we had a 'col- "lector.' The 'glory' is departed; yet in good hands Allahabad will "still show sport; I believe now is showing it.

"I have sadly digressed. As I have said, go below the big pool under "the rapids of Buroundah, and from thence to 'Pathurpore' near "'Koolsara.' A 1 fishing, but the water must be clear, and the angler "keep well out of sight; dark flies are the best, and I always used "them. Let me describe one that will take splendidly. But why "should I? 'The Rod in India' has christened it the Blackamoor.

"Then, again, we are now in the Allahabad district, Sohra to "Khurkha is splendid fishing ground the whole way, and there is a "place I do not quite remember, but think it is called 'Mai,' and is "close to 'Kohrar;' here I caught my best fish in nearly still water, "fishing just the break of the rapids; all these places are best reached, "I think, from the wayside railway station of 'Sirsa.' Any friend in "Allahabad could give information. The Beylun joins the 'Tons,' "and the fishing from Sohra to Khurkha and at 'Mai' is on the Tons. "In this latter river I was indebted to a brother sportsman for one of "the best flies I ever threw. We had to make them up, and he showed "me how.

"Body Austrian grey, silver tinsel, tail of two bustard feathers and "wings of the same. It is a splendid fly, and I am much indebted for "good sport to my friend. Here my experiences of Mirzapore and "Allahabad end. "DOON."

Extract from "The Asian," of October 14th, 1879.

"The next district I touch on is Jhansi. It is a fine sporting "district, deer, hares, grouse, and ducks are plentiful. Snipes "are not very plentiful, but still they are to be got with a little "trouble. Leopards are very numerous, but owing to the rocky "nature of the country not easily driven, and very wary. The fishing "is excellent.

"I am not quite certain of the distances, but the Pahooj river runs "about 3 miles from Jhansi, and holds some of the finest trout I have "ever seen. The Babarie, about 4 miles on the opposite side, "almost beats it, and the Betwa and Dessaun give fine Mahseer.

"Everything, however, in these streams must be taken at 'the "'tide.'

"The Betwa and Dessaun are raging torrents till October, and "then you must be down and get all you can of fishing or the streams "simply 'dribble,' and 'still-water' fishing is all that can be had. "The Babarie and Pahooj clear rather rapidly, especially the former, "and I hardly know prettier trout-fishing than the Babarie affords. "As both these streams are minor ones, the best fishing is to be got in "a break of the rains. I used always to go past the cavalry lines, "through a gate in the Custom's hedge, and down to the stream "where it cuts the Oorcha or Tehree road. Fish *down* stream. You "get splendid fun. Do not despise the water because it is rather "sluggish at places, and does not *look* deep. Lower and about 4 miles "from Jhansi off the Burwa Sagar road, is the best and deepest pool; "but though there are numbers of fish in it, I do not remember ever "to have taken there one good trout. No reason why others should "not, but it was puzzling.

"Oorcha, the ancient capital of the Raja of Teekumgarh or "Tehree, has a wall old and broken, in parts made of loose rocks and "boulders piled up, and I fear to say of how many miles in circum-"ference. It is 7 miles, probably. A Gazetteer would simplify "matters. The ruins are grand. Here we had many a merry party, "and many a jolly day. The Betwa runs close under the old temples, "and fish are fairly numerous, though I have never seen one above "8 lbs. The rapids are splendid, and there is a dam below the old "city, which was once unbreached, but has been neglected, and now "has one or two rifts in it, and the waters pour through in wild "disorder. Many a good fish have I taken there.

"Most successful was a fly I describe now. Body orange wool, "gold twist, yellow tail and yellow wings, with a 'taste' of red on "the shoulders. It is very killing.

"Another. Body dark yellow, tag of peacock harl, wings black "with a few peacock harl in it. I found, however, bright English "Salmon flies take well too.

"Then the country above Oorcha is splendid. The scenery all the "heart could desire, and the Betwa winds through forest lands, now "one united stream, and now through several channels, sometimes "clear of trees, and more often bordered by them thickly. Fishing "is grand, and so is it all on to the bridge over the Jhansi and "Lullutpore road. I would like once again to camp up the Betwa's "banks from Oorcha to the bridge on the road, and fish the old pools "Just above the bridge, too, is one of the finest pools in the river. It "is a 'still' pool, and requires *fishing*, but has given good sport. I "have given no fly for the Pahooj or Babaries, but here they are, and "I am indebted to a knowledge of the first to a friend about those "parts:—

"1. Body red, silver twist, wings black, tipped with white (the "common Myna will furnish this or the Turkey), hook rather small.

"2. The 'red spinner.'

"3. The 'black spinner,' with silver twist. I found gold twist "answer too.

"The above are probably the best flies, but there may be others.

"My experience of Jhansi dates only over a year. There are others "there who, if they would, could give better information. Then the "Dessaun. I hate the river! There are lots of fish in it, though I do "not think so many as in the Betwa, but I never could get a bag "out of it.

"The 'Ghat' off the road from Jhansi to Nowgong, about 38 miles "from Jhansi, and 15 or so from Nowgong, is the place I would choose "to try my luck. From thence one can fish some rapids about a mile "and a half down stream, and some two miles up stream, besides what "fishing one could get immediately above and below the Ghat itself. "Very fine trout are to be had above and below the 'cold weather' "bridge. There is a good pucka road from Jhansi to Nowgong, and "on both banks of the river, bungalows, permission to occupy which "has never, to my knowledge, been refused.

"Then there is Mow, near Raneepore, about 30 miles from Jhansi, "and 8 miles from the Ghat. You *must* pass Mow, if my old friend "will let you get to the Ghat, and there, though there *is* a dak "bungalow, with a 'call' or without one, the chances are you will "not be allowed to occupy it, but be most hospitably entertained, and "*welcomed* by as good-hearted a man, and as jolly a sportsman as ever "stepped. What is more, he would beat most fellows into 'fits,' with "a gun, and just pride himself on showing you the best sport to be "had all round his place, so one cannot do better than visit Mow, if "thereabouts.

"Chirgaon is about 18 miles, if I rightly remember, from Jhansi, on "the Jaloun road. There is here a road bungalow, but the good "fishing ground on the Betwa, which is about 3 miles from Chirgaon, "is at and about a place called Goolara, some 3 to 4 miles on the "Jhansi side of Chirgaon.

"The fishing from Goolara to Dhunna is magnificent, but you "must 'tent' it, and remember, that though your 'rises,' and probably "'takes,' will be numerous, the fish will very seldom exceed 7 lbs. I "do not remember ever trying *spinning*, but from what I saw of fish "in the pools from high banks, my impression is, they do not run to any "greater size in the rivers of Jhansi and Lullutpore than 12 to 15 lbs. "My experience of these districts is respectively about a year each, "and therefore I am open to correction, but I think that the instances "of fish caught over 10 lbs. (Mahasir) are rare. But after all, there "is more fun and greater enjoyment in playing a 10 lb. or 6 lb., with "a light rod and fine tackle, than *working and worrying* on for a big "fish with rods and tackle that might be described as 'Piscatorial "Woolwich Infants!' No more now from yours. "DOON."

Extract from "The Asian," of 28th October, 1879.

"It is best now to journey up country, and before going elsewhere, "let us take the Eastern Doon. Many know it well, and will "remember happy hours along the banks of the Ganges, the Song, and "the Sooswa.

"The Song flows behind the Kalunga Hill, once crowned by a "fortress, famous for its defence by the Goorkhalies. From Dehra "you go to Kalapani, and thence over the hill to a tributary stream, "following which down its junction with the Song, gives the first "pool I have tried.

"Here in August, September, and a part of October, good fish are "to be taken, up to 8 lbs., at any rate, though larger are in the waters, "and may be got by spinning. I once saw a fish certainly over 30 lbs. "in this stream, but nothing would tempt him.

"All down the Song the fishing till October is good, but after "that there is but little water in it, and, indeed, it almost dries up "altogether.

"The Sooswa flows past Kansaras, a place once famous for all "kinds of game, but now its glory has departed. Fine Trout and "Mahseer fishing is to be had all down the Sooswa, and where the "Song and Sooswa join is a splendid pool with heavy fish.

"Jamun Khatta, below the junction, is well worth staying at. "Good trout and good Mahseer, and plenty of them. Down the river "some few miles, you get to the junction of the Sooswa and Ganges, "and here are splendid fish, as large as any river in India can furnish; "but here spinning pays best.

"Up near the hills, where the Ganges leaves the Himalayas, is "Tuppobun, with its splendid scenery and grand pools. Lower down, "Rickee Khase, with equally good water, and so on, till you come to "Hurdwar, with its 'Myapore Bridge,' the 'Bund,' and 'Dam,' all "well-known ground.

"The fish, though, are getting more and more shy, and it is not "always a 'bag' to be made. Under the Myapore Bridge, hundreds "of swallows have their nests, and many a large fish has been caught "with a swallow, or rather martin (as I believe they are) tied on to a "hook, and used as a bait.

"I rigged up a very large hook in imitation of a swallow, and "tried it, years ago, but only bagged one fish. They do not seem to "take freely now. The 'escape' (I called it the 'Dam') is a fine "piece of trolling water, but one has to be careful spinning, as there "are 'snags,' or were—I speak of days long ago.

"Below Hurdwar is Kunkhal, but unless the escape is open, few "fish will be risen, though lower down, the pools deepen, and just "above the bridge of boats at Jheesnmwalla Ghat, in one morning "before breakfast, I happily landed two fish over 20 lbs. each, and "three others, none under 10 lbs.; a good morning's work!

"Lower still, down towards Asufgurh, one day's bag reached "146 lbs., the best fish weighing 27½ lbs. This water is splendid "fishing, and once again may I tread its banks. Further down yet "Mahseer are to be got, but only one ever rewarded my efforts with "fly. Bait fishing must be resorted to. The places to fish are the "'Kooties.' Fakirs build themselves small habitations on the Ganges, "and they generally wash their grain in the river, even if they do "not throw the remnants of their dinner into it; but often they *feed* "the fish, and a hook baited with atta is sure to give sport.

"But at the Ghat, over the Ganges between Bijpore and Meerut, "another kind of sport may be had—very exciting in its way, and "hard work too.

"When the bridge is 'up,' in the cold weather under the oldest "boats, the 'gonch' may be seen clinging on by feelers to the bottom. "It struck me they could be *speared*, so a friend and myself sent down "our canoes, armed ourselves with barbed spears, made so that the "heads should *slip off* the handles, and drove down to the Ghat. The "spear heads had about 20 yards of stout cotton string attached, and "to the end of the rope an inflated (bullock's) bladder. When we "saw the gonch, the spear was sent 'home,' and the shaft withdrawn. "The fish at once went off, and the bladder keeping on the surface "showed his course. We followed in canoes, and taking extra spears, "gained the bladder and pulled up our prey, finishing him as best we "could. One morning my friend and myself killed three gonch thus, "all about 80 lbs. If this sport can be got at one bridge, I see no "reason why not at every one on the Ganges and Jumna, and other "streams too, for gonch abound down country, but I must say I have "never tried it anywhere else but at that one bridge.

"Mahseer are to be got down the canal too. The falls toward "Roorkee are good places, and especially to Puthri Bridge. Here, "trolling with 'Chulwas,' I have caught 18 lb. fish, never anything "larger. But Mahseer are to be had lower still. In the Meerut "district, under the falls, I have taken them with the *fly*.

"Mahseer have been taken, too, with bait at Fatigarh and Cawn- "pore, and lower, I believe; but at the two places named, I have "*seen* them caught.

"At Bijpore, and at all the bridges lower down, the butchwa take "the fly freely, and are to be taken up to 2 lbs. in weight. A dark "fly seems the best.

"DOON."

Extract from the "Asian," of December 23rd, 1879.

"Fishing in Laour.

"I have just got back from Laour, where I went on a fishing trip, "and had very fair sport.

"Extract from my diary:—

November 19th, got nil, lost 4 fish.
,, 20th, ,, 1, lbs. 19, lost 3.
,, 21st, ,, 2, ,, 30, 36.
,, 22nd, ,, 6, ,, 46, 31, 41, 25, 13, 12.
,, 23rd, ,, 2, ,, 44, 30.
,, 24th, ,, 2, ,, 24, 32.
,, 25th, ,, nil, gave the good pools a rest, and tried some new water.
,, 26th, got 3, lbs. 18, 58, 55.
,, 27th, ,, 3, ,, 29, 29, 62.
,, 28th, ,, 8, ,, 16, 54, 20, 33, 7,* 32, 33, 26.
,, 29th, got 2, ,, 28, 26.
,, 30th, ,, 1, ,, 28, tried new water again.
December 1st, ,, 1, ,, 21.

"Of course, besides these fish, I lost several, of which I kept no "account. I got them all trolling with spoons 4 inches long. I tried "the fly, but without success.

"The river is called the Punateet, and runs out of the Khasia "Hills at Laour. To get to it, you have to branch off at Soonam-"gunge (on the Soormah) and go by boat to a village called Elamgao. "here you can get dingies and boatmen to take you up the gorge "where you must rough it in a grass hut. It is a beastly unhealthy "place. Every time I go there, all my servants are knocked over with "fever. I got it once myself, but on that occasion I was there for six "weeks.

* "I never saw a Mahseer like this before. Back and fins perfectly black, a game "little head, and very thick through. He astonished me, as before weighing him I "took him for a fish of about 4 lbs. He fought like a little devil, and showed as "great a disinclination to be landed as other fish of 12 or 15 lbs.—L. J."

Extract from the "Asian," of 25th May, 1880.

"*Fishing from the Simoor Territory to the Nepal Boundary.*

"I have fished all the rivers in this tract, except the Sarda, which "is the Nepal boundary.

"To begin: On the west, there is the Bata stream that runs from "below Nahan to join the Jumna at Bata; about 1 mile from the "junction up stream are two holes that used to be capital fly-fish "places. I have known 80 fish taken with a single rod in one day "out of these two holes. My largest take from there was 36 fish, but "I only tried for the larger ones. I once saw a 6 lb. Mahseer caught "there with *atta*, but from 2 ozs. to 2 lbs. is the usual thing with fly, "and both Mahseer and trout are caught. The trout (so called) is "also a species of carp, but he is a very game, handsome fish; "occasionally fish of other sorts are caught that look like roach.

"We used to have our fancy flies, but I am of opinion that "Indian fish generally take a fly in mistake for a young fish or "fry; I say generally, as I have seen them taking an insect often "such as locusts, larva of insects, and flying ants.

"Red and black palmers are favourites, and a sort of red palmer "with a tail is my especial. He is made of a single hackle feather "of the jungle-fowl or red game; that and a black one and a fly "with white body, dirty yellow tail, and florican or houbara wing.

"The Jumna is a splendid river for fly or spinning. I have "been told that pure white and pure yellow flies are the best in "this river, but I have found the ordinary* ones do very well indeed. "This river seems a favourite one for Mahseer; when the dirty water "of the melted snows come down in May, making the Jumna as dirty "as the Thames, large bags are made. The river is shallow in the "parts mostly fished over, and perhaps the fish see the lure more "readily than in deeper streams. The old town of Simoor, said to "have been deserted 1,000 years, is on the banks close to the lake. "Portions of the paved streets and many gods, etc., are still to be seen "lying in the jungle. The Jumna is a good river for monsters. The "Tons very bad fishing always. I have not gone in much for the big "river fishing, as to be successful, you must have Mullahs with Senai's "(inflated skins), and I never fancied this mode of fishing. The Arson "has yielded many fish to my rod, and all with fly. I prefer the first

* I do not understand what is meant; I have a shrewd suspicion one is as good as another, and perhaps a good deal better. I have already said my say as an unbeliever in the matter of salmon flies.

"and last mentioned fly for this river; up to 5 lbs. is the usual weight, "but fish of 15 to 20 lbs. have been caught in it. Snipe are very "fond of the edges of this river when going up or down country. I "have forgotten the large fish at the Pounta temple on the Jumna; "they are to be had with *atta* I believe. This is a Sikh temple, and "so is the Gurse Dwam at Dehra. A large trout 4¾ lbs. was caught "in the Arson, near the mouth, when I was there; it was the largest "by 1¾ lbs. that I have ever seen.

"The Luswa is a splendid stream for fly, and also the Song. I "have taken many dozens out of these two streams, the average of a "good day in the cold weather, is from 15 to 25 fish, average 1 lb. "each. I once bagged in one hole 18 trout, averaging nearly a pound, "and one small Mahseer; 5 lbs. is about the largest one can hope for, "until May, but during May and June, large fish are caught in both "streams, but fever is said to be very prevalent in those months. The "Song is the only decent sized stream I know of in these parts "that is not subject to floods; it principally drains Jhils, so the "supply of fish is steadier than elsewhere, and the water even in "the cold season is comparatively warm.

"The Ganges, 'The Mighty' has the monsters. Ask 'Moun- "taineer' to tell you how to catch them, as he manages to fetch "them out when others don't. He tells me the great art is to "pitch the bait as far out as possible. He also uses only small "Mahseer, about 2 ozs., when he can get them, in preference to any "other bait. The natives catch large fish with a very cunning "dodge; the line is wound on a roundish wheel; the end of the "line is weighted with a small stone, say 2 lbs. weight; the hook is "tied to a snooding about a yard long, and baited with a small fish; "sufficient line is unwound, and the stone swung round and round "until let go with a jerk, it flies into mid-stream; the line is then "tightened, and tied with a bit of thread to a forked stick, and all is "ready, the snooding allowing the bait to lay down stream. The fish "when taking the bait has to break the thread before he can run, and "that hooks him, and he is left to play himself, as most fish are caught "in this way at night.

"Fish may be caught with *atta* in the Ganges readily, Mahseer "generally, but at times another fish, something like a cross between "a Sauli and a Goonch, is to be had. I saw 'Mountaineer' catch "three at Rikhikare. Trout can be taken with fly and Mahseer also. "Trout in all rivers like a muddy bottom. One year I saw the "Ganges dry opposite a village, except in the pools, and I had great "success with the fly. Mahseer are caught by the natives as "far down as Nagal Ghat, and I had one a short distance above that "place.

* * * * *

"The Ramgunga I have fished a good deal. The largest taken "in that river by me with fly, is 5 lbs., and the largest when trolling, "29 lbs. I wrote to your paper at the beginning of the season to say "that fish had been killed, now there are a plentiful supply of young, "but nothing over 8 lbs. has been killed this year with the rod and "line as far as I know, but I saw a few big fish in one hole. I had "a fine morning last month at the smaller fish with fly. There were "shoals of the small climbing fish going up the river, similar to those "seen on the bank at Myapur; they are brown above, and white "beneath. I put on a home-made fly of these colours, and got 13 fish "weighing 23 lbs. in a short time; this I consider very good with the "fly. I lost a long time with the first fish, as when hooked a large "Gooneh and a huge Mahseer ran at him in turns, but he was about "1 lb. in weight, and the water very rapid, and they made a mess of "him, never getting a fair hold. I don't suppose I could have done "much, if either had hooked themselves, as I had only a light trout "rod and fine tackle. I have made some other good bags, but none "so heavy in proportion. A native boy taught me how to catch Sauli "the other day, and we bagged 18 in about one hour. I could not see "that my fine tackle had any advantage over his coarser line. "The plan is to bait with a bit of meat, and lower the bait to the "bottom, near a weed, and sit still until the fish runs away, then "strike, and out with him. The fun was so fast, that I did not "even open a sketch book I took out with me. The fish were of two "kinds, one a very ugly big-headed beast, of a uniform dirty olive "green colour, with the two side fins barred brown and black; the "other a mottled chap with not so large a head. Both have the fin "extending from the vent round the tail to the shoulder, and they "are very good eating; they were all small. Next time I will try "for bigger ones in deeper water; they have large mouths with strong "erect teeth, and often dropped off the hook when landed.

"The Kosi is a good river for fish, but bad for fishing, as con-"tracts are given yearly to the natives to poach it. There are "many other small streams with large holes in them, that have "good fly fishing with light tackle. The Commissioner's Hole at "Ramnagur, on the Kosi, is a good place for fishing. A few may be "had daily with *atta*, a few with live bait, and in the evening a "fly, but the fly must look something like a young fish, as the time "to catch with fly is when the young fish that have been kept back all "day by the people from the town coming for water, try to pass round a "rocky bluff in the hole, when the stream strikes them, and carries "them out a short distance, then the Mahseer rush at them, and make "the water boil. I have seen this at other places, and if you can manage "to get a fly there just as the boil is ceasing, you probably get a rise. "Watching the proceedings from a high bank above, after the rush is "over, three or four of the small fish will be seen twisting about in "the water, injured by fins or tails, I suppose; and quite old stagers of "Mahseer will be seen gleaning the injured ones, and I always imagine "in these cases that fly is mistaken for fish,—at all events it is a sure "time to catch.

"PALE FACE."

* * * * *

Sialkot.—N. tells me the Poonch is within a night's run, and the Cheenab, where Captain—— caught 294 lbs. in one day's fishing.

Poonah.—O., from Poonah, speaks of running out to the Koomowlie, a small river, but *extraordinarily* deep, averaging 60 feet deep, with the bottom honeycombed with rocky cells and grottos, and holding Mahseer of 50 or 60 lbs. Dav too, is spoken of by the same correspondent as near Poonah. He caught some sort of carp-like fish there up to 25 lbs., with the ground-nut for bait. Another day, in three hours, he caught there six fish, weighing 75 lbs. I cannot trace the places on the map, but they are probably easily discoverable by people in the locality.

MAHSEER FISHING, NEAR ROORKEE.

Extract from "The Asian," of 25th November, 1879.

"A few words now about Roorkee, and how to get there. It "is situated on the Ganges Canal, 24 miles from Saharunpore, a "station on the Scinde, Punjab, and Delhi Railway. Dâks are easily "procured for going and coming. The head-quarters of the Bengal "Sappers and Miners are always at Roorkee, also the head-quarters "and a wing of a European regiment. The Thomason Civil Engineer- "ing College is also located there, likewise the Government Canal "Workshops and Foundry, where you can get anything from a sewing- "machine needle to a wrought iron bridge. The angler can also get "artificial baits, gaff hooks, landing net rings, check winches, and other "metal fishing appliances made to order there. The dâk bungalow is "a comfortable one, within a stone's throw of the canal, and all "supplies are easily procurable. As all the fishing is either in the "canal or close to it, a small tent is useful for camping out in. There "are bungalows all along the canal bank, and leave to occupy them "can usually be obtained. There are no boats procurable to fish out "of,—at least there were none when I was there, but at nearly all the "falls there are long piers stretching out from the main piers of the "bridges, on the down stream side, accessible by steps from the road-"way of the bridge. At the end of these piers the angler is in the best "possible place for spinning, as he is just at the end of the broken "water made by the fall above, and just above the places where the "big fish usually are. The best time to fish is during the cold "weather. I did not get there till March, but even then I had quite "as good sport as I had hoped for. As the canal water comes from "the Ganges directly the snow water comes down from that river, it "also gets into the canal, and puts an end to the fishing. It made its "appearance at the time I am writing about, on the 25th March. I "certainly got several fish after that date, but no large ones, and by "the end of the month the fishing was quite at an end.

* * * * *

"I rode on to Hurdwar, and my tent was pitched close to the "camp of the Royal Engineer Officers, who were out there making "pontoon bridges for the pilgrims to cross the river. The dam "across the Ganges (for the purpose of turning the water into "the canal) is about a mile below Hurdwar, and the place is called "Mirepoor.

* * * * *

"I was at Mirepoor seven days, and during that time I caught "25 Mahseer, varying in size from 2 lbs. up to 15 lbs. I did not fish "all day, or every day either, but had quite as much sport as I wished "for.

* * * * *

"F. M. M."

BURMAH.

Extract from the "Madras Times," of 29th July, 1878.

"On page 85 the author invites 'contributions, which will be "'thankfully received.' I am thus emboldened to offer the following "remarks, premising that my experience is confined to fishing in "Burmah, Assam, and Sylhet. . . . There is capital shooting "and fishing in Cachar; moreover, the Cosseyah and Jynteah Hills "are easily got at, and the climate there is equal to Coonoor.

"The late Dr. Jerdon assured me there were some twenty-seven "varieties of Mahseer; but in general only three are recognised in "Assam and its dependencies. They are called the Useel Mahseer (the "true Mahseer), the Boga Mahseer, and the name of the third I forget. ". . . The upper part of the body to the central meridian line is "almost a golden brown, the fins red, whilst the lower part is bluish-"silvery: the lips, especially the upper, are very thick, the upper can "be uncurled. It is out and out the handsomest of the Mahseer, and "gives the most sport. . . . Mr. Thomas appears only to have "fished for these fish from the bank; a far more killing mode is to "troll out of a boat. Whether the Madras boatmen are capable of pro-"pelling a boat up rapids I don't know, but the Karens, Burmese, and "Cosseyahs will take a light boat up frightful rapids with perfect "safety. The plan is to trail your bait a good 50 yards behind the boat, "and the sport is thus very exciting. As Mr. Thomas justly remarks, "the large Mahseer are bottom-feeders and in clear streams, whilst the "smaller fish can be seen swimming about midstream, the small fry "near the surface; the monsters keep near the bottom, so if you want "big fish, fish deep. The fly is most killing in shallow rapids; a man "should wade in pretty deep, and, if a practised hand, he will kill "many fish, but few of them will be above 10 to 14 lbs., and the "greater number a good deal less. In the Dehra Dhoon, they are the "most gaudy flies, but where I have fished, the most killing fly was a "medium sized No. 4 or 5 semi-circle hook, dressed like the cock-o'-"the-walk as described by Mr. Thomas at page 101. For smaller fish "the smoky dun was most killing.*

"For spinning I have found nothing equal to a large spoon. . . . "In the waters of the Upper Burhampootra—especially near Suddyah—

* These two flies, Cock-o'-the-walk and Smoky Dun, were mentioned in my first edition; the former on the authority of "K," whose letter about fishing on the Poonch will be found among the extracts on fishing localities, and the latter on the recommendation of a fisherman who had killed many Mahseer before I had ever seen one, and who, while admitting certain merits in the Blackamoor, still fancied the Smoky Dun much more.

The Cock-o'-the-Walk.

Of this fly all that K. says is "by far the most deadly fly—indeed, the only one "that appears to tempt them—was Madras jungle cock feathers in the wings, if "with silver body, all the better." K. does not say anything about size, so I will take the liberty to suggest the same as for Blackamoor, to wit, a No. 2,0 and 2 Limerick hook, but especially No. 2.

This fly may be the more readily believed in, as the neck feathers of the Madras jungle cock are general favourites, are used more or less as a set-off in many salmon flies, and are at the head of the poll in Norway; even those Norwegians who know

"Mahseer are very plentiful and run to a very large size. The best "fishermen in Assam, in my day, were the late Capt. Hood—Robin "Hood of the Field—and Col. Combes—10-bore of the *Oriental* "*Sporting Magazine*. The latter especially made very large bags, "but he preferred the fly, and he has caught with it, I believe, fish "up to 40 lbs. in weight, but he is the only one I ever heard of per- "forming such a feat, whilst with the spoon and dead bait they have "killed fish up to 70 lbs. in weight. For some years I carried on an "active warfare with Farlow; he would not make his treble hooks "strong enough; at last I got him to make the hooks Mr. Thomas "alludes to in his book. Many a fish have I lost, and many an "anathema have I hurled at Farlow's head because he would not credit "that a Mahseer is capable of doubling up the strongest Salmon or "Pike hooks. I have had the hooks straightened, too, many a time, "but at last we came to an understanding, and Farlow is now by "far the best man to go to for not only hooks, but for every descrip- "tion of tackle.

"Besides the Mahseer, we used to catch what the Bengalees call "Bassah, and the Burmese Nga Memein. It is allied to the cat fish, "and has no scales; it is delicious eating, and takes a fly or a spoon "readily. This fish can be caught in great numbers in the Shoayghein "river; it does not give much play after being hooked. As for murrel "I have seen thirteen varieties exposed for sale in the market at Terriat "Ghat, at the foot of the ghaut, leading up to that moist place Cherra- "poonghe, with its fifty feet of rainfall in the year. . . .

"My first trip towards Sylhet was in 1869, when General Blake "was with us. My journal of this trip is not here, so I speak from "memory alone. He, Ommanney, and I started in November. We "went first to Nurting, where we shot duck, teal, and snipe; then to "Jawai (Jynteah Hills,) and so on across the Hills to the Darrung "river. . . . In the depths of the pool below we could see in the "clear limpid waters not one Mahseer, but literally thousands. . . . "Ommanney caught a couple of fish. . . . The Cossyah boats "are very roomy, very buoyant, and are easily propelled by the

no other English, being still able to introduce the word jungle cock, or yungle cock in their Norse recommendation of the right fly to use.

The Smoky Dun.

This fly is of one colour all over, a smoky dun colour, the colour say of smoke ascending from a damp wood fire, a dusky fisherman's blue or ash colour with just a perceptible touch of light dull yellow or dun in it. Wings and body the same, with a tag and three or four turns of silver twist, and a tail of peacock's back feather. Hook No. 2,0 or 2 Limerick, particularly the latter.

"muscular arms of these Cossyahs. I got hold of a capital fellow, "the only word of English he knew was 'wind up,' which he "kept repeating whenever we came to a rapid, where there was "danger of losing the spoon, or when I struck a fish. We tried in "the vicinity of our encamping ground, but though we could see the "fish in dozens, they would not look at our baits. We could ascend "the river only about a mile, and were then stopped by waterfalls. I "went up as far as I could without getting a bite; I had to go through "these rapids. Coming back I struck a trout-like fish at the edge of "the rapid, and it was drowned before we got into smooth water.

"Below our camp, towards the plains, the river was navigable for "about two miles, when it was partially dammed up by the Cossyahs. "There were alternately rapids and reaches of deep water. In one "place which we called the gorge, it was at least 50 to 60 feet deep, "with the steep hills rising abruptly out of the water's edge. I went "down to the obstruction without a bite; coming back I put on my "largest spoon, weighted it heavily, and in the centre of the gorge struck "a large fish which immediately took out 50 yards of line. After "several rushes, I got the boat moored in a sandy nook and gradually "drew the fish towards me. General Blake now joined me and stayed "with me till the fish was killed. We could watch its every move-"ment: it did its best to release itself from the hooks, it would be "almost on its side, and rub its mouth into the sand. Presently a fish, "every bit as big as himself, came by to see what the commotion "was about, the hooked fish went at him like a tiger, taking out some "forty yards of line. The sun was well up, the glare very unpleasant, "and the perspiration pouring down my face and almost blinding me; "yet I stuck to my fish, and, after upwards of an hour's struggle, got it "into the shallows, where 'Wind up' cleverly relieved him. It "weighed just 28 lbs., and was, perhaps, the handsomest fish I ever "caught, and gave the most trouble to kill. The next day I went below "the weir, and, amongst other fish, caught one about 35 lbs., but killed it "in about a quarter of an hour. Lightfoot, of the 44th, and Charley "Wilson, of the Artillery, an old school-fellow of mine, joined us, and "we remained fishing in these waters three more days, and then went "partly across country, and partly by water to Jynteeapore, and thence "back *viâ* Jowar to Shillong, putting up some woodcocks *en route*.

"I cannot give full particulars of this trip, because, as I have said "before, my journal is not by me. But in 1870, early in September, "Col. Hicks, Ommanney, Baurne, of the 44th, and I, started for these "diggings *viâ* China Poonghe. I need not enter into details of our "march. At Jerreah there is a river, which used to be, some years "ago, full of Mahseer, but it has been so poisoned of late years by the "Cossyahs, that very few fish are left. The river is full of limestone "rocks, and if you strike a fish, you cannot afford to play it, as it is "more than likely to get into a hollow rock, when you have to cut "him adrift. We commenced to fish on the 14th. O. with a spoon "only caught two fish, 1 = 3 lbs., 1 = 2½ lbs., and 14 small fish with the "fly; I got one 3 lbs. only. On 15th, Baurne caught 1 = 5 lbs., "1 = 3 lbs., and 1 = 2 lbs. Col. Hicks, 1 = 8 lbs. and 1 = 3 lbs. I "had to cut one adrift that got under a rock, but caught three "weighing respectively 20 lbs., 9 lbs., and 2 lbs., all on the same spoon. "Ommanney 1 = 3 lbs., 1 = 2 lbs., and a lot with the fly.

"On Saturday we moved towards the Darrung river, and tried a "cross cut. Owing to the dams constructed by the Cossyahs we had "great difficulty in getting into a branch river, which was connected "with the stream we wished to get to. After an infinity of trouble to "get to Lakat, we sent for boats to take us on, and put up for the "night on a sandbank. During the night we heard fish jumping "about, but never thought for a moment that there were Mahseer so "far down in the plains. Early next morning, on starting, I threw out "my line, without thinking for a moment I should hook anything, but "in a second I had struck a very heavy fish. The others crowded "round my boat, some declaring I held the fish too taut, others that "I gave it too much line; I paid no attention, but worked the fish my "own way. At last it kept turning over, belly uppermost, and a "beauty it looked too, with its large red fins and tail; it was reduced "to the last gasp, and was almost within striking distance of my two-"pronged spear, when it gave a last convulsive struggle, and, in "turning over, got its body across the line, one beastly hook snapped, "and the other two straightened, and off went my monster! Om-"manney and I were together, fishing with exactly the same tackle, "which was in fact mine. We all got our lines out at once, I kept "having all the luck. It began to rain, Baurne had gone on ahead, "with Colonel Hicks. As our boat approached a rapid, we saw "Baurne coming down it, fast to a very big fish, with all his line out. "As he passed us I struck a heavy fish which I bagged in half an hour; "no sooner was my spoon in, than I had another fish, a 22-pounder, which "I also landed. Baurne passed us in a very despondent mood, having "lost his monster. Our hut this time, thanks to Major Stewart, also "a good fisherman, was built on the plains side of the gorge, near the "weir. We arrived here at 10 A.M. with the following bags:—Colonel "Hicks 9 fish weighing 43 lbs., largest 13 lbs.; Baurne 6 fish, 27 lbs., "largest 11 lbs.; Ommanney 1 fish, 6 lbs.; I with 5 fish weighing 66 lbs., "the largest 32 lbs. The size of this fish was 3 feet 9 inches long, "2 feet in girth. In the afternoon Colonel Hicks caught 1 = 16 lbs., "2 = 4 lbs. each. I caught 1 = 9, 1 = 2, 1 = 7, 1 = 5, 1 = 1½ lbs. "B 1 = 4, 1 = 10 lbs. Ommanney 7 fish = 47 lbs., the largest 26 lbs.

"Monday morning Col. H. 1 = 4, 1 = ½ lb. I, 1 = 12, 1 = 9½, "2 = 4 each, 1 = 3 lbs. Baurne 1 = 8 lbs. O. 1 = 8 lbs. In the "evening I caught 1 = 41 (4 feet 3 inches long, 2 feet 3 inches girth), "1 = 4 lbs. Col. H. 1 = 7 lbs. Tuesday morning, O., 1 = 30, "1 = 20 lbs. Col. H., 1 = 1½, 1 = ½. I. 1 = 7, 1 = 5 lbs. We "then moved back to the sandbank near Lakat, fishing our way back. "It was almost dark, that is night, when we got there. There was a "bright moon, if I remember aright. Opposite to the sandbank, "another river joined the Lakat stream. Always remember when "fishing to fish a little below the junction of two rivers; if one comes "out of the hills close by, and the other through a stretch of plains, so "much the better, the fish will assemble at the mouth of the warmer "stream in search of food. As fast as we could throw in our lines, "though dark, we had a fish on; for a while my spoon was jammed "without my knowing it, and as it did not spin I caught nothing, but "as the others were catching them as fast as possible, I carefully "examined my bait, put it to rights, and at once hooked a whopper. "We caught altogether off this bank as follows:—

"Om., 2 = 17 each, 1 = 6, 1 = 8, 1 = 10½, 1 = 11.
"I. 1 = 25, 1 = 3½, 1 = 14, 1 = 6, 1 = 3, 1 = 31.
"B., 1 = 14, 1 = 4, 1 = 2, 1 = 11, 1 = 3½, 1 = 2¼, 1 = 10.
"Col. H., 1 = 10, 1 = 3½, 1 = 11, 1 = 4½, 1 = 7.

"Could any one wish for better sport, and the greater part after the "sun set, and in a place where it was thought no Mahseer existed? "I won't weary your readers with further details of sport. Baurne "and the Colonel left that night, and Ommanney and I followed early "next morning. My tackle, for a time, was again jammed. Om- "manney killed in a couple of hours, 1 = 26, 1 = 22, 1 = 20, 1 = 14, "1 = 4, whilst I got 1 = 14, 1 = 6, 1 = 4. So much for sport "within a day and a half's journey of Cachar, a few hours from Silchar, "two days from Shillong. May this be of use to your readers, and to "Mr. Thomas in particular, whose acquaintance I have not had the "pleasure of making, except through his excellent little treatise.

"PHOONGHEE."

AFGHANISTAN.

Kurrum.—There is Mahseer fishing in the Kurrum Valley. W. T. F. ("Asian," 25th Nov., 1879), took them up to 5 lbs., knew others who had killed them up to 10 lbs. and 12 lbs., and does not think they run over 15 lbs. there. He considers the river to be full of fish. It is easily commanded by an 18-ft. rod. He killed with gilt spoon and black fly, and had other flies carried away. The fishing stops as soon as the snow begins to melt on Safaid Koh, about March.

D., in the "Field" of 26th June, 1880, gives a long description of fishing in this valley.

The following from a friendly fisherman, the killer of the huge freshwater shark, has reached me too late to be compared with the manuscript and put in its proper place. I can only throw it in at the end of this chapter in the hope that it may prove useful to some.

Localities in the Punjab.

DELHI DISTRICT. *Okla Weir* 7 miles from Delhi. *Jumma Bridge. Head of Canal escape*, 3 miles from Delhi.

AMBALA DISTRICT. *Dadopur* (head of West Jumma canal) there is a dàk bungalow at Jagadri on S. P. & D. Railway, 5 miles distant.

Ropar (head of Sirhind canal) canal and dàk bungalows.

SIMLA DISTRICT. Various places on the *Giri, Sirsā, and Gambar* Rivers. It will be necessary to take a tent.

JULLUNDER DISTRICT. *Eastern Beyn*, 4 miles from cantonments.

HOSHIARPUR DISTRICT. *Mokerian*, on the Beas, police bungalow.

GURDASPUR DISTRICT. *Batāla* tanks (private). Various places on Beas. Tent required.

LAHORE DISTRICT. River *Ravi and old bed* of the same near the town.

GUJRANWALA DISTRICT. The Chenab near *Wazirābad* where there is a dāk bungalow. It is a Station on the P. N. I. Railway.

JHELAM DISTRICT. Several places in the Jhelam River. The junction of the Poonch and Jhelam Rivers where K. fished is best known. Near the fishing ground is *Tangrot* bungalow, 8 miles from Ratyal Station, P. N. I. Railway.

RAWAL PINDI DISTRICT. The hill streams at *Chirā*, *Kirpa*, *Kahūta* (police bungalow), and many other places. Also the River *Sohān*.

KASHMERE. *Hatti*, on the Murre Route, bungalow.

Sopur, exit of Wulār Lake, bungalow.

Banair, Marshy ground where the Jhelam falls into the Wulār Lake, 3 miles from Hajan, where a tent may be pitched.

Pandritan. 2 miles above the visitors' bungalows at Srinagar.

Korwinee. 4 miles from Islamabad, where there is a bungalow.

Pawzgam. 3 miles north of Aishmakām encamping ground. River Liddar.

C. S. KIRKPATRICK.

CHAPTER XXV.

A PLEA FOR RIVER FISHERIES.

Seth Green, the noted pisciculturist, says: "Expend one thousandth part of the sum spent in tilling the land in tilling the water, and fish may be sold in our markets at two cents a pound.—Report of the Commissioners of Agriculture.—WASHINGTON, 1870.

I HAD intended in the foregoing pages to embody, in a more popular form, all the piscicultural information contained in my Official Report of 1870; but finding that I have failed in some respects, I subjoin extracts from that Report. As the Report dealt primarily with my own then District, South Canara, its name comes frequently in; but the reader will recognize that the remarks on the peculiar formation of the rivers have equal applicability to other rivers of the West Coast of India; and that almost all the other observations have a general, quite as much as a local, pertinence in India:—

Rivers.

6. It will be convenient to treat first of the rivers and then of the sea, and in elucidation of remarks that will follow, it may be well to seek attention to the general features of the rivers of South Canara. The district lies between the sea and the high plateau of Mysore and Coorg; most of its rivers consequently take their rise in those provinces, and, as long as their course lies therein, they are beyond the jurisdiction of the Collector of South Canara. Though rapid and rocky at their sources they are tortuous at their mouths, and subject to much tidal influence. They would seem to be the natural result of the marginally noted formation of the district. Furthermore, Canara and its boundary hills are the first land that meets and receives the full force of the south-west monsoon, and the annual rainfall on the coast is 130 inches. On the hill sides of the interior it is probable that

Hindu mythology says that the whole of South Canara was formerly under the ocean, the boundary of which was the edge of the Mysore plateau; and that the sea was dried up by a flaming arrow of the god Parasurâma. Modern science robs the fable of its poetry, but leaves it its groundwork of truth, by ascribing the existence of Canara to volcanic action. There are also extensive littoral upheavings of evidently recent date.

it is considerably heavier. Almost the whole of this rain falls within a period of four months, consequently the rivers are subject to very marked fluctuations, mighty and lasting swellings to which the freshes on English streams bear no comparison. An approximate idea of the size of these rivers may perhaps be best conveyed to the English mind, by stating that of the two rivers which debouch at Mangalore, the Netràvaty alone owns several tributaries, each of which is as large as the Thames above tidal influence, and many of the salmon rivers of England are puny indeed in comparison with those treated of in this report.

Poisoning of Rivers.

7. It may be interesting to commence this subject with a notice of the substances used for poisoning the rivers. They are:—

Croton tiglium,
Anamirta cocculus,
Capsicum frutescens,
and *Kàre Kài* (Tulu), a *Posoqueria*, probably *nutans* or *longispina*.

8. Though very considerable progress has been made within the last two years in stopping the annual wholesale poisoning of the rivers, much still remains to be done. As long as fish can be easily captured in large quantities by this means, so long will this species of poaching be popular. In the wilder forest-locked parts of the interior it is not easy to observe and check it, and when the sympathies of the village authorities and police are with the people, it is doubly difficult.*

Pro. Govt., dated 27th Nov., 1868, No. 2 982, para. 3.

11. The destructiveness of poisoning is more extensive than at first sight appears. Though there may be many pools in a river, there are a few, at intervals of four or five miles, which are specially affected by the larger sorts of fish. These are generally the deepest

* In districts in which it is not discountenanced by the authorities, it is openly done in inhabited parts.

and longest; they are sometimes as much as twenty feet deep and a quarter of a mile long. They are generally cooler from being overshadowed with trees and more or less overhung with rocks. Their very depth also would keep them cooler than the wide shallows, extending for miles together, and in the height of the hot season, of a few inches only in depth, under a tropical sun. Their depths afford also concealment, and probably greater facilities for escape from otters. To bottom feeders, which the large fish mainly are, they must also yield more food than the shallows. They are natural resting places for the spawners, as shown below.

Paras. 51, 52.

12. These pools are well known to the villagers, are all distinguished by local names, and are selected as the ones for poisoning; consequently the poisoning of one of these pools is pretty nearly equivalent, as far as the bigger sorts of fish are concerned, to the poisoning of four or five miles of river.

13. Thus, whatever may be the cause of larger sorts of fish congregating in the deepest pools, the fact remains that they do so, and that it is taken advantage of for their poisoning. It may also be taken advantage of for their protection.

Para. 53.

14. But the chief sources of most of the Canara rivers are on the western ghâts of Mysore and Coorg, and to these it is that the best fish migrate for spawning purposes. Efforts to stop poisoning, and to protect the fry, must therefore be incomplete, till the same measures are adopted in Mysore and Coorg. It is obvious that, to be treated successfully, the rivers must be treated as a whole, no matter what territory they run through. It may seem unreasonable to object to the Coorgs and Mysoreans destroying the fish within their own countries; but it should be borne in mind that they cannot stop the effects of their poison abruptly at their boundaries: the tainted river will roll on. They also will benefit, as well as Canara; for if they spare the fry which are to descend and stock its rivers, those same fry, when grown, will not fail to revisit them annually, crowding up in increased numbers to spawn. In short, Mysore, Coorg, and Canara possess, more or less in common, one water farm, which, to be cultivated to advantage, must be worked in unison. At present, however, these people poison the fish and way-lay the descending fry in innumerable cruives.

Fry in Rivers.

20. But whether the poisoning of the waters, or the capture of the fry, be the more fertile source of ruin to the rivers it is hard to decide. Dr. Day and I have already urged that too much importance can scarcely be attached to the suppression of the practice of destroying fry wholesale. It has not been possible to obtain an exactly accurate account of the number of small-meshed cruives used in the district of South Canara, but there are sufficient data for concluding that there were at least 1,050 on the one river, the Netrávaty, with its affluents. If it be calculated that every one of these cruives captures on an average 3,000 fish in a day then there are as many as 94,500,000 tiny fry destroyed for no adequate purpose in a single month in one river alone. To say what may be the total number thus destroyed in the course of a year in all the rivers of Canara would be beyond my arithmetic. These closely-woven bamboo cruives then have been forbidden and vigorously hunted out of the rivers. It is not to be concluded that they have been entirely got rid of, far from it; there are clearly many remote places where they are freely used, and the water bailiffs sought are wanted as much for this purpose as for stopping poisoning. Still a considerable impression has already been made.

21. The consequence has been that the most ignorant, and therefore the most obstinate, opponents have been convinced by the testimony of their own senses, and have exclaimed, to use their own words, "truly, the river is everywhere *bubbling* with fry;" and, what is still more to the point, their practice has not belied their words, for they have taken to fishing on grounds that were before considered profitless.

22. Though this is nothing more than in my former paper I anticipated would be the natural result of the simultaneous stopping of poisoning and prohibition of the use of closely-woven cruives, still the actual sight of the result has surprised even my sanguinely expectant self. Two years' discouragement of poisoning, and one years' discouragement of fine cruives, have worked such a change that it has been demonstrated, beyond the cavil even of the ignorant and of the interestedly opposing, that marked advan-

tages can be reaped from the adoption of these two simple measures alone.

27. An outspoken critic gave it as his very decided opinion that pisciculture in west coast rivers, that are at one time in high flood, and at another a mere driblet, was "all gammon." He is probably not singular in his opinion. His objection, therefore, ought to be answered. This very variableness in the rivers, instead of being an insurmountable difficulty, would seem to be the most convenient arrangement that could possibly be desired. When the south-west monsoon commences, the rivers are at once in flood and continue so for four months, subsequently diminishing by slow degrees. This enables the grown fish, Mahseer, to ascend to new feeding grounds in the forests, which are quite inaccessible to them at other times, and ten-pound fish are to be found half way up the Mercara Ghât. In the high waters the big fish linger till the gradually subsiding streams warn them to drop gently downwards. The early spawners linger the longest to secure shallow waters for spawning; this done, they keep dropping gently downwards with the continually decreasing waters, and before the spawn they have deposited is hatched, they are probably completely cut off from their fry; so that till the commencement of the same monsoon in the following year, they cannot return to devour them. The fry thus not only have the heads of the rivers securely to themselves, but they have them also beautifully accommodated to their puny strength, the impassable torrent having become a mere driblet of an inch or so in depth.

Say 2,500 feet high.

28. Though the variation in the size of the Canara rivers is much greater than the changes in English rivers, it is at the same time much more regular. Though Canara has in a year 130 inches of rainfall to swell its rivers, and a tropical land and irrigation to waste them, yet they each come in their regular season. Almost the whole of the 130 inches falls during the prevalence of the south-west monsoon, which commences with June, and lasts about four months. This monsoon ended, there are only such moderate rains as cannot affect the rivers. This monsoon ends, then, with September, and from that time the rivers continue to subside steadily till the following June. The fish, Mahseer, spawn in the interim, and the spawn is safely hatched, and the fry are somewhat

grown, before the recurrence of the annual floods in June. There are thus no unseasonable floods coming down as in England, after the spawning time, and carrying away the spawn; and when they do come in June, they seasonably sweep away the obstacles, in the shape of temporary irrigation dams, which would otherwise prevent the spawning fish from ascending.

Para. 33.

29. In respect, therefore, both of the extremes of change, and the regularity of the change, the Canara rivers have an advantage over the rivers of England.

30. But while Providence has thus beautifully arranged to shield the fry from their voracious parents, they are by that very arrangement placed entirely at the mercy of short-sighted man, and the necessity for prohibiting all closely-woven cruives can scarcely be too strongly insisted on.

Fry in Rice Fields.

33. But the beautiful arrangement spoken of in paragraphs 27, 28, and 29 lays the tiny fry at the mercy of improvident men in yet another way. While the south-west monsoon prevails the ample rainfall on this coast supplies abundant water for irrigational purposes, and the rivers are the while too turbulent to be diverted. But as the dry season commences, and water is wanted for the irrigation of the second crop of rice, the rivers have settled down to more manageable proportions, and near their sources it becomes an easy matter for the farmer to collect the boulders in the stream, lay them in a line across it, and after filling in the interstices with shingle from the bed, to stop the whole with clay and bushes from the banks. A temporary and inexpensive, yet effective, dam is thus run up annually by every farmer who has ground conveniently situated for irrigation. Though it is completely swept away by the first flood in the next south-west monsoon, it lasts throughout the hot weather, throughout the lifetime of the fry, and the river or rivulet being thus completely cut off, is diverted entirely into an irrigation channel. As it is the instinct of the grown fish to ascend the rivers to spawn, so is it the instinct of the fry, as they grow, to allow themselves to drop downwards with the stream to

The fry of fourteen sorts have been

identified. How many more there may be that enter the rice-fields cannot be as yet said.

deeper wider waters. Down they glide therefore, day by day a little way, feeding as they go, and unconscious that they are already in an irrigation channel which can end only in a rice-field; and thus it is that the channel-fed rice fields swarm with fry of apparently all descriptions.

34. This would be no misfortune if even here the fry were left to themselves. The rice grows in fields which have been carefully levelled by man, and partitioned with narrow and shallow embankments, so as to economise the water, and spread it over the largest possible area. From a piscicultural point of view the whole stretch of rice-fields has the appearance of a vast and admirably constructed nursery. A whole river or rivulet has been turned on, a river too which has been stocked with ova, the water has been economised to the utmost, the depth regulated exactly to suit the fry, large predatory fish thoroughly excluded, the whole manured, ploughed, and planted, so as to provide the maximum of insect life, with the desired medicum of varying shade under the growing rice; and the area of the nursery is measured, not by the inch or foot, but by the acre or square mile. In this extensive nursery, therefore, which costs the pisciculturist nothing, the fry thrive admirably, and still following their instinct go feeding dawdling downwards with the stream. This takes them leisurely from rice-field to rice-field, and in the direction of the waste water; which of itself not unfrequently runs into the river again, or might almost always be contrived so to run. But at each drop from rice-field to rice-field, the cultivator places a basket made of finely split bamboos, having a wide mouth, a narrow neck, and a wide bottom. It lets the water pass but stops every single fry; and what was an admirable nursery, becomes one vast trap for destroying the majority of the fry in the river. So highly are these juicy morsels appreciated that no peasant fails to place a basket at every outlet.*

Frogs, however, find their way in in great numbers, and are destructive. See Para. 81.

The area irrigated under all the river dams in the district is

* The fry of that valuable sea fish, the Hilsa (*Clupea Ilisha*), which, after the manner of the Salmon, ascends Indian rivers to spawn, shares the same fate when seeking in Tanjore to gain the sea by descending the Cávèry.

estimated at 39,962, or, in round numbers, 40,000 acres, or more than 60 square miles of nursery. Calculating from a very low average of the number of fry contained in 50 acres, this area must contain in all probability considerably more, and certainly not less, than 283,500,000 of diminutive fry, which are annually destroyed for a comparatively insignificant number of juicy curries.

36. This is the destruction of fry under the river dams alone, without taking any account of the numbers which enter the rice-fields from hill streams, from the annual overflowings of the river in certain localities, and which enter marshes from the rise of the tide in the estuaries. The numbers of these two latter there are no means of computing, but they may safely be put down at about the same as in the dam-fed rice-fields. These also are destroyed, most of them, in the same way as the fry of the rivers, and some in other ways to be described in connection with sea-fish.

Para. 122.

37. The almost innumerable hosts of fry which enter the rice-fields from the hill streams have been excluded from the above calculations, because they are the fry of small fish, for though every rill of a foot in breadth teems in the season with minute fishes they are apparently only the fry of minnow, loach, and such like small fish, the destruction of which is, perhaps, not of much consequence, as there are probably enough of them intermixed with the larger sorts of fry from the rivers. Still it is worthy of note that the smallest sorts of fish seek the smallest rills to spawn in, and struggle up them to astonishing heights at the commencement of the monsoon; and it may remain a question whether the larger predatory fish would not be benefited by any protection extended to their natural food.

38. Omitting these, however, the annual destruction of fry in the rice-fields and marshes may be fairly put down at not less than 567,000,000. This is not unavoidable or accidental destruction, but it is wilful, reckless, and preventable. Some of these fry, it will be remembered, are capable of becoming fish of 10 and 20 pounds in weight.* Many more will run to two and three pounds,

* This is in Canara rivers. In larger rivers like the Càvèry, the Toonga-budra, and the affluents of the Ganges, we might safely say that many grow to 50 lbs., 100 lbs., 150 lbs., and 200 lbs. in weight, though there is no difference in their size when fry.

and very few comparatively to less than two or four ounces. It seems fair to assume for the purpose of calculation, that on an average the fry weigh at an early age not less than a grain each, and are calculated to grow to one pound weight. Is it worth while to turn these grains of meat into pounds, or, in other words, to allow them to multiply themselves by 7,000, for that is the number of grains in a pound. Is it worth while to turn 567,000,000 grains, or 81,000 pounds, of meat into 567,000,000 pounds, or 253,125 tons, of good food? Though the average weight attained, and consequently the multiple employed in this calculation, be reduced by a half or three-fourths, to meet the destruction by fish preying on each other, the figures which will remain will still be sufficiently indicative of the largeness of the results obtainable from the protection of fry. And against this reduction may be advanced the argument that, by maturing so many more fish, the number, which are to produce ova in succeeding years, will also be greatly increased.

Though every care has been taken to make the numerals in this paragraph, and in paragraphs 20 and 35, as correct as possible under the circumstances, and to err on the side of moderation, rather than of possible exaggeration, still large multiples of comparatively small multiplicands are generally more or less fruitful of error, and these figures should consequently be relied on only for the purpose for which they have been introduced, that of presenting an approximate idea of the amount of food destroyed.

39. This, be it remembered, is the destruction of fry computed to be still continuing. It was much greater before the discouragement of the finely-twined cruives in the rivers, which alone must have destroyed vast numbers. If the calculation made in the preceding paragraph were applied also to the fry spoken of in paragraph 20, there might be conveyed a more adequate idea of the extent of the destruction foolishly wrought.

Para. 20.

40. If, then, the machinery for destruction is so great, and it is possible not only to stay its destructiveness, but even to use it as a machinery for propagation, should not the opportunity be availed of?

41. In the matter of pisciculture something has already been gathered from the Chinese. This intelligent, though uncommunicative, people have long practised it, and as they also have rice-fields, it is probable that they have thoroughly studied how to overcome irrigational obstructions. On this, the main Indian

difficulty, much valuable information might probably be obtained from them. It is not likely to be found in books, for they are not the class of difficulties to attract the attention of a European or American. Personal enquiry on the spot, by one interested in the subject, is what would seem to be required. Such an one can probably be found among the regiments or residents there stationed.

Legislation for Fry.

42. But private interests are concerned in the rice-fields, and the question arises, how they will be affected? The agriculturists will doubtless be much discontented if they are prevented from enjoying the juicy morsels which they have been accustomed to obtain with such ease, and they will certainly think it very hard that they should not be allowed to eat even the little bits of fish in their own fields. But will they be right in thinking themselves aggrieved? It would seem that they will have very little, if any, more right to complain than has the English miller. They are like each other in diverting the rivers for their own benefit, and of each of them the request made would be the same, namely, that they should do it without injury to the fisheries. The Indian farmer may, like the English miller, claim that he has a prescriptive right to the water, and that it is no part of his business to protect the fry. It has, nevertheless, been decided against the English millers, equally with the companies or persons in charge of artificial channels for navigation, or for supplying towns with water, that they shall put gratings so as to prevent the passage of salmon fry to their destruction, and that, failing to do so, "they "shall incur a penalty not exceeding 5*l.* for every day" of delay and "a penalty not exceeding 1*l.* for every day" during which they may fail to maintain them when erected. Would it be unjust in the public interests to make the same demand of the Indian agriculturist?

43. But the Indian farmer cuts off the whole stream, and leaves no downward passage at all, except through his own fields. The option, therefore might be given him, "either "you must leave a fair passage in the river for "the fry and put a grating before your own artificial channel, or if

Para. 33.

"you *must* have every drop of water in the river and make "the only passage run through your own fields, then you must "leave that passage unobstructed to the fry." Whichever alternative is accepted the result is the same, fry are not to be entrapped in the rice-fields. As with salmon in England, therefore, it should be made illegal to "place any device for obstructing their passage."

44. It may be argued that the analogy of the Indian farmer and the English miller is faulty in one respect, the former having the use of the water itself, while the latter has a right only to its passing power. But the principle at the root of both cases is the same. The real question is whether or not private interests are to yield to public advantages; whether it is necessary that they should yield, and what amount of hardship the yielding will entail. As regards the hardship involved, the expense to which the Indian agriculturist will be put will be as nothing to that of the English miller; the loss of much appreciated morsels will be a vexation, and the fact of their being replaced by fish becoming more plentiful is not likely to be taken into account. On the other hand, the necessity for the measure may be judged of by the destruction now carried on in the rice-fields. Though in the case of freshwater fish it might be possible to arrange, by gratings at the commencement of the channels, to keep them in the river till the monsoon came and carried away the temporary dams, still they would be in many respects very unfavourably placed; and in the case of sea-going fish, like the *Clupea ilisha*, there seems no other way of protecting their fry from total extermination, for reach the sea they must, and they have no other way but through the rice-fields. Therefore it would seem unavoidable to prohibit the entrapping of fry in the rice-fields.

Para. 35 to 40.

45. It will further be desirable to make provision for a way being kept open for the fry eventually to rejoin the river by means of the waste water. This will frequently be found to have arranged itself, though in some places it will be susceptible of improvement by a very little labour, while in others it may be a little expensive to open a satisfactory communication. Most of these places again are liable to get a little out of order from being trodden by cattle, and from other causes, and may at the commencement of the monsoon require the most trivial repair to keep them in order. In those cases in which the labour entailed is

really nil, or next to nil, the responsibility of maintaining them in order might be thrown on the cultivator. In other cases a contract could be made with the cultivator to make and maintain any desired communication. Which cases should be thrown on the cultivator, and which should not, might be decided under the orders of the Collector of the district, as such subordinate matters are by conservators and commissioners in England. The Collector's decision might also be subject to appeal to the Board of Revenue, as are the decisions of commissioners to the Home Office, or in their place to an Inspector General of Pisciculture for the Presidency.

46. It may at first sight seem arbitrary to cast this labour on the farmer, but it is not requiring more of him than is exacted of the mill-owner in England. The latter is called on to make repairs to prevent leakage, when such wastage of water from the main stream is considered to interfere with the safe passage of the salmon. The chief ground of the demand would seem to be that the necessity for it arose out of the action of the person on whom the call is made. In the case under consideration it is the diversion of the water by the farmer that has caused the necessity for providing other passage for the fry.

47. In maintaining the channel, practically no one can have less difficulty than the person always on the spot, to whom also there will not be wanting enough of opportunities for throwing seemingly accidental obstacles in the way. For instance, what is easier than to remove a plank and lay the blame on the force of the stream; what is easier than to scrape the shingle together in a mound across the waste water so that the little stream shall percolate through it, and none of it be able to run over. By this means the fry would be effectually prevented from getting down to the river. The farmer deprived of the fry to which he had been accustomed would be not at all unlikely to retaliate in some such manner. And who is to fix it upon him? It would be generally impossible. It is therefore necessary to make him responsible for the maintenance of the passage for the fry.

48. It will be similarly desirable to fix the same responsibility on the man who contracts to do the same for a consideration, for if a suit is to be filed in the civil courts for every breach of such contract, the fry will not survive "the law's delay."

49. These, and other things necessary for the protection and improvement of the fisheries, cannot be done without law; a rough sketch of a draft* Act is therefore enclosed in Appendix F. It need hardly be mentioned that it would be impossible for such a draft to be made complete and legally accurate by one who has not at command for reference the already existing Indian enactments on matters which must be provided for, matters such as jurisdiction, commutation of fines, collection of taxes and rents, together with provision against abuses therein. All that has been aimed at, therefore, has been to aid those whose proper duty it may become to draw up a law on the subject by a sketch indicative of such requirements as strike the writer and might not strike the reader. The little work, marginally noted, may also be found useful as showing what has been done in the matter in England, Scotland, and Ireland.

The Laws relating to Salmon Fisheries in Great Britain, &c., by Thomas Baker, Esq., B.L., &c. London: Horace Cox, "Law Times" Office, 10, Wellington Street, Strand.

50. Apart from the question of legal accuracy and completeness, it will be remembered that the subject of this report is the fisheries of the South Canara district alone, and that consequently it is beyond my province as well as my opportunities to make proposals about any other; though the proposals contained in this report will probably be found to have applicability to other west coast rivers also, and other seas and estuaries. It is obvious that in the Madras Presidency alone, further provision will be required for differing circumstances on the east coast and in the interior. In reference to these, the opinions of the several Collectors, and of Dr. Day, who has visited their fisheries, are doubtless before the Board. In connection with the innumerable reservoirs therein, it may be allowable, however, to throw out, in passing, the suggestion, that instead of constructing them as our engineers do with the sluice so placed as annually to drain out the very last drop of water, it might be wiser in all fresh constructions, and when possible in repairs, to follow the example of Hyder, who so placed the sluice that after all the water available for irrigational purposes had been drawn off, there was still left in the reservoir some

* Some of these proposals have been slightly modified in a letter submitted to the Madras Government in November, 1879, which is not public property, so I am not at liberty to quote it

six or ten feet of water at the embankment, and this water served in the dry season, and more especially in times of drought, the treble purpose of feeding wells and thus supplying drinking water to the inhabitants, of watering the cattle of the agriculturists, and of keeping alive a nucleus of fish wherewith to re-stock the reservoir by natural breeding on its refilling at the commencement of the rains. The manner of constructing and repairing reservoirs, and the restrictions necessary to prevent netting when they are so low that it is next to impossible for the fish to escape extermination, are among the matters to be considered in any legislation calculated to meet the requirements of the east coast and interior, equally with those of the west coast.

Fry in Pools.

51. Before quitting the subject of fry, it will be well to guard against misconception on one point. It has been said that the whole Para. 33. river is frequently diverted into the rice-fields, and that none of the fry in the rice-fields escape destruction. Para. 34. It would be a not unnatural conclusion that it is meant to be conveyed that all the fry in the river are thus destroyed; and so it would be if the spawning Paras. 27, 28, 29. places alluded to were the only ones, and if the fry had not sometimes intermediate water deep enough to satisfy their descending instinct. But fortunately the fish do not all spawn by one rule, so as to make their fry all dependent on the accident of the successful or disastrous issue of a single arrangement. The Mahseer apparently go on spawning at different localities for three months. Many will thus be below the dams when spawning, and many again will be below the upper dams, and have miles of deep water in which to live between them and the lower dams. This is the case at *Sirùli.* There are four miles above and 12 miles below it, altogether 16 miles, without a dam across the river. Within this space there are many deep pools, which tempt the big fish to stay, and which shelve gradually up to very shallow water running over sand, gravel, or shingle. The shallow water at the tail of these pools is not, after the spawning time, liable to any great fluctuation in depth; for, however low the water in the river, the water in the pool must necessarily rise to the same level

before it can flow over at all. Consequently the tails of pools form favourable spawning beds, and being not unfrequently followed by a long scour, the fry have a very fair chance of escaping their devouring parents, who, after spawning, have returned to deep water nearer the head of the pool, a furlong or a quarter of a mile, more or less, away from their fry. These are the fry that, having kept out of the rice-fields, used to be caught in the numerous basket-work cruives set in the river. These are the fry which have peopled the river since those cruives have been removed, and since the poisoning of these pools has been checked.

Para. 20, *supra*. Also para. 11 of my former Report in Pro. Madras Government, Revenue Dept., 27th Nov. 1868. Nos. 501–506.

Paras. 21, 22.

52. Seeing, then, that the larger pools are not only the hot-weather resorts of the larger fish, but frequently the birth-place of the fry also, the mischief done by poisoning them and tainting the scours below, is greater than at first sight appears; for fry as well as big fish are poisoned.

Para. 11.

Stock Pools.

53. But though poisoning be reduced to a minimum, the fact of the larger fish being driven out of the rest of the river by the lowness of the water in the dry season, and compelled to mass themselves in the pools, will still be taken advantage of for netting them. At that time parties of Moplahs make expeditions as far as Sirady, 50 odd miles from Mangalore, prepared with boats and sets of large nets to fish all the pools; and so great are their takes that traders come down from Manzerabad and the neighbourhood to purchase, slightly salt, and carry into the interior, the fish that are in excess of the local demand. Weavers, and others who are not fishermen by trade, turn out in force, unite all their nets in one, and sweep these pools. There is the danger, therefore, of the river being over-netted, and an insufficient stock left to supply spawn the next year. It would be well, therefore, to select a few of these pools, and in them to prohibit netting altogether.

54. That there might be no needless anxiety as to which were prohibited pools, and no idle excuses of having netted them by mistake, they might be distinctly marked, at a trifling cost, with the Queen's broad arrow, cut on the rock. An

The cost of this precaution is estimated at 100 rupees, and entered in Appendix C.

arrow on each side pointing up stream from the tail of a pool, and an arrow on each side pointing down stream from the head of the pool, would indicate that all between them was reserved from nets.

55. The pools would have to be selected not only with a view to their being convenient to the fish and fry, but also with some reference to their being convenient to protect. Pools in the neighbourhood of the land or house of the head of the village would be preferred; and for the extra duty of throwing his ægis over them a trifle might be added to his very meagre pay. Six rupees a year for each head of a village thus employed would probably come to somewhere about 300 rupees a year out of the fishery rents. Without some payment it cannot be expected that the duty will be well done for a continuance.

56. Fortunately there are already two places on tributaries of the Puiswany and Netràvatty where the fish have, in the priests of the temples at Thodikàn and Cicilly, friends as stout as were the monks of old. They have a legend that their god Ishwara performed a journey from Kailàsa to Thodikàn on the back of a Mahseer. These fish, therefore, which are fortunately the best fish in the river, are considered sacred, and no man is allowed to harm them in any way, and the priests and pilgrims feed them. The consequence is that they are exceedingly tame and numerous. They crowd together till, for 20 yards round the temple steps, fish of all sizes, from eight pounds downwards, are packed as thickly

NOTE.—This feeding and protecting of Mahseer at Hindu temples is, I find, a common practice. I have observed it in other places in the Madras Presidency, and in the Mysore Territory, and have heard of it in more places again, and also in Northern India, notably at Jubbulpore. The fish are always Mahseer, for, the simple reason that the food given by Hindus is always grain, and the Mahseer being the largest fish that feed on vegetable matter, soon assert their strength over the smaller fish, which you may see giving place to them.

It may be interestingly noted here that, as a friend points out, Martial had observed similarly fed fish,

"Piscator fuge, ne nocens recedas,
Sacris piscibus hæ natantur undæ," &c.

and that Xenophon mentions the sacred fishes of the river Chalus, a tributary of the Euphrates—

"*χάλον ποταμὸν πληρῆ ἰχθύων
μεγάλων καὶ πραέων, ὃυς ὁι Σύροι
θεὸυς ἐνόμιζαν καὶ ἀδικεῖν ὀυκ ἔιων.*"

The river Chalus full of big tame fish, which the Syrians held as Gods, and would not allow to be ill-used.

in the river as sardines in a tin, scrambling over each other's backs into the air, and up the stone steps, and taking food out of the very hand. One was caught for identification in a saucepan, and immediately released again.

Close Season.

73. The Board has desired to know whether a close time should be enforced. The circumstances of the South Canara rivers differ so widely from those of English streams that it does not seem necessary to follow the home example in this respect. The monsoon floods render it practically impossible to net for four months in the twelve, and the body of water still in the river makes it scarcely worth while to net for three months more. Netting is generally delayed till the large fish are driven by the general lowness of the rivers to congregate in the pools. If a few stock pools are reserved, and fixed engines prohibited, a close time may, as far as the fisheries are concerned, be safely dispensed with.

Para. 53.

Para. 72.

Size of Meshes.

75. The meshes of the nets now used in the rivers and in the sea are of all sizes, from three-quarters of an inch to twenty-four inches in circumference; the Government has ordered the prohibition of nets with meshes of less than four inches in circumference; but very many sorts of fish, both in the rivers and in the sea, never grow to a size to be entangled in such nets. To prohibit smaller meshes, therefore, is to prohibit netting for these fishes, and to cut off from the people a large percentage of the food in the waters. Properly to appreciate the effect of this order, it is only necessary to observe how large a fish can escape through a mesh 4 inches in circumference, and how many sorts of fish there are that are seldom or never large enough to be caught in such meshes, and how numerous those sorts of fish are.

Pro. Bd. Rev. No. 3,823 dated 28th May, 1869, Govt. Order thereon, 25th June, 1869, No. 1,812.

76. The ultimate effect on the fisheries would probably be still more unfortunate. The smaller sorts of fish having immunity from netting must disproportionately increase on the larger netted sorts. Nature has arranged that the larger predatory fish shall

balance the smaller, and thus maintain due proportions; but if one sort is netted by man, and the other sort has immunity, the balance is disturbed, and the larger fish are no longer able to maintain their position. It is true that the predatory sorts of fish are not few in number; but their numbers must none the less have been calculated by nature with reference to the number and prolificacy of the smaller sorts of fish. But, however well calculated they may be to keep the latter within due bounds, they must cease to be able to do so when their relative position is as altered as it must be, by netting the larger fish and not netting the smaller. The balance is disturbed by the netting being thrown into one scale only. The mischief of the balance being disturbed lies in the fact of much of the insect life in the waters being the common sustenance of both large and small sorts of fish. If the latter disproportionately increase on the former they monopolize this food; and the larger fish, and especially their young, are starved. Minnows have starved out trout. It has been a question whether it would not improve the Thames fisheries to allow again a certain amount of netting of the smaller fishes. If this can be a question on a river which is crowded every day with hundreds, and perhaps thousands, of professional and amateur anglers, armed with the best of tackle, it must surely be beyond a doubt in a country where there are no amateur anglers, and the professionals are few indeed, and very rudely equipped.

Para. 25.

77. On both these grounds, therefore, it would seem that the size of the meshes to be prohibited should be reconsidered. The object should be not to interfere with the netting of fishes which are always small, and only to protect from premature capture the young of such as are calculated to grow to a large size. Two inches in circumference is found to be the size of mesh most convenient for the capture of several sorts of small fish which are the most abundant in the Canara rivers. These are fishes, that when at the size to which they ordinarily attain, would escape through a mesh 4 inches in circumference Their ordinary size is, nevertheless, such that but few fish are able to prey on them There are no sorts, it would seem, but those given in the margin, that would be large enough to prey on

These are of the sorts numbered 3, 8, 9, 12, 19, 21, 22, 23, 27, 30, 31, 36 in the list given in Appendix G.

Nos. 17, 18, 24, 25, 26 in the same list.

them when mature; and of these sorts even only one individual in a thousand would be grown enough to make of them a comfortable mouthful. Furthermore, even those fish which can eat a larger fish than their neighbours can, not unfrequently take smaller ones by preference. There would be few indeed, then, of the predatory fish that would habitually prey upon the fish which can be taken by the 2-inch mesh and escape the 4-inch mesh. As they are not only not required, then, by the larger fish, but would also be likely to injure them by out-numbering and starving them, and especially their young, if given immunity from the netting to which the larger sorts are subject, would it not be advisable to add them to the food of the people, and to that end to permit a mesh calculated to catch them? Such a mesh, it is repeated, is one 2 inches in circumference.*

78. While advocating the allowance of a mesh of this size in rivers, it would seem undesirable to allow any smaller ones; for if there be no restriction placed on the size of meshes, it is probable that the fry of large fish will be captured along with the smaller kinds of fish; for below a certain size it is not always so easy to recognise the young of large fish, at least not so easy as to be able at once to pick them out and return them to the water alive, not easy enough to be able to detect them at a glance in the fisherman's or salesman's basket, not sufficiently easy to justify the magistrate in presuming *mala fides* against the destroyer thereof. If no meshes less than 2 inches in circumference be allowed, there will be no difficulty about recognition, and the fry of the larger sorts can be returned to the water. Again, the restriction of smaller

Para. 79.

meshes will have the effect of leaving the smallest sorts of fishes as food for the bigger ones. These will scarcely be able to increase on and injure the larger ones by competition for food, for the fish that never grow large enough to be captured by meshes of 2 inches in circumference are more easily kept under by the predatory fish, because there are more fish that are large enough to prey upon them, and because more of them are required to satisfy the largest. It is not likely, moreover, that they will prove unequal in numbers to feed the larger

* In larger rivers, perhaps 3 inches would be better, because the predatory fish are larger.

fish, for they are very numerous and as prolific as they are small, and in addition to them there will always be the immature fish of the sorts proposed to be surrendered to the two-inch meshes. Moreover, if both these fail to suffice, it is still easy to multiply *ad infinitum* the supply of these smallest fish by protecting the produce of hill streams.

End of Para. 37.

79. If, then, meshes of all sizes from two inches in circumference upwards are allowed for the capture in the rivers of small sorts of fishes, provision will have to be made for the protection of the larger sorts of fish liable to be caught therein, and this might be done by making it obligatory to return to the water all the following fish:—

In the Rivers.

Those numbered in the list in Appendix G.

1, 2, 5, 6, 7, 17, 18, 24, 25, 26, 33, 34 } When of 9 inches in length or under.

80. The objection may be raised that few fish once caught are likely to be returned to the water, and that consequently it will be more practical to prevent their being ever caught. But a sweeping prohibition of small meshes will, it has been urged, be more baneful than advantageous to the larger sorts of fishes, and the system here advocated is the one followed in England, and by the aid of punishments for offenders and rewards for informers might soon be set working in India.

Spawning Time.

81. The spawning times of all fish are probably subject to some variation in different years; the observations of a single year are, therefore, not to be implicitly relied on, though carefully made. There has also been considerable difficulty with some fish in capturing them at all times for examination. But of the fish shown in the following table sufficient

Appendix G.

numbers have been caught and examined from time to time to make the seasons set against them very fairly reliable.

82. Not only do some fish of a sort spawn early and some late, but the same individual seems to spawn two or three times, and, perhaps, oftener in a season. In October or November a Mahseer generally contains three distinct sizes of roe, and the two larger sizes are mostly shed before January. Whether they have been laid in two batches or from time to time as they became mature, cannot be certainly stated, and it remains to be seen whether the minute ova which are still in the fish in January are matured and laid before the monsoon, or are the nucleus of the next year's crop. It seems probable that these fish do not accomplish their spawning operations in as short a time as salmon, but lay a few eggs from time to time as they ripen, and that this lengthened spawning may be a provision to meet the variableness in the rivers. Several Indian fish have also been ascertained to spawn twice a year at distinct periods, with an interval of several months between, and more fish may do this than we are aware of. Here, then, is unusual fertility, as well as adaptability to changing rivers.

Roach carry two crops of roe at one time, and a laying fowl, it will be remembered, contains the yolks of the eggs of many days to come in different degrees of advancement.

Particularized in Appendix G.

83. It will be seen from column 11 of the accompanying table, that though there are in the rivers some fish or other spawning in every month of the year except August, the very great majority of the small fish spawn in May, June, and July (a few of them repeating the performance in October, November, December and January), and that the spawning time of the mass of the big fish extends over September, October, November, December, and January, but is chiefly confined to December and January.

Appendix G.

Spawning.

84. The quantity of spawn contained in each fish has been but slightly tested. As far as examination has been made, Indian fish seem to be as prolific as others.

A Mahseer of	6¼ lbs.	contained	13,219 eggs,	which is	2,115	to the pound.
,,	11¼	,,	10,587	,,	941	,,
,,	6	,,	9,444	,,	1,574	,,
,,	5¾	,,	12,440	,,	2,163	,,
,,	3½	,,	4,350	,,	1,243	,,
,,	5	,,	6,034	,,	1,206	,,
	Average ..	..	..	..	1,540	

85. It may be interesting to know that here as elsewhere some fish build nests among the rushes at the margin of the water, deposit their eggs therein and keep guard over them like a stickleback. Others exhibit parental affection, swimming always close below their offspring and attacking everything that comes near them. This they do till the fry are about three inches long, when they turn on and eat them themselves if they do not disperse. Others, again, spawn in the sand, in the gravel, and even on rock. But all that has been ascertained will be found particularized against the different fish in column 11 of the list of fishes in Appendix G. An attempt to discover the period of incubation is also noticed below.

Nandus marmoratus.
Nandus malabaricus.

Ophiocephalus striatus.
Ophiocephalus marulius.
Ophiocephalus diplogramme.

Para. 94.

Food of Fishes.

86. What has been ascertained of the food of different fishes is also shown in the accompanying table. This has been gathered, not from hearsay, but from the contents of the intestines. This is interesting as showing the sustenance necessary for their increase and their influence on each other. Some fish seem to be almost entirely herbivorous, and they find an ample supply of freshwater weeds * on all the rocks in the rivers. Others prey on their brethren, and others again are omnivorous, and none more so than the Mahseer. For the purposes of this report the fish are classed in the accompanying table with reference to their food, and consequent influence on each other.

Appendix F.

87. The teeth in the throat of the Mahseer seem unusually

* Six different sorts of *podostemaceæ* have been gathered in flower and seed, but the names of only two of them have been ascertained. These are *Moriopsis hookeriana* and *Dalzellia pedunculosa*.

powerful. They are required to be so to crush freshwater snails, and crabs the size of the palm. They would make very short work of breaking a finger bone. They are also somewhat more pointed or carnivorous than is usual with the Carp species. This peculiar formation of their teeth accords with the observation that small fish also form a large portion of their food. Specimens of their teeth are submitted. The gall-bag, too, is unusually large. It is much prized by the country people as a remedy in cases of stomach-ache, cholera, and puerperal fever.

Ampullaria glauca L.
Paludina Bengalensis.
One of *Unio* species.
Limnea stagnalis.
Planorbis Indicus.
" *Coromandelina.*"

Two of *Corbicula* species.

88. Except in the neighbourhood of the coast, the rivers are generally fringed with forests, the foliage of which yields no scant supply of insect life; the overhanging bamboo swarms with small moths, and a bush that springs up in the bed of the river as it dwindles teems with various flies. The dhoop drops seeds as big as a bantam's egg, which, with the different seeds at different seasons of many descriptions of trees and the bamboo rice, are greedily devoured by the expectant fish. The Cyanite rocks, with which the rivers abound, are covered with many sorts of water crickets, and the freshwater weeds are alive with shrimps and beetles. The tender roots of trees and the leaves of the lilies in the shallows are freely found in the intestines of some fish, and others are filled to repletion with the simple green leaves of certain overhanging trees, well known to the natives, and used as ground bait before netting. Here in the tropics vegetation by the waterside is rank, and insect life is in profusion, so that the food supply of the Canara rivers can well bear comparsion with the best waters of colder climes; and there seems no limit on this score to the number of fish that these rivers are capable of sustaining.

Vateria Indica or Vegetable tallow tree.

Podostomacia.

Valisneria spiralis.

92. Frogs do some mischief among the fry, but they have themselves enough of enemies. In the water the Murral (*Ophiocephalus*) feeds almost entirely upon them, generally lying close under the banks for this purpose, and on land, mongooses, snakes, kites, crows, and paddy-birds assist in suppressing them, while water-snakes follow them in

Hylorana malabarica; hylorana florescens; rana cyanophlyctis (*Schn*) an unnamed species of *polypedates.*

both elements. The frog is, however, mentioned here as a creature to be carefully excluded from artificial nurseries.

The most troublesome is the common brown one (*rana cyanophlyctis.*)

93. The ova also have their enemies here as elsewhere. The small insect forwarded in spirits was, when taken, very busily engaged tossing the ova up, and turning it round and round, and apparently tearing it open. At 5 o'clock in the afternoon the eggs had evidently been only just deposited, for the male was seen moving away, and the milt had not yet cleared off. Not one of these insects was then visible, but early the next morning the hollow was full of them. How keen, then, must be their sense for discovering ova. In three days not an undestroyed egg was to be seen, the empty egg cases only were there. Tadpoles and small fry and a crab and the larvae of other insects were also there on the second and third days.

This was seen by two natives set to watch all day in turns. They did not observe unobserved, nor sufficiently intelligently, and so did not discover the intents of these visitants.

94. Some ova were speedily removed from the river, and carried in an earthen pot of water to a place where they could be kept under the intelligent observation of a gentleman, and there they were transferred to a finely-woven basket which was partially immersed in shallow water, so that there was a constant gentle stream through it from percolation, but no access for intruders. The same insects quickly gathered round the basket but could not find ingress. The mouth of the basket was also covered with muslin. Mr. J. Russel, who conducted this experiment, has sent word that these ova also failed. This opportunity for discovering the period of incubation of the ova of Mahseer has therefore been unfortunately lost.

95. Men search in the rivers for hillocks wherein spawn has been left, gather the ova and make it into cakes, which are considered a delicacy. The eggs of the kari and kalmuri are highly prized. (Nos. 1 and 3 in Appendix G.)

96. Here also lice-like parasites are found adhering to the gills and scales of the Canara Mahseer. Specimens were preserved in spirits, but the bottle met with an accident.

I was informed by Dr. Day that they are a variety of fresh water *Algæ*, hitherto not met by him, and as yet unnamed.

Molluscs.

105. But fishes are not the only food contained in the rivers. There are tons and tons of molluscs which are collected with great ease by the women and children. They are not to be despised in this country while similar articles of food are prized in England and France. There is a growing demand in England for limpets and periwinkles, from 150 to 250 bushels of periwinkles being sold in a day in London alone. A farm for the artificial propagation and sale of edible mussels has been worked for seven centuries in France, and it must have been profitable or it would scarcely be in existence. But whether these shell-fish can be artificially propagated, or in any way protected at certain periods, with advantage, is a matter yet to be ascertained. The *Velorita*, which is the most numerous, and the most substantial eating, and is eaten also in Japan, has no byssus wherewith to attach itself; and the mark on one side shows that it lies on the mud with one edge upwards. The method followed for propagating oysters and mussels would therefore seem inapplicable.

Cyclas.
Cerithium; two of the species.
Nerita.
Corbicula; one of the species found within tidal influence, and two others in the fresh water.
Velorita cyprinoides (Gray), of the family *Cyrenidæ*.
Unio.
Limnea stagnalis.
Ampullaria glauca L.
Planorbis Indicus.
" *Coromandelina.*
Paludina Bengalensis.

Practical Water-farming, by William Peard, M.D., L.L.B., pages 239, 211.

The Preservation of Ova in Mud.

106. The possible utilization of sun-dried mud for suspending the progress of incubation in ova in tropical climes, was proposed in my last report. It is a subject, the investigation of which would have been particularly interesting to me; but it has not been fairly within the scope of the experiments sanctioned by Government. The process could only be tested by collecting fecundated ova, and hatching them side by side with other exactly similar eggs that had been enclosed for varying periods and in various ways in mud; and as the propagation of fish by an artificial process was expressly excluded from the experiments sanctioned, the amount of time and attention that would have been required for the collection and treatment of ova could not be withdrawn from other subjects.

107. It is hoped, however, that it will be considered a proposal of sufficient importance to warrant its thorough investigation and application to practical purposes as the study of pisciculture advances in India, and in this hope the paragraph on this subject is extracted from my former report and placed in the appendix in order that it may be consulted if desired by any one inclined to make the experiment. Australia, Burmah, and the warmer parts of China and America also, are probably in latitudes equally suitable to the trial, and in these places there is no lack of persevering and successful pisciculturists.

Sea Fisheries.

110. The observations hitherto made in this report have had reference only to the rivers. But the sea fisheries of this district are more fruitful and more important. It has been computed that an acre of uncultivated sea bottom yields every week a larger supply of food than an equal extent of good land carefully tilled will produce in a year. The weight of fish and of beef annually consumed in London is in no great disproportion. In Canara, fish are almost the sole meat food of the people.

Report of Sea Fisheries Commission.

Para. 26.

122. There are marshes by the riverside that are flooded by every high tide. The fry of sea-fish frequenting the estuaries are in the habit of coasting along the very edge of the rivers, and running into all shallow places. When the tide rises over these marshes the fry go in with it, probably finding more insect food amongst the swamp grass, and on the freshly inundated land. But when they think to return with the ebbing tide, they are met by long lines of close wattle and fine leaf basket work, that allows the water to pass, but not the fry. At every tide in the day time the fry are thus waylaid, and left high and dry, thickly strewn in long lines, whence they are carried away in basket loads. The mullet suffer much in this way. They are a desirable sea-fish, and the wholesale destruction of their fry in this manner should be prevented.

123. It has been thought in England that the numbers of sea-fish frequenting a shore were greatly affected by the over-fishing of

their natural food, the shrimp. The mullet lives largely on shrimps and sand-worms. A small plot of some four or five acres in the Mangalore estuary was therefore buoyed off, to be left undisturbed for shrimps to breed in. This might, perhaps, be done with advantage in every estuary.

Pisciculture to be made a Separate Department.

153. If the receipts obtained by the above proposed means do not equal the expenditure, exception cannot fairly be taken on that ground, for it is not reasonable to expect that a Government, any more than an individual, can commence a new undertaking without some outlay at the first. The only proper question is, what amount of outlay is called for, and promises a reasonable return. This amount being placed to the debit of pisciculture in India, there is good ground for confidence that at no distant period it will be repaid with interest. It will be much more satisfactory that pisciculture should be fairly put upon its trial by the keeping against it of a strict profit and loss account, much more satisfactory than that the proceeds should be lost sight of as hitherto, by being merged in the general revenues, and that every outlay required for its proper advancement should be so sparingly doled out as to defy success, and should be looked upon as an encroachment on the Imperial revenues. If piscicultural accounts had, as now advocated, been hitherto kept separate, there would be now a weighty balance in their favour, for large sums have been annually taken therefrom from the very commencement of our rule in India, and have been applied, without any return whatever, to other purposes; have been absorbed into the Imperial revenues.

CHAPTER XXVI.

A PLEA FOR SEA FISHERIES.

> "And God said, 'Let the waters bring forth abundantly.'
> And God blessed them, saying, 'Be fruitful and multiply, and fill the waters in the seas.'
> 'And have dominion over the fish of the sea.'"—
>
> GENESIS i, 20, 22, 28.

To those who have travelled with me thus far from a love of the subject the following plea for Indian Sea Fisheries may prove not uninteresting. I quote it as I do the previous Chapter, in the hope, moreover, that there may rise among my readers, others who hereafter may succeed in forwarding the cause of pisciculture in India. Dr. Day has laboured much and left the scene with nothing set on foot for practical pisciculture. I have done my little all for 12 years, and am not sanguine of anything being done before my retirement. Though it come not in my time, still I cannot abandon the hope that come the day will. If these two Chapters aid in any way in advancing it either by instigating others to take an interest in the subject, or by aiding ever so slightly any that may hereafter take it up, they will not have burdened my book to no purpose. The report to be now quoted was written on the receipt of the thousand and one questions circulated by the late Famine Commission.

A PROPOSAL FOR MAKING INDIAN FISHERIES A MEANS OF ALLEVIATING INDIAN FAMINES.

Numerous and exhaustive though the questions are which search and probe for information valuable to the alleviation and prevention of famine, nevertheless there is a source of food supply for millions which has altogether escaped attention, and that although it is a source of food supply which,

(i.) Has a special relevancy to the famine enquiry, in that it is utterly uninfluenced by the severest and most protracted drought;

(ii.) It yields a very large supply,

(iii.) A throughly wholesome one,

(iv.) A self creative one, only needing harvesting,

(v.) An inexhaustible one,

(vi.) One not confined to any particular locality, but surrounding the whole peninsula of India,

(vii.) One that provides also its own highways for carriage,

(viii.) One that is incomparably more fertile than any land,

(ix.) And spreads its harvest over a longer period;

I mean the sea.

2. There is another source of food supply that has all the recommendations of the above, except the 5th and 6th, and in those also it falls short only in a very minor degree,

(x.) While it has the further special advantage that it penetrates miles inland,

I mean the estuaries.

3. In the rivers and lakes we have,

(xi.) A less reliable, less extensive food farm, but one capable, nevertheless, of supporting millions, one by no means to be neglected, one still immeasurably superior to the land;

(xii.) And one to be found spread over much of the interior country.

(xiii.) This whole water farm requires incomparably less outlay, incomparably less time, to bring it into bearing than any known land farm.

(xiv.) This fertile food farm further yields in its very refuse, the means of fertilizing land farms;

(xv.) And adds to the non-edible yet food-purchasing products of the country.

4. Though they may fail possibly from the treatment they receive at my hands, these broad assertions are, I believe, capable of irrebuttable proof. Many of them seem, however, to be so self-apparent that I hesitate to dwell on them for fear of idle prolixity calculated to weary rather than convince. Still these very truisms have not been practically acted on as if they were believed. I hope,

therefore, that I may be forgiven the following remarks, although they may contain nothing new, and aim only at putting well known facts in such juxta-position as to convince and move to action.

5. I shall hope to establish every one of the fifteen propositions above set forth, and if this is done successfully, I shall, I trust, enjoy the satisfaction of seeing a Government which is in downright earnest to alleviate and prevent famines, availing itself of a means at once so potent and so inexpensive.

6. That the sea is not assailable by drought even in the tropics is a point not likely to be contested. The same will be conceded of estuaries. These are my main points as regards famine.

7. As regards the non-tidal rivers and lakes it may be safely asserted that there are in India hundreds and thousands of square miles of them, millions of acres of them, that have never been known to succumb to the severest longest drought that ever visited India. They, as well as the sea and estuaries, are a perennial source of food supply, unassailable by drought.

8. There are rivers and lakes again that dry up, some of them annually, some only in famine years. For even these this much may be advanced, that in their very drying up they yield their all, and that if the land farmer will abandon the cultivation in favourable years of every field that is barren or in danger of being barren in time of long continued drought, I too will throw all my like fields out of the category. He will not do it. He will take his risks and try his best with them. I will be more liberal as far as the data at my command will allow me. I will throw out of my calculations such uncertain sources of supply, for I am not dealing here with pisciculture generally in ordinary or favourable years, but wish to keep strictly to my subject—famine alleviation and the sources of food supply that may be relied on at all and the worst seasons. I wish further to eliminate all objects of suspicious doubt, objects which might cast a shadow larger than themselves, and thus injure the rest of the argument. I wish to be well on the safe side of reliable truth. I would rather sacrifice the larger half of my position to secure a thorough working belief in the minor half than endanger the whole by endeavouring to establish the whole. I am satisfied that, if the minor half that I shall put forward is accepted, the rest must in course of time force its own

acceptance. Belief in the subject will come by seeing. I only use the parallel of the land to aid the appreciation of the value of the water farm.

9. This much, as to my first and main point, unassailableness by the severest drought, reliability in times of the worst famine.

10. If instead of taking my remaining propositions in the exact order in which they stand, I turn next to the fertility of the above sources of supply, I shall hope the better to gain an interested reading for the minor conclusions; for I must show the productiveness of the farm before I can hope for a contemplation of its extent and accessibility and cheapness of working, &c.

11. I begin with the sea, I shall quote from the very best authority, from the Commissioners selected by the British Parliament to report on the sea fisheries of the United Kingdom, selected presumedly for being previously the best informed persons on the subject, and persons whose judgment was to be most relied on by the nation in such a matter of public wealth. They, after having further informed themselves by enquiring of the persons best qualified to give them information, and after having laboriously recorded the answers to no less than 61,831 questions, give the following as one of their conclusions:—

"The produce of the sea around our coasts bears a far higher "proportion to that of the land than is generally imagined. The "most frequented fishing grounds are much more prolific of food "than the same extent of the richest land. Once in the year an "acre of good land, carefully tilled, produces a ton of corn, or two "or three cwt. of meat or cheese. The same area at the bottom of "the sea on the best fishing grounds yields a greater weight of food "to the persevering fishermen every week in the year. Five "vessels belonging to the same owner, in a single night's fishing, "brought in 17 tons weight of fish, an amount of wholesome food "equal in weight to that of 50 cattle, or 300 sheep. The ground "which these vessels covered during the night's fishing could not "have exceeded an area of 50 acres."

12. Not without careful consideration can such an astounding assertion have been arrived at by such men to be printed in a Parliamentary Blue Book, and presented to the scrutiny of the numerous experts and the far more numerous opponents of pisciculture throughout the country. I claim for it, therefore, that

it shall be accepted in its entirety without any reservation, and I shall base my calculations upon it as closely as I can. I have not quoted piecemeal to suit my own argument, but exactly as the passage stands.

13. Here we have broadly the conclusion that certain favourable acres of sea bottom, though wholly untilled, unmanured, unprotected by man, but habitually despoiled by every contrivance that skill and wealth can bring to bear on them, and that for years and years past, still continue to yield an inexhaustible annual crop of food fifty-two times as heavy as good land carefully tilled can be made to bear—still continue to yield fifty-two tons of food per acre per annum.

14. It has been objected here that it requires to be known what proportion of the sea bottom these favourable acres constitute. I reply that it is not known even in English, much less in less-fished Indian seas. In England fresh localities are constantly being discovered. A sandy bottomed shallow is the general desideratum, and it will be seen from the liberal reductions made below that I have confined my calculations as far as possible to such localities (para. 35). It will be seen, also (para. 52), that while advancing this calculation as not unworthy of thought, I am still content myself to rely definitely for the strength of my position on the very much lower and, I conceive, unchallengeable calculation of 332,683 tons of fish per annum, an amount of life preserving food equal to the support of three and a half millions of men for a year. And when all is done I have further shown (paras. 56 and 57) that I have used figures, as I have used parallels, only to draw exact attention, to gain a definite working belief in the real magnitude of the neglected food farm at our doors. If in the end that broad fact is heartily conceded as a great reality, then it matters little what minor deductions several thinkers may make at different places.

15. The one night's special fishing above recorded gives a produce of one ox or six sheep per acre per diem. Where is the acre of land that could yield the same? If calculated for the year, omitting Sundays, it would show 106 tons per acre per annum. Neither is it so extravagant as it would seem to extend the daily catch over the year by a multiple of days, for the weight of evidence is in favour of trawling not being exhaustive, but rather the reverse, improving the fish by stirring up the insect life at the bottom, and,

perhaps, also by capturing the predatory fish, which are less fertile as a rule, than those on which they prey, and consequently suffer most by equal capture.* If one trawler is known to be making a good catch, other vessels do not avoid that ground as fished over, but follow over the same ground by preference. There are other methods of fishing also which, being specially applied to the capture of predatory fish, are, in their results, specially beneficial to the fishery generally.

16. A friend objects to this calculation, saying that because five boats were employed, the total should be divided by five. I say, as well might you divide the produce of an acre of land by the number of men it takes to reap it. The present question is not the reaper but the acre; to the reaper we will come hereafter.

17. However, it is not my intention to rest at all on this special night's fishing, which shows 106 tons per acre per annum. I only put it forward as the Commissioners have done, just to show that the previous calculation of 52 tons per acre per annum is not an exceptional, but an average one, on the most frequented fishing grounds. On the contrary, I shall further subject even this average calculation to liberal reductions, as will be seen hereafter.

18. Nor will I turn aside to calculate the cost of fishing an acre of water so as to show the profits of sea fishing. Exact data are wanting. It is enough for our present purpose, the feeding of the masses, to adduce that the Commissioners thought it highly profitable, as will be seen in the next paragraph: and this their conclusion is based on ample grounds found in the body of their report.

19. But before passing on to my own calculations, I will quote the next paragraph, the conclusion which the Commissioners themselves draw from the facts which they have arrived at:

"When we consider the amount of care that has been bestowed "on the improvement of agriculture, the national societies which are "established for promoting it, and the scientific knowledge and en-"gineering skill which have been enlisted in its aid, it seems strange "that the sea fisheries have hitherto attracted so little of the public "attention. There are few means of enterprise that present better

* In the Sea Fishery Report for Great Britain, 1879, predatory fish are estimated, if I remember rightly, to destroy fifty times as many fish as man does.

"chances of profit than our sea fisheries, and no object of greater "utility could be named than the development of enterprise, skill, "and mechanical ingenuity, which might be elicited by the "periodical exhibitions and publications of an influential society, "specially devoted to the British fisheries."

20. These are the same conclusions in the main as I shall draw hereafter; but I quote the Commissioners for conclusions as well as facts, for deductions as well as data, in order that I may gain for my subject the superior weight of such authority.

21. On this basis I pass on to apply the data and the conclusions as closely as I can to our Indian position. To apply them exactly is not possible, for they are not sufficiently full and accurate. If there were data that the sea fisheries of England yielded so much on an average per lineal mile of shore, the calculation could be readily transferred with some degree of accuracy to India. If there were even information as to the whole take of sea fish in England there would be no great difficulty in drawing a parallel. But there is not. The Commissioners themselves, in their report for 1866, deplore the deficiency and suggest means of supplying it. Whether this has since been done I have at command no means of knowing. They write: "With the exception of the "statistics of the northern herring fishery collected by the Scotch "Fishery Board, there are no means of ascertaining even approxi- "mately the annual yield of fish on the coasts of the United "Kingdom. The only facts we have been able to obtain were returns "of the fish traffic on several of the great lines of railway, by which "the fish is transported from the fishing ports to the markets"

22. Then there are twelve lines of rail carrying, in 1864, 122,813 tons of fish.

23. We have elsewhere, in the same report, the statement that at Scarborough, so plentiful were the herrings sometimes, that from 700 to 800 tons were said to be sent thence into the interior of the country by railway in a single day. This, it will be observed, was over and above the local consumption, and Scarborough would surely eat more fish in a day than Madras. This, too, was seemingly over and above the takes of the French and Dutch boats. And this represents between a half and a third of the weight of grain carried daily by rail from Madras to the interior in the time of famine; the average carried from 17th February, 1877, to the

end of December, 1877, the famine time, being 1,817 tons per diem.

24. In another place we have the calculation that trawl vessels alone, "irrespective of the vast quantities of herrings, sprats, shell-"fish and of other descriptions of fish, which are supplied by other "modes of fishing," annually supply to London alone about 80,000 tons of trawled fish.

25. Of beam trawlers it is said: "Leaving out of consideration "the minor ports then, and taking account only of the Thames, Yar-"mouth, the Humber, Ramsgate, Brixham, Plymouth, Liverpool, "Fleetwood, and Dublin, not fewer than 955 sail of trawlers of "between 40 and 60 tons are employed in the North Sea, the "Channel, and St. George's Channel. These vessels are manned by "at least 5,000 souls; they represent a capital of, at the very "lowest estimate, £1,000,000, and they supply the daily market "with probably not less than 300 tons of fish, valued at from £1,500 "to £2,000."

26. Thus we have 300 tons a day, which, omitting Sundays, means 93,900 tons a year, and this from beam trawlers alone, and from English trawlers alone, and from nine localities alone.

27. Thus one single mode of trawling supplies 93,900 tons a year: several modes of trawling supply London alone with 80,000 tons a year, without taking any count of any of the other methods of fishing, though one alone of them, seining, is so successful, that a single port, Scarborough, sent inland a surplus for a time of 700 to 800 tons a day. Twelve lines of rail carried in a year 122,381 tons of fish. These calculations take and can take no note of the numbers carried inland by carts from every fishing village, of the numbers taken off by French and Dutch boats, of the numbers consumed on the coast.

28. These numbers, though a palpably deficient return of the fish farm of our English coast, still serve to open the mind to its magnitude. Without some such preamble, I could not expect a moment's faith for the figures that I shall have to set forth with reference to India. I may add that, had I wished to show large figures, I might have quoted from other sources; but they do not seem to me to be so precise as the official report, so I have confined myself to the Blue Book.

29. But, I may be asked, what ground have you for drawing a

parallel? How do you know that the Indian seas are as prolific of fish as the English? Have you herring, pilchard, or sardine, mackerel, and cod fisheries as in England? We have not the fisheries to any extent, but we have the fish; and I take it upon me to assert that, as far as our knowledge goes, there is every reason to believe that the Indian seas are as prolific as the British. The presumption is rather that they are more so. As regards fresh-waters I think there is no doubt that the balance is heavily in favour of India.

30. To enter into much detail would be wearisome. It will probably suffice to say that while the Carp runs in England with difficulty over 20 lbs., it is to be found of 200 lbs. weight in India (*Barbus tor*). The Sardine or Pilchard is on our Indian coasts in plenty (*Clupea Neohowi*). Herrings too we have, the one that ascends our rivers (*Clupea ilisha*) is incomparably a finer fish than the Yarmouth celebrity. In Mackerel, *Scomber kanagurta*, and some thirty *Carangides* or horse-mackerel are more or less relatives and represent quantity if not quality. Against the Cod we may fairly pit the Seir (*Cybium lineolatum*, and *C. Commersonii*) and several others, as well as the excellent salting fish *Polynemus tetradactylus* and *Polynemus Indicus* and others; but I surely need not go further into some hundreds of varieties of Indian fish, They are sufficiently set forth in the works of Dr. Day, and I do not think it can seriously be doubted for a minute that our Indian seas are quite as productive of fish as the seas of colder climes.

31. I had written thus far when a friend objected with pertinence that the natural enemies of the fish here, as compared with those in England, should be taken into account. I must admit it. Setting aside porpoises, dog-fish, and other sorts common to both, we have in India large predatory animals which they have not, in the form of sharks and crocodiles. But I do not think this is an argument that our fisheries compare badly with English fisheries, but rather the reverse. I think the presence of these monsters indicates that their functions are necessary to the maintenance of the balance of nature, or, in other words, that the Indian seas and rivers are more prolific than the English, and that when man enters on the field more fully and diminishes these, his competitors in the work of slaughter, the yield of other fish will be still more favourable.

Sharks are largely eaten as it is, and they might be much more freely caught and utilized to the benefit of both the capturers and the fishery.

32. Given their fertility, the next question is their fertile area. Taking the lineal measurement of our Indian shores, how far out may they be held to be fertile? As they are untried fields, I can only go back to the analogy of our English fisheries, of which more is known. There they have near-shore fishing and deep-sea fishing, net and line fishing of every description from the very shore outwards. The question is how far out? Trawlers of different descriptions fish at different depths, and I find it in evidence in the same Blue Book that deep trawlers fish in water of 23 to 24 fathoms, and the Dogger bank is girdled in their Chart by a 20 fathoms line of soundings.

33. On this I have taken a marine Chart of the Indian Coasts, and commencing from above Kurachi on the West, going round Cape Comorin, not Ceylon, to beyond the mouths of the Ganges on the East, I have at every degree taken the distance out to sea, at which I find marked sounding from 20 to 24 fathoms. I have generally been nearer 20 than 24 fathoms, always erring on the side of moderation. Then adding up their total and striking an average, I find it gives me an average distance out to sea of 26 English miles. But as I found my average very much swollen by certain exceptional localities, in which for about 250 miles in length it was necessary to go 46, 57, 80, and 89 English miles out to sea before the 24 fathoms depth could be reached, I considered it fairer to a general average that these exceptional localities should be thrown out. This reduced my average to 14 English miles.

34. These measurements are from latitude 8° to latitude 26° on the West Coast, and from latitude 8° to latitude 21° on the East Coast. I have no means of carrying them further; but the area is sufficiently extended to make it fairly applicable to all India and Burmah.

35. But trawlers ply on soft sandy bottoms not rock, and though I believe that with few exceptions there is sandy bottom all round our Indian Coasts, still I prefer to be rid of the possible objection by a liberal concession. On the bare possibility I will throw off a belt of two miles all round the coast, which amounts to an area of 9,222 square miles; albeit, this should not in fairness

be thus summarily discarded, for rocks yield crustaceans and shell-fish and insect life-rearing seaweed. This leaves me with still an average belt of 12 miles of fishing ground.

36. To find the length of this belt, an opisometer has been run round the coast at about a mile from shore, so as to take no count of indentations. The result is a length of 4,611 English miles.

37. Then 4,611 miles long, multiplied by 12 miles broad, gives a sea fishing area of 55,332 square miles, which, reduced to acres, gives 35,412,480 acres of sea bottom good for fishing.

38. We have above (paras. 11 and 17) allowed an annual produce of 52 tons an acre. But that was "on the best fishing "grounds," though they were at the same time "the most frequented "fishing grounds." How may I obtain a calculation for all fishing grounds? I have already stated that I believe the Indian seas are better for fishing than the English, being almost all sandy bottomed. However, if I consider that half of them are utterly barren, and so reduce my average from 52 to 26 tons an acre, I shall surely have satisfied the most exacting.

39. Then 26 tons an acre will, over 35,412,480 acres, give me an annual possible produce of 920,724,480 tons of fish.

40. But India has its monsoons, so that for two and a half to three months in the year on the West Coast, and for a less period on the East Coast, it is dangerous for small boats to put to sea. I will take a three months' cessation of sea fishing all round both coasts, and reducing my calculation by one quarter, claim only an annual harvestable produce of 690,543,360 tons of fish.

41. But if I am to draw an exact parallel, I am entitled to claim that the the water farm of which I speak, the sea, as being utterly unassailable by drought, shall be compared not with the land generally, but with only so much of it as is in a like position, as is not liable to be affected by drought. In the Madras Presidency I find that 4,004 square miles, or more exactly 2,535,063 acres, are put down as irrigated in a manner that makes them safe from drought.

42. This is not my calculation, but that of the department whose business it is to indicate it. It is arrived at as follows:

District.			Area in Square Miles.	Irrigation System.	Area actually Irrigated, Sq. Miles.
Malabar	..	..	6,002	There are no permanent irrigation works, but there is a trustworthy monsoon	604
S. Canara	..	..	3,902		302
Tanjore	..	..	3,654	Cauvery Delta	1,175
Trichinopoly	..	..	3,515	Cauvery Channels	121
S. Arcot	..	..	4,873	Coleroon Channels..	111
Coimbatore	..	..	7,432	Bowanny Channels	42
Godavery	..	..	6,224	Godavery Delta	836
Kistna	..	..	8,036	Kistna Delta	367
Tinnevelly	..	..	5,176	Tambraparni	164
Nellore	..	..	8,462	Pennar Anicut	84
North Arcot	..	..	7,139	Palar Anicut	33
Kurnool	..	..	7,358	Irrigation Company's Canal ..	115
Cuddapah	..	..	8,367	do. do. ..	27
Chingleput	..	..	2,753	Chembrambaukum and Red Hill Tanks	23
Total	..	..	82,893	Total	4,004

43. These rough calculations of square miles reduced to acres would be 2,562,560, but the exact amount is 2,535,063 acres of land in the whole Madras Presidency so irrigated as to be safe from famine. The reported yield on this acreage, both from 1st and 2nd crop cultivation combined is, I find, 4,324,580,186 lbs. This is the yield in the Famine year when there was an enormous stimulus to cultivation on safely irrigated acres, a stimulus so great that the cultivated area under the Irrigation Company's Canal increased eight-fold. Nevertheless, I take it as the best case that can be made out for rice. This weight above given, is the weight of unhusked paddy, and if we make the usual deduction of one-third for husk, we shall have 2,883,053,458 lbs., or, say, 1,287,077 tons of rice per annum, against the safe water farm of which I speak, which for no culture whatever bears from the sea alone 690,543,360 tons of fish.

44. If I wished to be more particular, I should be entitled to go still a step further and examine what is the comparative value as food of the tons of fish and tons of rice. The following percentage table will give it :—

	Quantity of Nitrogenous flesh-forming ingredients.	Quantity of non-azotized heat-giving principles.	Quantity of mineral matter.	Quantity of Carbon.
Fish	14·00	7·00	1·00	9·15
Rice	5·43	84·65	0·52	36·00

45. It is obvious that in nitrogenous alimentary matter fish is a little more than two and a half times as rich as rice, or, in other words, will serve, in this respect, to support two and a half times as many human beings.

46. This table indicates also that fish and rice are good complements of each other for mixture towards the composition of a dietary, the one being rich in what the other is poor in, and I put this forward to meet the objection that men cannot live on fish alone. True: but it matters not to my calculations whether a certain amount of fish will suffice by mathematical calculation to alone support a million people, or mixed in practice with nine times as much other food to keep alive and in working health ten millions. The result is the same; an additional amount of food representing the lives of one million has been thrown into the supply market, and it serves by so much to make the other food go further, let alone that it also cheapens it.

47. I may add that in a country where the diet is chiefly of vegetables, salt is more required than elsewhere, so that salt-fish would meet a want. In practice there is a call for it. In Trichinopoly, for instance, as well as other places, it sells for twice the price of cheap butcher's meat. If in demand even as an expensive luxury, much more should it be so if made cheap and plentiful. That it is not cheap at present is attributable, I think, to the supply being unequal to the demand; for in the fish-curing yards salt is given by Government at cost, not monopoly, price. Curing, however, as well as fishing, stands much in need of development, while it must fairly be admitted that if salt-fish cannot be made cheap, it fails as a famine-preventive food, still it is contended that with plentiful cheap fish, cheap salt, cheap labour, and cheap rail and sea carriage, the presumption is that it can be made cheap. It may also be admitted that if salt fish are only an appetizing relish rather

than a hunger-satisfying food, they must again be held to be a failure as regards the object of the present paper. But it is contended that there is no insuperable difficulty in the way of salting fish any more than there is in the way of salting pork or beef, so as to fit it to form a substantial part of a health and strength and life sustaining meal. The several manners of curing form only one of the minor difficulties to be overcome. The manner of curing is calculated very much to follow the demand.

48. I am told there are parts of India in which the fish-eating portion of the population is comparatively small, almost *nil*, and I think the general idea is that it is so in this Presidency also. But it is not. The majority are vegetarians by compulsion of circumstances, not by rule of creed. Taking the last Census report, and going very carefully through the castes, I find that more than 90 per cent. are of castes that may and do eat meat when they can get it.

The total population of the Madras Presidency, including the Native States of Mysore, Travancore, Cochin, and Poothocottah, is given as 39,565,777. Of these 35,903,807 are meat eaters, which is a proportion of 90·7.

The way in which the calculation has been arrived at is shown in an enclosure.

49. But I may be told my calculations are purely theoretical. The fish are in the sea. You cannot count and weigh and eat them there. True. That is the very point of my argument. I say the harvest is there, and we will not reap it. I will go further, I will admit that the calculation indicates only the vastness of the farm standing there before us ready to be reaped. It stands as vast impenetrable forests have stood in times past, inviting the axe and the plough of the settler to utilize their wealth of productiveness. But it differs from them in not needing so much outlay, and in being inexhaustible. It stands as a sea of corn inviting you to put in the sickle, aye, to turn in all the reaping machines you can, and do nothing but reap; for clearing, tilling, sowing, are all unneeded. It may take years before you are able to reap a tenth or even a fiftieth part of it, still it is as well to run the eye over the standing crop, estimate its value as approximately as possible, and consider in earnest whether it is not worth while to make a real commencement at harvesting it, an effort worthy of the crop

before us. Halve, quarter, decimate, my figures, make what deductions you like, and still the food farm is surely large enough to attract the attention of Government. That is my object.

50. Having thus scanned prospective possibilities, and not improbable possibilities either, but a calculation carefully reduced at every turn to bring it within reliable limits, I turn now to a calculation based on a wider range of actuals, a range taking in every adverse circumstance possible, and utterly excluding all grounds for casting on it any suspicion of being a sanguine or theoretical calculation. The same Commissioners write: "We have, "however, a more full return for the last three years, embracing "nearly the whole line of coast from the Firth of Forth, on the "North, by the East, South and West Coasts of England to the "Solway on the West, which is of a very satisfactory character."

This is a return of the quantity of fish forwarded by twelve lines of railway in 1862, 1863, 1864. The object of the Commissioners was to know whether or not fisheries were declining from over fishing, and the return showed very satisfactorily that they were growing rapidly. The return, though very satisfactory from that point of view, is far from complete for the purpose of the present enquiry, as will be shown below, and as the Commissioners themselves regret in the following words:—"With the exception of "the statistics of the northern herring fishery collected by the "Scotch Fishery Board, there are no means of ascertaining, even "approximately, the annual yield of fish on the coasts of the "United Kingdom." Incomplete, and evidently far below the truth, though they are, I take the figures. The return of these twelve lines for the last year (1864) was 122,381 tons of fish carried inland. The distance of this line from Solway to Firth of Forth, taken in the same way as I have taken it for India, is, I find, 1,696 miles. The return of 122,381 tons being divided by 1,696 miles, gives 72·15 tons per lineal mile of coast. Taking the coast of India and British Burmah at 4,611 miles, and multiplying it by 72·15 tons, we have a yield of 332,683 tons. This is a very different conclusion certainly from the 690,513,360 tons at which we arrived before. But the larger calculation represented the total harvest which the sea is seemingly capable of yielding. The minor calculation represents the equivalent to the actual yielded in England for transport inland by rail, after deducting—(1) all not caught for want of fishing stations along the whole coast, for want of sufficient and good implements of capture, from the presence of non-fertile acres, from stress of weather; (2) all caught by the French and Dutch boats and taken away; (3) all taken inland to intervening towns by cart or any means other than railways; (4) all consumed on the coasts; (5) all exported in salt to foreign countries; and (6) all used as manure.

51. Thus, it will be seen, that this return, however satisfactory and sufficient for the enquiry prosecuted by the Commissioners, is glaringly incomplete for the present purpose. It is obviously very far from representing the whole actual take of fish, which is what is here wanted. It is palpably much within the mark. In nevertheless accepting these figures just for the sake of the argument, it must be admitted that they are so accepted only in lieu of any more approximate data, and that they are well beyond any further depreciation.

52. If even this calculation, after all these deductions, be applied as a parallel to the average of the Madras Presidency, which is considered safe, then we have 332,683 tons of fish against 1,287,077 tons of rice, which is a little more than one-fourth; or, if the comparative nutriment of the two sorts of food is taken, more than one half. This 332,683 tons of fish, be it remembered, is all for inland carriage by rail, and is equal to more than half of the amount of rice carried inland by the Madras Railway during the Famine pressure of 1877. From 17th July, 1877, to 31st December, 1877, 585,233 tons of grain, almost without exception rice, if, indeed, it was not all rice, was the amount carried inland from Madras. If the relative nourishment of this 332,683 tons of fish be considered, it is the equivalent to 831,707 tons of rice, or more than all that was carried by rail from Madras, more by 246,474 tons of grain. Who will say that such an additional supply of food for the country would not have saved many lives. At 1½ lbs. of grain per man per diem, it would have sufficed for 1,380,018 working men for a year; or if it be allowed that fish is 2½ times as nourishing as rice, for 3,450,043 working men for a year—say, for nearly three and a-half millions for a twelvemonth.

53. I would wish next to turn to the estuaries, but am deficient in definite proof of fertility, and utterly at a loss for data of their area. As regards fertility, I should point for analogy to the salmon

fisheries, whose value is patent to all. But I am met with the objection that we have not, and cannot possibly have, any salmon fisheries in India. We have, however, a very valuable sea fish, the Hilsa (*Clupea ilisha*) which, like the Shad of America, ascends our rivers after the manner of the salmon in England. Now I find from Government Order, 28th June, 1878, No. 984, that one single locality on one estuary of the Ganges supplied of this single fish alone, the Hilsa, and that within three months, and salted, for the return refers only to the fish salted at a single curing yard, no less than 19,300 maunds. It is also mentioned that there was a large simultaneous demand for fresh Hilsa carried by rail to Calcutta and elsewhere. What it was is not given, but if we put it down at not less than the salted supply, we shall have 38,600 maunds, say 1,418 tons.

It may fairly be thence concluded that the tonnage of fish to be annually taken of all sorts, specially such as Mullets and *Megalops Cyprinoides*, and at all times, and from all the estuaries of India, must be very considerable indeed; but I have no data whereon to arrive at the roughest approximation. I can only omit it, merely drawing attention to the fact that the quantity of food here omitted from the calculation must be very large indeed.

54. As regards such of the rivers and lakes as are unassailable by drought, I am again unable to give such accurate data of the fertility of an acre as may serve whereon to base calculations. I can only show generally extreme fertility far in advance of any land. The American Pisciculturist, Seth Green, writes: "Expend "one thousandth part of the sum spent in tilling the land in tilling "the water, and fish may be sold in our markets at two cents a "pound." Dr. F. Buckland says, that a salmon worth about as much as a prime fed sheep can be bred for one farthing. As regards India, I may instance the following experiment of my own. Taking advantage of a pond, of about two or three acres, being cleaned in 1875, I re-stocked it myself with carefully selected sorts of fish. I spent 2 rupees. I put in not more than 2 lbs. weight of fry. I gave 18 months' rest. I flung in half a handful of snails to breed. I did nothing else. More than 4,000 lbs. weight of fish are now annually taken out of that pond without making any impression on it. I should mention that the 2 rupees spent included also the carriage of the fry from a distant river. Intrin-

sically what I turned in were worth about 2 annas, say three pence. This result came of judicious selection, of not trying to rear predatory and non-predatory fish, wolves and lambs, on the same farm.

55. What multiple, then, may I be allowed in comparing the fresh-water farm with the land. Mr. Green says, 1,000. Dr. Buckland's calculation comes to much the same. My experiment to about 250. Dropping hundreds and thousands, I might surely ask a modest ten, and, multiplying the acres of fresh water, thereby show again some millions of tons of fish producible from them. But in their case some trifling outlay would be necessary on legislation and protection. They are not quite like the seas waiting only to be harvested.

56. And, after all, of what avail are figures? They serve only to reduce platitudes to points, hazy notions to definite conceptions. And figures, too, lie under the suspicion of being misleading under large multiples. I have therefore studiously endeavoured at every turn to steer so far within the truth, that the very figures which I have put forward, are only to be considered as roughly approximate estimates. Every multiple has been unfairly reduced. The length of line, as taken by an opisometer, is rough in the extreme, and hundreds of miles within the mark. The depth to which the breadth of coast line has been taken is far within the mark, the favourable localities being without reason thrown out, and undue allowance made for possible rock, and again for possible barrenness, and again a liberal allowance for stress of weather. In the second minor calculation for the sea all the deductions, obviously existing in the return have nevertheless been accepted. The fertile estuaries have been taken no count of; and the hundreds and thousands of miles of perennial fresh water have been allowed to drop out, while the areas of fresh water not unassailable by drought have been altogether discredited, though they, too, might be made to yield no mean returns in ordinary years.

57. I had thought to compare the produce of the sea, the estuaries, and the rivers unassailable by drought, with the whole of the produce of the land, both that considered safe against famine from being reliably irrigated, and that also that could only be relied on in ordinary years. I had meant to throw in also the rain-watered "dry lands." But of what avail are further calcula-

tions? They would only weary. Such calculations as have been brought forward, I have felt compelled to adduce for the purpose of reducing platitudes that make no impression to points that leave a mark.

How else could I draw exact attention, how else gain a definite working belief in the real magnitude of the food farm at our doors? There is food for millions.

58. While quoting from the report of the Sea Fishery Commissioners passages that suit my argument, I must in fairness, not omit to quote also the one single passage that seems to militate against sea fisheries being a preventive of famine.

With reference to Ireland, where the fishermen are mostly farmers, who fish only when not farming, the Commissioners write: "The great decline in the number of the fishermen we "believe to be wholly due to the effects of the famine in 1848, "and the subsequent emigration. It might have been anticipated "that during the famine the fishermen at least would be secure "from its ill effects, and would not only have plenty of food them-"selves, but would be the means of diverting starvation from "others. But such was not the case; it was found that the people "would not live wholly on fish, nor would they, out of the small "means remaining to them, buy fish in preference to meal or "potatoes; the fishermen, therefore, suffered, not only from the "loss of their own crops of potatoes, but from want of a market for "their fish. They shared to the full extent in the sufferings of the "famine, and as most of them became physically incapable of "going to sea, it was frequently found that men were starving, "while fish were in abundance on the coast. In many parts of "Ireland, the fishing population has not yet recovered from the "depression and ruin caused by the famine; and the subsequent "emigration, by taking off the youngest and ablest of the fisher-"men, and leaving behind the old, the feeble, and the incompetent, "has still further operated, not only in reducing the numbers, "but in lowering the average condition of those who remain "behind."

59. These are awkward facts and unexpected. All I can do is to set against them the equally stubborn fact that our experience during the present famine in India has been the opposite. While other classes have been starving, the fishermen have done well. I

have enquired of the Collectors of the Maritime Districts of the Madras Presidency, and they have obligingly supplied me with information of which the following is an epitome. The Maritime Districts are Ganjam, Vizagapatam, Godavery, Kistna, Nellore, Madras, Chingleput, South Arcot, Tanjore, Madura, Tinnevelly, Travancore, Cochin, Malabar, South Canara. Of these, Travancore and Cochin are Native States, from which I can get no information, and from South Arcot, I have no reply as yet; so that there remain twelve districts, the reports from which I epitomize. Above they are in their coast order. Below I will class them according to the tenor of their replies; two unfavourable; two depending on the grain trade; and eight favourable on fishery grounds proper.

Tinnevelly.—It is conceived that there were fewer fish in the sea than in former years, and that consequently the fishermen suffered as much as any other class.

Vizagapatam.—The sea fishermen suffered as much as other classes, especially from the prohibition of the use of earth salt. Efforts to induce a use of Government salt failed. They emigrated largely.

Madras.—The sea fishermen in this District profited in large measure by the liberal hire given them for landing rice, which was a more lucrative avocation than fishing. This, however, is scarcely an objection, for it points in the direction of the usefulness of a body of seafaring men to our mercantile marine as will be seen below.

The take of fish was probably less from the fishermen being otherwise occupied, but the price of fish seems to have remained unaffected, in spite of the high price of grain. This might naturally be expected to result from the non-salting of fish for the interior, in consequence of the highly profitable employ of landing grain having absorbed all energies; and the quantity of spilt grain, which the boatmen daily got in their boats, was so ample, that the fishermen themselves did not eat as much fish as in ordinary times, and the surplus thus saved, was left to the local public.

Chingleput.—The sea fishermen flourished, but it was probably more from hire and gleaning in landing grain than from actual fishing.

Ganjam.—The fishermen, it is said, are certainly better off than the ordinary coolies.

Godavery.—The sea fishermen of the District have certainly not suffered during the present famine. They have, they say, derived no benefit from it, and the Collector is inclined to think they have not benefited much.

Kistna.—The Collector thinks the seafaring fishermen have not suffered so much as others, though at the same time the distress on the coast was not so great as it was inland.

Nellore.—The fishermen flourished, and there was little or no distress amongst them during the famine, but there was an important thing to help them, the Canal was being made, and at one time there were as many as 41,000 coolies on it distributed all along the coast. This gave the fishermen an unusually good market, and when their fishing failed, they could always get a day or two's earthwork on high wages.

Tanjore.—In this District there was never real famine, but very nearly famine prices in the midst of plenty, because the grain was going as fast as it could be carried to famine Districts. Men who had been used to add to their daily meal, the luxury of a little salt fish as a relish, were compelled by the price of grain to abandon the tasteful dainty. The fishermen had to pay the same prices as others for grain, and complain that they suffered equally in that they had to barter a full meal of fish for a mere pittance of grain. But this seems to be an admission that to those who were content with it, fish-food was cheap, and an admission also that the fishermen could afford to exercise a preference in the food with which they sustained life. They and their children were in better case than their neighbours.

At Negapatam they were largely used as in Madras for landing grain, but the above remarks refer to the coast line of the District generally.

Madura.—The Madura Collector says that the sea fishermen escaped the great distress felt by the inland population, owing this escape to the facility with which they could take fish, and his Salt Deputy Collector says, that from his personal knowledge, and from enquiries, he is able to say that they prospered and benefited their neighbours, though he adds that fishing was not so successful in parts of the coast as it used to be at other times, implying that the famine has affected, not the take from, but the very fishes in the sea. This same conclusion is drawn in Tinnevelly also. But it is a conclusion difficult to accept, and needs some proof.

Malabar.—The fishermen did not suffer as a class during the famine. Though the captures were not as abundant as usual, they fetched good prices. Fishermen were not to be seen begging. Though it cannot positively be said that they flourished, yet it can be said that there was no distress among them, such as afflicted the Irishmen. "The fish supply undoubtedly helped us through our "difficulties in the famine. The Collector dined on fresh sardines "brought by rail, 80 miles inland, and the inland fish trade carried "by porters, got a great impetus." The fishermen were also advantaged by employ in landing grain.

South Canara.—The sea fishermen profited by the increased sales of fish, though the article was cheap, but they lost, owing to the high prices of rice and other necessaries of life, so that on the whole they were not more prosperous than ordinarily, but were perhaps less pinched than others of the poorer classes.

60. I take the general result of this to be that they saved themselves and aided their neighbours. There was the same result when I was Collector of that District myself in the scarcity in 1867. It is reported that Pilchards were more than usually plentiful. I can state from my own knowledge that they came in the same unusual numbers in 1867.

61. Thus we have briefly two districts from which come reports unfavourable to the usefulness of sea fisheries during the famine, and ten districts from which the reports are favourable. Of these ten two may be eliminated on the ground that the welfare of the fishermen is attributable rather to the grain trade than to fishing, the remaining eight can report more or less favourably, some very favourably.

62. The curious statement coming from Tinnevelly, Madura, and Malabar, that there were less fish in the sea that year, is met by the exactly opposite experience in South Canara. I presume that the scarcity, or plenty of fish, was in no way influenced by the drought on land, but resulted from the habits of migratory fish.

63. On the whole, I think, the Indian experience during the famine, sufficiently neutralises the fears to be entertained from the experience in Ireland, and that if our Indian experience is so far favourable even with the present appliances, and almost utter absence of salting, much more favourable results may be looked for

if we can induce an improvement, both in the fishing and the curing, with, perhaps, also some additional means of carriage inland in branch railways likely to be started in connection with the grain traffic from the coast.

64. It is not to be forgotten that in salting fish, large quantities of oil can be saved and added to the wealth which represents the means of purchasing food.

65. It is not to be forgotten that the offal of fish, the refuse which is otherwise thrown into the sea, and only serves to scare the better fish, and draw the predaceous ones, makes excellent manure. It is prepared and used in America, under the name of "fish chum." It is also prepared of the fish condemned at Billingsgate as bad, or, as it is there called, diseased. It is already sent in an offensive unprepared way to our coffee estates. It could easily be prepared so as greatly to increase its value. By this means can the refuse of the seas be made to fertilize, and add to the yield of the land.

66. It is not to be forgotten that fish are captured on the very highway for carriage, the sea, whence they can most cheaply be transported to any rail-fed or road-fed port. They are also captured where salt is made, or easily carried to them. So that in both these respects they are better situated than food grown in an interior district not tapped by rail or canal.

67. It is not to be forgotten that by improving the fisheries, we shall improve the fishermen also. In England this is a very important matter as aiding the manning of our naval and mercantile marine. As we have used Indian soldiers, it is possible we may be glad to have Indian sailors available. They are already used in the merchant service. In the famine their aid for landing grain was found indispensable, and their numbers all too small: improved sea fisheries would provide against such a difficulty.

68. My third proposition is that fish are a wholesome diet. This is surely about as well known as my first one, that the sea cannot be dried up by a famine.

69. The fourth proposition is, that the supply of fish from the sea is inexhaustible. This is the burden of the whole Blue Book from which I have been quoting. This very question was the origin of the appointment of Parliamentary Commissioners. Men's minds were exercised by the fear that over-fishing and injurious

modes of fishing were destroying our fisheries. The Commissioners have heaped up a mass of incontestible evidence to the contrary. Briefly their conclusion may be summed up in their own words: "This return shows, in 1863, an increase of 11 per cent. over 1862; "and in 1864 of 12 per cent. over 1863. It is particularly interest-"ing as bearing upon the alleged falling-off of the take of fish on "the Eastern Coast of England, where, instead of a decline, there "is shown to be an annual increase exceeding 10,000 tons."

70. But fish decay, I am told, and will not bear carriage in this tropical clime. This difficulty can be remedied by salt in India, as it is by ice in England. The question is further discussed in remarks on fish curing in connection with the experimental farm proposed.

71. Again, I may be reminded that there are already fishermen in India, and that their takes are considerable. May be they are, but comparatively they are perfectly insignificant, grains or ounces against tons. It would take too long to examine in detail their means of capturing. It will suffice to say that, as far as I am aware, they do not even know what a trawl net is; their nearest approach to it is very poor; and to speak antithetically our steam launch is represented by their catamaran or raft, formed of four or five logs lashed together. Still they are a hardy race of whom much might be made to the advantage both of themselves and their neighbours.

72. In the above remarks I trust the fifteen propositions set forth at the commencement have been supported.

73. Time and space forbid me to dwell on the profits to the fishermen, and especially to the capitalists. It would be premature to dwell on the details of the measures to be adopted. It is also too large a subject to be worked out in the scraps of time toil-somely saved from the pressure of current duties, which same want of time is submitted as an apology for the shortcomings of this paper. Suffice it here to say that undivided, consecutive, untiring attention and study will need to be given to the subject, if practical useful results are to be expected for the benefit of our fellow creatures: a fitful policy of general interestedness can produce no fruits. This, however, is no more than I had the honour of pointing out more than ten years ago. It is earnestly hoped that the present famine may suffice to induce the Government to take

definite action in this matter of food supply. Not one farthing will it need to advance for the purpose. The produce of the now mismanaged fisheries, which is injudiciously merged in the general revenues, is sufficient to build them up into an incalculable blessing to the Empire.

74. But in conclusion I will once more strengthen myself in the weight to be attached to the opinion of the Sea Fishery Commissioners, requoting from them the following: "When we "consider the amount of care that has been bestowed on the improve- "ment of agriculture, the national societies which are established "for promoting it, and the scientific knowledge and engineering "skill which have been enlisted in its aid, it seems strange that the "sea fisheries have hitherto attracted so little of the public atten- "tion. There are few means of enterprise that present better "chances of profit than our sea fisheries, and no object of greater "utility could be named than the development of enterprise, skill "and mechanical ingenuity, which might be elicited by the "periodical exhibitions and publications of an influential Society "specially devoted to the British Fisheries."

If they could write this of England, and that, too, at a time when the general idea was that there was over-fishing, surely their words apply with ten-fold force in far more backward India.

75. On writing the above, I am asked, and it is natural that I should be asked, "What definite steps I advocate that the Govern- "ment should take to utilize the supply of food furnished by "the sea and rivers?"

Such a question cannot be answered off-hand, or if it be, the answer must be subject to so many qualifications as to make it lack the required definiteness.

I do not think it is possible for any man, or even for any Commission of Experts to advise the Government off-hand without a great amount of previous local enquiry, nor do I think that the advice given can possibly be final. It must be progressive over a course of years. I will indicate below the lines which I conceive such inquiry should follow, and I think the conclusion will be that the most advanced scientist in Europe of ichthyology and pisci-culture must be incompetent, without much previous local inquiry, to tender off-hand sound practical advice as to the steps which the Government should take; in fact, I am confident that a prudent man would not undertake it. We have only to look around us and read the record of so many English Companies started on the most promising theories, seemingly well-considered by eminently cautious experts, and yet ruined by some little unforseen hitch inherent in the country; we have only to consider this to be satisfied of the importance of having exact knowledge of the native and the country, as well as of the fish. It is necessary that we should have a knowledge, not only of the native of one particular country, but of the several natives, the several nations, peoples, and languages inhabiting India. A knowledge of their fishing habits, present means, progressive capabilities—a knowledge of their appliances, and the best way of adapting to them the improvements to which Europe has attained, a knowledge of the Indian seas, their depths, bottoms, currents, winds, ports, in order to judge of the lines, nets, and boats most desirable to use—a knowledge of the markets, how to reach, and how to influence them—a knowledge of the existing methods of curing, and the reasons therefor, together with the wisest way of improving them, and of surmounting the difficulties offered by the salt monopoly. These subjects of enquiry present themselves as primary considerations with reference to the sea alone. Then the estuaries and the rivers must be studied. To enforce the necessity for close study and consideration of the peculiarities thereof, would require that I should re-write much that has been written by Dr. Day and myself in our several reports. The natural peculiarities of tropical rivers, the artificial difficulties introduced by irrigational structures, and they are many, fish-passes, wholesale fish-poisoning, indiscriminate destruction of fry, varying regulation of the size of the mesh, the use of cruives, and other fixed engines; and these points require local study of the best method of meeting them. The fish-pass question alone is one of much greater difficulty in India than it is in England, as the enclosed letter with its years of antecedent correspondence may serve to indicate. He must be a bold man, therefore, who ventures to tell the Government exactly what it should do before he has had the means of locally inquiring. Some little opportunity for such inquiry I may have had, but it has been very limited—limited to the Districts in which I happened to be employed in revenue administration, limited to the hours and the seasons I could save from prior revenue and magisterial duties, limited therefore, very limited, both as to locality and time. If such defined industries as iron mines, cotton-mills, saw-mills, and so forth, have repeatedly broken down for want of prescience of local difficulties, much more is a like danger to be guarded against in an industry which is to spread itself over so wide an area as all India, and to be applied to such much less controlable elements as natural forces, animal life, human beings.

76. My conclusion, then, is that the first step which the Government should take is to appoint an officer who shall be able to give the whole of his undivided attention to the mastery of practical difficulties; they are neither few nor insignificant, and the *vis inertiæ* to be overcome at every turn is alone so great, that such an officer will have before him a truly Herculean labour. If he is resolved to leave marks of success within a reasonable time, he will not fail to find his best energies and his patience taxed to the utmost.

77. Whether there should at first be one such officer for all India, or one for each Presidency, I am doubtful; but if there be only one, I think he should work in the direction of systematizing a scheme by which each Presidency should eventually have charge of its own fisheries, for if the industry grows as it should, the Fisheries of a Presidency, like the Salt, the Police, the Agriculture of a Presidency, will be as much as one head can manage. Each Presidency should also, for the purpose of extension, have the control of its own funds, the proceeds of its Fisheries. At the outset it may be possible that some small allotment may be needed from Imperial Funds, but I do not anticipate it.

78. Any officer or officers appointed to the duty should, I think, give attention to all the local peculiarities which I have above indicated, to the drafting of a law, to the creation of an experimental Farm, to the organization of so much Establishment as may be found absolutely necessary for the protection of the Fisheries, to the writing of the very simplest and briefest possible manuals for the guidance of those employed in the advancement of Fisheries.

79. With Ichthyology or the classification and nomenclature of fish, I do not think we need concern ourselves; that is being well done by Dr. Day, the late Inspector-General of Indian Fisheries, and even in his retirement, and at his private cost. Not only should no counter effort be made in that direction, but any possible

assistance in the supply of new specimens rendered, so that he may make his work as complete as possible. Our business is the eating of fish by the masses, and for want of a better term, I will call our way to it practical pisciculture.

80. But I do not propose any fish cultivation in the sea, for the sea needs no culture, only harvesting; and the harvesting properly conducted is in itself a means of culture. It is a general and obviously necessary rule in nature, that the predatory classes propagate their species less rapidly than those preyed on. It follows that improved fishing, if applied equally to both classes of fish, must most affect the class that has the less power of recouping itself, to wit, the predatory. The result is increased immunity and multiplication of the minor species, and thus it comes about that in large measure, man takes the place of predatory fish, or, in other words, the Fishery is improved.

81. Neither do I propose artificial cultivation of the fresh-water fish, but rather assistance of the natural reproduction by protection from wholesale poisoning, by regulation of the size of the mesh, and other protection of fry from indiscriminate slaughter. The best practical methods of applying such protection, and adapting their details to various rivers will have to be studied.

82. For harvesting the sea, I think it would be well to have an experimental and model Farm. It is found necessary in agriculture, and I think that in this country it is equally necessary in aquiculture or pisciculture. I think it is necessary that we should show the native fishermen what can be captured by our English methods. We may talk as long as we like about trawls and trots, and so forth, but they will not give practical heed to us till they see the fish brought ashore. Then they may wish to know more about them, and then we should be able to show them the implements in work, and allow them to copy them exactly.

83. But I would wish to guard against the thoughtless plunging into English, Dutch, or French means of capture, without first thoroughly studying their suitability to Indian seas, and men, and means. I am inclined to think that one reason why agriculture has for ten long years made so very little progress in this Presidency at least, if not in other parts of India, is that it commenced by too little regarding the native and the country, and aiming at the introduction of a too full blown and English stereotyped agriculture.

For instance, it is not to be concluded that because steam launches are the most profitable means of fishing in England, they must necessarily be so in India.

Fuel is more expensive here than in England, which is an argument against steam, but winds and currents both run in the same direction on the coast from which I write, so that working against the current or getting back to port against the wind, will both be difficult, nay impossible, without steam. It is a question of which the *pros* and *cons* must be worked out experimentally. A small steamer could, perhaps, be lent for the purpose of a trial. I believe all the Government vessels are screw-steamers. Shift could nevertheless be made for a trial.

84. But I do not think that one Fish Farm will suffice for all India, any more than one Agricultural Farm. I think that at the very commencement there should be one in each Presidency. Considering the areas sought to be influenced, this is very little; also it will be valuable that they should help each other by comparing notes of progress and practical difficulties from time to time. This they will naturally do if they all report to, and are under the eye of, one central officer equally interested in all, and keeping all informed of the progress of the others. At the same time healthy emulation will be encouraged, and a wider knowledge acquired.

85. The native craft used in fishing are of many sorts, from the catamaran upwards, and it would have to be seen which could best be adapted to the use of large English nets, and native nets themselves would have to be compared for the purposes of adaptation to the boats, to the seas, to the men, to the fish.

86. The introduction of cotton in place of hemp in nets might seem a minor matter, nevertheless it worked a perfect revolution in English sea-fishing, because a boat that used to carry 960 yards of netting can now carry 3,300 yards. It might do the same in India. We have now cotton-mills in India that could make the nets by machinery even more cheaply here than they can in England.

87. An equally important branch of the Farm would be to teach how best to cure fish for the Indian market, how to express and send to market oil, how to prepare fish manure. Each one of these is an important industry in itself; the three combined are still more so.

88. The chief fault of the present Indian curing seems to be

that it does not ordinarily commence till after putrefaction has set in. Fish are also dried in the sun rather than cured with salt, so that with the least moisture in the atmosphere they smell most offensively. And they will not travel far.

Then, again, fish are cured so very dry and hard that they are only eaten in very small quantities as a salt relish. Objections are loudly raised to the insurmountable obstructiveness of the salt monopoly. It is idle to run a tilt against that infinitesimal indirect poll tax which, as such, has so much to commend it, and is far too important a source of revenue to be sacrificed. Let it be a business of the farm to show in practice that it is not an insurmountable difficulty. The giving of salt cheap in curing yards has already been conceded by Government. The difficulty is to bring the salt to the fish out at sea immediately they are caught, for when caught far out at sea, they must necessarily in this tropical clime be putrid before they get ashore, and this difficulty prevents fishing any distance from the shore. I have seen fish being brought in covered with maggots. As fish are put into wells of water and kept alive, and into wells of ice and kept fresh in England, so I believe that they might be put into wells of strong brine in this country, and that brine may be given cheap under certain regulations without any fear of salt smuggling. They could not evaporate it into salt on board, and it would be very nearly as difficult to make salt out of it on shore as it is to make salt of the sea water or earth efflorescence; so that no new difficulty to the salt monopoly would have been introduced.

89. The curing of fish stands very greatly in need of fostering. It should not be forgotten that there was a time when English fish salting suffered from like difficulties. Adam Smith says, that before the repeal of the Salt laws, although salt used for curing was exempted from duty, yet, to protect the revenue, so many Regulations were enacted that many of the fishermen chose to use taxed salt rather than comply with the rules. The character of our salt fish had also to be maintained by Government supervision, and a Government brand. It should not surprise us, therefore, that Indian fish curing stands in need of encouragement, especially when we consider the chronic depression firmly established by long years of suppressive salt monopoly, and the very recentness of the one concession made. It cannot be expected that an industry so long

dead will at once start into life and vigour without something more than simple sufferance, without some active fostering. At present there is no one specially interested in watching its practical difficulties and helping it over them. At most we have an order of Government, and a stray Native Deputy Collector fitfully energetic, and that without knowledge. We have no one continuously interested in it and watching, and steadily assisting it in the way of progressive improvement and extension. I note, as shown in my letter above* quoted and enclosed in connection with fish-passes, that one single officer has in one place and in one season of three months brought about the curing of from 77,000 Rs., to 96,000 Rs., say on an average 86,000 Rs. worth of fish. Does not this encourage the hope that like fostering in many places might contribute markedly to swell the amount of cured fish sent into the interior.

90. At the very outset, also, I think it would be well to have some statistics of how we stand now, so that we may test the growth of our fisheries, the results of our measures.

91. As to whether any and what nominal or other tax shall be put upon the fishermen whereby to find funds for the advancement of fisheries, is a question for consideration.

92. While I have insisted so strongly on the value of local knowledge, it will not be concluded that I in the least undervalue fish knowledge; on the contrary, it is only on science that any local enquiry can profitably be based. That proposition is, I hope, self evident. It were easy to enforce it by instances of grievous injury already done in more places than one in India by misguided but well-intentioned energies, and the extraordinary suicidal proposals of friendly but ignorant supporters of pisciculture. It were easy but unkindly, to particularize; and as no practical good would be gained by detail here, I trust the general position may be granted that any one entrusted with all the duties above indicated should have a previous knowledge of fish generally, and of Indian fish in particular, and a concurrent knowledge of the country and people. This last would be a very great advantage indeed as indicated by the stress which I lay on local knowledge and the correct attainment of it.

* Omitted here as too long.

93. The officer or officers appointed to lay down the first lines of Pisciculture in India should, in my opinion, meet these requisites. Those that follow, if well selected, can acquire their knowledge in the course of their duties.

94. But no officer can do justice to the task without books of reference, and as I am asked to give an opinion what definite steps Government should take, I venture to submit that the first thing it should do is to form in each Presidency a Piscicultural bookshelf, containing a complete record of all that has been done and is being done in the several branches of fish industry in different parts of the world. We want all the information we can get about nets, lines, boats, steam-launches, and all other appliances for capturing fish in the sea, in the estuaries, in the fresh waters; about the different methods of curing and packing fish for human consumption, and for manure; about oil extracting; about artificial fish breeding, and in this respect the American experience is valuable; about the laws and rules made in different countries to suit different circumstances. I cannot find, and I have searched, that the Government of this Presidency* has a single book of any real value on the subject, and never have I been able to get the smallest particle of help from any Government bookshelf in this matter. I have had to be entirely dependent on my own private library, lamentably meagre though it is. The officer charged with the task of organizing the Indian Fisheries should be given a very liberal discretion in the formation of a library.

95. The existing museums, by devoting a section thereto, can do something hereafter towards the education of those employed in aiding the advancement of the industry, and the several Superintendents will doubtless co-operate kindly when the time arrives.

* I have since learnt that there are some books about fish in the Madras Central Museum, but whether they are of the sort required, is the question. I fear they are not.

CHAPTER XXVII.

STRAY CRUMBS FOR THE NATURALIST AND PISCICULTURIST.

"And this our life, exempt from public haunt,
Finds tongues in trees, books in the running brooks,
Sermons in stones, and good in everything."—
As you like it. Act ii, Sc. 1.

Page

INDEX.

Page

HARRISON AND SONS, PRINTERS IN ORDINARY TO HER MAJESTY, ST. MARTIN'S LANE.

CPSIA information can be obtained
at www.ICGtesting.com
Printed in the USA
LVOW04s0709180716
496705LV00013BA/236/P